MW01051377

THOMAS McKELVEY CLEAVER

MEDITERRANEAN SWEEP

The USAAF in the Italian Campaign

OSPREY PUBLISHING
Bloomsbury Publishing Plc
Kemp House, Chawley Park, Cumnor Hill, Oxford OX2 9PH, UK
Bloomsbury Publishing Ireland Limited,
29 Earlsfort Terrace, Dublin 2, D02 AY28, Ireland
1385 Broadway, 5th Floor, New York, NY 10018, USA
E-mail: info@ospreypublishing.com
www.ospreypublishing.com

OSPREY is a trademark of Osprey Publishing Ltd

First published in Great Britain in 2025

A catalog record for this book is available from the British Library.

ISBN: HB 9781472863454; PB 9781472863461; eBook 9781472863478; ePDF 9781472863423;
XML 9781472863430; Audio 9781472863447

25 26 27 28 29   10 9 8 7 6 5 4 3 2 1

The quotations from Michael McCarthy are from Michael C. McCarthy, *Air-to-Ground Battle for Italy*
(Maxwell AFB: Air University Press, 2012).

Maps by www.bounford.com
Index by Mark Swift

Typeset by Deanta Global Publishing Services, Chennai, India
Printed and bound in Great Britain by CPI (Group) UK Ltd, Croydon CR0 4YY

Osprey Publishing supports the Woodland Trust, the UK's leading woodland conservation charity.

To find out more about our authors and books visit www.ospreypublishing.com. Here you will find
extracts, author interviews, details of forthcoming events and the option to sign up for our newsletter.

For product safety related questions contact productsafety@bloomsbury.com

CONTENTS

LIST OF ILLUSTRATIONS AND MAPS

ILLUSTRATIONS

Joseph Heller plays the role of "Pete, a replacement bombardier," in the training film *Training In Combat* directed by First Lieutenant Wilbur Blume and made between September and December 1944. (Wilbur Blume Collection)

First Lieutenant Wilbur Blume directs a scene for the film *Training In Combat*, one of several he made for 340th Group CO Colonel John Chapman, which Blume called "a boondoggle." (USAF Official)

Colonel Robert D. Knapp led the 321st Bomb Group in North Africa, Sicily, and Italy before being promoted to command the 57th Bomb Wing, despite being initially thought to be too old for combat. (USAF Official)

On February 15, 1944, B-17s and B-24s of the new Fifteenth Air Force, as well as Twelfth Air Force B-26 Marauders, B-25 Mitchells, and A-20 Havocs, bombed the Benedictine abbey atop Monte Cassino, established as the first monastery of the Benedictine Order in AD 529 by Benedict of Nursia. (USAF Official)

Mount Vesuvius erupted on March 25, 1944, part of a series of increasingly violent eruptions in 1906, 1929, and 1944. (USAF Official)

A Caterpillar tractor driver attempts to scrape away volcanic ash from Pompeii airfield as Mount Vesuvius continued to erupt a week after the initial blast. (USAF Official)

The 340th Bomb Group was based at Pompeii airfield just north of the volcano when it erupted on March 25, 1944. All 88 bombers were destroyed, with their plastic canopies melted and fuselages filled with hot volcanic ash. (USAF Official)

This B-25J of the 12th Bomb Group was given a publicity paint scheme celebrating the downfall of Mussolini in Italy and promising the same to Japanese emperor Hirohito. The Mitchell is flying over the Bay of Naples in the spring of 1944. (USAF Official)

Avignon bridge was where Joseph Heller had "the daylights scared out of me," which became the "Help the Bombardier!" scene in *Catch-22*. (USAF Official)

Production of the Fiat G.55 "Centauro" (Centaur) came too late to equip units of the Regia Aeronautica before the surrender of Italy in late 1943. (Chronicle/Alamy Stock Photo)

Tents like this one used by a crew in the 340th Bomb Group on Corsica were the main living quarters for most American airmen in the Italian campaign from September 1943 to the end of the war. (USAF Official)

Most of the maintenance on aircraft of both sides during World War II was done outside. Ground crews became very adept at coming up with simple rigs that were easy to move from plane to plane for heavy work up to and including an engine change. This is a rig used by the 310th Bomb Group on Corsica. (USAF Official)

The Brenner Pass rail line ran from Bologna in the Po Valley to Munich, Germany, an eight-hour, one-way trip. (USAF Official)

B-25s of the 321st Bomb Group bombed the Galliate bridge in the Po Valley in October 1944 during the final Allied ground offensive to break the Gothic Line in 1944. (USAF Official)

The transformers at Trento, in the southern approaches to the Brenner Pass, provided all the power for the electric trains the railway used. (USAF Official)

Rovereto, at the entrance of the Brenner Pass, was the most difficult target to hit in Operation *Bingo*. (USAF Official)

P-47D-30 Thunderbolt "Torrid Tessie" of the 350th Fighter Group. It was part of a formation escorting bombers from 57th Bomb Wing during Operation *Bingo* in the spring of 1945. (USAF Official)

On April 16, 1945, Lieutenant Vladimir Sandtner of the Air Force of the Independent State of Croatia defected to Italy. He landed at Fano airfield just as Dan Bowling was taking off to lead a major mission, barely missing Bowling's B-25. The 321st's ground crews later sold the Bf-109G-10 to an RAF unit for three cases of Scotch whiskey. (USAF Official)

MAPS

FOREWORD BY COLONEL USAF (RET.) RALPH WETTERHAHN

Much of the history written about World War II focuses on the major air campaigns, the turning points such as at Midway, Guadalcanal, D-Day (Normandy), and the invasions of the Philippines and Okinawa. The struggle for control of the air also involved many important side shows. The holding actions during the dark days of 1942 over Sumatra, Malaya, and Java, the Aleutian campaign against the northern Kurile Islands, the North African campaign, and finally the Mediterranean campaign all played crucial roles in eventual victory. *Mediterranean Sweep* is a bold attempt to raise the consciousness of readers and historians to this epic air campaign.

For many, D-Day, June 6, 1944, is thought of as the time when Allied forces first set foot on Fortress Europe. The truth, of course, is Allied forces landed on Italian soil at Salerno on September 9, 1943, during Operation *Avalanche*. That history has for the most part fallen through the cracks. Yet, the impact of this haphazard invasion cannot be overstated. The landings came as no surprise to the Germans. At Paestum, 25 miles south of Salerno, a German loudspeaker just behind the landing area proclaimed in English: "Come on in and give up. We have you covered." Politics, missed opportunities, and the steadfast "unconditional surrender" mantra all combined to make the Italian surrender effort chaotic.

Early on, many of the Allied fighter aircraft involved were less capable than the German Bf-109 and Fw-190s. Additionally, the scarcity of replacement parts and crews made for sluggish progress.

Despite the difficulties, the P-38 Lightning groups fought a battle against the odds in making the twin-engine plane the primary US fighter type in the Mediterranean Theater of Operations with 37 P-38 pilots becoming aces during their time in the Med. Only 12 Spitfire pilots achieved that rank, along with ten P-40 Warhawk pilots.

The little known and less heralded A-36 Mustang (precursor to the P-51 Mustang) made its own mark in ground attack service over the Italian battlefield and was awarded a Distinguished Unit Citation for saving the *Avalanche* invasion.

Later in the conflict, the P-47 Thunderbolt proved crucial in taking over the ground attack role. Its rugged construction became legendary in surviving heavy battle damage. The 57th Fighter Group P-47s had been so successful in Operation *Strangle*, blocking German supplies coming through the Brenner Pass, that famed Hollywood director William Wyler – who had made the acclaimed documentary the year before about *Memphis Belle*, the first Eighth Air Force B-17 to survive 35 missions – brought his film crew to Italy to film the P-47 group's story for a second documentary. The result was the film *Thunderbolt*, which was finally shown in the United States in 1947.

Of particular personal interest are the actions by historic squadrons, Rickenbacker's "Hat in the Ring" Squadron, the 94th, plus the 71st and 27th Squadrons, all of which I would later be assigned to while at Langley Air Force Base, Virginia, from 1976–82. Current or former Air Force fighter pilots will likely read about a particular squadron during this period in the war that later he or she would be assigned to.

Following the Normandy invasion, mission tours for air crew in bombers and fighters would be extended in the face of personnel and equipment shortages, and would make their way into one of the most famous novels of World War II, Joseph Heller's *Catch-22*, about B-25 Mitchell bombing missions over Italy, a great companion read to this effort.

What could have been a cake walk securing Italy turned out to be a hard-fought campaign due to political and military complications. Between September 1943 and April 1945, 60,000 Allied and 50,000 German soldiers died, with overall Allied casualties at approximately 320,000 and the Germans at 336,650. But by keeping the German forces defending the "underbelly" of Europe, the D-Day forces at Normandy had an easier time of it, despite the difficulties encountered there.

Tighten your shoulder straps and seat belt as you begin reading *Mediterranean Sweep*, because you're in for a fascinating ride.

Ralph F. Wetterhahn
Colonel USAF (Ret.)

AUTHOR PREFACE

The war in Italy between the invasion at Salerno in September 1943 and the German surrender at the end of April 1945 was a disaster – militarily, tactically, strategically, and geopolitically. It was a near-catastrophe for Italy itself.

The reasons for this state of affairs are many, but two facts stand out.

The first is that no Allied military leader wanted to fight a war in Italy. Once Sicily was taken, the Mediterranean sea lanes to the Suez Canal were secure. Everyone correctly saw that the main battle to defeat Nazi Germany would take place in northwestern Europe; a war in Italy was a distraction from that main event. However, when the Sicilian campaign ended, everyone also knew that the cross-Channel invasion was around a year away at the earliest. As Churchill pointed out, giving the enemy a year's respite to rebuild the Wehrmacht and create defenses that really would be an "Atlantic Wall" might guarantee Allied failure in 1944. In the end, the Italian campaign was fought because there was no immediate alternative.

But the campaign was fought by the Allies with one hand tied behind their backs – by early 1944, the best units from the North African and Sicilian campaigns were withdrawn and transferred to the UK, where they would prepare for the coming invasion. Additionally, the units – both ground and air – that were committed to the Italian campaign had a lower priority for replacements of men and material than the units preparing in Britain and later fighting across northwestern Europe. One veteran of the 57th Bomb Wing – the unit in which Joseph Heller served and later memorialized in his novel – recalled, "*Catch-22* was real – they didn't call it that, but it worked just like the book says." The tour constantly changed; not because of arbitrariness on the part of the unit leadership but rather because they could not obtain replacements for aircrew who completed their tour; this was the case in every United States Army Air Force (USAAF) unit in Italy.

Thus, the Allies were not able to land a knockout blow against their enemy until the very end – the result of an air campaign that constituted the most successful battlefield interdiction campaign in the history of the US Air Force, the only time success was achieved in this role in World War II, Korea, or Vietnam, and which has strangely been forgotten by the Air Force since its success disproves that service's main argument for its existence as a separate service.

The second reason was a failure of political and military leadership on the part of the Allies. This led to an inability at important points to take advantage of situations that might be favorable to the Allied goals if the correct actions could be taken in a timely manner. This was, unfortunately, never the case from beginning to end.

At the outset, when the Italian government attempted to end the Italo-German alliance and make peace with the Allies, the Allied demand for "unconditional surrender" hamstrung a response to the events in Rome in the summer of 1943. "Unconditional surrender" sounded good on the American domestic political scene, which was why Franklin Roosevelt had publicly proclaimed that as the Allied goal in the war. In practical terms, it meant the Allies could not act to support political and military forces on the other side who saw the writing on the wall and were willing to take action to end things on their side. This "strategy," based on a need for public relations, made at a time when civilian support for the war was flagging in the United States, ultimately meant an additional 18 months of war in Italy, a likely additional year of war against Germany, and the atomic bombing of Japan – which despite 80 years of official mythology to the contrary did not in fact end World War II. The policy and strategy of "unconditional surrender" was President Roosevelt's greatest political mistake of his entire career.

Sadly, in spite of the heroism and commitment of Allied soldiers, sailors, and airmen fighting in Italy, their heroic effort was undermined by military leaders who were unworthy of the men they led. This was nowhere more obvious than the decisions made by Fifth Army commander Major General Mark W. Clark; indeed, he ranks on the incompetence scale with Civil War General George B. McClellan, coupled with his inability to separate his ego from the needs of the campaign. At the point where the Allies could have ended the war in Italy with the capture and surrender of the German Tenth and Fourteenth Armies in the aftermath of the final Allied breakout from Cassino in May 1944, Clark personally added a year to the death, destruction, and suffering of all involved in Italy when he changed the orders for VI Corps, which was two days away from linking up with the British Eighth Army to surround and cut off the two German armies from further retreat and thus end Axis resistance in Italy. Instead, he diverted VI Corps to "liberate" Rome, which was at the time undefended and an open city. Clark was known to those in the Fifth Army he commanded as "Markus Clarkus" for his obsession over taking Rome; he actually went to the length of asking General Eisenhower to delay the Normandy invasion so that his "victory" could be "properly celebrated"! While Allied troops marched through the streets of Rome, the German armies escaped to the Gothic Line in northern Italy where they would hold out for ten months.

Eventually, in December 1944, leadership of the Italian campaign was finally handed to someone who knew how to do the job: General Lucian K. Truscott, Jr. As Captain Dan Bowling, a B-25 pilot in the 321st Bomb Group of the 57th Wing, later wrote, "the air we breathed was different after General Truscott took command." Following the end of the war in May 1945, General Truscott did something no other Allied commander ever did when he apologized to the men lying in the graves at the American cemetery in Nettuno, Italy, for any mistakes he might have made that put them there, and promised them that if he ever met someone who thought the Italian campaign was worthy of praise, "I'll be sure to set him straight on that."

Despite Allied leaders treating the war in Italy as secondary, despite poor leadership, the men who fought and died in the Italian campaign wrote a record of sacrifice and accomplishment second to none, regardless of the difficulties they faced from the enemy and their own commanders. This book is their story.

Thomas McKelvey Cleaver
Encino, California
2024

ITALY, 1943–45

Key airfields
Volturno Line
Barbara Line
Bernhardt Line
Gustav Line
Hitler Line
Gothic Line

GERMANY

Innsbruck

AUSTRIA

SWITZERLAND

Brenner Pass

Trento
Ala
Vicenza
Campoformido
Udine

Malpensa
Bergamo
Verona
Venice
Villafranca

Milan

Po River

YUGOSLAVIA

ITALY

Ferrara

Genoa
Bologna
Cesenatico
Rimini

La Spezia
Vernio
Forli
Fano
Falconara
Ancona

Pisa
Florence
Leghorn
Pontedera
Jesi

Siena

Montalto di Castro
Perugia

Piombino
Orvieto
Grosseto
Viterbo

Orbetello
Littoria
Pescara
Ortona

Corsica
Tarquinia
Centocelle
Guidonia
Adriatic Sea

Civitavecchia
Termoli

Ajaccio
Furbara/Cerveteri
Rome
Ciampino

Nettuno
Cassino
Grazzanise

Anzio
Fondi
Pomigliano
Foggia

Cisterna
Benevento
Bari

Castel Volturno
Pompeii
Gioia del Colle

Capodichino
Naples
Montecorvino
San Pancrazio

Sorrento
Seretella
Taranto

Sardinia
Salerno
Paestum
San Donato
Galatina

Sele
Ionian Sea

Villacridro
Rocca Bernardo
Crotone

Decimomannu

Cagliari
Tyrrhenian Sea

Pizzo

Milazzo
Palmi

Palermo
Messina

Trapani
Sicily
Gerbini
Catania

Bizerte
Lentini

Mateur
Tunis

Grombalia

N

TUNISIA

0   100 mile
0   100km

I

OPENING BELL

By mid-July 1943, it was obvious the Germans and Italians were defeated on Sicily. That week, the last air units departed for the Italian mainland. While no one in the forward units involved was exactly certain what the future of the war in the Mediterranean would be, the fact the enemy was now concentrated on the Italian peninsula meant that the air war would focus on those enemy airfields.

In the weeks between the end of fighting on Sicily and the Salerno invasion, the Twelfth Air Force's three P-38 fighter groups would see some of the heaviest fighting they had experienced in the ten months since Operation *Torch* had brought American fighting units to the Mediterranean Theater of Operations.

The 14th Fighter Group had been rebuilt over the spring of 1943 following their heavy losses earlier in the North African campaign. In March the group finally was fully equipped with a third fighter squadron, the 37th Fighter Squadron, commanded by former "Flying Tiger" Major John Gilpin Bright. In late March P-38G Lightnings and pilots taken from the 78th Fighter Group in England arrived in the group, while 15 experienced flight leaders from the 1st Fighter Group were transferred to the 14th following completion of their tours in the 1st Group. Major Joel Owens, a seven-victory P-38 ace from the 1st Group's 27th Fighter Squadron, transferred in as group executive officer at the end of March. Fellow 27th Fighter Squadron aces Captains Bernard Muldoon and William Newman were posted as commanders of the 48th and 49th Squadrons respectively. The pilots had all been expecting to return to the United States following completion of their tours. When they were informed by XII Fighter

Command General Joe Cannon that they were staying in-theater and transferring to the 14th Group, Major Owens recalled that none of the pilots thanked the general for this "splendid opportunity." The group had re-entered combat in early May just before the Axis surrender. By the end of the Sicilian campaign, the group was fully experienced. Major Owens recalled that the 14th was "essentially a new group" when they re-entered combat, and that the experienced group and squadron leaders and other flight leaders meant that the unbloodied pilots from the 78th Group were soon considered successful combat pilots.

In late July, the 14th moved to Sicily where they took up residence at Lentini airfield, a former Regia Aeronautica base. At the same time, the 82nd Fighter Group moved to a new airfield at Grombalia, near Cap Bon in Tunisia on July 30, completing the move by August 4. Grombalia was the northernmost airfield on Cap Bon that could support P-38s. The 1st Fighter Group remained at their base at Mateur, Tunisia.

The Allied air forces began attacking targets on the Italian peninsula in mid-July. The first big mission was flown against Naples – the main port supplying Axis forces in Sicily – hitting the docks, railroad marshalling yards, and industrial area. On July 15, the 1st Group's 94th Fighter Squadron was tasked with dive-bombing a bridge near Catania, to block Axis retreat on Sicily.

July 19 saw the first bombing of Rome, with the bombers concentrating on outlying Littorio and San Lorenzo rail yards and Ciampino Airport. The mission included all Twelfth Air Force bomber squadrons, led by B-17s of the veteran 97th Bomb Group, accompanied by B-24s, B-25s, and B-26s. It was considered so important that Twelfth Air Force commander General Jimmy Doolittle flew as co-pilot in the lead bomber. The 321st Bomb Group's commander, 45-year-old Colonel Robert D. Knapp, led the Mitchells, flying left seat in the lead ship.

The rail yards at Foggia in southeastern Italy were hit on July 22. Missions alternated between supporting Allied forces on Sicily and attacking strategic targets located on the Italian mainland.

The afternoon of August 7 found the 82nd Fighter Group's 96th Fighter Squadron escorting four of the newly arrived B-25G Mitchells from the 310th Bomb Group, which were armed with a modified 75mm pack howitzer cannon mounted in the bombardier's tunnel, while the rest of the nose was now metal, mounting two .50-caliber M2 machine guns. The Mitchells were searching for enemy shipping in the Gulf of

Eufemia between the harbors of Pizzo and Palmi, supported by eight Lightnings loaded with bombs. The low cloud ceiling meant both the fighters and fighter-bombers had to operate at the same low altitude as the bombers, which meant trouble if the enemy decided to contest the mission. The Mitchells managed to find some shipping in Pizzo harbor and scored hits with their big cannons.

Suddenly, two Fw-190s and two Bf-109s popped out of the cloud cover above and attacked the bomb-carrying P-38s; pilots salvoed their bombs and turned into the enemy fighters. Flight Officer Frank Hurlbut and Second Lieutenant Don Warr each scored hits on the Fw-190s. Both crashed into the sea below, but not before one had fatally damaged the P-38 flown by element leader Second Lieutenant Richard Drayton, killing him. Hurlbut managed to tag onto one of the Messerschmitts and damage it. Considering he had recently been released from hospital and was still not fully recovered from what he described as a "full-blown case of malaria" that left him feeling "very weak and somewhat out of it," his quick reactions were admirable, saving the rest of the squadron.

The Sicilian campaign officially ended on August 17, when Allied forces entered Messina. What the Allies did not know at the time was that the Germans had managed to evacuate 38,846 troops and 10,356 vehicles including 94 assault guns and 50 tanks, along with 14,946 tons of fuel and ammunition from Messina to Calabria between August 1 and 16. Additionally, 18,168 wounded were evacuated, to later rejoin the fighting. The Italians had evacuated 60,000 troops while 137,000 had surrendered to the Allies. In the aerial battles over Pantelleria and Sicily, the Luftwaffe had lost 1,678 aircraft written off to all causes since the surrender in Tunisia; this was one-third of all Luftwaffe losses on all fronts in this period.

The P-38s of the 96th and 97th Squadrons escorted B-25s to Benevento, in Italy, on August 20, and the enemy came up for a fight once again. Shortly after the formation crossed the Italian coast headed to the target at 1330 hours, ten Bf-109s dove from out of the sun, shooting down a straggling 97th pilot. During withdrawal 15 more Fw-190s jumped the Lightnings. The 96th's Second Lieutenant CO Johnson was ready for them and quickly turned in behind a *Schwarm* (flight of four aircraft) of Fw-190s, shooting down one and damaging another. He got on the tail of a third and lost several thousand feet chasing the enemy who tried to evade. He finally got the fighter in his sights long enough to open fire and hit the pilot just as he climbed out of the cockpit. Johnson's squadron mate Second Lieutenant Larry Liebers shot down another Fw-190 for his seventh, and last, victory before completing his tour eight days later. Two other Lightning pilots were posted missing in action; total claims for the encounter were four destroyed and two damaged.

One of the most celebrated Lightning missions of 1943 was the surprise raid flown by the 82nd and 1st Groups and a squadron from the 14th Group to hit the large complex of eight enemy airfields in the plains surrounding Foggia in east-central Italy on August 25. The widely dispersed airfields in the complex operated some 200–250 enemy aircraft; the wide dispersal made conventional bombing ineffective, hence the decision to send a massive fighter force to hit the enemy. The mission was different from any flown before, since they were ordered to execute a low-level strafing attack to destroy as many enemy aircraft on the ground as possible, reducing the force that could oppose the Salerno invasion.

South Pacific veteran Lieutenant Colonel George M. MacNicol, the 82nd's new deputy group commander, was overall mission leader. Takeoff began at 0630hrs. The 82nd was joined over the Gulf of Tunis by the 1st and 14th Groups, creating an aerial armada of more than 150 P-38s. To ensure surprise, MacNicol led the formation at wave-top height across the Sicilian Narrows, using a navigator's compass between his feet to stay on course. They crossed Sicily, then flew northeast across the Italian peninsula, then north across the Gulf of Manfredonia to just below the city of the same name, where they turned southwest toward Foggia, 20 miles distant. Nearing the city, the individual squadrons proceeded on to their assigned target airfields.

Approaching at more than 300mph and just 20 feet above the ground, it quickly became apparent they had achieved complete surprise as they flashed over the airfields, opening fire and destroying 34 enemy aircraft while damaging many others.

MacNicol led the 97th and 96th Squadrons over Foggia Satellite Airfield Number 7; he spotted an Fw-190 attempting to take off and hit it just as it got airborne; the enemy fighter cartwheeled over the ground before it exploded. The Lightnings claimed five other aircraft destroyed, including a C.202 by Second Lieutenant Sammy E. McGuffin of the 97th and a Ju-52/3m by the 96th's First Lieutenant Lee Solem; his P-38 was badly damaged by antiaircraft fire and he wasn't sure if he was going to make it home. He did make it to the refueling and emergency stop in Sicily, where he spent the night. This was Solem's 50th, and last, combat mission. When he left for the States shortly after, his score was three destroyed, one probable, and four damaged in the air and the Ju-52/3m as his only strafing victory. Three pilots of the 96th Squadron and Flight Officer Urban F. Stahl of the 97th attacked Airfield Number 9, where Stahl claimed four Ju-88s that caught fire when he hit them.

The 95th was the most successful squadron, destroying 11 aircraft on Airfield Number 3, including a Ju-88, a Bf-109, and a Ju-52/3m credited to First Lieutenant Guido Lucini to add to his two previous aerial victories. Leading a flight of four, First Lieutenant Tom Hodgson strafed a C.202 and then encountered airborne enemy aircraft. He recalled:

When we were over the far edge of the field, we broke up the line abreast formation and bunched together, with me leading the way. I looked around to check the other three ships, and at that instant I saw two of them hit the ground. For a moment I thought it must be flak, but then as I watched, the third ship went in and I could feel shots hitting my airplane. I saw two Macchi 202 fighters that had trailed us across the field. I was the only one left of my flight. I gave my ship hard left rudder and turned into them, but they got away. Then, because I was pretty well banged up myself, I hit the deck and beat it home.

The 82nd's 95th Fighter Squadron claimed 21 enemy aircraft destroyed on the ground, plus several more damaged. The 14th Group claimed 50 aircraft destroyed between them. As the Lightnings headed away from the airfield complex, B-17s escorted by the rest of the 14th Group bombed the complex, destroying 21 aircraft and damaging an additional 43 aircraft. Five P-38s were reported missing in action, including the three claimed by Major Johannes Steinhoff, *Kommodore* of JG 77.

Major George Rush, group operations officer, led the P-38s of the 1st Fighter Group. Surprise was complete as the Lightnings flashed over Satellite Airfield Number 6, catching mechanics and armorers working on the fighters on the ground below, and in hangars and shops on the field. As the P-38s opened fire, enemy aircraft sagged to the ground, caught fire, and exploded. The group later claimed 47 aircraft destroyed on the field and 13 damaged.

Second Lieutenant Marcel Williams of the 27th Squadron was hit by flak over the field and forced to bail out onto the wrecked airfield, where he was quickly made prisoner.

The 94th Squadron's First Lieutenant Jack Hanton strafed a train after he departed the field; hit in one engine, he managed to make it to Sicily and land safely. A railroad station was strafed and a troop train at Potenza was shot up, with troops pouring from the cars to be cut down by the massed machine-gun fire from a flight of four P-38s. The Lightnings arrived back at their base at Mateur south of Bizerte in twos and fours, with several being forced to land on Sicily to refuel before crossing the Mediterranean.

Immediately upon return to Grombalia, Lieutenant Colonel MacNicol was personally awarded a Distinguished Flying Cross (DFC) for his leadership by Lieutenant General Carl Spaatz. The 82nd Fighter Group received its first Distinguished Unit Citation (DUC) for their part in the mission, as did the 1st Fighter Group. The next day, MacNicol assumed command of the 82nd; a week later Major William P. Litton, a West Point graduate and veteran of the Aleutians, became his deputy.

Two days later, on August 27, one of the 82nd's ranking aces became an unwilling guest of the Germans. One of the most aggressive pilots in the 95th Squadron, Second Lieutenant Louis Curdes opened his score by claiming three Bf-109s destroyed and another damaged in a fight over Cap Bon on April 29, 1943. Three weeks later he became an ace when he shot down two more 109s over the Sardinian town of Villacidro on May 19, with a C.202 shot down over the Gulf of Aranci for his sixth claim on June 24.

On August 27, Curdes claimed two Bf-109s destroyed in a major battle over Benevento, in southwest Italy, before a third shot down his wingman and hit one of his engines solidly. Heading for home on one engine, his fate was sealed when he crossed the Italian coast and his good engine took a flak hit. Knowing the Lightning was done for, he crash-landed on a beach a few miles south of Salerno, set the airplane on fire, and awaited inevitable capture. His adventures had only begun.

A week after his capture, on the morning of September 4, he and some other prisoners escaped but were almost immediately recaptured and sent to a maximum-security camp. Four days later, on September 8, the Italian government agreed to an armistice. Curdes and the other POWs were provided rifles and blankets by their former guards and walked away. Unfortunately, the prison was far behind the German lines; Curdes and the others lived as fugitives for the next eight months, helped by Italian partisans. On May 27, 1944, nine months after his capture, Curdes finally crossed into Allied-controlled territory.

On August 26, the 1st Group escorted B-26s to bomb Grazzanise airfield, with follow-up missions on August 27 and 28 to Caserta and Naples and the Battipaglia rail yards outside Naples on August 29. Enemy fighters engaged the Lightnings on all these missions, though only one P-38 was lost while a total of six Bf-109s were claimed.

Two missions flown on August 30 and September 2 proved costly to the Lightning groups. The Luftwaffe's Jagdgeschwader 3, 53, and 77 that had evacuated Sicily were now based in the Naples region. On August 30, they intercepted Allied bomber formations escorted by P-38s. While the enemy fighters were unable to inflict significant damage to the bombers, they inflicted the worst losses the 1st Fighter Group had experienced yet in the war.

The Lightnings were escorting B-26s that bombed the marshalling yards at Aversa, where they were attacked by a mixed formation of Axis fighters. The 1st Group was awarded its second Distinguished Unit Citation for its part in the mission; the combat account accompanying the DUC described the action graphically:

> Crossing the Italian coast, their formation of 44 P-38s was intercepted by approximately 75 aggressive and highly persistent enemy aircraft. Alone and unaided, the 1st FG engaged them, beating off wave after wave of enemy planes attempting to pierce the fighter defenses and break up the bomber formation. These courageous pilots fought a brilliant defensive aerial battle, destroying eight, probably destroying three and damaging three enemy fighters, while our own losses totaled 13 missing. Through their highly effective cover, the bomber formation was able to complete a highly successful bombing run unmolested, and return to base without the loss of a single bomber.

During the 1st Group's mission to Aversa on August 30, the 27th and 94th Squadrons were engaged by 25–30 enemy fighters, claiming three shot down but losing Lieutenants Rudnick, Winegar, Catledge,

Warren, and Phillips. While Phillips turned up the next day after an overnight stay on Sicily, no one knew the fates of the flight of four that went missing until Lieutenant Richard Catledge returned to the group in 1944 to give an account.

According to Catledge, the flight was hit five minutes before they arrived over the target as they crossed the Italian coast by enemy fighters that suddenly appeared out of the clouds. Lieutenant Warren called he had lost an engine, and the other three dropped back to cover him as they turned for home. Other enemy fighters spotted the crippled P-38 and its escorts, and the foursome were broken up when ten enemy fighters attacked. Catledge reported one went straight in, one pilot bailed out, and the third went down smoking. Catledge continued to engage the enemy until his right engine was hit. He was then hit by another Bf-109 that shot up the P-38, forcing Catledge to make a water landing in the Bay of Naples from low altitude, with the enemy fighter still on his tail and shooting. The Lightning immediately sank; he managed to open the canopy and swim out to the surface. Reaching shore, he was spotted by Italian troops and immediately captured.

He was taken to the same jail where Curdes was being held with other Allied aircrew, and took part in the first escape where they were quickly recaptured. He later joined Curdes in the second escape, after which they spent eight months hiding in the Italian hills until they were able to make contact with Allied units.

A total of 13 1st Group pilots from all three squadrons were reported missing after the battle on August 30. Fortunately, none of the Marauders the Lightnings were escorting were shot down.

On September 2, the 82nd Fighter Group was awarded its second DUC in 11 days, resulting from a similar mission to the same area. The group sent 74 Lightnings to protect 72 B-25s of the 321st Bomb Group that attacked Naples' Cancello marshalling yards. The 82nd engaged the same enemy units faced by the 1st Fighter Group on August 30, losing ten P-38s.

As the B-25s pointed their noses down to pick up speed for withdrawal after "bombs away," 15–20 enemy Bf-109s and C.202s attacked the 96th Fighter Squadron, initiating an old-fashioned turning dogfight. The Lightning pilots soon became embroiled in combat so intense that cries for assistance were heard from the embattled pilots. The Mitchells were on their way out of the target area, thus allowing the P-38 pilots to face the additional German and Italian fighters that joined the battle.

Pilots from the 95th Squadron had claimed several enemy fighters when they saw that the bombers were now well clear of the action. It was their turn to extricate themselves from the battle that drove them ever lower as the battle drifted toward the coast. This then became even more difficult when 30 more Axis fighters pitched into the fray, attacking the 96th Squadron, whose Second Lieutenant Fred Selle claimed three Bf-109s shot down while Second Lieutenant James Padgett collided with another Bf-109. Although Padgett parachuted successfully, the German pilot was killed when he failed to get out of what was left of his fighter before it crashed.

The 96th Squadron claimed 11 of the group's 23 victories, but paid a high price for this success with seven of the ten P-38s lost coming from the squadron. Second Lieutenant Leslie Andersen scored the first two of his eventual five aerial victories, claiming two Bf-109s shot down north of Ischia. Flight Officer Frank Hurlbut scored the last of his nine victories, claiming a Bf-109. He later recalled the fight:

We had fought our way down to the water so they couldn't hit us from below – only from the sides or from above. This gave us a little less to worry about. Two Me 109s in line astern dove down right next to me, then pulled up and away to the right. I broke into them as they came down, only to find that I had been suckered away from my flight, which had continued to the left, just above the water. Immediately thereafter, two other 109s attacked me from above. They were flying line abreast and came in to close range. I could see their guns flashing as I looked back and up through my canopy. At the same time, two more Me 109s, flying close together, were closing in from approximately 90 degrees directly above my canopy, firing as they came. I was in a maximum performance turn to the left and an extreme cross-controlled skid to the right. This was a trick I had learned that I used in combat many times. When enemy fighters were trying to hit me I would bank violently while cross-controlling, standing on the inside rudder and racking the aircraft into a turn. This caused the airplane to slide sideways and fly erratically in a somewhat different flight path from the direction it appeared to be going in. This technique probably saved my life once again, because even though all four enemy aircraft were right on top of me, and the water just below was churning from cannon and machinegun fire, they all completely missed me – thank God! As I was getting back with the other P-38s, another single Me 109 was down at my level. The pilot was banking around to the right and cutting directly in front of me. I straightened out my aircraft for a few seconds, led him with my guns and started firing. He flew right through my line of fire and then simply peeled over and went into the sea. I wasn't sure whether he had gone in because of my fire or had simply forgotten in the heat of battle what his altitude was when he peeled away.

According to German records, seven Bf-109s were lost, with five pilots missing. There is no mention of the Fw-190 claimed to have been destroyed. Italian records regarding the four Macchi fighters claimed shot down are unavailable. The missing German pilots included 67-victory *Experte* (ace) Leutnant Franz Schiess, *Staffelführer* of 8./JG 53; 17 of his credited score were P-38s, seven of which he claimed over the previous 13 days.

The German units that engaged the Lightnings on both these missions had many of the best *Jagdwaffe* (Fighter Force) pilots in the Mediterranean Theater, such as II./JG 3's Oberleutnant Gustav Frielinghaus, who claimed his 73rd and 74th victories, and 1./JG 77's Feldwebel Horst Schlick, who was credited with his 27th and 28th victories. Only two of the ten 82nd Group pilots shot down survived to become POWs.

The August 30 mission led to a re-examination of escort tactics. Since arrival in North Africa, the 1st Group had flown escort missions in 12-plane squadrons, with three four-plane flights weaving over the bombers. After August 30, this was changed to four flights and a total of 16 Lightnings, which changed the weave pattern so that one flight wasn't on its own and separated from the others. However, this created additional difficulties since the P-38 groups in Italy had difficulty keeping their assigned numbers, as new P-38 groups were assigned to the Eighth Air Force in England during the fall of 1943.

On September 4, the 1st Group made a strafing attack on the German fighter fields around Naples where the Bf-109s of JG 77 they had tangled with on August 30 were based. A second strafing attack was flown on September 6, at the conclusion of which the Lightnings landed at their new base, Dittaino airfield on the east coast of Sicily not far from Catania. This positioned them much closer to Italy to support the coming invasion at Salerno.

2

ITALY SURRENDERS

Germany and Italy had become allies in the "Pact of Steel" signed in May 1939. This agreement had nothing in it approaching the combination of leadership the Allies would display after the entry of the United States into the war. There was no combined German and Italian Chiefs of Staff committee to deal with differences between the two countries. The Italo-German alliance was officially described by the treaty as a pact between the German National Socialist and the Italian Fascist regimes; essentially, it was a personal union of Adolf Hitler and Benito Mussolini, each the head of government of their respective state and each supreme commander of his armed forces. Whatever agreements would be reached when tensions developed would be ultimately determined by the personal relations between the two.

Under the Oberkommando der Wehrmacht (OKW), each German service – army, navy, and air force – had its own commander and made its own decisions, often without consultation of the others. Hitler directed overall Wehrmacht operations for the first two years through the OKW; after he fired Walther von Brauchitsch and took personal control of the Oberkommando des Heeres (OKH) in 1941, he controlled operations on the Eastern Front through OKH while allowing the normal command through OKW on the other fronts. There was no over-all chief of staff who could plan all German strategy, taking into consideration the requirements of each service and each theater as regarded the allocation of available resources. Ultimate resolution of conflicting demands could be resolved only by Hitler, who had become more and more jealous of his power and suspicious of his generals following the failure of the initial German offensive in the East, which made it increasingly difficult for service leaders with independent minds to serve him.

In Italy, Mussolini's powers were almost as great, differing in that King Victor Emmanuel III was *Capo de Stato* (head of the state), and thus the individual to whom the personnel of the Royal Army, Navy, and Air Force were bound by oath. Mussolini was *Capo de Governo* (head of government) as *Duce* of the Fascist Party, to whom all party members – both civil and paramilitary – had sworn personal allegiance. Thus he had complete control of the executive branch of government. After 1939, Mussolini served simultaneously as Minister of War, Minister of the Navy, and Minister of the Air Force; the undersecretaries of the Navy and Air Force ministries were chiefs of staff of their respective armed forces, while the War Ministry had both an undersecretary and a chief of the Army General Staff. Bureaucratically, Mussolini maintained close control over the armed forces through their ministries.

The Italian constitution vested power of command over the Italian armed forces in the king as Marshal of the Empire. In 1938, Mussolini secured promotion to the same rank; when Italy entered the war in 1940, he took the commander-in-chief role by having the king delegate to him command of all armed forces operating on all fronts. Unlike Hitler, who increasingly micro-managed the Wehrmacht, Mussolini was not interested in details and exercised control at the strategic level only. The Stato Maggiore Generale (Armed Forces General Staff, or the Comando Supremo) had seven members who exercised no command or direct dealings with other staffs, serving as an advisory body to Mussolini as head of government. Each military service had its own staff: the Stato Maggiore Regio Esercito or Superesercito for the army; the Stato Maggiore Regia Marina or Supermarina for the navy; and the Stato Maggiore Regia Aeronautica or Superaereo for the air force. In 1941, Mussolini ousted Maresciallo d'Italia (Marshal of Italy) Pietro Badoglio as chief of Comando Supremo and appointed Generale d'Armata (General of the Army) Ugo Cavallero his successor. The service chiefs of staff became directly subordinate to the chief of Comando Supremo, which expanded into a huge organization, acting not only as Mussolini's command organ but also as the group that cooperated with the OKW. Comando Supremo controlled the operational theaters: North Africa, Russia, Greece, and the Balkans.

Unnoticed by Mussolini, the ousting of Marshal Badoglio, who was a popular leader in the armed forces, created a division between those officers who considered themselves apolitical professionals, and those like Cavallero who hitched their stars politically to Mussolini; as Italy faced military reverse after military reverse under this command structure, Badoglio's influence with the "professionals" grew, since he was not associated with the continual defeats.

On matters of interest to Italy and Germany, the two depended on the older and more traditional methods of cooperation between states allied in war: ministerial correspondence, military attaché reports, and periodic conferences between the two leaders.

While Hitler did have great admiration and friendship for Mussolini, the Italian leader did not reciprocate such feeling. As German predominance grew, Mussolini found Hitler's ascendancy galling. The professional militaries in both nations each retained their traditional views of the other. The Germans had a low estimate of Italian capabilities, recalling how Italy had abandoned the Triple Alliance with Germany and Austro-Hungary in 1914, then turned against the Central Powers in 1915; they also retained awareness that the major duty of the Italian Army since the establishment of the Kingdom of Italy in the mid-19th century had been defense of the Alps against the enemy to the north.

When Italy entered the war in 1940, Mussolini announced the two nations would fight a "parallel war," not a war of alliance, since each had the same enemies. Mussolini's moves in the Mediterranean, first against Yugoslavia and then against Greece, both of which required an intervention by German forces to rescue the hapless Italians from defeat, followed by the need to send the Afrika Korps to North Africa after the British gained ascendancy over the Italian forces there in 1941, contributed both to an increase in German contempt for Italian military capability and Italian dislike of being under German control.

Marshal Cavallero had personified the policy of close integration with Germany; the Germans in turn regarded him highly. But at the end of January 1943, Cavallero experienced a change of heart, brought about by the German accusation that Soviet success at Stalingrad was due to the failures of the Italian troops in the battle. Additionally, he objected when the Germans proposed that in the event of Allied landings in Italy, the Wehrmacht would assume command over the Italian units in the Balkans. It was too late. Mussolini suddenly dismissed Cavallero on February 1.

The day before, Il Duce had informed Generale d'Armata Vittorio Ambrosio that he was now head of the armed forces. When Ambrosio expressed surprise and a lack of interest in assuming the command, Mussolini declared, "We will divide the responsibility," and asked Ambrosio for his ideas. Ambrosio stated three conditions under which he would accept Mussolini's offer: lighten the organization of Comando Supremo; return as many Italian divisions as possible to Italy; and stand up to the Germans. Mussolini exclaimed, "*Benissima!*" to the final point.

Ambrosio thoroughly disliked the Germans and had a faithful protégé in Generale di Brigata Giuseppe Castellano, who hated the Germans violently and was predisposed to political intrigue. Ambrosio met Foreign Minister Count Ciano and, together with Generale di Corpo d'Armata Giacomo Carboni, made plans to end Italian dependence on Germany. Following Ciano's departure from the Foreign Ministry and the cabinet, he became the leader of the dissident Fascists and worked with Dino Grandi, Giuseppe Bottai, Roberto Farinacci, and others who were critical of Mussolini's leadership. Though Ciano had negotiated the Pact of Steel, he personally detested the Germans and never really believed in the treaty. He was sufficiently detached from political reality to believe he could force Mussolini from office and still maintain the Fascist Party's power. The others shared his hope that they could rid themselves of Mussolini and find a way to make a separate peace with the Allies that allowed them to maintain their positions of power. Increasingly, they came to see the only way to do this was through the king.

The military party coalesced around Ambrosino. Most of the officer class were non-political professionals whose oath of office was to the king; in the case of conflict between fascism and the monarchy, they would consider their oaths to the king to be paramount. Ambrosino saw the war as unwinnable as early as February 1943 and favored terminating the alliance with Germany in order to cut Italian losses and save both the army and the monarchy. The general believed if Mussolini was given the unvarnished truth, he would see the logic of ending the alliance and the war. When he did so, Mussolini declared he would "march to the end" with Hitler. With that, Ambrosino finally agreed with General Castellano that Il Duce would have to go.

By March 1943, Castellano had drawn up detailed plans for a coup d'état in which Mussolini and all the Fascists still loyal to him would be arrested. Ambrosino concluded the idea was premature, which led

Castellano to show it to Ciano, who locked it in his safe. Ambrosino then went to the king and laid out the real facts of the situation with regard to the war. Castellano continued his efforts to foment a coup and received assurances from Renxo Chierici, the head of the national police, that he would not intervene in any actions to come.

As all this was taking place, former Prime Minister Ivanoe Bonomi began working in December 1942 to convince the underground political opposition that the Liberals, Christian Democrats, Socialists, Labor Democrats, and Communists must ally to rid the country of Mussolini and the Fascists. The Liberals – the most conservative party in the opposition – were in favor of a complete outlawing of the Fascists and a restoration of parliamentary democracy as it had existed in 1922. In March 1943, the parties agreed to support the Liberals' position for the duration of the war.

In April, Bonomi discovered through contacts with the British minister to the Holy See that Britain supported a political solution favoring retention of the monarchy and steps to rebuild the pre-1922 parliamentary system. When he learned that the British had not rejected contact with Ciano and the dissident Fascists, Bonomi became concerned that a surrender that saw the Fascists remain in power might be accepted by the Allies. An appeal for action was made to the king in mid-May, to which he did not respond.

Bonomi met on May 26 with the Duc d'Acquarone – the king's private secretary – where he presented a plan to arrest the leading Fascists and remove Mussolini from power. This was transmitted to the king, who continued to vacillate. Victor Emmanuel III had largely withdrawn from public life following his appointment of Mussolini as prime minister in 1924. He was by nature cautious, timid, and secretive. He had, however, become skeptical of continuing the war as early as November 1942, following a long meeting with Ciano in which he asked detailed questions about the conduct of the war and the attitude of the British toward Italian withdrawal from the conflict.

On June 2, Bonomi received an audience with the king, during which he laid out the political and military situation as an impending disaster and argued that the king did have the power to remove Mussolini and that the necessary political and military support for such an act was present. The king did not respond then, or in a meeting with Marshal Badoglio on June 10.

Unknown to those who met with him, on May 15 the king had presented Mussolini with three memoranda regarding how he wished the prime minister to proceed. The first dealt with the Axis military forces, pointing out their weaknesses; the second dealt with the growing Allied power and the lack of potential success in continuing resistance. The third laid out a desired course of action that concluded: "It is necessary to consider very seriously the possibility of separating the fate of Italy from that of Germany whose internal collapse can come unexpectedly like the collapse of the German Empire in 1918." The king indicated he wished to terminate the German alliance, but only with German consent. Mussolini replied that he did not know how he could accomplish this.

By mid-June, when the Duc d'Acquarone revealed to several leading Fascists that the king was thinking of replacing Mussolini as prime minister, there was no dissent. By the end of June, the dissident Fascists and the military party were ready to move, awaiting only action on the part of Victor Emmanuel III.

All of this domestic political maneuvering took place against a backdrop of the previously cordial relationship between Comando Supremo and OKW ceasing in the months after February 1943, as part of a general shift by Mussolini toward greater independence from Germany. The wartime spirit of comradeship in arms vanished. What seemed at first to the Germans to be obscure Italian political intentions in the Balkans excited a suspicious Hitler that his Italian allies were plotting "treason" against the Axis.

Italy's lack of raw materials and the industrial capability to support modern warfare now exacerbated the country's previous weaknesses, which could not be successfully solved by increased German aid, since Germany was beginning to encounter economic difficulty as the Allied Combined Bomber Offensive began to make its presence felt in the war. By March 1943, production of both armored fighting vehicles and trucks for transport started to experience shortages that would never be made up. Following the losses experienced on the Eastern Front at Stalingrad and thereafter, and in North Africa, the Luftwaffe was no longer a dominant force other than in the defensive role against Allied bombers over Germany itself.

The death knell of the Axis was quietly sounded in May 1943, when the Battle of the Atlantic took a decisive turn with the introduction of microwave radar that allowed Allied submarine hunters to spot U-boats without the Germans being able to detect the Allied radar, resulting in U-boat losses that soon became intolerable.

In April 1943, Hitler and Mussolini met for the first time in over a year at Klessheim Castle outside Salzburg. At the meeting, Hitler admitted that Germany could not increase its military aid to Italy. Relations were further strained when Mussolini suggested an end to the war in the East through a negotiated settlement with Stalin. The Fascist regime in Italy was secure only as long as prospect of victory existed. Victory without German power was hard to imagine. Mussolini's domestic power was declining.

Following the failure of the Klessheim Castle conference, Mussolini concluded the war could not be won. By the time of his mid-May meeting with the king, he had dismissed the capable members of his cabinet and replaced them with more dedicated Fascists, making the thug Carlo Scorza secretary of the Fascist Party with orders to return to the violence of the 1920s to maintain power. Despite these measures – or perhaps because of them – defeatism spread through Italian society. In March, 50,000 workers in Milan had gone on strike, demanding support for their bombed-out families. On May 1, for the first time since 1924, labor unions marched in May Day parades and rallies calling for an end to the war.

As the political crisis in Italy moved toward final resolution, the Allied demand for "unconditional surrender" made the plans difficult; in March, President Roosevelt had stated through the Holy See that the Allies would not accept any attempt at a negotiated surrender made by Mussolini. The king had to finally face the fact that if he wished to end the war, he had to remove Mussolini without delay regardless of what the Germans thought or did.

Surprisingly, with the Allies in Sicily across the Straits of Messina from Italy in July, Hitler became convinced their ultimate goal was to use their Sicilian base to invade Greece and the Balkans, invasion targets he and OKW had identified as the most likely as far back as April 1943 while the North African campaign came to a close. Both regions were more important to the German economy than Italy was, with the Balkans being the major source for bauxite, copper, and chrome. Knowing the difficulty his forces would face in defending these targets, due to the poor transportation facilities in the Balkans,

Hitler would, a year later, unilaterally withdraw German forces, when Greece and Yugoslavia were abandoned. He was also aware of and understood Churchill's desire to move into eastern Europe to forestall the Soviets, taking advantage of the fact that his Bulgarian, Romanian, and Hungarian allies were not that committed to the Axis cause. Hitler was increasingly concerned with events in Italy, since he foresaw that if Italy left the alliance, he would be forced to give the Mediterranean higher priority over the Eastern Front.

Following the Axis surrender in North Africa, Rommel was sent to Italy in June to take command of Army Group B, with the possibility of occupying all of Italy in the event of an Italian surrender. Hitler promised Rommel six infantry and *Panzergrenadier* divisions, two panzer divisions, and two *Fallschirmjäger* (Luftwaffe paratroop) divisions that would be transferred from France, and two panzer divisions transferred from the Eastern Front. The German tank losses at Kursk in July precluded transfer of the two Eastern Front divisions.

Rommel advised Hitler that Italy could not be defended without the Italian Army, advocating a retreat by German forces to a fortified line in the northern Apennine mountains south of the Po Valley, stating that from such a position, the Allies could be held at bay from entering the Reich from the south. This was set aside when the decision was made to move German troops into Sicily to reinforce the Italians.

The underground political opposition had already been in contact with Badoglio. In a meeting with Bonomi back on July 14, the marshal had agreed the new government would need the support from all the anti-Fascist parties – Liberal, Christian Democrat, Socialist, Communist, Actionist, and Democracy of Labor – and that the correct solution was a politico-military cabinet, which would eliminate fascism and break with Germany if the coup was to be recognized by the Allies. When Badoglio presented this to the king the following day, the monarch refused, remarking that prearranged coups had little chance of success in Italy, since people were not in the habit of keeping secrets; with that he terminated the audience.

For his part, Victor Emmanuel III wished to keep fascism in power for the time being if he was to dismiss Mussolini, desiring gradual political changes only. Recognizing that Badoglio was popular enough with the Italian people to be seen as a viable alternative if Mussolini was dismissed, the king was also concerned that the dissidents in the

Comando Supremo were too committed to appealing to the British and might agree to making the political changes necessary to receive a positive response from the Allies more rapidly than he considered reasonable.

On June 17, Badoglio informed Bonomi of his conversation with the king and said he did not concur with a coup based on political forces only, and that if the king did not come to accept the proposal he had made, he would withdraw his support. On July 18, the marshal's personal representatives met in Switzerland with the British ambassador to inform the British that Badoglio wished to make contact with the Allies. That same day, the king's private secretary Acquarone let it be known the king was ready to act against Mussolini, but that he wanted the government that was installed to be composed of non-political civil servants. This alarmed the underground political opposition, since the dismissal of Mussolini without the creation of a government the Allies would take seriously would leave the question of the German alliance unresolved.

On July 19, Hitler met with a dispirited Mussolini in Feltre in northern Italy. There, he lectured his Italian ally that Italy must adhere to the "voice of history" and continue the fight. Such was not to be. On his return to Rome the next day, Mussolini informed Ambrosio that he now planned to write Hitler to request a formal termination of the Pact of Steel.

Watching Mussolini's abject performance when meeting with Hitler, Ambrosio informed him that it was impossible under current conditions to defend Italy and offered his resignation, which Mussolini refused to accept.

The morning of July 20, Badoglio met with Bonomi and announced his agreement to the king's demand for gradualism. Bonomi immediately met with Acquarone and argued that such a policy of gradualism would not work, since a government of nonentities would be seen as enemies by the Fascists, and would not receive support from the opposition or from the Allies since it would include no known anti-Fascists. Additionally, the Germans would have no doubt regarding the ultimate goal of whoever replaced Mussolini; delaying the act of denouncing the alliance would only give the Germans time to take action against the new government.

Mussolini's failure in the meeting with Hitler and the Allied bombing of Rome on July 20 finally brought the king to agree with Badoglio's original proposal to arrest Mussolini and form a government composed of known anti-Fascists.

Despite offering his resignation, Ambrosio continued negotiating with the Germans to reinforce Sicily and make an all-out fight for the island, with the decision to do so made the night of June 21. On June 22, OKW informed the Comando Supremo that the 29th Panzergrenadier Division would be sent to Sicily and offered other units.

On June 22, the king met with Mussolini and attempted to induce Mussolini to offer his resignation for the good of the country, pointing out that he had become the focal point of enemy propaganda and public opinion, which prevented the government from taking action to preserve Italy from German occupation. Mussolini refused. Following the meeting, Acquarone informed General Castellano that the king had definitely decided to appoint Badoglio to succeed Mussolini, and that the plans should be firm for creating the new government by the time the king met formally with Mussolini on July 26; Castellano began planning to make the arrest then.

To prevent a rising of the Fascist militias in the capital, Ambrosio ordered General Carboni – known for being anti-German and pro-Ally – to move the 10th (Piave) Motorized Infantry Division and the 135th (Ariete) Armored Division to Rome and take control of the units as a special corps for the protection of the government. By order of the king, no special measures were taken against a German reaction to the arrest; there would be no immediate denunciation of the Pact of Steel or immediate move to approach the Allies. Victor Emmanuel's dithering and reluctance to take the actions the situation required would soon create more problems than the arrest of Mussolini resolved. For his part, Badoglio said he would follow the king's orders regardless.

Surprisingly, Mussolini had already set the stage for his overthrow. Carlo Scorza, the newly installed Fascist Party secretary, had begun planning a series of mass meetings in the major Italian cities, where Fascist leaders would exhort the public to support the war effort. Dino Grandi – who in his younger years had been considered the only possible leadership alternative to Mussolini in the Fascist Party – took the opportunity and convinced the major party leaders not to participate. These men met with Mussolini on July 16 and expressed their dissatisfaction with the situation and proposed convening the Grand Council of Fascism. The day after he returned from the disastrous meeting with Hitler, Mussolini called a meeting of the Grand Council on July 24. Grandi, who knew of the king's decision to oust Mussolini, was able to line up a majority of the council to support a resolution calling on the king to resume command of the armed forces. Several signed, believing this would merely remove Mussolini from command of the military. Grandi and his allies hoped a majority vote on the resolution would be seen as an official lack of confidence in Mussolini's leadership and give the king the opportunity to replace Mussolini with support from the Fascist Party leadership.

The Grand Council convened at 1700 hours on Saturday, July 24. Grandi immediately put forward the motion that requested the king resume leadership of the government. The debate on the motion lasted nearly nine hours. At around 0300 hours on July 25, Mussolini acceded to Grandi's demand for a vote. With 28 members present, the motion carried 19–7, with two abstentions.

At 1700 hours the afternoon of July 25, the king met with Marshal Badoglio and formally appointed him prime minister. He then handed the marshal the list of cabinet members the king and Acquarone had approved; all were professional civil servants with no history of political involvement. Badoglio was informed he would only be in charge of civil affairs, while the king resumed his role as Commander-in-Chief of the armed forces. Badoglio was also handed two proclamations that had already been issued. The first was the official announcement of his appointment, while the second was a statement to the Italian people and members of the Fascist Party, informing them that the war continued and warning them not to continue agitating for major political changes in the government or for peace. The new government would be non-Fascist instead of anti-Fascist. In one stroke, Victor Emmanuel had squandered the move against Mussolini by creating a government the Allies would not see as a legitimate negotiating partner.

The next day, on July 26, Mussolini met with the king. He tried to argue that the council vote did not require his resignation as prime minister; Victor Emmanuel coldly informed him that Marshal Badoglio had replaced him. On leaving the palace, Mussolini found his car was no longer waiting. Accepting assistance from a Carabinieri officer, he was escorted to an ambulance and whisked away. He only realized when the ambulance was on the road out of Rome that he was under arrest. The Carabinieri quickly spirited him to the island of Ponza where he was placed in prison. After dominating Italian politics and society for 21 years, since the march on Rome in 1922, Mussolini's dictatorship was over.

Grandi remained in Rome, expecting to be part of the new government. He proposed going to Spain to meet the British ambassador, Sir Samuel Hoare, with whom he had enjoyed a warm prewar friendship. Instead, Grandi was used by the new government as a red herring; the Germans assumed he would replace Mussolini given his previous role in the party, and he was followed when he was eventually sent to meet with Hoare in early August. This allowed the actual Italian delegation to get out of Italy and meet with the Allies.

When news of Mussolini's arrest raced through Rome, a massive public demonstration of support for the event broke out, with people dancing in the streets and parading in support of the king. Mobs attacked Fascist party offices, tearing down Fascist symbols throughout the city. Everyone expected the new government to negotiate an immediate peace. No one paid attention to the fact that no Germans were seen in public.

Never was people's faith in the power of royalty to be more bitterly shattered.

Badoglio's government was secretly committed to one goal: making peace with the Allies. Officially, the new government reassured their German allies that Italy remained committed to the war. The German high command from Hitler down was initially surprised by the reported resignation of Mussolini, though Hitler believed from the first word he received of the event that the resignation was not voluntary. Despite the protestations of the new Italian government of their continued loyalty to the alliance, the Germans were not deceived. German Admiral Friedrich Ruge wrote, "Mussolini's resignation, accepted without protest anywhere, is the clearest possible proof of the almost total collapse of the Fascist Party."

So far as the German leadership was concerned, the only question was whether to act immediately with the forces on hand to capture the new government before it could act, or to wait for an Allied invasion, so they might be seen as the saviors of Italy. Hitler's first instinct was to respond to the fall of Mussolini by a lightning move to take control of Rome, using the 3rd Panzergrenadier Division, which was at Lake Bolsena 35 miles north of Rome, reinforced by the 2nd Fallschirmjäger Division that would be flown to Ciampino Airport from southern France. These units would arrest the king, Badoglio, and the new cabinet members, find out where Mussolini was being held, and restore him to power, which he believed would restore the prestige of fascism. Hitler felt such betrayal by Italy that in his rage he declared Vatican City and Pope Pius XII should be taken. Only the intervention of Joachim von Ribbentrop and Joseph Goebbels dissuaded him from ordering the action.

Ultimately, it was decided that Rommel – who had been removed as commander of Army Group B a few weeks earlier – would resume command and occupy northern Italy, where the defensive line later known as the Gothic Line he had originally advocated would be constructed as rapidly as possible. General Kurt Student would take command of the 3rd Panzergrenadier Division and 2nd Fallschirmjäger Division, with orders to take control of Rome.

Mussolini's overthrow took the Allies by surprise. Allied military leaders had first considered the question of an Italian surrender in April 1943. The Joint War Plans Committee (JWPC) considered three possibilities: civil war, collapse, or unconditional surrender. The issue was first publicly discussed at the Trident Conference, held in Washington May 12–25, 1943.

The Americans had argued that the conquest of Sicily and increased bombing of the Italian mainland might bring about the collapse of Italy without the necessity of an invasion. The British argued that only an invasion would ensure the collapse of fascism and its replacement by a pro-Allied government that would join the war effort.

Civil war was considered the least likely possibility, and little thought was given to what the Allied response would be should it happen. Collapse was considered possible due to Italian military reverses, German refusal of further military assistance, destruction caused by Allied air attacks, or a loss of faith by the Italian people in their leadership. Planners assumed – wrongly as it turned out – that in this situation, the Germans would likely withdraw from Italy. In this event, the Allies might occupy a defensive line in northern Italy, establish air bases in Italy, provide garrisons to maintain order, and provide economic assistance to the anti-German government.

The possibility that the Italian government might surrender was considered unlikely as long as the government was headed by Mussolini, who had been publicly branded a war criminal by the Allies. However, there was the possibility that Mussolini might be overthrown by the Italian government, which then might try to negotiate for an armistice.

British planners submitted a document stating that, in such event, the sovereign government of Italy would have to make a legally binding guarantee that all opposition against Allied military operations would end, and that Allied armed forces could make full use of Italian territory, facilities, and resources to prosecute the war against Germany.

This pragmatic position was rejected by the US Army Civil Affairs Division (CAD) on the grounds it did not include a call for unconditional surrender, which had become the publicly declared Allied position with regard to the three Axis powers in the Casablanca Declaration the previous January. The CAD submitted a counter-proposal that, following a surrender, the Italian government should cease to exist for the remaining period of war against the Axis, and that it be replaced by an Allied military government with full powers throughout Italy, with the exception of Vatican City.

The US Joint Chiefs accepted this CAD recommendation on June 29, 1943, and submitted it to the Combined Chiefs of Staff on July 2. The gap between the British and Americans was so wide – with the British taking the position that of course the Italians would be welcomed into the anti-Nazi coalition, while the Americans were constrained from Washington by the political view that American public opinion would not support anything other than unconditional surrender, making it impossible for the American government to agree with the British position – that there was no possibility of immediate reconciliation of views.

The Combined Chiefs referred both proposals to a newly created Combined Civil Affairs Committee on July 10. British members of the CCAC requested instructions from London, and on this point Allied direction of the war stalled. Thus, when it became known on July 27 that the Italian government was prepared to attempt such an armistice, the Allies were initially late to respond since the Combined Chiefs of Staff could not agree on an Anglo-American political program or military strategy.

The news of the surrender brought out differences between the Allies that had not been apparent before. Both Churchill and Foreign Minister Anthony Eden had come to detest Mussolini as a result of his bad faith actions before the war and in its opening stages. While they supported maintenance of the House of Savoy and the Italian monarchy, they also supported Italian efforts to cut all Fascists out of any power. The Americans had to deal with what the political attitude of the large Italian-American community would be toward actions taken with regard to the home country, which exerted a moderating influence on American policy.

Immediately on learning of Mussolini's dismissal and arrest, Eisenhower directed his staff to develop a simple set of armistice terms that would allow the Italians to cooperate with the Allies as quickly as possible, which he first set forth on June 27, the day after receiving the news of Mussolini's dismissal and arrest.

The ten-point armistice Eisenhower proposed was simple and direct. His terms were an attempt to meet an Italian request for armistice before an Allied invasion of the mainland, and he made no mention of unconditional surrender.

1. Immediate cessation of all hostile activity by the Italian armed forces with disarmament as dictated by the C-in-C, and a guarantee by the Italian Government that German forces now on the Italian mainland will immediately comply with all provisions of this document.

2. All prisoners or internees of the United Nations to be immediately turned over to the C-in-C, and none of these may, from the beginning of these negotiations, be evacuated to Germany.

3. Immediate transfer of the Italian fleet to such points as may be designated by the C-in-C Med., with details of disarmament and conduct to be prescribed by him.

4. Immediate evacuation from all Italian territory of the German Air Force.

5. Immediate beginning of the evacuation of German land forces from the Italian mainland on phase lines to be so prescribed by the Allied C-in-C that the evacuation from all Italy will be complete within one month. German forces in Sicily are not affected by this armistice and will either surrender unconditionally or will be destroyed.

6. Immediate surrender of Corsica and of all Italian territory, both islands and mainland, to the Allies, for such use as operational bases and other purposes as the Allies may see fit.

7. Immediate acknowledgment of the overriding authority of the Allied Commander-in-Chief to establish military government

and with the unquestioned right to effect, through such agencies as he may set up, any changes in personnel that may seem to him desirable.

8. Immediate guarantee of the free use by the Allies of all airfields and naval ports in Italian territory, regardless of the rate of evacuation of the Italian territory by the German forces. These ports and fields to be protected by Italian armed forces until the function is taken over by the Allies.

9. Immediate withdrawal of Italian armed forces from all participation in the current war from whatever areas in which they may now be engaged.

10. Guarantee by the Italian Government that if necessary it will employ all its available armed forces to insure prompt and exact compliance with all the provisions of this armistice.

On the afternoon of July 27, Churchill spoke in Parliament of the new developments:

We should let the Italians, to use a homely phrase, stew in their own juice for a bit, and hot up the fire to the utmost in order to accelerate the process, until we obtain from their Government, or whoever possesses the necessary authority, all our indispensable requirements for carrying on the war against our prime and capital foe, which is not Italy but Germany. It is the interest of Italy, and also the interest of the Allies, that the unconditional surrender of Italy be brought about wholesale and not piecemeal.

Interestingly, President Roosevelt made no mention of unconditional surrender when he first heard of Mussolini's downfall. He immediately cabled Churchill, suggesting that if the new Italian government attempted to negotiate a separate peace, the Allied response ought to be as close as possible to unconditional surrender, then follow the capitulation with good treatment of the Italian people. For his part, Churchill believed the destruction of the Fascist system would follow any negotiated peace, and submitted a proposed armistice closely resembling Eisenhower's, with the additional demand for the surrender of Mussolini and the leading Fascists to be tried as war criminals. Also on July 27, the British government informed the American government that either the king or Marshal Badoglio was an acceptable authority for the purpose of negotiating a surrender.

On July 28, President Roosevelt made a radio address about the Italian situation: "Our terms for Italy are still the same as our terms to Germany and Japan – 'Unconditional Surrender.' We will have no truck with Fascism in any way, shape, or manner. We will permit no vestige of Fascism to remain."

Chief of Staff General George C. Marshall informed Eisenhower that the British viewed his authority as limited to purely local surrenders, while an overall surrender of the Italian government involved political and economic conditions as well as military points. Eisenhower replied that there might only be a fleeting opportunity to gain all objectives, and it was his belief that obtaining Italian cooperation in seizing vital ports and airfields was paramount, and that if possible, economic and political matters should be settled later, allowing him to use military terms alone to rapidly bring the Mediterranean campaign to an end.

The sticking point between British and American proposals was whether or not the surrendering Italian authority should be allowed to remain in office. On July 29, the American CAD made clear that the British terms were unacceptable since they did not include a call for unconditional surrender. Roosevelt informed Churchill that he found General Eisenhower's proposed armistice terms "entirely acceptable." With this, he removed the requirement that the armistice include "unconditional surrender," though the Combined Civil Affairs Division was still operating on that demand. Roosevelt also did not believe it necessary to require Mussolini to be turned over as a war criminal if such a demand would delay an armistice. Roosevelt explained to the press when questioned on this point that he did not care with whom the Allies dealt in Italy, as long as that individual – "King, prime minister, or a mayor" – was not a member of the Fascist government and as long as Italian troops would lay down their arms, and as long as anarchy could be prevented.

On July 29, the British and American governments approved the following statement be broadcast to Italy:

We commend the Italian people and the House of Savoy on ridding themselves of Mussolini, the man who involved them in war as the tool of Hitler, and brought them to the verge of disaster. The greatest obstacle which divided the Italian people from the United Nations has been removed by the Italians themselves. The only remaining obstacle on the road to peace is the German aggressor who is still on Italian soil.

You want peace. You can have peace immediately, and peace under the honorable conditions which our governments have already offered you. We are coming to you as liberators. Your part is to cease immediately any assistance to the German military forces in your country. If you do this, we will rid you of the Germans and deliver you from the horrors of war. As you have already seen in Sicily, our occupation will be mild and beneficent. Your men will return to their normal life, and to their productive avocations and, provided all British and Allied prisoners now in your hands are restored safely to us, and not taken away to Germany, the hundreds of thousands of Italian prisoners captured by us in Tunisia and Sicily, will return to the countless Italian homes who long for them. The ancient liberties and traditions of your country will be restored.

In the end, the one thing the two Allies could agree on was to order General Eisenhower on August 2 to invade Italy at the earliest possible date. Eisenhower saw the political developments in Italy as creating an opportunity for bold action on the part of the Allies to rapidly seize the important points on the Italian mainland with Italian consent. He instructed General Mark W. Clark to prepare one division to sail directly into Naples harbor and seize the port in conjunction with a drop of the 82nd Airborne Division. Events would prove all this to be overly optimistic. While the Allies dithered among themselves over what to do, the Germans acted.

It was said during the war that only Winston Churchill wanted to keep fighting in the Mediterranean. There was, however, one other man itching for a fight in Italy.

Field Marshal Albert Kesselring first arrived in Italy in December 1941, having been appointed Southern Front commander. It was appropriate at the time to send a senior Luftwaffe commander such as Kesselring to take this post, since the primary German contribution to the Mediterranean war at that time was airpower. Kesselring had proven himself a very adept commander in the 20 months he had been in command: Luftflotte 2 – which he had commanded during the 1940 Blitzkrieg, the Battle of Britain, and the invasion of the

Soviet Union – came close to ending the British ability to use Malta as a base, and controlled the Luftwaffe units in North Africa. Since Kesselring's background was in the army, having joined the Bavarian Army in 1906, serving as an infantry officer during World War I and on the Reichswehr staff during the Weimar Republic before taking part in the creation of the Luftwaffe in 1933–34, he was easily accepted as commander by Erwin Rommel and the Afrika Korps. Derisively nicknamed "Smiling Albert" by the Allies, Kesselring was known to his troops as "Uncle Albert" in recognition of the importance he put on the welfare of his men. This reputation made him one of the most popular senior military leaders with the Wehrmacht rank and file. His frequent, generally unannounced, visits to the front lines added to this popularity. Additionally, he was respected by the officers who led the units in his command for being the only senior commander to visit the front in North Africa, where he listened to their reports and did his best to provide the support they needed.

After Mussolini's arrest, Kesselring planned to occupy all of Italy should the government surrender. Despite the professed loyalty to the Axis cause by the new government, the Germans were well aware of the intense negotiations Marshal Badoglio's government were involved in with the Allies. On August 1, Rommel's Army Group B began moving into northern Italy from southern France in accordance with Hitler's directive of July 30, doing so in small units so as not to alarm the Italians; nevertheless, tensions increased as the Wehrmacht operation movement continued over the following days.

Kesselring had long planned to defend southern Italy when the Allied invasion he considered inevitable occurred. By his command, German units on their way to North Africa were held in Italy when the surrender of Axis forces in Tunisia became inevitable. Kesselring also believed the Italian Army would remain loyal.

Kesselring believed Rommel had a closer relationship with Hitler than he did. Knowing Rommel's antipathy to fighting in southern Italy, Kesselring took the occasion of Luftwaffe paratroop commander General Kurt Student's arrival in Rome to plan a coup de main to arrest the king and Badoglio, to press his plans for an all-out defense of southern Italy. He stated his belief that if such a fight were made, using the geographic difficulties Italy presented to any invader for a campaign of attrition, forcing the Allies to pay in blood for every inch of territory taken in Calabria and Apulia, then he could hold Rome until the summer of 1944, thus delaying the Allied approach to the Reich.

Many German officers believed the Allies might attempt to land in northern Italy, taking a shortcut to assaulting Rome. Kesselring stated flatly the invasion would happen no further north than Naples, because Allied air units on Sicily did not have the range to support an invasion further north. He specifically said that the most likely invasion spot was Salerno, south of Naples; he advocated Salerno be occupied against such a move. Presciently, he also stated that after Rome fell the next summer, the army should retreat north to the line of fortifications in the Apennines that Rommel was in the process of constructing, which Kesselring believed they could hold "indefinitely" as long as sufficient supplies could be secured through the Brenner Pass.

Student was impressed by Kesselring's knowledge of conditions in Italy and by how comprehensive his plan to defend the peninsula to delay Allied advance was. He promised to inform Hitler of Kesselring's plans and position when he returned to Berlin.

Mussolini's birthday was July 29. Rumors flew through the streets of Rome that the Germans were preparing to seize the city. In an effort to discover Mussolini's whereabouts, German Ambassador Hans Georg von Mackensen and Field Marshal Kesselring met with Italian government representatives. Kesselring brough a special set of Nietzsche's works as a present from Hitler to Mussolini and asked to deliver it personally, but the Italians refused the gift and would not reveal where Mussolini was being held.

At the same time, the Comando Supremo received the news that German troops were massing north of the Brenner Pass and that units were moving toward the pass that had been used over the centuries by so many invaders to conquer Italy. General Ambrosio now faced the possibility of resisting the Germans on two fronts. That morning, he had appointed Generale di Corpo d'Armata Alberto Barbieri to command the newly created Army Corps of Rome, composed of the 12th "Sassari" Infantry Division, elements of the 21st "Granatieri" Infantry Division, Roman police forces, and African police troops, to support the units commanded by General Carboni, to oppose any German move to seize control of the city. Ambrosino ordered nearby Italian Army units in southern France and Slovenia to stand by to oppose any German move to cross the border in the Brenner Pass, and ordered placement of explosive charges along the railroad line. News of the Italian Army's moves in the north outraged Hitler when he learned of it; he issued orders to the Wehrmacht units moving into Italy to carry out their orders even if bloodshed resulted.

The crisis seemed at hand on July 30, when the 29th Panzergrenadier Division – which was authorized to move into Italy to reinforce the defenses in the south – began moving to the Brenner Pass along with the 44th Infantry Division, which was not authorized to make such a move. The German commander, General Valentin Feuerstein, met with General Alessandro Gloria, the Italian commander in the north, and informed him the German units would move into Italy by road, so as not to take up valuable rail space. The Italians saw through this move and refused entry. In Rome, Kesselring met with Badoglio to resolve the crisis, but Badoglio stated that military issues were beyond his authority. Kesselring went to Ambrosio and appealed to him as a fellow ally to allow the move; Ambrosio refused. The next day, the German units were ordered to cross the border after a final appeal by Kesselring to Badoglio, who repeated he had no power over military issues. Ultimately, the issue was resolved when General Emil von Rintelen, the German military attaché in Italy, met with Badoglio, who continued to protest that he intended to carry on the war and wanted to resolve the crisis at the border. Von Rintelen – who knew Badoglio was at the same time attempting to contact the Allies, and who also believed the war was lost, though he was not an active opponent of Hitler – understood Badoglio's difficulty. In the end, the 44th Infantry Division was allowed to enter Italy by train, which meant they were not able to take control of the border as originally planned. Therefore direct armed conflict was averted.

On August 3, OKW informed Comando Supremo they were moving additional Wehrmacht units into Italy in accordance with Hitler's decision of July 22 to reinforce Italian defenses against the Allies. Under orders from Badoglio, Ambrosio agreed to these moves. The moves were complete by mid-August, and the Germans were now in position to occupy Italy in the event of an armistice being announced.

The new Wehrmacht Tenth Army was activated on August 22, with the very capable General Heinrich von Vietinghoff in command. The army's force was composed of the German units Kesselring had held back from North Africa, and the units recently evacuated from

Sicily, along with the units that had recently moved into Italy. The two subordinate corps were positioned to cover potential landing sites north and south of Naples. XIV Panzer Korps was sent to the Salerno plain with the paratroop/panzer division "Hermann Göring," which was at approximately half strength due to losses in Sicily; they were backed up by the 16th Panzer Division holding the hills above the Salerno plain. The 15th Panzergrenadier Division and 16th Panzer Division were near Naples, while LXXVI Panzer Korps' 26th Panzer Division, 29th Panzergrenadier Division and 4th Fallschirmjäger Division were positioned further south, just north of Salerno.

While Kesselring made his moves to strengthen the German position in Italy, the Allies dithered over the question of what exactly to do with Italy. Bolder planners advocated using the coming confusion to take advantage of the situation and give a real knockout blow to the war. Unfortunately, there was no accurate information about Rommel's Army Group B, since German communications were conducted by telephone landline, shielding them from Ultra codebreaking.

A coup de main against Rome itself was suggested, with the 82nd Airborne landing at Ciampino Airport the day the surrender was announced, to take control of Rome. Further, this move would be supported by a landing at Nettuno, just west of Rome. The idea was abandoned due to there being no way to provide air support, since neither the Royal Navy nor US Navy could provide aircraft carriers and naval air units to give cover. The idea of an airborne landing continued into early September; General Maxwell Taylor landed at Anzio on September 1 and met with the Italian in Rome to plan the event. Unfortunately, the Italians could not provide sufficient loyal army units to support the intervention, while it was now obvious Kesselring's forces in the city were larger and more active than expected.

The Badoglio government desperately wanted to contact the Allies to find a way to negotiate peace. Raffaele Guariglia, the Italian ambassador to Turkey, had been named foreign minister when the Badoglio government was formed. Guariglia strongly believed peace must occur. Before leaving Istanbul on July 28, he asked the Turkish Foreign Ministry to convey to the Allied diplomatic representatives that he was returning to Italy to find a way to declare peace. On his arrival in Rome on July 29, he met with Badoglio and learned the true situation; the two men agreed that all contact and negotiations with the Allies must remain Top Secret. On July 31, Guariglia attempted to make contact with the Allies through the British and American representatives to the Vatican, but was told that both British and American diplomatic ties had been compromised and there was no way to communicate with their governments without the Germans learning of the move.

Guariglia then appointed the Marchese Blasco Lanza D'Ajeta, Counselor to the Italian Vatican mission and a godson of the wife of American Deputy Secretary of State Sumner Welles, as Counselor to the Italian embassy in Lisbon, Portugal, since D'Ajeta didn't rank high enough to excite German suspicions with his transfer. The British Vatican ambassador, D'Arcy Osborne, provided D'Ajeta with a letter of introduction attesting to his bona fides, for presentation to Osborne's cousin, Sir Ronald Hugh Campbell, the British ambassador to Portugal. D'Ajeta was under orders to make clear he did not have power to negotiate, but he was to provide the Allies with a full account of the situation in Rome and request immediate Allied assistance. D'Ajeta flew to Lisbon on August 3 and met with Ambassador Campbell the next day. He informed the ambassador that Italy was on the verge of a complete German takeover. In Rome, the Italian government waited for an Allied reply. With the British and Americans still far apart on how to proceed, there was none.

Guariglia also sent Alberto Berio, former Counselor to the Italian embassy in Istanbul, to Tangier in Spanish Morocco, to present the Italian case to the British Consul there that Italy wanted to negotiate. Berio was ordered to tell the British that the Italian government was a virtual German prisoner in Rome, to request that the Allies make a move in the Balkans to draw off German attention, and to plead that if an invasion of Italy was to happen that it come ashore as far north as possible. Again, there was no Allied reply to the Italian plea.

On August 5, the Germans had determined they could not take Rome in a lightning move, now that there were sufficient Italian military units in the vicinity to put up a serious fight if such a move was attempted. Additionally, General Kurt Student had been unsuccessful in discovering where Mussolini was being held. The two allies met in an atmosphere of mutual suspicion at Tarvis on August 6. The Italians were determined to maintain the public position that they were committed to the Italo-German alliance while they played for time to hear from their two messengers. The Germans arrived not believing a word their counterparts said. General Ambrosio complained that the German units that had entered Italy to reinforce the southern defenses were remaining in northern and central Italy; OKW commander General Wilhelm Keitel replied that any questioning of German good faith was unacceptable and that the Italians should be thankful Germany was coming to their assistance and insisted that northern Italy must be secured before the units could be sent south. In the end, the only agreement reached was that German units in southern Italy would be brought to full strength. Diplomat Leonardo Vitetti later explained that the Tarvis Conference was like Columbus' first voyage: "He did not know where he was going and when he came back he did not know where he had been or what he had done." On August 7, General Gloria reported that 30,000 German troops had crossed the Brenner Pass as of that day. The German intention to compel the Italian government to continue the war whether it wished to or not, to seize Rome and the Italian fleet, and to turn Italy into a battlefield for the defense of Germany was abundantly clear to the Italians after the conference. General Ambrosio recalled two more Italian divisions to Rome to defend the city against their "allies."

In the end, the Allies were only able to come to any resolution of the Italian attempt to surrender at the Quadrant Conference, held in Quebec August 17–24, 1943, where the principal Allied leaders could make definitive decisions. Additionally, the definitive decision made at the conference to remove seven first-rate Allied divisions from the Mediterranean as of November 1, 1943, and send them to Britain in preparation for the 1944 cross-Channel invasion would guarantee that the Allies would not be able to deliver a decisive blow against the German forces in Italy once the decision was made to invade the peninsula.

On the Italian side, the individual primarily responsible for pushing events to the point where a formal armistice was negotiated and signed was Marshal Castellano, who had believed from the beginning that Italy could only be saved by changing sides and joining the Allies. He detested Badoglio as an incompetent who had proven his ineptitude by his failure to recognize that it was impossible for Italy to rid itself of Mussolini and yet remain allied with Nazi Germany. General Ambrosio would go no further than Badoglio in pushing to end the alliance with Germany, and Badoglio would take no action except on the explicit word of the king. A proposal was made to send a direct representative of the government to the Allies, with power to negotiate an armistice if not a peace agreement, and the king was prevailed upon to name Castellano for the assignment. Castellano's main assignment was to convince the Allies to land far enough north that Rome could be quickly taken. He departed for Madrid on August 12, traveling under an assumed name as a minor consular official.

As of that date, half of Rommel's Army Group B was in Italy and the 44th Infantry Division controlled the Italian end of the Brenner Pass. None of the recently arrived German units had moved south of Rome, which was now surrounded by German units that were stronger than the defending Italian units. Having seen no movement on the part of the Italian government since the end of July, the Allies had resumed bombing missions in Italy after a week's suspension, including two missions against Rome.

Reports of the D'Ajeta and Berio missions were finally sent to London. Immediately prior to departing for the Quadrant Conference, Churchill dismissed both as having no substance other than "a desire that we should rescue the Italians from the Germans, and do so as soon as possible," as he wrote to Roosevelt when passing on the reports. Foreign Minister Anthony Eden continued to maintain that since the Allies had determined on a policy of unconditional surrender that the Badoglio government would have to first notify the Allies that Italy was surrendering unconditionally before any negotiations could proceed.

On August 12, President Roosevelt approved Eden's draft reply to Berio, which stated that the Allies were unwilling to negotiate and concluded: "Badoglio must understand that we cannot negotiate, but require unconditional surrender, which means that the Italian Government should place themselves in the hands of the Allied Governments, who will then state their terms. These will provide for an honorable capitulation."

Harold Tittman, chief assistant to the American representative at the Holy See, managed to get a report to Washington through the US embassy in Switzerland, reporting the current situation in Rome and reiterating that Badoglio was playing for time while Hitler decided whether or not he would occupy all of Italy, reiterating that time was of the essence for Allied action to prevent this outcome, and that in this situation Badoglio and his government could not take any unconditional action as required by the Allies.

Concurrently, General Eisenhower was planning Operation *Avalanche*, as he had been ordered to do on August 4. Unfortunately, the information D'Ajeta had memorized regarding the German reinforcement of the southern front and the presence south of Naples of two panzer divisions, was not communicated to Eisenhower's headquarters in Algiers. Had Eisenhower known the actual situation regarding enemy forces and taken that information into the planning of the invasion, the battle on the beaches of Salerno might have been far different.

Once in Madrid, Castellano met with the British ambassador, Sir Samuel Hoare. He stated that, while the Italian government was currently a prisoner of an "ally" with 13 divisions in the country, which had threatened to bomb Italian cities if the government attempted to leave the alliance with Germany, if the Allies would invade the Italian mainland the government was prepared to join the Allies in fighting the Germans. When Hoare asked what the Italian response was to the Allied demand for unconditional surrender, Castellano stated, "We are not in a position to make any terms. We will accept unconditional surrender provided we can join the Allies in fighting the Germans." Castellano departed Madrid for Lisbon that evening, after requesting that General Eisenhower send a military representative, to whom Castellano would provide detailed information on German dispositions in Italy. Hoare reported to London that the Italians were ready to surrender unconditionally if the Allies landed on the peninsula, provided they were allowed to join the fight against Germany. "Without these two conditions, the Italian Government will not have sufficient courage or justification to make a complete volte face and will drift impotently into chaos."

On receipt of Hoare's message, Anthony Eden advised Churchill against accepting the Italian proposal on the grounds it might create "political difficulties" for the Allies. Eden was referring specifically to President Roosevelt's public position against accepting any conditions to a surrender. Churchill messaged Roosevelt at Hyde Park, proposing that the Allies respond to Castellano's proposal by informing him, "The Italian Government should … resist the Germans to the best of their ability as soon as possible, pending arrival of Anglo-American armies," and suggesting this resistance could include freeing Allied POWs in Italian custody, cutting German communications in southern Italy, and sailing the fleet from La Spezia to Malta.

On August 17, the Combined Chiefs of Staff issued a draft "Suggested Action on Italian Peace Feelers," which would come to be known as the Quebec Memorandum. The draft suggested Eisenhower send two staff officers – one American, one British – to Lisbon immediately to meet Castellano, whom they were to inform that the Allies would accept the unconditional surrender of Italy on the conditions of the previously announced "short terms," with political, economic, and financial terms to be communicated later; while the Allies expected no "active resistance" on the part of Italy in fighting the Germans, Italy should take the actions possible to hamper German operations. In return, the Allies would restrict bombing to targets affecting the Germans alone. Hostilities would cease at a time to be determined by General Eisenhower; the Italian government was to proclaim the armistice at once and "collaborate with the Allies and to resist the Germans" by sending the navy, merchant shipping, and aircraft to Allied territory. Until the hour of the armistice, the Italians were to institute general passive resistance and minor sabotage against the Germans, safeguard Allied prisoners of war, prevent Italian ships and aircraft from falling into German hands, and prevent the Germans from taking over Italian coast defenses. If the Italians complied, Eisenhower would be authorized to soften the armistice terms proportionately with the scale of the assistance rendered to the Allies.

The terms of the Quebec Memorandum offered the Badoglio government little inducement to surrender past a general promise that the Allies would modify the terms of surrender in the future if Italy surrendered unconditionally on the eve of invasion and gave aid to that invasion. There were no answers to Badoglio's vital questions: were the Allies able, willing, and planning to occupy Rome, the seat of his government? Or would the surrender signal the German occupation of Rome and immediate establishment of a neo-Fascist Quisling regime?

The British were concerned that the "long terms" of the surrender were not spelled out. However, after Churchill and Eden conferred with President Roosevelt, the British Foreign Office informed the US State Department on August 23 that it was agreed the "long terms" would form the basis for all surrender discussion. While the State Department demurred, on August 26 Roosevelt stated that Eisenhower was strictly to use the "long terms."

Eisenhower was thus faced with conflicting orders: to invade the mainland at two locations, Messina and Salerno, with limited resources, then sweep 140 miles to Rome as rapidly as possible; and bluff Badoglio into surrender before the invasion while insisting on unconditional surrender. In the meantime, Allied intelligence had discovered that previous estimates of German strength and capability in southern Italy had been greatly underestimated; the plans for the Salerno invasion were radically wrong and there was no time to revise them.

In Italy, Marshal Kesselring advocated continued cooperation with the Italians while consolidating the plans to occupy the country, but to take no action until there was incontrovertible evidence of Italian double-dealing; doing so would allow him time to bring in sufficient armed force to hold the entire peninsula rather than retreat to the north precipitously. This was the German strategy during the final Italo-German military meeting at Bologna on August 15. The meeting was inconclusive, with both sides leaving convinced the other was not to be trusted.

On August 22, General Walter Bedell Smith, Eisenhower's chief of staff, met with Castellano in Lisbon and communicated the Allied position. Castellano was disappointed to see there would be no move to immediately occupy Rome; he asked technical questions about how the Italians were to demonstrate their "resistance" and was assured by Smith that the Allies did not expect the Italians to accomplish things beyond their ability. His questions regarding what sovereignty the Italian government would retain in light of the statement that Eisenhower was to establish a military administration of the country revealed that the Allies had little disposition to welcoming Italy to their ranks. The Italian government was to respond by August 28; if they had not done so by August 30, the Allies would interpret that as rejection of the terms.

Castellano realized it was too late for Italy to bargain. He returned to Italy with the Allied terms in a daring train trip across Spain and France, arriving in Rome on August 27; Badoglio was dismayed when he learned the Allied terms. The government concluded that Italy had no way out other than acceptance of Allied terms, regardless. The agreed-upon radio announcement that would be considered Italian acceptance of the terms to the Allies was not made on August 28; the king did not see the information until the next day. The king wanted to send a message that did not refuse the armistice while not accepting the conditions for surrender; Castellano informed him that the Allies required a yes or no answer, and that they were now 24 hours late in making that answer. Reluctantly, Victor Emmanuel gave his approval.

On August 31, Castellano and General Giacomo Zanussi arrived at the Palermo airfield on Sicily. General Smith bluntly informed him that the Italian position, demanding that the Allies land near Rome, was unacceptable; the choice for Italy was to accept the conditions offered or refuse. He pointed out that if the Italians refused, Eisenhower would lose his authority to modify the conditions later in light of Italian compliance, and that a settlement imposed by the Allies would be far less generous. While he maintained a position of "take it or leave it," Smith knew that an Italian surrender was crucial to any success of Operation *Avalanche*, given what Allied intelligence had discovered regarding the now nearly overwhelming strength of German forces against what the Allies could put on the mainland – 19 German divisions in Italy against three to five Allied divisions landed on the beaches, with a maximum buildup over two weeks to eight. If the 16 Italian divisions fought with the Germans, the invasion would fail. Over the next 72 hours, the armistice was hammered out at Cassibile, with Smith finally promising to drop the 82nd Airborne on Rome. Castellano and Zanussi returned to Rome. Meeting with Badoglio on September 1, they admitted that the Allies had rejected the demand for a landing near Rome. The marshal and other members of the government realized they had no choice. When presented with the terms on that basis, the king gave his assent. Castellano returned to Sicily on September 2; the atmosphere was cool when he was asked if he had the power to sign the armistice and replied that he did not. Radio messages between Sicily and Rome became frantic. Finally, at 1700 hours on September 3, Castellano received authority to sign the document; 15 minutes later the Armistice of Cassibile, in which Italy surrendered to the Allies and pledged to join the fight against Germany, was secretly signed.

That same day, the British Eighth Army crossed the Straits of Messina in Operation *Baytown*. The Italian government ordered the Italian Army units holding the position not to resist the Allies. The British landed without casualties.

The end result of King Victor Emmanuel's reluctance to decisively reject fascism and move to join the Allies, fear of the Germans on the part of the Italian government, and the lack of Allied unity over what to do with Italy in the immediate event of Mussolini's overthrow, would add 18 months and incredible suffering on the part of the Italian people to the cost of the war.

3

THE NEAR DISASTER OF OPERATION
AVALANCHE

Operation *Avalanche*, the amphibious landing at Salerno by the US Fifth Army and elements of the British Eighth Army and the Canadian Army, was the main attack Kesselring anticipated. The most rapidly planned of all Allied amphibious operations other than the invasion of Guadalcanal the year before, it was the closest to disaster – with the Allied commanders on the scene forced at one point to seriously consider the possibility of attempting a withdrawal under fire.

Kesselring had been correct that the range of Allied airpower based on Sicily would define the location of the invasion, and also correct that it would be Salerno, south of Naples. The only Allied fighters capable of supporting any action north of Salerno were the P-38 Lightnings of the three fighter groups and the two groups of A-36 Mustangs. Even at Salerno, the Spitfire-equipped units would only have fuel for 15 minutes over the beachhead, with the P-40 units being even less capable.

The Americans had made an attempt to live up to the promises made to the Italian government to land the 82nd Airborne Division in Rome, as Operation *Giant II*. Once the armistice was signed, 82nd Airborne commander General Maxwell D. Ridgway joined the meeting to specifically discuss what support such an operation would require from the Italians. General Ridgway was only too aware of the vulnerability of the slow C-47s, coming in at low altitude to drop troops, after the disaster at Gela in July, when a formation of C-47s carrying reinforcements for the initial paratroop drops were fired on by the ships of the invasion fleet with the loss of 23 aircraft with the troops they carried. Castellano assured those present that the Italians would secure the airfields and take control of the Rome antiaircraft defenses. He suggested troop landings at Littoria and Centocelle airfields, with heavy equipment delivered to Guidonia airfield.

The more aggressive planners on Eisenhower's staff were strongly in favor of a coup de main against Rome itself, landing the 82nd Airborne at Rome the day the surrender was announced to take control of the city and disrupt the Germans. This would have been supported by limited Allied landings at Nettuno of one armored division, with shallow-draft ships carrying ammunition and other supplies run up the Tiber River to the city itself. The armor would quickly move to Rome to support the paratroopers and the Italian forces who were to defend the city against the Germans. The only air cover that could have been provided for the operation would have been the three P-38 groups, all now based on Sicily; if sufficient supplies of 100-octane fuel could be provided, then other Allied fighters could also provide support, landing to refuel on the airfields that had been taken. The plan was audacious and risky, and depended on the Italians being able to disrupt German forces and hold them off from occupying major parts of the city.

After Ridgway consulted his planners, he was increasingly skeptical of the ability of the Italian forces to neutralize antiaircraft units and worried over how many German flak units were available. He also expressed concern about the ability of Italian forces to maintain control of the city, given that Castellano had admitted all units were short of ammunition. When he conferred again that night with Castellano, the Italian admitted it would be enormously difficult to silence every Italian-manned antiaircraft battery, and that Littoria and Guidonia airfields were surrounded by extensive flak batteries. He suggested as an alternative that the paratroops be landed at Furbara and Cerveteri airfields, which were further from Rome than those originally suggested.

After working overnight, a more detailed plan was presented on September 4. Initial forces would land on Cerveteri and Furbara airfields, with drops the next night on the Guidonia, Littoria, and Centocelle airfields, with the troops assembling on the western outskirts of Rome. The Italians would secure and protect the airfields and would man all the antiaircraft defenses, with the batteries given explicit orders not to fire at any aircraft during the two nights of the operation. Additionally,

Italian troops would block the approach of German units, provide local protection of the airfields before the landings, and assure unmolested passage of supply craft up the Tiber River to Rome.

General Maxwell Taylor, the 82nd's artillery commander, described the operation thus: "The airborne troops upon arrival will cooperate with the Italians in the defense of Rome and comply with the recommendations of the Italian high command without relinquishing their liberty of action or undertaking any operation or making any disposition considered unsound."

After discussing all this with Castellano and realizing the general could not make any firm commitments that would provide adequate protection and support to the landing, Ridgway became convinced the operation was a "tragic mistake" and protested strongly to General Smith. It was decided that the questions would be resolved by sending two American officers to meet with the Italians in Rome; their real purpose was to assess the actual feasibility of the operation.

Castellano had a final meeting with Smith, in which he tried to get a more definite date of the intended landings. All Smith would say was that the landings were scheduled to happen "in the next two weeks." Castellano then wrote a report to be returned to Rome in which he stated it was his belief the landings would happen between September 10 and 15, with the most likely date being September 12. Unfortunately, the Italian leaders accepted Castellano's guess as to the date as being definite and made their plans accordingly.

The Italian leaders in Rome did not agree with Castellano's assurances of active participation in fighting the Germans; they still wished to be passively rescued from the Germans by the Allies. The only orders they issued to Italian units in the three days after the armistice was signed were defensive in nature, with no orders to any commanders to cooperate with the Allies. The only troop moves ordered foresaw the units arriving in Rome on September 8, in the expectation of the Allied landing coming on September 12. When he received a copy of the plans for *Giant II*, General Mario Roatta – commanding troops in Rome – was flabbergasted and informed his superiors that the requirements for Italian action were far beyond the capabilities of any of his units; he stated that if his troops were capable of carrying out the tasks the Allied plan assigned them, "we would not require that the Allies land in Rome."

Regia Aeronautica aerial photos taken of the North African embarkation ports on September 4 and reports from Sicily convinced General Roatta that the Allies had no intention of landing the six divisions near Rome that he had been informed would happen, and that they would in fact land in southern Italy. He reported to Badoglio on September 6 that if his forces in Rome took any action in support of the landings, when they were so far away, he risked losing all his sway with the Germans cementing their control of central and northern Italy. The fact that the king had not yet agreed to have Italian forces actively cooperate with the Allies hamstrung all their decisions.

The result was that the night of September 6, Generals Carboni and Roatta, the commanders with responsibility for Rome, met with Marshal Badoglio and repudiated all of Castellano's assurances to the Allies regarding *Giant II*.

On the night of September 7, the 82nd's General Taylor and Colonel William T. Gardiner of Troop Carrier Command landed at Gaeta from a British motor torpedo boat, and were taken to Rome to confer with the Italian leaders. A final decision to put *Giant II* into operation – the 82nd was at the time in Italy preparing for the landings – would be made by General Taylor after he met with the Italians. Time was of the essence, since D-Day for Operation *Avalanche* was September 9. On arrival in Rome they were provided an expansive dinner, during which they found the Italians did not plan to meet immediately. The two protested that a meeting must take place as soon as possible.

General Carboni arrived at 2130 hours and proceeded to inform them that there were now 12,000 German paratroops around Rome, along with 24,000 troops of the 3rd Panzergrenadier Division accompanied by 150 tanks. He also stated the Germans had stopped supplying the Italians, and that his troops did not have ammunition for a battle lasting more than a few hours. He continued, stating his belief that if the government announced the armistice, the Germans would occupy Rome within a matter of hours, and that his troops could do little to prevent that; in conclusion he told the two Americans he believed they were going to land at Salerno, which was too far away to provide any support to the capital, and he advised against any action that would result in the Germans taking control of the capital.

Taylor and Gardiner demanded to meet Marshal Badoglio, and were taken to his villa, where they waited 20 minutes while Carboni met with the marshal. They were then taken into Badoglio's quarters. Taylor asked Badoglio if he was aware of how much action the Allies had taken in response to Castellano's information. Badoglio replied that the situation had changed without Castellano's knowledge, and that it was now impossible to make such an announcement the next day, or for the Americans to land in Rome. In response, Taylor said he would act as a messenger for any response Badoglio wished to communicate to the Allied leadership.

Badoglio wrote out his message: "Due to changes in the situation brought about by the disposition and strength of the German forces in the Rome area, it is no longer possible to accept an immediate armistice as this could provoke the occupation of the Capital and the violent assumption of the government by the Germans. Operation Giant Two is no longer possible because of lack of forces to guarantee the airfields. Badoglio."

Taylor sent a message with Badoglio's: "In view of the statement of Marshal Badoglio as to inability to declare armistice and to guarantee fields GIANT TWO is impossible. Reasons given for change are irreplaceable lack of gasoline and munitions and new German dispositions. Badoglio requests Taylor return to present government views. Taylor and Gardiner awaiting instructions. Acknowledge. Taylor."

The messages were sent at 0200 hours on September 8. Worried that they might take too long to decode after receipt, Taylor sent the emergency message he had been instructed to use to cancel the airborne landings: "Situation Innocuous."

As Taylor and Gardiner prepared to return to Palermo, the Italians asked if General Carlo Rossi could accompany them to explain to General Eisenhower in person why the Italians were forced to act as they were and requesting a delay in the invasion until September 15. At the same time, a four-part message from Eisenhower to Badoglio, outlining all the Allied plans and intentions, had been sent but not yet seen by Badoglio. Had it been read, it would have been clear that Rossi's trip would be fruitless. Nevertheless, he accompanied the two Americans on their return, with the trip made in an Italian air force transport direct to Bizerte.

Taylor discovered on arrival in Bizerte that he had arrived before the message he had sent and the one from Badoglio had been decoded. General Eisenhower was making plans and issuing orders in accordance with the belief that *Giant II* was going ahead. The Salerno invasion would go ahead in 24 hours without a paratroop landing inland to help secure the beaches while the 82nd went on to Rome. Eisenhower was enraged by the Italian decision when Taylor informed him of it.

Castellano was brought into a meeting with Eisenhower, Admiral Andrew Browne Cunningham, General Sir Harold Alexander, and a number of other high-ranking Allied officers. He later told his aide he felt like he was at his own court-martial. Eisenhower read Badoglio's message, which shocked Castellano. Eisenhower then stated that if Badoglio did not announce the armistice as planned, it would be taken as evidence of bad faith on the part of the Italian government and the armistice would be rescinded. Castellano argued that something unexpected must have happened in Rome to have this occur. He was desperate to maintain the armistice. Eisenhower read the message he intended to send to Badoglio, which concluded: "Plans have been made on the assumption that you were acting in good faith and we have been prepared to carry out future operations on that basis. Failure now on your part to carry out the full obligations to the signed agreement will have the most serious consequences for your country. No future action of yours could then restore any confidence whatever in your good faith and consequently the dissolution of your government and nation would ensue." Eisenhower then dismissed Castellano.

In the aftermath of the meeting, Eisenhower informed the Combined Chiefs of his decision. When it was communicated to Churchill and Roosevelt, both agreed with his decision. Since it was imperative the 82nd not proceed as planned, General Lyman Lemnitzer flew directly to Sicily with the cancellation order. Due to faulty navigation by his pilot, Lemnitzer did not arrive at the division headquarters at Licata until troops were actually boarding the aircraft. Sixty-two C-47s had already been loaded and taken off and were circling the field when Lemnitzer arrived.

At 1830 hours on September 8, 1943, General Eisenhower's message regarding the invasion was broadcast by Radio Algiers despite Badoglio's failure to announce the armistice.

This is General Dwight D. Eisenhower, Commander-in-Chief of the Allied forces. The Italian Government has surrendered its armed forces unconditionally. As Allied Commander-in-Chief, I have granted a military armistice, the terms of which have been approved by the Governments of the United Kingdom, the United States, and the Union of Soviet Socialist Republics. Thus I am acting in the interests of the United Nations. The Italian Government has bound itself by these terms without reservation. The armistice was signed by my representative and the representative of Marshal Badoglio and it becomes effective this instant.

Hostilities between the armed forces of the United Nations and those of Italy terminate at once. All Italians who now act to help eject the German aggressor from Italian soil will have the assistance and support of the United Nations.

No confirming announcement came from Rome. After waiting ten minutes, Eisenhower authorized Radio Algiers to broadcast the approved version of Badoglio's announcement: "The Italian Government, recognizing the impossibility of continuing the unequal struggle against the overwhelming power of the enemy, with the object of avoiding further and more grievous harm to the nation, has requested an armistice from General Eisenhower, Commander-in-Chief of the Anglo-American Allied Force. This request has been granted. The Italian forces will, therefore, cease all acts of hostility against the Anglo-American forces wherever they may be met. They will, however, oppose attacks from any other quarter."

Minutes after the Radio Algiers broadcast of Badoglio's statement, General Roatta called Kesselring's headquarters at OB SUD (Southern Command HQ) twice, demanding to speak to Kesselring, who came on the phone at the second attempt. Roatta swore on his honor as an officer that he had known nothing of the government's plan to surrender to the Allies; Kesselring thanked him for the assurance and hung up. Neither believed the other. Kesselring responded by ordering execution of Operation *Achse* to disarm Italian Army units and occupy important positions. At nearly the same time, Roatta ordered the three Italian army corps that defended Rome to man roadblocks around the capital, telling them that German troops departing should be permitted to leave, though any German columns approaching Rome were to be stopped. The heart of the order was that "All units are to react energetically against any attempt to penetrate [into Rome] by force or against any hostile actions whatsoever." Unlike what the Allies expected, the orders were entirely defensive. While rumors of the Italian surrender had begun circulating in Rome on September 7, the actual announcement took the Germans by surprise. The German embassy staff began burning papers immediately while they attempted to organize an evacuation of the embassy. By 2100 hours, Ambassador Rudolf Rahn took his staff aboard a special train that departed for the Brenner Pass.

Shortly after midnight on September 9, General Ambrosio issued an order backing up Roatta's original order, specifically ordering the entire Italian Army, "Do not in any case take the initiative in hostile acts against the Germans." This was immediately followed by the reception of reports at Comando Supremo of German paratroopers attacking the Piacenza Division near Anzio. This was soon followed by reports that the 3rd Panzergrenadier Division was moving against the Ariete Division, which was unable to move its tanks due to lack of fuel. In response, Roatta ordered his three corps defending Rome to close all barricades and forcibly oppose any German moves. Within the hour, a telephone conversation between the German Foreign Office and the Rome embassy was intercepted that created alarm when it was learned that the 2nd Fallschirmjäger Division was disarming nearby Italian units and the 3rd Panzergrenadier Division was now marching on Rome. In the meantime, Badoglio remained silent in the face of all these movements. His failure to directly order resistance meant the Germans would have no difficulty occupying Italy.

Throughout the early morning of September 9, increasingly serious reports were received at Comando Supremo detailing a German attack against Rome: 2nd Fallschirmjäger Division advanced against the Granatieri Division to the south; German units moving against strongpoints on the Via Ostiense and Via Laurentina; a clash between the Ariete and 3rd Panzergrenadier Divisions. At 0330 hours, the German XVII Korps at Velletri informed the Italians that the 15th Panzergrenadier Division was marching on Rome along the Via Appia and was 100 kilometers north of the city. Carboni informed Roatta that a defense of Rome could not last beyond 24 hours.

Shortly before 0400 hours, Roatta met with Ambrosino and Badoglio in the presence of Crown Prince Humbert. The two reported that, if the Allies had landed near Rome, they would have ordered full-scale resistance; in the absence of such landings, Ambrosio informed Badoglio and the crown prince that if the Italian government was determined to flee Rome it should happen as quickly as possible, since only the Via Tiburtina remained open.

Badoglio then met with Victor Emmanuel II, who had been informed of the situation and quickly concurred with the decision to remove the government from Rome. By 0500 hours, Badoglio and the royal party were ready to leave; they departed in a five-car convoy. The other Italian officials most at risk of arrest by the Germans for their role in the surrender were ordered to rendezvous as quickly as possible with the king's party at Pescara. Roatta and Ambrosio left in the same vehicle at 0545 hours, leaving General Carboni in charge of the Italian forces still resisting the Germans in the city; Carboni issued orders, then went home and changed out of his uniform into civilian clothes, then left the city at 0600 hours in the company of his son and two junior officers. The rest of the senior government ministers had left the city by 0815 hours. Interior Minister Umberto Ricci was left in control of the civil government in the capital. In North Africa, no one at Allied headquarters knew that the Italian government had fled Rome.

The Germans moved decisively. Rommel's Army Group B disarmed all Italian units in northern Italy. The morning of September 9, Kesselring ordered Italian units in the south to go home. With this, the Italian Army disappeared overnight as the Germans took further prosecution of war in Italy entirely in line with their interests.

While all this happened, Hitler – who up to this point agreed with Rommel about not fighting in southern Italy – was on the verge of ordering German forces in southern Italy to withdraw to the region of Rome to defend against the possible Allied move. The evening of September 8, just before the Radio Algiers broadcasts, Kesselring had bowed to the inevitable and told his forces to make preparations for evacuation if the order was given, while continuing to hold position. That night, following the broadcast, Hitler changed his mind. At 0300 hours on September 9, Kesselring was ordered to oppose the Allies in southern Italy in accordance with his plan to make the Allied armies fight for every inch of territory south of Rome.

Had the Allies waited to invade until September 12 – the date the Italians expected the invasion and the date the Wehrmacht was using to coordinate their withdrawal plans – Hitler's order would have been given the morning of September 9. Tenth Army would have been in the middle of withdrawing from southern Italy; opposition to the invading Allies would have been nearly impossible.

Planning for Operation *Avalanche* had been complicated by the wide geographic separation of the principal commanders, making ongoing meetings that could make decisions immediately in light of new information impossible; by uncertainty regarding what units – military and naval – would be assigned to the operation; and by the short time available to pull things together. There were only two months between "D-Day" for Operation *Husky* and that for *Avalanche*, which took place only 23 days after the end of the Sicilian campaign.

Vice Admiral H. Kent Hewitt commanded the invasion fleet as Commander, Allied Naval Force (Western Naval Task Force) for Operation *Avalanche*. In 1953, he wrote of the decision to land at Salerno:

> To the south of Naples, however, the Gulf of Salerno offered a long stretch of beach, with excellent gradients for the most part and clear approaches. While fighter planes here would not be able to remain long on station, reasonable air cover was practicable, particularly if augmented by some naval aviation. From the military point of view, Salerno had the disadvantage that the whole beachhead area would be under enemy observation from the high land which ringed it and that an advance to Naples would have to be made over the high ridge which separated the Salerno from the Naples plain.

Fifth Army's attack plan called for two assaults: one in the northern part of the Gulf of Salerno, between Salerno on the north and the Sele River that bisected the invasion beaches by the British X Corps on a two-division front; the other – south of the Sele River – would be made on a one-division front by the US VI Corps. Three US Ranger battalions and two Royal Marine Commandos, commanded by the famous Colonel William Orlando Darby, would cover the (northern) left flank, securing the mountain passes from Maiori and Vietri sul Mare to the plain of Naples.

This plan led to the establishment of two naval attack forces: the British-led Northern Attack Force, commanded by Commodore Geoffrey Oliver, RN, would land X Corps and the Rangers and Commandos. The Southern Attack Force – under Rear Admiral John

Hall, Commander Eighth Amphibious Force – would land VI Corps. Importantly, none of the divisions assigned originally to VI Corps had prior combat or amphibious experience; the decision to land on a one-corps front was dictated by assault shipping limitations. The 36th Division was placed under intensive amphibious training by the Eighth Amphibious Force, with the 34th Division assigned as a reserve carried in the first follow-up convoy. The veteran 45th and 3rd Divisions were also assigned to VI Corps for the invasion. The British X Corps – commanded by General Brian Horrocks – was built around the 46th and 56th Infantry Divisions with the 7th Armoured Division as corps reserve.

The problem created by geographic separation of commanders was demonstrated by the fact that Commodore Oliver was at Tripoli, while Admiral Richard L. Conolly was at Bizerte. On August 22, General Horrocks was so badly wounded in a German air raid that he had to be replaced by General Sir Richard McCreery. The 46th Division would be transported in landing craft from Bizerte, while the 56th Division would depart Tripoli in landing ships, small, fast assault transports, and landing craft. The 36th Division would depart from Oran. Due to lack of availability of some component units, none of the initial assault divisions was complete.

The naval units assigned to Operation *Avalanche* were experienced, well-trained veterans of *Torch* and *Husky*; however, the majority of the army units assigned would be engaged in their first real combat role. The Army Service Command Oran unit assigned to load the assault transports and cargo ships of the 36th Division was not only unfamiliar with the principles of combat-loading for an amphibious operation but also ignored the Army transport quartermasters who had been trained by Eighth Amphibious Force. The result was unfortunate delays and controversies that need not have happened. The unsafe loading of cargo vessels, such as loading ammunition and cased inflammables in the same hold, would lead to losses that would have been avoidable had those who knew what they were doing been in charge.

Planning air support for the invasion was greatly improved from what had been the case in Operation *Husky*. The Northwest African Coastal Air Force was responsible for aerial anti-submarine protection and combat air patrols for the Western Naval Task Force during the voyage from the North African ports of embarkation. Once the task force was north of Sicily, this protection was provided by the Northwest African Tactical Air Force, whose units were based on Sicily; as soon as practicable, these units would move to captured Italian airfields. Twelfth Air Force promised to maintain at least 36 fighters over the invasion fleet and beaches during the daylight hours. Only the P-38 and A-36 had the range to allow them to operate over Salerno and as far north as Naples for any appreciable time. Carrying one drop tank and one 500 or 1,000-pound bomb, the P-38 could maintain cover over Salerno for an hour. The A-36, carrying two 500-pound bombs and capable of air combat with ordnance gone, could provide a similar cover. The Spitfire – the best Allied air supremacy fighter – could only operate over the invasion for 20 minutes using a 45-gallon drop tank, and only ten minutes if it engaged in combat. Allied planners expected to take several Italian airfields during the first hours of the invasion, which would allow shorter-ranged aircraft to support the invasion from D+1; this proved over-optimistic, with only two airfields available ashore by D+3.

The Northwest African Strategic Air Force (NASAF) commenced a series of heavy attacks against enemy airfields within range of the assault area on September 2, and expanded the attacks against enemy lines of communications connecting that area. In order not to give the enemy information that would pinpoint the invasion site, the attacks were made over a geographically wide range of targets, with those against the actual targets being in the minority to avoid premature disclosure of the real objective.

September 5 saw the first of the invasion convoys begin departing North Africa, with the last steaming out of harbor on September 7. On September 7, D-2, Ultra intercepts revealed large numbers of Do-217 bombers being moved from the south of France to the Foggia airfields, located just across the Apennines from Salerno; German aerial reconnaissance had obviously spotted the convoys as they crossed the Mediterranean. At 2230 hours that night, the British convoy came under attack by He-111 torpedo bombers of III./KG 26, but fortunately no damage was done.

Ultra picked up many enemy sighting reports throughout the day of September 8 as the convoys came together in an invasion fleet. The first air attack on the slow landing craft convoys that were at the head of the fleet due to their slower speeds came at 1400 hours. The

British LCT 624 was hit and sunk at 1650 hours. The Northern and Southern Attack Forces of the Western Naval Task Force commenced their respective approaches to assigned positions and areas in the Gulf of Salerno at 2000 hours, with "H" hour scheduled for 0330 hours on September 9.

As had occurred in Operation *Torch*, the assault was made under cover of darkness without prior naval bombardment, other than a minor one in the Northern Area just before the landing craft hit the beach. At 0315 hours, fire support groups of the Northern Attack Force opened gun and rocket fire on the northern beaches. As requested, there was no preliminary fire on the VI Corps beaches. Fifth Army commander Lieutenant General Mark Clark had decided to forego a traditional preliminary air and naval bombardment so as to maximize surprise. There was none. The Germans were ready and able to respond. VI Corps ran into trouble from the start, since enemy tanks were in position behind the beaches. Troops on Yellow and Blue Beaches were pinned down nearly all day. When the first wave of the American 36th Infantry Division approached the beach at Paestum, a loudspeaker just behind the landing area proclaimed in English: "Come on in and give up. We have you covered." With the two VI Corps beaches under immediate, sustained, heavy enemy fire, they were quickly closed down and were out of communication with the rest of the force for part of the day.

The British 46th and 56th Divisions landed alongside the 36th, right into the four battle groups of the 16th Panzer Division. Fortunately, when word spread of the immediate German response, Allied warships offshore commenced a bombardment and the British divisions fought their way ashore with that support.

Heavy enemy artillery fire raked the beaches throughout the day from positions in the hills behind the beaches, delaying beaching of following waves due to the considerable damage inflicted on landing craft and LSTs (Landing Ship, Tank). One beached LST in the southern zone engaged enemy tanks. Beaches became congested with landing craft beaching and then waiting to be unloaded by troops that weren't where they were supposed to be. Some had to be retracted under gunfire, still loaded, a particularly difficult maneuver.

The Royal Navy monitor HMS *Abercrombie* – armed with two 15-inch naval cannon in a turret originally designed for HMS *Furious*

– provided heavy firepower to defend the Allied forces on the southern beaches, along with the cruisers and destroyers of the Southern Support Force, and the LCGs (Landing Craft, Gun) that were effective in keeping the defending German forces from overrunning the beachhead. The naval gunfire allowed VI Corps to reopen Yellow and Blue beaches again. Unfortunately, *Abercrombie* struck a mine and was damaged in the late afternoon.

All three P-38 groups had moved up to Sicily to provide cover for the invasion. The 1st Fighter Group had moved to Dittaino airfield on the east coast of Sicily on September 6. Dittaino was 200 miles from Salerno, which allowed the group to stay over the invasion beaches for an hour, even with only one drop tank and carrying a 500-pound bomb on the other wing pylon. The 1st Group's patrol area, codenamed "Pears, Peaches and Apples," covered the area from the Sorrento peninsula to Agropoli at the southern end of the Gulf of Salerno. During the invasion, each of the group's squadrons would fly two to three missions per day, in formations of eight P-38s from two flights per mission.

Second Lieutenant Frank Lawson had a most memorable mission on September 9. He and several other P-40 pilots had been assigned to the 1st Group at the end of August, despite having no experience with the P-38 other than – as he later said – having seen pictures of them. Lawson had only 250 total flying hours when he arrived in the group. He was able to get in three training flights before finding himself assigned to the first mission in support of the invasion. After being instructed in how to turn on the airplane's lights, he managed a pre-dawn takeoff over the burning P-38 of his element leader, who crashed on takeoff. The other new guy flying wing on the flight leader managed to crash into the side of Mount Etna. To top it off, he lost sight of the flight leader in the darkness.

Lawson flew on to the invasion beaches, confused in the dark. When he was suddenly surrounded by flak bursts just after first light, he discovered, on looking down as the sunlight finally hit the ground, that he was over Naples. He turned back to the invasion and arrived overhead just at the moment when the entire fleet opened fire. With the arrival of daylight, he finally found his flight leader and the two completed the patrol. They nearly attacked a Seafire they came across, having been told in their preflight briefing that they would be the only fighters over the invasion beach and that any single-engine aircraft they came across would be hostile. Following that, the two flew back to Dittaino and landed safely.

During one afternoon mission flown by the 94th Squadron on D-Day, First Lieutenant James Dibble flew lead with first-timer Second Lieutenant Stan Wojcik flying wing. Dibble received a call from a forward observer to strafe German reinforcements spotted in a valley 30 miles inland. When the four Lightnings dropped into the valley and made their run, they were met with antiaircraft fire from below, the hills to both sides and even from the hilltops shooting down at them. Dibble was shot down and killed, while Wojcik's P-38 was set afire and he was badly burned before he was able to bail out to become a POW.

The group flew ten missions on September 10, D+1. The 71st Squadron's evening patrol was hit by Bf-109s over the Gulf of Salerno. Second Lieutenant Stanley Stuber was hit by flak and forced to bail out over Capaccio where he was rescued by an infantry unit. His wingman, Flight Officer Joe Boyd – a former "flying sergeant" who had wangled a transfer from Troop Carrier Command after many turned-down requests – was on his sixth mission in P-38s. Boyd's left engine was shot out in the first pass, along with all his electrical systems. Without instruments, he managed to get to Sicily in the last light of day. With Mount Etna finally in sight, his good engine ran out of gas and he ditched the Lightning offshore. He was swept out to sea by the current, and by chance was picked up at midday on September 11 by a British motor torpedo boat that was searching for a downed RAF pilot.

Dittaino airfield had no equipment available for servicing the Lightnings, and ground crews were forced to refuel the fighters from 5-gallon gas cans. The situation was similar for the other Lightning groups. With the failure to capture airfields ashore as originally planned, the need for the P-38s to provide cover was even more critical than originally expected.

The 82nd Group had moved to Maddalena-Gerbini Satellite Field No. 2, with all aircraft and ground crews arriving by September 7. The first mission in support of the invasion was flown the next day, September 8, when two flights each over three missions provided air cover for the fleet as it approached the Bay of Salerno.

Widespread air combat didn't occur during the invasion until September 11. This was likely due to disruptions on the German side involved in taking over bases from the Italians. The first Luftwaffe *freie*

Jagd (Free Hunt – a fighter sweep by a squadron or group looking for targets of opportunity) was flown by Bf-109s from the veteran I. and II./ JG 53. The 82nd's 97th Squadron was patrolling over the invasion fleet when they were hit by the Germans. Despite being badly outnumbered, the Lightning pilots claimed five Bf-109s shot down and two damaged.

Squadron operations officer Captain Gerry Rounds scored one of the Bf-109s, which took his score to five, making him the group's 17th ace, this despite taking hits that knocked out the hydraulic system and resulted in his making a wheels-up landing that pretty much wiped out the Lightning. Afterwards, he recalled:

The controller vectored us towards what they called eight bogies. When we arrived where the controller said the bogies were, we saw 12 airplanes in what looked like a typical P-40 formation – flights of four, with all in line abreast, a little off to our right. Just before reaching the abreast point, they turned into us. At the same time, 12 more came down from the rear, making it a perfectly coordinated attack. With our eight against their 24, the situation looked a little one-sided, with us on the losing end. After the initial attack, we formed a Lufbery in two directions; we were meeting P-38s of our own outfit head-on, in vertical banks. We had to stay and fight, but we weren't worrying about it because we had full gas tanks, having used our belly tanks on patrol and dropping them the minute we started to attack. The '109s dived down at us in pairs, but as soon as they got within range, there was always a P-38 meeting them head-on; no matter how they came in, someone was always in position to level out, fire a burst and get back in the circle. They dropped off one by one, and after about ten minutes, when they'd lost five, they decided they'd had enough and started for home.

Second Lieutenant Sammy McGuffin scored his first victory in the fight despite having an engine shot out. The next day he claimed an Fw-190 when his patrol ran into a mixed formation of 12 Fw-190s and Bf-109s.

The 14th Fighter Group moved into Lentini airfield in Sicily at the beginning of September. Over the three days preceding the invasion, the group flew sweeps over enemy airfields in the vicinity of Naples; between September 6 and 8, the pilots claimed ten enemy fighters shot down by 12 pilots in all three squadrons. Like the other two

Lightning groups, the 14th flew three missions a day over the invasion fleet and the beaches. The P-38s carried a 1,000-pound bomb and a drop tank, allowing them to provide support to the troops on the ground. Lieutenant Harry Crim recalled that each mission could last up to three hours over the invasion area, depending on how much ammunition they had.

British fleet carriers HMS *Illustrious* and *Formidable* provided air cover for the invasion until airfields ashore became available. Their Martlet IV fighters looked enough like Fw-190s at a distance that when Lieutenants Walter Brower and Hank Alm of the 14th's 37th Fighter Squadron spotted a flight of Martlets over the Bay of Salerno, they misidentified them at first. Brower later recalled they were vectored into "a real beehive of aircraft." Alm jumped one radial-engined fighter thinking it was a Focke-Wulf that Brower quickly recognized as a Martlet. When he called to Alm not to fire because it was "a Grumman," he was misunderstood as saying "German," and Alm opened fire until Brower yelled again and was understood correctly. The Martlet made it back to its carrier, where the landing hook pulled out on touchdown due to the damage inflicted by Alm.

Unfortunately, interception air cover over the invasion fleet itself was the responsibility of Force V, the aircraft carriers commanded by Rear Admiral Sir Phillip Vian, RN. This force was composed of the Royal Navy maintenance carrier HMS *Unicorn* – temporarily assigned to operational duties the ship and its crew were not prepared or trained for – with the Seafire-equipped 809, 887, and 897 Squadrons; the escort carriers HMS *Hunter* with 899 Squadron and 834 Flight; *Stalker* with 880 Squadron and 833 Flight; *Attacker* with 879 and 886 Squadrons; and *Battler* with 807 and 808 Squadrons. Admiral Vian had no experience or knowledge of leading a carrier group; he was honest enough to admit later that his lack of experience contributed to the difficulties experienced by Force V. The Seafires were originally to provide air cover only for the invasion's first day, with land-based units flown into airfields that were expected to be quickly taken. However, the strong enemy response prevented the taking of any airfields; Montecorvino airfield was only captured on the fourth day.

The Seafires have been excoriated in histories of the Salerno invasion for their many operational losses in landing accidents and their inability to successfully oppose the Luftwaffe's fighter-bomber response. This is unfair to the aircraft and their pilots for several reasons. First, the squadrons had only transitioned to the Seafire over the three weeks before the invasion, which meant the pilots lacked experience; pilots had an average of 15–20 hours' flight experience each in the Seafire. Adverse operating conditions were exacerbated by the lack of wind coupled with the fact the escort carriers had a top speed of 17 knots, which meant there was barely enough wind over the deck for operations. Additionally, Force V was forced to restrict their operations to a limited area.

The escort carriers had to move to the extreme eastern end of the operating area, then hope to build up to full speed in a westward run while leaving sufficient space to slow down and turn around while remaining inside the operating area; during the run, aircraft would either be launched or taken aboard, though the ships were often unable to exceed 15 knots in this situation, making operations even more fraught. Writing in his memoir, *Action This Day*, Admiral Vian stated, "The problem was how, with so little speed, and whilst remaining within our area, to have the ships back at the leeward end in time for the next flying operation."

While *Illustrious* and *Formidable* operated Martlets, which could have been used on board the escort carriers which were all experienced in operating that aircraft, the Seafire was chosen over the Martlet because of its higher speed at low altitude, which ostensibly made it better at intercepting enemy fighter-bombers attacking the fleet.

Sorties of 85 minutes had aircraft in the combat zone for 60 minutes with the remaining 25 spent in launch and landing. The escort carriers could only launch four Seafires each cycle, given the time they had at maximum speed before having to slow to remain in the operating area. HMS *Unicorn*, which was never intended to be used as an operational carrier, could handle eight per cycle.

The mist that covered the sea to an altitude of 500 feet throughout the invasion made interceptions difficult due to the fact the attackers came out of the east, flying from the Italian mainland at low level. Thus, the fleet radars had difficulty picking them up due to the ground clutter immediately behind, which masked the attackers and made fighter direction difficult, while the pilots had difficulty visually spotting their opponents.

On D-Day, air operations began at 0615 hours and ended 13 hours later at sunset with 265 sorties flown. D+1 saw 65 Seafires able to give air cover to the beleaguered beachhead, flying 232 sorties in which the defenders successfully disrupted more than 40 attacks. While leading a flight of four Seafires, Lieutenant Commander W. C. Simpson, commanding officer of 897 Squadron, spotted four Bf-109s at 12,000 feet. Simpson shot down two while his wingman damaged a third and one Seafire was lightly damaged. D+2 saw the least wind, but another 38 raids were intercepted in 160 sorties, though by the end of the day there were only 39 Seafires left operational. The Seafires flew dawn patrols on D+3, with land-based fighters which were finally able to operate from Montecorvino airfield by midday and take over all responsibility for air defense. Overall, the Seafires' main success was their ability to force the enemy fighter-bombers to drop their ordnance prematurely in order to evade interception, after which they could outrun the defenders at low altitude.

The mist also made it difficult when pilots had to land aboard the carriers. In the end, over the four days the fighters were responsible for fleet air defense, of 109 Seafires in the 11 squadrons 70 were written off. The fighters flew 713 sorties during these days, with 32 deck-landing crashes in which the aircraft was completely written off. Undercarriage failure from being slammed onto the deck too hard claimed another 17, while a further 24 sustained distortion of the rear fuselage from bad landings that overstressed the A-frame arrester hooks. Four were lost to engine failure. HMS *Unicorn*'s fighters experienced 21 losses, attributed to turbulent air over the flight deck caused by the carrier's larger island. Overall, the Seafires performed above expectation, flying as many as four sorties per aircraft per day, though they had been expected to only fly twice each on the first day. The Seafires only claimed the two shot down by Lieutenant Commander Simpson and four damaged.

In response to the invasion, German air attacks started early, with the first appearing over the invasion fleet at 0417 hours on September 9; they continued in strength throughout the day and into the night, with 12 or more attacks in all. The American tug *Nauset* was hit in the first attack and again during the second attack at 0615 hours, when it exploded and sank. The minesweeper *Intent* was damaged by the explosion of the *Nauset*, and other nearby shipping was damaged. The British cruisers HMS *Uganda* and *Delhi* collided and damaged each other as they maneuvered in a smoke screen during the final evening air attack in the Northern Area. While the attacking German aircraft gave most attention to ships in the

Northern Area, those in the Southern Area did not escape. Major General Edwin J. House, commanding XII Air Support Command, appealed for attacks by the strategic bombers against the airfields the enemy planes were using at Naples, Benevento, and Foggia.

By the end of D-Day, lead elements of the Allied forces could look down on the plain of Naples but were hard-pressed to hold their position. That night, the Hermann Göring and 15th Panzergrenadier Divisions arrived at the battlefield. Fighting was intense over the next three days as Kesselring fed more units into the battlefield from as far north as Rome in addition to the units south of Salerno. Allied reinforcements were restricted by the limited availability of transports to unload in the crowded anchorages, and the predetermined build-up schedule that had been based on the planners' anticipation of how the battle would develop.

The evening of September 9, Kesselring asked Rommel to send him the two Panzer divisions of Army Group B but Rommel refused on the grounds he could not risk their loss if he was to successfully defend northern Italy after the forces in the south were defeated.

September 10, D+1, began with a night air attack between 0100 and 0200 hours, before the moon set. Heavier attacks were resumed at first light and continued throughout the day, with 14 attacks recorded before the last, which happened just before midnight. Fortunately, the Seafires were reinforced by A-36 Mustangs and P-38s based on Sicily, with the result that only minor damage was done due to the valiant work of the fighter cover and the effective use of smoke cover. Over 20 enemy planes were reported as having been shot down. In spite of this air activity, and the request by General House for an extra P-38 squadron from 1630 to last light, the commanding general of the North African Tactical Air Force, from his position back in Tunisia, was proposing that fighter cover be reduced in favor of increased fighter-bomber attacks on enemy road communications.

September 11, D+2, opened with the usual daylight air attack, with determined attacks being made by Fw-190 fighter-bombers and by Ju-88 bombers in both the Northern and Southern Areas to support the German drive against the beaches that had become possible as the German reinforcements had arrived in the battle area sooner than the Allies could land reinforcements. Incredibly, XII Tactical Air Command had determined that air cover over the invasion beaches could be reduced to allow additional strikes against the airfields the Luftwaffe was using. Fortunately, the decision was rescinded in the face of continuing reports of enemy resistance.

While naval gunfire support had been crucial for the Allied forces during the first two days of the invasion, the Luftwaffe countered on the third day with attacks by Do-217K-2 bombers of III./KG 100, carrying "Fritz-X" radio-guided anti-shipping bombs. The deployment of these weapons on September 11, 1943, was the first time that precision-guided air-dropped or launched weapons were used on a large scale in combat. Fritz-X was an armor-piercing weapon designed for use against warships, while the Hs-293 was effective against transports and invasion ships like LSTs. The Fritz-X required that the aircraft that dropped it keep the weapon in sight in order for the bombardier to control it to hit its target while maintaining slow steady flight; this exposed the Do-217s to attack by defending Allied fighters. The Fritz-X had to be dropped from a minimum distance of 5 kilometers from the target, from a preferred altitude of 18,000 feet and no lower than 15,000 feet.

These bombs had first been used against the Italian fleet after it departed La Spezia to steam to Malta and surrender. Six Do-217K-2s, each carrying one Fritz-X, attacked the fleet. The flagship, the battleship *Roma*, was hit by two of the missiles and near-missed by a third. The second hit set off the battleship's magazines, which exploded and sank *Roma* with the loss of 1,393 crewmen. *Roma*'s sistership *Italia* was also damaged by two hits, but managed to evade a third attack and eventually arrived at Malta.

At 1000 hours on September 11, the American light cruiser USS *Savannah* (CL-42), which was providing gunfire support to the units ashore, was hit by a Fritz-X that penetrated "C" Turret, killing the turret crew when it exploded in the lower ammunition-handling room. The blast tore open a large hole in the lower hull immediately beneath the turret, opening a seam in her side, and blowing out all fires in her boilers. Heroic damage control efforts left *Savannah* dead in the water with her bow nearly awash. Engineering crews were finally able to re-light her boilers after an eight-hour effort and the ship was able to get under way to Malta. The explosion and consequent damage in the engineering spaces killed 197 crewmen and injured 15. Four sailors were trapped in a watertight compartment for 60 hours before the surrounding compartments were pumped out to rescue them after the cruiser arrived in Grand Harbor, Valletta, Malta, on September 12. USS *Philadelphia* (CL-41) was also targeted by a Fritz-X that missed her, exploding 50 feet away from the cruiser.

Three days later, on September 14, the Royal Navy cruiser HMS *Uganda* was hit by a Fritz-X that penetrated through seven decks and straight through her keel before it exploded just under the keel. The concussive shock of the underwater explosion extinguished all of *Uganda*'s boiler fires, killing 16 crewmen. The cruiser took on 1,300 tons of water and had to be towed to Malta for repairs.

Two days after that, a Fritz-X hit the battleship HMS *Warspite*, penetrating six decks before exploding in the number four boiler room, extinguishing all boiler fires and cutting off power to all ship's systems while blowing a hole in the double bottom. A second Fritz X near-missed the ship, holing her at the waterline. *Warspite* took on 5,000 tons of water; though the damage she suffered was extensive, only nine crewmen were killed and 15 wounded. She too was towed to Malta; repaired sufficiently to steam to Britain for further repair, *Warspite* was out of action for nine months and was never completely repaired.

The Luftwaffe also deployed the Henschel Hs-293 rocket-powered glide bomb from Do-217K-2s of II./KG 100 for use against unarmored transports and LSTs. The transport SS *Bushrod Washington* was hit by an Hs-293 on September 14, while offloading a cargo of gasoline, and set afire. The next day, SS *James W. Marshall* was set afire by an Hs-293 or Fritz X while offloading fuel. The hospital ship HMHS *Newfoundland* was also struck by an Hs-293 and so heavily damaged that the ship was eventually scuttled by a torpedo from USS *Plunkett* (DD-431), along with the transports SS *Delius* and SS *Dulverton*, which was so heavily damaged that the ship was finally scuttled.

On D+3, the airfield at Paestum that had been captured on D-Day was finally cleared and able to operate aircraft. Around noon that day, Seafires were flown in and were able to mount patrols from the field over to the invasion, returning to their carriers that evening. The airfield at Montecorvino was still bombarded by enemy artillery and unusable. However, two airfields opened in the British sector on D+4; with these airfields, Allied fighters were finally able to operate more or less continuously over the battlefield.

The 86th Bomb Group (Dive) had moved to Barcellona airfield, a dirt strip in what had been a vineyard west of Messina on Sicily, at the end of August, to bring the A-36s as close to Salerno as possible. Starting on September 1, the group flew several missions a day to the invasion area, where they attacked troop locations, gun positions, rail and road traffic, road junctions, bridges, and any shipping they came across, both with pinpoint dive-bombing and strafing attacks. Twenty-four-year-old Major Paul Streigel, commander of the 309th Bomb Squadron (Dive), was killed on September 2 when his A-36 was hit in its vertical dive by a heavy-caliber flak shell and disintegrated over Lemezia. The popular Streigel was replaced as squadron commander by Major Justin "Mickey" Gunnison.

The group was originally scheduled to begin operations ashore from Sele airfield immediately south of Paestum on D+1, but the airfield was not captured and made operational until D+3. An advance party from the 527th Fighter-Bomber Squadron went ashore on September 12 to establish Sele as an operational base, but 30 minutes after arrival they were hit by a dozen Fw-190 fighter-bombers. Once at Sele the ground echelon was subjected to repeated bombardment, and an attempt to land the rest of the ground echelon on the field by C-47s was driven off, with the field under infantry attack; that night, German patrols passed through the position. The A-36s were able to rearm and refuel to extend their time over the battlefield even though the Germans had the airfield under observation, and such landings and movements frequently attracted artillery fire, though operations continued despite this; the German positions attacked by the A-36s were so close that the ground crews could observe the results of what the aircraft they had armed and fueled accomplished. It was not until September 16 that the group finally was able to move all three squadrons to Sele for permanent operations. The other A-36 unit, the 27th Fighter-Bomber Group, had been the first to take the A-36 into action during the Pantelleria campaign in June 1943.

On September 9, the 522nd Squadron's First Lieutenant Michael Russo became the first A-36 pilot to shoot down an enemy fighter when he shot down an Fw-190F fighter-bomber. He followed that on a later patrol the same day with a Fieseler Storch observation plane spotted over the battlefield. The Storch was a particularly difficult target due to its ability to fly at a speed as low as 40 knots. The next day when the group attacked German airfields, he spotted a Ju-52 that had taken off just after he had released his bombs and shot it down. In December 1943, he would go on to shoot down two Bf-109s over Rome to become the only ace pilot flying the Allison Mustang.

On September 10, the 27th Group's A-36s stopped a German armored thrust toward the invasion beaches with a devastating pinpoint dive-bombing attack that blocked the advance of three panzer units and established the A-36's reputation in combat in an action which resulted in the award of a Distinguished Unit Citation for saving the invasion. The 86th Group was also active on September 10, when Captain John Harsh led the 312th Squadron, destroying ten of 14 Ju-88s lined up for takeoff on the airfield at Gioia del Colle.

Confusingly, the 86th was redesignated a fighter-bomber group on September 12, with the 309th Squadron becoming the 525th Fighter-Bomber Squadron, the 310th the 526th Fighter-Bomber Squadron, and the 312th becoming the 527th Fighter-Bomber Squadron.

On September 16, a flight from the 527th Fighter-Bomber Squadron flew north in search of targets of opportunity; south of Rome they came across an airfield that had been bombed the day before by B-17s, leaving several wrecks on the field. Just as the A-36s arrived overhead, they spotted 24 Bf-109s that had just landed and had not yet been dispersed. Lieutenant John Gee remembered that the flight immediately dived on the enemy fighters, scoring three direct hits and two near misses. "All you could see was parts flying through the air and dust," he recalled. Despite defensive AA opening up on them, the Mustang pilots strafed the field as they pulled out of their dives. They returned to Sele to claim 12 Bf-109s destroyed by bombing and strafing.

When a second airfield was opened at Sele on September 18, the 27th quickly moved up from Sicily. Unfortunately, the weather broke on September 19, with rain off and on for the rest of September, which turned both airfields into muddy morasses that limited operations for both A-36 groups.

The 33rd Fighter Group moved up from Sicily to Montecorvino airfield in the Salerno beachhead on September 13. The pilots quickly found themselves in the thick of the fighting, with their primary duty being defense of the Salerno beachhead from Luftwaffe fighter-bombers. The pilots were spoiling for a good fight and acquitted themselves well over Salerno. Over the period September 15–17, they claimed 14 Bf-109s and Fw-190s destroyed for the loss of only one

P-40. All three squadrons scored victories; the top scorer was Second Lieutenant Morgan S. Tyler of the 59th Squadron, who claimed two Bf-109s destroyed.

Life on a front-line airfield was difficult for the ground crews. The landing was rough, and the crews were subject to attacks from Ju-88s while working on their aircraft. Additionally, the field was within artillery range of the enemy who shelled the area without warning. Dust played hell with the Merlin engines. The Luftwaffe made three raids a day – at breakfast, lunch, and dinner, plus night raids by night-attack Stukas.

While the 52nd Fighter Group continued to be stuck in Northwest Africa Coastal Command flying defensive patrols over convoys from North Africa to Sicily, the 31st Fighter Group, which had established themselves as the top USAAF fighter group in air combat over Sicily, moved to Milazzo airfield in northeast Sicily on September 2. The airfield turned out to be a "dust bowl," in which succeeding flights had to wait a full ten minutes for the dust to settle from the takeoff of a flight of four Spitfires sufficient to allow sufficient visibility to take off. The field was also subject to crosswinds that created further havoc with takeoffs; none of this was helped by the additional fact that the airfield surface was very uneven, leading to accidents taxiing on the field. The arrival of a shipment of 90-gallon belly tanks on September 5 was warning the group would be involved in the coming invasion. Later that day they learned they were to move to Montecorvino airfield in the invasion area, with the advance ground party landing in Italy on D-Day. In the event, despite several false alarms, Montecorvino wasn't taken for a week and the advance party remained offshore in two LSTs.

The 31st's 307th Squadron flew cover for the invasion, taking off before dawn on September 9. Lieutenant Fields spotted a Do-217 moments after the squadron arrived over the invasion and attacked it. The rear gunner's fire was effective, and Fields was forced to belly land his Spitfire on the beach. Picked up by an LCVP (Landing Craft, Vehicle, Personnel) and taken to a ship in the invasion force, he would not return to the group for a week.

The 308th Squadron flew the second D-Day patrol. The pilots had difficulty using the 90-gallon belly tanks, which sloshed once they were down ten gallons or so, which made the Spitfires wallow in flight. The 309th Squadron flew the third patrol of the day, six Spitfire Vs at

6,000 feet and six Spitfire IXs at 17,000 feet. The patrol spotted two different formations of German fighter-bombers, but in each case the targets were hit by patrolling RAF Spitfires before the Americans could get close enough to open fire. The flight to and from Sicily to Salerno took an hour, leaving the Spitfires a maximum of 30 minutes over the invasion, even with the larger belly tanks.

The Spitfires finally saw combat on September 10, when the 12-plane patrol from the 309th Squadron spotted a mixed enemy formation estimated at 45 Bf-109s and Fw-190s. The squadron attacked despite the size of the enemy formation, and Captain Shafer scored a Bf-109 in the first pass while damaging the element leader. His number 3 and 4, Lieutenants Burton and Hughes, shared the second enemy fighter shot down. The enemy pilots showed little inclination to stick around and fight, jettisoning their bombs and turning back when they spotted the diving Spitfires.

On September 11, the 31st's advance party from the 308th Squadron landed in Italy, to find that Montecorvino airfield had not yet been taken and was being shelled by enemy artillery. The 309th's Lieutenant Lupton was hit over the invasion beach by groundfire and made a forced landing at Sele airfield, which had just been captured, becoming the first Allied pilot to land in Italy. The rest of the squadron completed their patrol without coming across the enemy.

The ground party found themselves in the middle of more combat than any had seen since the retreat from Thelepte during the Battle of Kasserine Pass in North Africa. During the night of September 12–13, they were dragooned into manning a roadblock in the expectation of a German breakthrough; at dawn all considered themselves fortunate that the British Army had stopped the Germans before they arrived at the 308th's roadblock.

The dust at Milazzo played havoc with the Merlin engines. On September 14, three Spitfires were forced to make emergency landings at Sele with engine failures. With these losses, the 307th was down to five useable Spitfires. A patrol from the 309th Squadron spotted 20 Italian fighter-bombers approaching the invasion beaches, but the Italians dropped their ordnance and turned back. Despite a long chase to the limits of their gas supply, the Spitfires were forced to turn back for Sicily without any score. Another patrol from the 309th was more successful, when Lieutenant Weismuller, flying a Spitfire V, caught a formation of Fw-190F fighter-bombers at low level and shot down one. September 15 saw one Ju-88 shot down on the final patrol of the day. That night, the advance party hid in a walnut grove as the enemy shelled the area.

Finally, on September 18, Montecorvino airfield was declared secure and operational. However, the group did not arrive at the field until September 20, since September 19 had seen bad weather as the rains arrived in southern Italy. Within minutes of the first 308th Squadron Spitfires touching down at Montecorvino, six Fw-190 fighter-bombers arrived overhead and bombed the field. Fortunately, they missed the Spitfires. The rest of the 308th's Spitfires arrived the next day, followed by the 309th and 307th Squadrons on September 22.

P-40s finally arrived in the Salerno battlefield on October 2, when the 57th and 79th Fighter Groups moved into the newly operational Foggia airfield complex. Both groups had provided support for the Eighth Army's landings in southern Italy in early September before the main landing at Taranto. The 57th had found the Luftwaffe in the "toe" and "heel" of Italy operational in strength and in a mood to fight, engaging in several air battles in the midst of providing fighter-bomber support to the ground forces. The 57th became the first USAAF fighter group based on the Italian mainland when they moved across the Straits of Messina to the landing ground at Rocco Bernardo on September 18. The two P-40 groups moved on to Gioia del Colle airfield outside Taranto in mid-September.

Fifth Army had been delayed in getting its backup units ashore and was short of infantry when the German counterattack was launched on September 12. Two battalions of the 36th Infantry Division were overrun by two German battle groups in the afternoon and nearly wiped out, with the enemy only stopped by US artillerymen firing their guns at point-blank range over open sights, and naval gunfire. The attack crested at a makeshift position that was rapidly created, manned, and held by artillerymen, drivers, cooks, and clerks. The battle continued throughout the night and through September 13.

At the height of the battle, Clark and his staff spent the night of September 13–14 seriously considering the possibility of being forced to evacuate under fire. Fortunately, the 82nd Airborne Division, which had been held on Sicily for the possible Rome operation, was able to drop two battalions of the 504th Parachute Infantry Regiment into the beachhead at 2100 hours on September 13, the operation marred by the 3rd Battalion being dropped over the Salerno plain with the majority of the paratroopers dropped behind enemy lines. The two battalions provided the necessary reinforcement to stabilize the immediate situation, while the other two regiments were dropped the next two nights.

Over the course of September 14, German attacks were thrown back and the enemy forced to retreat with heavy casualties on both sides. That night, every Allied bomber in North Africa and Sicily hit enemy positions in the surrounding hills. The next day, the Hermann Göring Division attacked on high ground east of the beachhead. The Germans were stopped by naval gunfire including the 15-inch guns of the battleship HMS *Warspite*. B-25s of the 321st and 340th Groups flew low-level battlefield bombing attacks against the Germans.

The British sector of the invasion was stabilized on September 15 when the 7th Armoured Division came ashore to provide the necessary armor to withstand and throw back the German offensive there that had gone on over the preceding three days.

On September 15, Hitler – impressed with the results at Salerno – agreed with Kesselring that a delayed fighting withdrawal was the correct strategy. Kesselring obtained permission from Hitler to prepare a defensive line on the Volturno and Rapido rivers north of Naples, which he called the Bernhardt Line. This would allow the Germans to mount a counteroffensive against Apulia, if it turned out that the Allies did intend to attack the Balkans and withdrew forces for that operation from the Italian front. This latter argument was probably decisive with Hitler, who was always "offensively minded," in his decision to allow Kesselring to stand and fight.

Despite the Allies withstanding and throwing back Kesselring's counterstrike, the Germans continued their determined drive down the Sele River Valley; German armor threatened to break through to the beach and drive a wedge between X Corps and VI Corps on September 16, which was stopped by the British 7th Armoured. Even with this, the situation ashore and afloat was far from favorable.

With the Allies managing to hold in the face of the German attacks, the enemy went over to the defensive the evening of September 16, when Kesselring allowed Tenth Army commander General von Vietinghoff to break off contact and begin a fighting withdrawal over the next month that would end with occupation of the Bernhardt defenses that would stymie further American advance through the end of the year. Tenth Army had come within an ace of defeating the Salerno invasion. The 16th Panzer Division's stubborn initial resistance, and the German ability to reinforce by land faster than the Allies could land their backup forces, had almost tipped the battle, even with Rommel's denial of the two armored divisions. This level of resistance had not been anticipated by the American planners. It was a failure of imagination that would unfortunately be repeated in months to come.

By September 18, D+9, the Allied position ashore began to look still better, although enemy artillery was bothering the Uncle beaches and the port of Salerno was still closed. The 3rd Division – veterans of the Casablanca landing and of the Sicilian campaign – finally were able to come ashore.

The P-38 groups, which had been mounting squadron-sized attacks on the Luftwaffe units at the Foggia airfield complex, each mounted a major group-sized attack on the airfields on September 18.

Again, the 82nd's Lieutenant Colonel MacNicol led the strike at the head of the 97th Fighter Squadron; he was credited with the destruction of two unidentified single-engined fighters. Deputy group commander Major Bill Litton flew with the 96th Squadron; he and Lieutenant Selle were each credited with one destroyed. Captain Hugh M. Muse Jr., commanding the 95th Squadron, claimed a Ju-88. The 82nd lost three P-38s to flak.

Twenty-three 14th Group Lightning pilots claimed destruction of seven Ju-88s, two Bf-110s, one Fw-190, and one Bf-109 by strafing. The 37th Squadron's Lieutenant John Garbett shot down a Ju-52 that had just lifted off when the P-38s appeared overhead. The Lightnings also shot up an 88mm flak battery, several trucks, and ten railroad cars. The 49th Squadron's First Lieutenant Marin Faust was hit by intense and accurate 37mm AA and was killed when he crashed on the enemy airfield.

The 1st Group's P-38s attacked another satellite airfield and claimed seven German fighters destroyed in their strafing run. When they returned to Catania at midday, they received orders to return to Mateur airfield in North Africa to give the ground crews a chance to catch up on maintenance issues with the Lightnings after having flown 87 missions between September 9 and 18 in support of the invasion.

On September 19, the Allies attacked toward Naples. On September 22, the 3rd Division took Acerno, followed by Avellino on September 28. On September 27, the British Eighth Army captured the airfield complex at Foggia.

On September 25, D+16, Salerno port was finally pronounced out of range of enemy gunfire and the port was pronounced open. A rebellion by the people of Naples forced a German withdrawal, and Allied forces entered the city on October 1.

On October 4, both Kesselring and Rommel were summoned to Hitler's headquarters to present their views on a possible counteroffensive. Rommel overestimated the Allies' amphibious capabilities and stated his belief that a line too far south was a danger for which he did not want to assume responsibility, though he did admit that the Bernhardt Line could be held with half the divisions necessary for a stand in the northern Apennines. Hitler and his advisors believed the Italian invasion was a diversion; that once the airfields at Foggia were operational, the Allies would finally turn to their real objective in the Balkans. Rommel's "negative attitude" toward making the fight in the south convinced Hitler he was no longer "reliable"; Kesselring was authorized to finish the Bernhardt Line. Hitler signed a formal order keeping Kesselring's and Rommel's commands separate, with both functioning directly under the Oberkommando der Wehrmacht (OKW). While Hitler liked Kesselring's fighting attitude, he did not yet completely accept Kesselring's optimism about holding the Allies south of Rome for six to nine months; the same order instructing Kesselring to build up and hold the Bernhardt Line instructed Rommel to complete construction of a strong defensive line in the northern Apennines, while he was ordered to send reinforcements south. Kesselring had won a major victory in the battle of concepts that would define the rest of the war in Italy.

Finally, there was the question of what to do with the former ally Germany had just occupied. Otto Skorzeny had rescued Mussolini, who had been moved to Castel Gandolfo in northern Italy, on September 12. With Mussolini now completely dependent on Hitler and the Italian Army disbanded, the Germans proceeded to establish a Fascist puppet regime, known as the Repubblica Sociale Italiana, or RSI. Italian military units composed of loyal Fascist volunteers, including an air force, the Aviazione della RSI, were authorized. After all Luftwaffe fighter units were evacuated from Italy to defend the German homeland following the fall of Rome, these Italian fighters would become the sole aerial opposition to the Allied air forces.

The chief of the new Italian army was Marshal Rodolfo Graziani; he met with Hitler on October 9 to discuss the manner in which Italy would again participate in the war. German-occupied Italy would be treated as a "friendly" country; the Fascist government would have a measure of independence outside of large areas designated as "zones of operation," where the Germans would control both the fighting and the local population.

Between October 4 and November 6, Hitler vacillated regarding who should be given supreme command in Italy; he swung from Kesselring to Rommel and back to Kesselring. When he asked Rommel whether he thought he could defend the Bernhardt Line and hold Rome and central Italy, Rommel demurred. Hitler then appointed Kesselring Commander-in-Chief Southwest (i.e., the Italian Theater) and Army Group C. The order affirmed that "the Bernhardt Line will mark the end of withdrawals." Hitler had made the final decision as to the manner in which the rest of the war would be fought. Rommel was transferred to France on November 21, to assume responsibility for the defense of the Atlantic Wall against invasion.

Hitler's decision set the stage for the bloody battles of the Rapido River, Monte Cassino, and the Anzio beachhead over the next six months. Had he not decided to reappraise the strategic defense of Italy, all would likely have fallen to the Allies after light skirmishes or perhaps even unopposed.

The "easy pickings" in Italy were not easy to pick at all. After Salerno, Allied planners turned their focus to northern Europe. General Dwight D. Eisenhower left for England in January 1944 to become Supreme Commander, Allied Expeditionary Forces, for the Normandy invasion. He took with him the 1st Infantry Division, "The Big Red One," veterans of North Africa, Sicily, and Italy, as well as the 82nd Airborne Division, the most experienced American paratroop division. For the rest of the war, Allied forces in Italy would become progressively weaker and weaker against their German opponents as men, material, and equipment were diverted to operations aimed directly at German defeat.

The Italian campaign had been opposed as a diversion of resources by the leaders responsible for winning the war. Handicapped by poor leaders who were consistently out-generaled by Kesselring and von Vietinghoff, the campaign stalled after the failure at Rome to block the German retreat, until competent leadership was finally appointed in December 1944. Between September 1943 and April 1945, 60,000 Allied and 50,000 German soldiers died, with overall Allied casualties approximately 320,000 while the Germans lost nearly 336,650.

Kesselring told his Allied interrogators after the war that he firmly believed that if Rommel had acceded to his request to send the two armored divisions, he could have defeated the Allies at Salerno. When one considers just how close the fighting was, adding two experienced armored divisions might well have tipped the balance in the Germans' favor.

The bloodbath at Salerno was just a taste of what was to come. By mid-October, the Germans were ensconced in the Bernhardt Line while the Gustav Line centered on Cassino further north, which blocked the advance to Rome, was completed. The Allies were held at the Bernhardt Line following the rains of November and the blizzards and drifting snow of December.

In the end, the war in Italy was fought because it was there.

4

KESSELRING'S TOLL

Field Marshal Kesselring had promised Adolf Hitler that if his plan to fight the Allies in southern Italy was adopted, he would make the invaders pay for every inch of Italian soil they gained in blood, and that he would prevent the Allies' taking Rome until the summer of 1944. The field marshal was as good as his word. The Allied armies would suffer terrible casualties as they fought to break first the Bernhardt Line on the Volturno River, which was accomplished in December 1943, followed by the Gustav Line, the main German defensive line in southern Italy, running from the Tyrrhenian Sea to the Adriatic Sea along the Garigliano and Rapido rivers to the west and the Sangro River to the east. It was defended by 15 German infantry, paratroop, *Panzergrenadier*, and panzer divisions, fortified with small arms, artillery, pillboxes, machine gun emplacements, minefields, and barbed wire. Breaking the Gustav Line would take nearly all of the first half of 1944.

"Sunny Italy" was anything but in the fall and winter of 1943–44; the Allies were barely out of the Salerno battlefield before the rains that heralded the coming of winter began in late September and only became stronger in October, before winter snows began to fall in the mountains in November. Most Americans who fought in Italy recalled afterwards that the rain and snow turned the country into a sea of mud that made passage by any vehicle other than a tank nearly impossible. Sherman tanks frequently became angels of mercy to Allied supply convoys as they dragged "Deuce-and-a-Half" trucks to solid ground after the convoy floundered in mud up to the axles.

The Allies had three potential alternative routes by which to reach Rome. On the Adriatic Front, the Eighth Army could advance to Pescara, then take Highway 5 – the old Roman Via Valeria – which traversed the Adriatic coast to Rome. On the western side of the Apennines, along the Ligurian coast, the American Fifth Army could follow Highway 7 – the old Roman Appian Way – along the west coast; however, they would then have to cross the Pontine Marshes south of Rome, which the Germans had flooded. The third alternative was to take Highway 6, which ran north to Rome but further inland, through the Liri Valley.

Kesselring expected the main line of the Allied advance to be along Highway 6, and thus he set his defensive lines accordingly. The Bernhardt Line was the first major German defensive line the Allies had to force their way through after moving out of the Salerno beachhead and breaking through first the Volturno Line and then the Barbara Line.

The Volturno Line – the southernmost German defensive position – started at the Volturno River just north of Naples, running to the east through the Apennine mountains along the Biferno River to Termoli in the east on the Adriatic coast. The British Eighth Army broke through these defenses in the Battle of Termoli that began on October 3 when the British crossed the Biferno. The battle became desperate after the bridge across the Biferno collapsed following the transit of five tanks of an armored force which was to support the 78th Division's 36th Brigade that had landed at Termoli. The German 16th Panzer Division moved east to face this force, which was now cut off from reinforcement from the southern side of the Biferno. While the troops on the northern side of the river were forced on the defensive over October 4, by October 5 a Bailey Bridge had been constructed that allowed tanks of the British 7th Armoured Division to cross the river. That evening, 78th Division's 38th (Irish) Brigade arrived by sea at Termoli, and the German attack the following morning was narrowly repulsed in desperate fighting. By late morning on October 6, troops attacked the German positions, and by late afternoon the German units began to fall back to the next prepared defenses on the River Trigno, the Barbara Line.

The night of October 12, the US Fifth Army attacked across the Volturno. German units using rearguard tactics were able to slow the American advance, skillfully using the mountainous terrain – which favored the defense – and conducted a fighting withdrawal over the rest of the month to the Barbara Line, the next line north, which Fifth Army reached on November 2. The American units had breached the Barbara Line on the Tyrrhenian Sea side of the Apennine mountains by November 9. The Wehrmacht forces then fell back to the Bernhardt Line.

These defenses were an outlying spur of the Gustav Line, the main German defensive position south of Rome. Both lines began at the mouth of the Garigliano River, with the Gustav Line following that river inland to the junction with the Rapido, where it then turned north up that river to Cassino, which was the center of the defenses. The Bernhardt Line linked a series of strongly defended mountains – Monte la Difensa, Monte Camino, Monte Lungo, and Monte Sammucro, further to the east. The line consisted primarily of fortified hilltop positions, and was an outer shield to the Rapido Valley protecting the Mignano Gap – a 6-mile-long mountain pass, between mountains on both sides that were 3,000 feet high – which was the entrance to the Liri Valley, the best route from Naples to Rome along Highway 6. The Bernhardt Line was not as strong as the Gustav Line, being intended only to delay the arrival of the Allies at the Gustav Line, which was the primary German winter line. In the event, the Gustav Line would hold against the Allies until May.

The poor weather also had a negative effect on the Allied air forces, with both Twelfth Air Force and the British Desert Air Force limited in the support they could provide to the troops attacking mountain strong points. The Luftwaffe, while less of a threat than it had been in North Africa or Sicily, still rose to contest Allied air superiority, with night-raider Stukas adding to the discomfort of the troops on the ground with unexpected attacks on anything moving in the darkness.

Following the Italian surrender and the Allied success at Salerno, there was considerable action in the eastern Mediterranean in late September and the month of October. Aerial reconnaissance had found by October 1 that the Luftwaffe was building up its force in Greece. Some 250 fighters and bombers were found on airfields in eastern Greece, with another 100 at airfields around Salonika, on Crete, and in the Dodecanese. These airfields were close enough that the enemy could strike the newly captured Foggia airfield complex in eastern Italy and the port of Bari. The fighters in the Dodecanese threatened British forces that had landed on Cos, Leros, and Samos islands. The Allied air forces struck these Greek fields beginning on October 4.

Many Italian garrisons on the islands in the Aegean Sea south of Greece opposed the German presence. Winston Churchill had hoped that by taking these islands, Turkey might be influenced to enter the war on the Allied side. While British forces landed on several of the Dodecanese islands, German forces, acting with typical efficiency, moved faster than their Allied opponents and recaptured several of them. The German capture of Cos, which had an airfield that controlled the islands in the immediate vicinity, forced the British to evacuate. With British airpower unable to challenge this German response, the island of Rhodes was secured and turned into the major Luftwaffe base in the region. Three Stuka units were either based at Rhodes or flew to the island to use it as a staging post for their attacks on Allied warships and shipping. Several Royal Navy ships were heavily damaged by the Stukas and were evacuated to Egypt in early October.

To counter this Luftwaffe threat, P-38s of the 14th and 1st Fighter Groups moved from their base at Sainte Mare du Zit 30 miles south of Tunis to the RAF secondary field Gambut, outside Tobruk in Libya, 8 miles from the Egyptian border, on October 4. This brought the Lightnings in effective range of Rhodes and the rest of the Dodecanese. The 14th's 37th Squadron arrived at Gambut after dark; having been delayed in their takeoff, they landed in nearly pitch darkness and almost came to the edge of a precipice right beside the airfield, having not been informed of the danger before their arrival.

The Lightnings began providing air cover to the Royal Navy the next day; however, the Luftwaffe managed to avoid the fighters for the first three days after their arrival. On October 8, the Stukas caught the sloop HMS *Peacock* and crippled it with near misses. The next day, British and Greek ships were attacked in the Scarpento Channel southwest of Rhodes by Ju-87Ds of II./StG 3, which launched all 26 of the *Gruppe*'s Ju-87s to strike the Allied ships after radar confirmed the 1st Group's P-38s had departed. With the P-38s gone, the Stukas went after the destroyer HMS *Panther* and sank it, then damaged the light cruiser HMS *Carlisle* so badly that it never put to sea again after surviving the journey to Alexandria.

At the height of the attack, Major William Leverette arrived at the head of seven P-38s. They had flown on the deck across the Mediterranean to avoid being picked up by German radar, and their presence was a complete surprise to the enemy. Two P-38s had been forced to abort, leaving Leverette with four P-38s of Red Flight, while White Flight leader First Lieutenant Wayne Blue led a three-fighter formation. Blue's trio stayed high to provide top cover while Leverette led his four P-38s in a diving attack on the vulnerable Stukas, which had no fighter cover. Leverette later wrote in his combat report:

> On 9 October 1943 our squadron took off at 1030 hours with nine planes to cover a convoy of one cruiser and four destroyers. Two were forced to return because of engine trouble. We sighted the convoy at 1200 hours approximately 15 miles east of Cape Valoca, on the island of Scarpanto. The convoy had been attacked and the cruiser was smoking from the stern. I took position at 6,000 feet out of range of the ship's AA. During our first orbit around the convoy, while flying a southwesterly course at 8,000 feet, Lieutenant Homer Sprinkle called out, "Bogies at one o'clock, slightly high, approaching the convoy from the northwest."
>
> We immediately changed course to pass behind the bogies and began a gradual climb. Shortly thereafter, we identified the bogies as approximately 25 Ju-87s in three flights. My flight attacked the Ju 87s at about 1215 hours. We immediately dived to the left and attacked from the left quarter. I attacked one in the rear of the formation, firing at about 20 degrees and observing smoke pouring from the left side of the engine.

As Leverette broke away to the left and upward, the rest of the Stukas immediately jettisoned their bombs. "I attacked a second enemy aircraft from the rear and slightly below. After a short burst at about 200 yards this enemy aircraft rolled over and spiraled steeply downwards. After breaking away to the left again and turning back towards the enemy formation, I saw both enemy aircraft strike the water."

Leverette then attacked a third Ju-87. "I fired just after the rear gunner opened fire. He ceased firing immediately and the pilot jumped out, although I did not see the 'chute open." He flew through the formation and attacked a fourth Ju-87 with a deflection shot from 30 degrees. "I observed cannon and machine gun hits in its engine. Large pieces of cowling and parts flew off and the engine immediately began smoking profusely as the enemy aircraft started down."

Leverette broke away climbing to the left, then came around and opened fire on a fifth Ju-87. "The canopy and parts flew off, a long flame immediately shot out from the rear of the engine and left wing root and the rear gunner jumped clear of the enemy aircraft." Leverette continued on past that Stuka into the formation and hit a sixth dive bomber from the left and below. "I was forced to roll partially on my back to the left to bring my sight onto the enemy aircraft, opening fire at close range. I observed full hits on the right upper side of the engine, which immediately began to smoke." While Leverette broke away to the left, his element leader saw the Ju-87 strike the water. Leverette then went after a seventh Stuka, attacking from behind and slightly below. "The rear gunner ceased firing after I hit him with a short burst. The enemy aircraft nosed downwards slightly and I closed to minimum range, setting the engine on fire with a full burst in the bottom of the fuselage." The dive bomber then angled down, which prevented Leverette from breaking away by climbing. "In attempting to pass under the right wing of the aircraft, three feet of my left propeller sliced through the enemy aircraft." With its tail gone, the Stuka flipped crazily into the sea below.

The Lightnings continued their attacks on the enemy formation until the Stukas crossed the south coast of Rhodes at 1230 hours and the Americans were all out of ammo. The final victory tally for the 37th was 16 Ju-87s destroyed and five claimed probable or damaged, along with a single Ju-88 that strayed into the aerial battlefield and was also shot down. All seven Lightnings returned safely to Gambut.

Bill Leverette's claim of seven victories in one engagement was the top score by a USAAF pilot in Europe during the entire war, and resulted in an immediate award of the Distinguished Flying Cross. His element leader, Second Lieutenant Henry Hanna, became an "ace in a day" with five Stukas shot down, while Hanna's wingman, Second Lieutenant Homer Sprinkle, claimed three destroyed and a probable. According to German records, II./StG 3 lost seven Stukas in the fight, with two more written off in crash-landings on Rhodes. One of Leverette's pilots counted 14 splashes in the water during the fight. Despite the discrepancy between claims and actual losses, II./StG 3's combat effectiveness had been seriously depleted by the loss of at least nine of its 26 Stuka dive bombers.

Once Allied fighters were based on the Italian mainland, it changed the tactical situation for the Luftwaffe fighter groups. In October, Oberst Günther Freiherr von Maltzahn, JG 53's *Kommodore*, was promoted to *Jagdführer (Jafu) Oberitalien*, commanding all German fighter units in Italy. Tactical commander was renowned fighter leader Oberst Eduard "Edu" Neumann, formerly *Kommodore* of JG 27 in North Africa. Von Maltzahn and Neumann would lead the Luftwaffe's defensive battles until the summer of 1944, when most of the fighter units were withdrawn to Germany following the fall of Rome, to join the defense of the Reich.

JG 77 was assigned primarily to air defense; Jagdgeschwader 4, 51, and 53 were tasked with supporting ground operations on the Cassino front, and at Anzio following the January invasion; these three units were also responsible for providing fighter escort to the *Schlachtgruppen*, the Fw-190-equipped fighter-bomber units.

The 82nd Fighter Group moved their P-38s from Sicily to San Pancrazio/Salentina airfield, a former Regia Aeronautica base on the heel of the Italian "boot," but only remained there a week, flying eight missions. On October 6, the 82nd was given a mission to strafe the airfield outside the town of Araxos in southern Greece; the 96th Squadron provided high cover while the 95th and 97th Squadrons attacked the target. They were again led by Lieutenant Colonel MacNicol, leading the 97th; he destroyed an unidentified single-engine fighter and damaged an Fw-190 fighter-bomber. The group claimed seven enemy fighters destroyed in the air and seven damaged; all the aerial scores were by pilots from the 97th.

On October 8, the 95th and 96th Squadrons escorted B-25s of the 321st Bomb Group to hit Athens' Eleusis airfield. As the Mitchells left the target, 12 JG 27 Bf-109Gs attacked the 95th Squadron from above and behind; the running fight over the Gulf of Corinth resulted in claims for two confirmed victories and four damaged for two P-38s lost.

On the afternoon of October 9, the 97th Squadron escorted four B-25Gs from the 310th Bomb Group on a sweep over the Adriatic. One flight of four spotted a lone Ju-88 and shot it up before it crashed. Since the 82nd did not award shared victories, pilots in such circumstances had to come to an agreement regarding who received official credit; in this case, the four cast lots to see who received official credit and Second Lieutenant Bob Williams was given the score.

On October 10, the group moved 20 miles to San Donato airfield, near Lecce, which they would call home for the next three months. The field was also known as Aeroporto Galatina, and was – like San Pancrazio – a prewar base with concrete runways.

The group escorted the 321st Bomb Group to Argos airfield in Greece on October 14. A formation of eight Bf-109s from III./JG 27 was spotted near the target; Major Muse's flight from the 95th Fighter Squadron bounced four in a fight in which Muse claimed one destroyed and one probable, but number four in the flight fell to the enemy fighters. Six days later, the Lightnings flew a combination escort and dive-bombing mission, taking Mitchells from the 321st to the marshalling yard at Nis, in Yugoslavia. The yard was heavily damaged and the Lightnings strafed a nearby airfield, claiming three enemy aircraft destroyed and eight damaged. Lieutenant Colonel MacNicol claimed an SM.82 transport.

On October 22, the 82nd took the 321st back to Eleusis with the Mitchells, where they were jumped by 20 JG 27 Bf-109s as the Mitchells departed the target. The 96th Squadron's Second Lieutenant Hiram C. Pitts claimed a Bf-109 destroyed while the 97th's Second Lieutenant Paul F. Jorgensen claimed a second, while three Fw-190s were claimed as damaged. The next day the group flew a strafing mission to the airfield at Tirana, Albania, where the 97th Squadron gave cover while the 95th attacked the field, claiming four destroyed and five damaged. Flight Leader First Lieutenant Claud E. Ford, one of the group's original staff sergeant pilots, spotted a Ju-52/3m in the landing pattern and shot it down.

One of the 82nd's final missions in Twelfth Air Force was their first high-altitude, long-range strategic escort, with 48 Lightnings covering B-17s and B-24s on their outbound leg to bomb Weiner Neustadt in Austria; the P-38s provided escort as far as Lake Balaton in Hungary, but the enemy made no appearance before their departure.

On October 27, the 97th Squadron flew a strafing mission against the airfield at Podgorica in Yugoslavia. Three enemy aircraft were destroyed and seven damaged. Enemy fighters attempted to engage the Lightnings as they headed for the Adriatic, but nothing came of the attempt. The final Twelfth Air Force mission was flown on October 31, with the 97th Squadron again strafing an airfield outside Tirana, Albania. As they headed toward the sea, several Bf-109s made an attack, with three shot down in a confused battle.

The 1st Fighter Group fought their final battles as part of XII Fighter Command on two missions at the end of October. On October 21, all three squadrons provided escort to B-26s bombing targets in Italy. As the Marauders dropped their bombs and headed away, the group was jumped by a mixed force of 15 Bf-109s and Fw-190s; the Lightnings accounted for five Bf-109s and one Fw-190 but lost three pilots. Two days later, on October 23, a similar mission was flown. This time the 27th Squadron bore the brunt of the enemy attack by 20 Bf-109s; three were claimed shot down for the loss of one P-38. On October 29, the group received orders to transfer from Mateur, Algeria, to Cagliari airfield on Sardinia.

Leverette and Hanna were XII Fighter Command's final P-38 aces as a result of their one-sided fight. At the end of October, the three P-38 groups were absorbed into the new strategic Fifteenth Air Force on its formation, effective November 1, 1943. Throughout the fighting in North Africa, as well as the Sicilian and Italian invasions, the P-38 groups had fought a battle against the odds in making the Lightning the primary US fighter type in the MTO, with 37 P-38 pilots becoming aces during their time in Twelfth Air Force while only 12 Spitfire pilots achieved that rank, along with ten P-40 pilots.

The 325th "Checkertail Clan" had been transferred to the Northwest African Strategic Air Force on the basis of their excellent performance as part of Twelfth Air Force's 2nd Air Defense Wing in the Pantelleria and early Sicily campaigns. During that time, in 110 missions, the group had scored an impressive 128 victories for the loss of only 34 P-40s, a victory/loss ratio of 4:1, despite a relatively slow start when they had entered combat in May. During that time, they had escorted 1,100 B-17s, B-24s, B25s, and B-26s, without a single bomber lost while under their protection. The P-40-equipped group was the only single-engine fighter group in NASAF. Following the victory in Sicily, the only Axis target in range of the P-40s was Sardinia; the Checkertails spent August 1943 escorting B-25s and B-26s on the softening-up campaign against Sardinia, which was a thorn in the Allied side with the number of Axis air units based on the island's many airfields. Additionally, Sardinia was a staging base for German and Italian bomber missions to hit the North African ports. Jimmy Doolittle's orders to the group were to fly a mission a day to targets in Sardinia that the 325th picked out for maximum opportunity to take on the Luftwaffe and Regia Aeronautica units, and also disrupt transport and communications.

Captain John Watkins described the Sardinian period as "our gentleman's war. We set our own time and place to fight. We ranged up and down the island, staging dogfights in the best Hollywood style. We divebombed power stations, bridges and factories."

On August 28, the group was jumped by 26 Bf-109s while dive-bombing a factory; those who had not yet bombed jettisoned their ordnance and turned into the enemy. When the sky cleared of airplanes, the Checkertails claimed seven destroyed, three probables, and two damaged, for only two P-40s damaged, though both had to belly in when they returned to Sicily. Watkins scored a double and was awarded a Distinguished Flying Cross for having turned back when he spotted another squadron under attack. Diving into the enemy formation, he shot down the leader and damaged the wingman of a *Rotte* ("pack" of two planes) diving on the other squadron, then turned into a *Schwarm* of four attacking other P-40s and scored another shot down with the leader badly damaged.

On September 2, the 14th Group was scheduled to provide top cover for the Checkertails as they dive-bombed Decimomannu airfield, but the P-38s never showed up; this was not the first time such a thing had happened. When he returned to base, group CO Bob Baseler had the ground crews ready "Hoiman," the nickname for a captured Bf-109G the group maintained. He took off and flew to what he thought was the 14th's base, and commenced to beat up the airfield during dinner hour. When those below recognized the silhouette of the Bf-109 – paying no attention to the fact it was painted black with red control surfaces with Allied stars on the wings – the air was filled with food and mess kits as they scattered in all directions seeking cover. An hour after Baseler returned from the flight, the 1st Group's CO, Colonel Ralph Garmin, landed his P-38 and came to the Checkertails' headquarters, demanding to know who had buzzed his chow line. "They're still trying to get some of them out of the shelters!" he exclaimed. Fortunately, Garmin and Baseler had been squadron mates before the war in the 94th Pursuit Squadron. Baseler apologized for mistaking the airfield and explained the group was tired of P-38 "cover" that didn't show up. Garmin promised to get in touch with the 14th and 82nd Groups and straighten things out. There were no more missed rendezvous.

On September 7, Captain Harold H. Crossley flew the final mission of his tour, leading a flight in a fighter sweep over Sardinia. No enemy aircraft were seen, but on the way home he spotted a large seagoing tug towing four barges. Leading the flight in line-astern, he dove on the barges and opened fire. "All of a sudden, I heard a noise like things banging on a tin roof and I smelled gunpowder. Then I looked down and realized these barges had targets on them – the tug was towing them to give the coastal batteries practice! Boy, were we in a spot! They were shooting everything and we had to go and fly right into their sights. I thought to myself, 'All right, you sap, this IS your last mission!'" Fortunately for Crossley and the other three, the enemy gunners were as surprised by their appearance as they were to find themselves in the situation. After sinking the barges, the four P-40s stayed low and headed out to sea. When Crossley landed, his ground crew took one look at all the bullet holes and flak holes in his Warhawk and sent it to the junkyard as a total loss.

The group's final P-40 missions were two escort flights to cover C-47s flying the Allied delegation to Decimomannu on September 17 to take the surrender of the Italian garrison. On September 18, the Checkertails flew to Mateur airfield in Tunisia and turned their P-40s over to the 324th Fighter Group. Late in the afternoon of September 18, the first Republic Aviation tech reps landed on the field. The 325th discovered they were the first P-40 group in the MTO to re-equip with the Thunderbolt, supplies of which had finally arrived in North Africa as production finally was sufficient to meet the needs of the P-47 groups in the Fifth Air Force in New Guinea and the Eighth Air Force in Britain, allowing the big fighters to appear in the skies over the Mediterranean. The 325th spent the rest of September and the first two weeks of October studying the manuals and listening to lectures on their new mounts by the tech reps. On October 11, Colonel Baseler landed the first Thunderbolt at Mateur. Over the next week, the rest of the P-47s arrived, and by October 31, the Checkertails were declared operational. The next day, they joined the three P-38 groups in the new Fifteenth Air Force.

The veteran 57th Group, based on Sicily, had provided air cover for the British Eighth Army's landings at Taranto. They had provided support from Sicily until they moved to Rocco Bernardo landing ground on September 19. A week later the group transferred to the modern Gioia del Colle airfield near Taranto before moving on to the Foggia complex on October 2 following capture of the airfields by the Eighth Army.

The 79th Fighter Group moved their P-40s from their base at Palagonia airfield in Sicily to the mainland on September 16, taking up residence at Isole landing ground, 15 miles southwest of Crotone. The Italians had been in the process of upgrading the landing ground to a more permanent air base; they left hangars, administration buildings, and barracks. The ground crews, who had not slept indoors since they arrived in North Africa a year before, quickly took possession of the barracks buildings while the pilots continued living in tents.

Within an hour of touching down, the group flew 43 ground support sorties for the Canadian division that was attacking Potenza, which was captured four days later. That evening, the group was entertained by Jack Benny's USO troupe which had arrived on the field while the first missions were flown; Benny's troupe were the first to put on a USO show on mainland Italy. The next day the group began flying "road recce" missions looking for enemy vehicles as far north as Benevento.

On September 20, 12 P-40s attacked a German convoy. Lieutenants Charles Cummings, Frank Nicolai, and Robert Davis were all hit by ground fire that forced Cummings and Davis to make forced landings at Santa Maria where the 33rd Group was now stationed. Davis's P-40 was hit in the engine and he was compelled to bail out a short distance from where they had hit the German convoy. He fractured his left arm when it got entangled in the shroud lines on landing, but was lucky to find that the first person he ran across was a farmer who had lived in New Jersey and spoke English. Taken to the farmer's home, the townspeople brought food and he stayed overnight. The next morning the commander of the local Carabinieri arrived to offer help. When he learned of Davis's injury, he brought a local doctor, who was dissuaded by the police captain from reporting Davis to the Germans. With his arm now set, Davis spent the next three days at the farmer's home. On September 24 he was moved to another home. The next morning the town was liberated by the British, and Davis was able to return to the 79th on October 22.

The British advance was rapid enough that on October 1, the group moved to Pisticci, southwest of Taranto from Isole. They only stayed there three days before moving on to a landing ground known as Penny Post, one of the fields in the Foggia complex, before moving on to Salsola, a grass strip in the complex. The extended bad weather that began in October leading into winter meant that few missions were flown. As the rains came, the Italian landing grounds, which were either dirt or grass strips, became muddy fields that made operations from takeoff to landing and taxiing on the field both difficult and dangerous.

Many of the American units made efforts to restore damaged enemy aircraft to flying status. German fighters were used to give pilots experience in air combat maneuvering with them, while Italian fighters were restored purely for flying, since many of them had excellent flight characteristics. The 79th Group had restored many enemy aircraft in North Africa and Sicily, but their achievement in restoring a Ju-88 that required an engine change, replacement propellers and wheels, restoration of brake lines, replacement of instruments, and some sheet metal work – accomplished over six days during a driving rainstorm – was a remarkable achievement by the ground crews. Once restored to flight, the plan was to use it to transport liquor and foodstuffs from North Africa. Higher authority had other ideas. Major Fred Barsodi, commander of the 86th Squadron, was due to depart after completing his tour. He flew the bomber to Tunis, where Generals Jimmy Doolittle and Carl Spaatz gave him and co-pilot Captain Pete Bedford a large German flag to present to General Arnold. Flying by way of Marrakech and Dakar, then across the Atlantic, the Ju-88 landed at Miami on November 6, 1943, after 51 hours' flying time. The Ju-88 eventually made a "grand tour" of the United States as part of the fourth war bond drive.

On October 16, the 99th Fighter Squadron, which had been attached to the 324th Fighter Group during the Pantelleria and Sicilian campaigns, was transferred to the 79th Group. At the time, Benjamin O. Davis was testifying in Washington to a Senate Advisory Committee about the scathing report written about the unit. The combat performance of the black squadron was criticized as poor, based partly on information supplied in a memorandum by Colonel William Momyer, commander of the 324th Group. The memorandum claimed that "the consensus of opinion seems to be that the negro type has not the proper reflexes to make a first-class fighter pilot." It went on to recommend reassignment of the 99th Fighter Squadron away from the front lines.

On October 29, First Lieutenant Charles "Jazz" Jaslow – one of the last original pilots in the 79th – flew his 80th and last mission of his tour, which he would also remember as his most memorable, leading two flights of P-40s to attack shipping in the port of Torino. As the Warhawks turned for home, they ran into a towering thunderhead and were swallowed up in darkness and driving rain. Dropping low enough to see the waters of the Adriatic through the rain, they flew south; reaching the checkpoint to turn for Foggia, they confronted a solid wall of rain with zero visibility. They were ready to belly land on the beach when one flight member recalled seeing an abandoned British airstrip near Termoli. Arriving overhead, the field was deserted. Jaslow landed and luckily was able to stay on the muddy strip as he locked his brakes and slid the length of the short strip. The others landed successfully, but it was two days before the field was dry enough after the rain passed for them to fly out and return home.

All of southern Italy had now been liberated, but the Allies now faced the Volturno Line, the first of Field Marshal Kesselring's prepared defensive positions, which held the northern side of the Volturno River. The Allies faced a bloody advance in constant contact with the enemy, exactly as the field marshal had promised Hitler they would. The month of October saw both Fifth and Eighth Armies slowly advance and hammer through these defenses. Without the close air support of XII Air Support Command and the RAF's Desert Air Force squadrons, this advance would have been nearly impossible. The Mustangs of the 27th and 86th Groups were able to provide outstanding close support near Allied ground positions, due to the accuracy in dive bombing that the A-36 was capable of.

With the onset of bad weather beginning to hamper operations over Italy in October, Twelfth Air Force units started venturing across the Adriatic Sea to hit targets in Greece, Albania, and Yugoslavia. The P-40's limited range restricted the 57th to missions against targets along the Yugoslavian coast, going after enemy shipping and other targets of opportunity. On October 21, ten 66th Fighter Squadron P-40s on an anti-shipping patrol spotted six Ju-87 Stukas near Vodice, Yugoslavia. With mission leader First Lieutenant William P. Benedict in front, the pilots destroyed all six German dive bombers without loss. Four days later, on October 25, the group moved to Amendola on the Adriatic coast, putting them closer to Yugoslavia, from where they would fly dive-bombing, strafing, patrol, and escort missions for the next four months.

While aerial opposition was waning as the Luftwaffe withdrew unit after unit from the Southern Front to reinforce the air defense of Germany, the fighter-bomber pilots still faced danger from the always-growing concentration and skill of German antiaircraft defenses. On

November 6, the 65th "Fighting Cocks" lost three P-40s over Metković, Yugoslavia. One was flown by Second Lieutenant Henry Hunter Barker Jr., who had originally joined the Royal Canadian Air Force before Pearl Harbor but returned to the US afterwards, joining the USAAF and arriving in the 57th in time to make the trip to Africa on board *Ranger* in July 1942. A 23-year-old veteran of the group's operations in Egypt and across North Africa and Sicily, Barker was hit by flak and shot down on his third pass over the city. He was secretly buried in the local graveyard.

The 57th was one group that made certain that the ground crews, without whose unsung efforts nothing could happen, received recognition for their work by being allowed to put a name of their choice on the right-hand cowling of the airplane they cared for, as well as getting passes for R&R back to Cairo, as the pilots did. The 57th's crews were highly professional. Herb Gluckman, a 66th Fighter Squadron flight chief who was one of the earliest assigned members of the squadron, recalled how the ground crews operated:

Each squadron was divided into three flights – A, B and C – with a flight chief responsible for the mechanical maintenance of the eight airplanes in his flight. A crew chief and assistant crew chief were permanently assigned to each ship. The flight chief oversaw the work of the 16 mechanics and made sure routine inspections were performed as close to periodic schedule as possible. He frequently had to juggle those schedules because of the squadron's need for aircraft to fly missions. We had the authority to ground a ship if we felt maintenance was being stretched to the point that pilot safety might become an issue. We couldn't pull rank like that too often though.

Essentially, the responsibility of the flight chief was to "keep 'em flying" by plotting aircraft availability, and this often involved his interceding, on behalf of a crew chief, with a specialty section of the squadron service staff when severe technical problems arose such as when a ship came back shot up, arranging for sheet-metal men to fix things. Or arranging to move an airplane to our engineering section for an engine or wing change due to combat damage, during which time the chief would reassign that crew temporarily to help the guys of another ship who were overloaded with work. We met with

armorers, radiomen etc., to coordinate their needs with the down-
times we were scheduling for individual planes. We frequently rolled
up our sleeves and pitched in with the "grease monkey" work, either
because a crew was stumped by a problem or to help rush the work
along so as to meet the squadron's mission schedules.

Of course, the flight chief had to always keep an eye on the
squadron's need of airplanes so as to be able to fulfill upcoming
mission requirements – how many aircraft were needed, when and
did they need to be configured for a long-range mission? If so, he had
to make sure belly tanks were hung on those aircraft assigned for that
mission. We also had to know how many missions were scheduled for
the day, and with how many aircraft, which determined which crews
to put the pressure on. And with all that, a wise flight chief would
also attempt to build and maintain a sense of esprit de corps within
his small group for the purpose of developing a smooth-running and
effective unit. Generally, the compact group of 17 or 18 men – some,
mere boys – did work smoothly together, and voluntarily helped each
other when needed.

So far as the working hours were concerned, it was simple –
sun-up to sundown, seven days a week, no holidays or overtime.
And that was everyone. We had no hangars in which to do our
maintenance, nor lighting facilities with which to perform work after
dark, therefore all work had to be done during daylight hours. Of
course, we wouldn't have used lights even if we had had them. We
got enough nighttime visits from uninvited guests as it was without
pinpointing our location for them.

The workload gradually got heavier the longer the aircraft had been
in service. The P-40F and L models that were powered by the Merlin
had ceased production back in March 1943, which meant there often
was not a replacement available. This led to creativity on the part of
the crews in keeping things working by taking parts from aircraft that
had been damaged beyond repair, turning them into "hangar queens."
The group created unofficial "medals" that were awarded to crews who
set records in maintaining their individual aircraft, which added to the
high morale in the ground echelons.

Following the 325th Group's re-equipment with the P-47, the 57th
Fighter Group received its first P-47s a few days after Thanksgiving. After

a week spent checking out in the Thunderbolt, the 57th took their new mount on its first combat mission on December 5, when each squadron contributed three P-47s and four P-40s to escort 36 B-25s from the 321st Bomb Group on their return from attacking Split harbour, in Yugoslavia. Due to engine problems, one P-47 returned early but the eight others patrolled over Split. No enemy aircraft appeared, and the fighters did not spot the B-25s.

Capitalizing on the increased ordnance-carrying capacity of the P-47, the 57th's next missions were involved with maritime interdiction in the Adriatic and along the Dalmatian coast of Yugoslavia. On December 16, the group flew their 1,000th mission, a sweep over the Pelješac peninsula. Eight P-47s from the three squadrons took off at 0900 hours from Amendola, headed northeast across the Adriatic. With one abort for engine trouble, the remaining seven made landfall just west of Zabrde after flying by dead reckoning 120 miles over open sea. They strafed targets between Zabrde and Ston, 3 miles to the south, setting fire among some supply sheds outside Ston. They then turned northeast toward Drace, in search of targets of opportunity. Spotting activity around some buildings north of Drace, they made a strafing run. As they pulled out of the run, the Thunderbolts were bounced by eight Bf-109G-6s from IV./JG 27, led by Leutnant Wolfgang Lang.

In a fight over the shoreline, ranging from sea level to 1,000 feet, the P-47 pilots turned into their attackers and shot down four of the enemy fighters, while the rest turned away. First Lieutenant Alfred Froning claimed two of the Bf-109s, which brought his score to six, making him the 65th Squadron's second ace. Froning later described the fight:

I was leading the top flight of three P-47s. We had just pulled up from strafing Ston and were at 1,000 feet. Lieutenant Monahan called in one snapper. As he dove on the enemy aircraft, a second Me 109 closed on his tail. I was above and behind him, and closed in for a dead astern shot at a range of 250 yards. I opened fire and observed pieces and smoke trail off his Me 109. The enemy pilot tried to pull up and I continued firing. He then half rolled at 900 feet and went straight into the water burning. As I broke away, two cannon shells hit my right wing, causing my right wheel to drop and set the wing on fire. I tried turning, but my ship was crippled, resulting in my tail getting shot up. I hit the deck, trying to evade the Me 109's fire.

Immediately, two more Me 109s jumped me. The three of them then ran a gunnery pattern on me from line abreast astern. I took hits all over the aircraft. Two of the Me 109s left, while the remaining ship turned onto the tail of another P-47 that crossed our path. I turned about and fired a 30-degree deflection shot, gradually closing it down to line astern. I observed approximately three or four feet of his left wing fly off, as well as the balance of his tail section. He was throwing out much white and black smoke. He was at 400 feet and started to roll over on his back in a 60-degree dive. When last seen, he was at 150 feet, apparently out of control on his back, smoking. This aircraft was observed to crash into the sea.

First Lieutenant Harold Monahan also claimed two Bf-109s destroyed without being hit:

Upon completion of our strafing attack, three of us saw 15-plus Me 109s. I attacked one flying on the deck. He did a chandelle up to the left and I followed, shooting all the time. Smoke began to pour from him when 400 feet above the sea. Looking back, I saw him crash into the sea. I then sighted one on my left and did a 90-degree turn, firing a long burst at close range. I then had to break off as another Me 109 was closing in on me. I turned into him but did not engage. I then looked to my right and saw the Me 109 that I had previously engaged go down in smoke and crash. The pilot bailed out.

As the enemy disappeared, the P-47s turned north toward Trpanj, then back across the Adriatic. While Froning's Thunderbolt was fairly well shot up, he managed to stay with the others and coax the fighter back to Amendola. This was the first time anyone in the 57th had experienced the P-47's toughness, which allowed it to keep flying despite serious battle carnage, a trait that pilots would come to rely on.

A second mission – flown by 66th Squadron pilots in P-40Fs – that took off an hour after the first engaged a similar force of Bf-109s just south and east of Froning's flight. The Warhawk pilots claimed three Bf-109s destroyed, one probable, and three damaged.

A third mission later that day, flown with a mixed force of P-40s with P-47s flying top cover on a search for shipping along the Pelješac peninsula, saw the Warhawks strafe several troop concentrations between Viganj and Orebić, before they spotted and destroyed a locomotive pulling seven rail cars. There was no aerial opposition for the P-47s to worry about.

On December 17, another mixed-squadron formation of eight P-47s and 12 P-40s flew another shipping interdiction mission. Inbound leg at 10,000 feet, the P-47s surprised five Bf-109s. They attacked in line abreast from dead astern. Two Bf-109s were shot down immediately, and a third that attempted to intervene after the 64th's Lieutenant Liebing shot down the first was shot down by Lieutenants Charles Leaf and Hugh Barlow, while Lieutenant Warren Shaw shot down the second solo victory. Liebing remembered, "One of them made the mistake of lagging behind, so I snuck up to where I could get a shot at him. I got him in my sights for a 60-degree deflection shot. I saw the tracers going out toward him. He seemed to fly right into them, and all of a sudden he wasn't there. He had blown right up in mid-air." They then continued their assigned interdiction mission, spotting and strafing a 75-foot barge and a 200-foot cargo vessel before they touched down back at Amendola at 1615 hours. It was later learned that one of the German pilots shot down was 188-victory Hauptmann Joachim Kirschner, *Gruppenkommandeur* of IV./JG 27. While he managed to successfully bail out, he was captured by partisans of the 29th Herzegovinian Striking Division and executed.

The group spent the rest of December hunting Axis shipping. While more Thunderbolts were issued to the group in early 1944, the remaining December missions saw P-40s flying as the strike element, while the available P-47s flew top cover.

The 86th Group's 525th Fighter-Bomber Squadron had been operating from Seretella landing ground since late September, while the 526th and 527th Squadrons remained at Sele landing ground, which they had moved to immediately after the Salerno landings. Seretella was 10 miles south of Salerno, and close to the Volturno front, allowing the 525th Squadron to fly strikes against rail and motor transport from the Volturno River area all the way to Rome. In early October, the 526th Squadron moved up to Seretella and operated with the 525th for a week before moving on to Pomigliano d'Arco airfield, 15 miles south of Naples. The 527th replaced them at Seretella for a week beginning October 14, before moving on to Pomigliano on October 19. The 525th Squadron moved up to Pomigliano on November 20. The group would remain there until the end of April 1944. At Pomigliano, pilots lived in the Hotel Lago Maggiore in Naples, which was the first time they had access to permanent indoor living since the group had left the United States. On several occasions, when pilots left for the airfield in the morning, overnight guests they left in bed looted the rooms. The 31st Fighter Group, whose pilots shared the hotel with the 86th's pilots, had arrived at Pomigliano in mid-October, when the rains had turned the dirt runway at Montecorvino into what was recalled as a "swamp." Pomigliano would become increasingly popular as the rains of fall turned into the snows of winter, leaving its concrete runway operational throughout.

The 86th Group made a strong effort for pilots of the three squadrons to fly their own assigned aircraft on missions if at all possible. Lieutenant George Palmer recalled, "We took great pride in seeing our name under the canopy and our name for the airplane on the nose. The crews who maintained the airplanes also took tremendous pride in their assigned aircraft and its accomplishments. This resulted in a friendly competition between the ground crews as to whose airplane flew the most missions without any write-ups." The crew of "Baby Carmen" in the 526th were the winners when their Mustang rang up its 200th mission without an engine change.

When Palmer and 17 other replacements arrived at Sele in early October, there was only one A-36 available that was not already assigned to a pilot. "We new pilots put our names in a hat, and luckily mine was the one chosen. I inherited 'Midnite,' which got its name from the crew chief, Ken Barnes, who had named the plane after a black puppy in a litter of six from 'Taffy,' our squadron mascot who had adopted us in Algeria."

The 526th Squadron flew nine different missions on October 18, roving patrols looking for targets of opportunity that resulted in two airfields being strafed with many aircraft destroyed, as well as many trucks and other vehicles strafed on the roads. Enemy fighters rose to oppose the Mustangs, and Lieutenant Forst was credited with two Fw-190s, with First Lieutenant Mike credited with a third.

On October 25, group executive Lieutenant Colonel "Smitty" Tarrant led four Mustangs on an armed reconnaissance – known in group parlance as a "wreckie" – north of Rome. Catching a train stopped at a station near Orte, Tarrant and his wingman shot up a string of boxcars.

When element leader Lieutenant Brown made a following attack, he was immediately rewarded on opening fire with a violent explosion that sent smoke and flames 5,000 feet into the air when an ammo wagon was hit. Caught in the blast at an altitude of 150 feet, his A-36 flipped over on its back and went straight in, the guns still firing. Tarrant was more than 1,000 feet away from the explosion, but the entire left side of his Mustang was caved in, while all the plexiglass in the canopy on that side was blown into the cockpit, jamming the controls until he was able to recover at the last moment. Tarrant managed to fly the badly damaged A-36 back to Pomigliano, where it was found that every stringer and bulkhead on the left side was bent or buckled and the left wingtip bent as well. The fighter-bomber went straight to the junk heap.

On the ground, the first attack toward the Bernhardt Line began on October 31, when the US 3rd Infantry Division attacked the Barbara Line, bypassing Presenzano and heading directly for Mignano. Following a quick victory there, they attacked Monte la Difensa, but were forced to abandon the attack on November 10. While the 3rd Division was thus engaged, the 34th and 45th Divisions waded across the Volturno on the night of November 2–3. Venafro was captured by the 45th Division, while Pozzilli fell to the 34th Division. This success gave the Allies control of the upper Volturno Valley. At the same time, 3rd Division commander Major General Lucian Truscott, Jr. sent the 30th Infantry Regiment around the 45th Division sector to attack Monte Rotondo from the east; this was captured on November 8.

To the right, the Germans still held Monte Cesima and the area of high ground between the Volturno and the Mignano Gap. The other two regiments of the 3rd Division attacked Monte Cesima from the south on November 4, facing a counterattack from the German VI Paratroop Regiment's III Battalion; they were unable to push the Americans back, and Monte Cesima was firmly in Allied hands by November 5. This allowed the 34th and 45th Divisions to move through the Barbara Line up to the Bernhardt Line.

That day, the British 56th Division attacked Monte Camino. They made slow progress up the mountain but were able to successfully fight off three German counterattacks by troops of the 15th Panzergrenadier Division on November 8. The British attack began running out of steam on November 10. As division commander General Templer prepared to send his third brigade into the fight on November 12, he was ordered to halt by General Mark Clark, who didn't believe the mountain could be held. He suggested a temporary retreat, and the British pulled back during the night of November 14.

Further to the Allied right, the US VI Corps pushed the German 305th Infantry Division back at Monte Pantano, in the mountains north of Pozzilli. The 26th Panzer Division moved into the mountains on November 8, taking over the lines to the right of the 305th Division's sector. The 29th Panzergrenadiers were also moved to the front between November 11 and 16, replacing the German 3rd Infantry Division in the Mignano Pass and Mount Sambucaro north of the gap.

General Clark became worried that Fifth Army was in danger of being destroyed by the constant attacks. He asked General Sir Harold Alexander for permission to pause, which was granted, and the Allied offensive came to a halt on November 15. The Allied divisions were given until the end of November to recover before they continued the offensive against the Bernhardt Line. The Allies had captured the mountains guarding the Mignano Gap, which controlled the approaches to the main Gustav Line positions behind the Garigliano and Rapido rivers.

November saw the Italian Theater begin losing out to Operation *Overlord*. That month the experienced British 7th Armoured Division and the American 82nd Airborne Division departed Italy for Britain where they would prepare to fight in Normandy. The US 1st Armored Division and the 1st Special Service Force – a specially trained US–Canadian mountain warfare unit – replaced these units. December saw the 2nd Moroccan Infantry Division arrive.

In November, the "tour" in the 86th Group was extended from 80 missions to 90. This would become common in the Italian campaign, as replacement aircraft and pilots were diverted to "the main event" that was being prepared in Britain. Following the Normandy invasion, mission totals for aircrew in bombers and fighters would be extended in the face of personnel and equipment shortages, and would make their way into the most famous novel of World War II, Joseph Heller's *Catch-22*. As operations on the Italian mainland intensified, the A-36A suffered an alarming loss rate, with 177 falling to enemy action – primarily ground fire – by the end of February 1944.

The 86th and 27th Fighter-Bomber Groups were both experiencing difficulty keeping their A-36s operational in sufficient numbers to meet operational demands. Only 500 A-36s had been produced, of which

300 were assigned to the MTO as original equipment and replacements for the two groups. In addition to the two Mediterranean-based groups, A-36s equipped one squadron of a third group that had been sent to the China–Burma–India Theater in the summer of 1943, with the other two squadrons flying P-51A fighters. There was a fourth group in the United States assigned to training. Each group was authorized a strength of 68 Mustangs, which came to 272 A-36s. Given operational attrition and accidents, by the fall of 1943 the two groups in Italy were down to 60 aircraft each. Eventually, in late January 1944, it became clear that only one group could continue operating the A-36 with the assets available. In a meeting at XII Tactical Air Command HQ that month, the decision of which group would continue with the A-36 was made by a coin toss. The 27th Group came up short. They began transferring to P-40s in late January while the 86th Group absorbed the remaining Mustangs. This was only a temporary solution, since the Warhawks were also in short supply. Most of those given to the 27th were hand-me-downs from the 57th Group after they became the second fighter group in the Mediterranean Theater to re-equip with the P-47 Thunderbolt in late November 1943.

The 86th Group continued to fly close air support missions for ground troops as they forced their way north. Postwar reports claimed that the A-36s were not used as dive bombers, and that the dive brakes were wired shut. In truth, the dive brakes were wired shut on the A-36s used in the stateside training group and the A-36s that found their way to the China–Burma–India Theater, where they were primarily used as fighters. Stateside training resulted in some alarming accident rates, with the A-36A at one point having the highest accident rate per hour of flying time of any USAAF aircraft. The most serious incident involved an A-36A shedding both wings when its pilot tried to pull out from a 450mph dive. Combat units were ordered to restrict the approach to a 70-degree "glide" attack and to stop using the dive brakes, but the order was generally ignored by experienced pilots. However, the 86th continued to provide pinpoint dive-bombing strikes and was considered so accurate that they bombed closer to Allied ground forces than any other ground support aircraft. Utilizing the dive brakes, which allowed a 90-degree vertical dive on the target from 12,000 feet, with speed limited to 390mph, the A-36A had terrific accuracy. Pilots soon discovered that extending the dive brakes after "peel off" led to unequal extension of the brakes due to varying hydraulic pressure, thus inducing a slight roll that impeded aim. The proper technique was to deploy the brakes before entering the dive; when this procedure was used, pilots achieved very consistent results. Regardless of the myths, the truth is that the A-36A was very successful as a dive bomber, with a reputation for precision attacks right on the front lines.

The second attack against the Bernhardt Line was part of a larger Allied offensive that was to begin on November 20 with an Eighth Army attack on the Sangro Line on the Adriatic Coast that was to cross the Sangro Line, break the Gustav Line, and advance to Pescara, then move up the Pescara Valley to threaten Rome from the northeast. This would be joined by Fifth Army's attack to break the Bernhardt and Gustav Lines and advance into the Liri Valley. At that point, two divisions would land at Anzio, where those troops and the advancing troops from the south would trap the retreating Germans. As it turned out, this plan was over-optimistic.

The Sangro was in flood, with soft, muddy approaches, when the Eighth Army attacked the Sangro positions on November 20, forcing the British 78th Division to build a half-mile-long road across swampland to the edge of the river before they could construct a Bailey Bridge to cross the river. Once across, they then were forced to build a road off the riverbank, with all this done under heavy German fire. Two days of heavy work saw the Bailey Bridge completed; once across, the German 65th Infantry Division was almost wiped out. On November 23, more heavy rain caused the Sangro to rise again, washing away the bridges.

The British attack on the Sangro was supported by the P-40s of the 57th Fighter Group, which dive-bombed the German gun positions while the road was constructed and the Bailey Bridge assembled. German flak claimed several of the P-40s, the first personnel losses the group had suffered since the Sicilian campaign.

Eighth Army was forced to pause the attack until November 27, when the rain abated and allowed the 8th Indian Division and 2nd New Zealand Division to cross the Sangro. The British units now faced two fresh German divisions that had been moved into the area from Mignano and the north of Italy. Beginning on December 4, a bitter battle was fought on the line of the Moro River, which delayed the British forces' reaching the outskirts of Ortona until December 19. The British had thus penetrated the Gustav Line and faced German units determined to hold on as long as possible. The resulting battle of Ortona, fought between December 20 and 28, saw the heavily defended town captured by the Canadians, but the fighting brought the Eighth Army offensive to an end when it began snowing.

Fifth Army began its main attack on December 1, with the first objectives being Monte Camino and Monte la Difensa to the left of the Mignano Gap. The battle commenced following a massive two-day aerial and artillery bombardment of both positions, with almost continuous daylight attacks by B-25 and B-26 bombers, along with fighter-bomber attacks with tens of thousands of rounds fired between November 29 and 30. Following this, the British 46th Division took Calabritto at the foot of Monte Camino the night of December 1.

The next night, the main offensive began with the British 56th Division attacking Monte Camino; the troops reached the summit overnight. Between December 3 and 5, German counterattacks pushed them off the summit twice, but they finally took and held the peak on December 6.

As this happened, Monte la Difensa and Monte Maggiore were attacked by US II Corps, beginning with a bombardment by 925 guns. While the enemy was fairly secure in their stone defences on the mountains, the barrage cut them off from the rest of the German army. The 1st Special Service Force attacked Monte la Difensa; they found an unexpected route to the top that allowed them to ambush the garrison. They then fought off a series of counterattacks until the enemy finally commenced a withdrawal the afternoon of December 8, after the British secured Monte Camino. At the same time, the US 36th Division's 142nd Infantry Regiment took Monte Maggiore, supported by an effective artillery bombardment.

Later that morning, the newly arrived 1st Italian Motorized Group advanced to take Monte Lungo – the last mountain in the middle of the gap – while the US 36th Division attacked the village of San Pietro, north of the gap. While the Allies were confident these positions would fall easily, it quickly became clear neither would be simple. The Italians were forced to fall back by noon, with 84 dead, 122 wounded, and 170 missing of the original 1,700 troops. The 36th Division fought a long, costly battle at San Pietro which lasted until the night of December 16–17, when the Germans withdrew following the capture of Monte Lungo.

With the Allies now in control of the mountains in the heart of the Bernhardt Line, the German Tenth Army withdrew to the Gustav Line. There were still a few more bloody battles before the Allies were able to move all the way up to the Rapido River, but this came quickly after the last mountain east of the river was abandoned when Allied troops took positions surrounding it on three sides. It was clear the Allied armies were too exhausted to continue advancing into the Gustav Line, not to mention the end of December saw major snowfall in the mountains.

While the fighting intensified, the Luftwaffe flew one of its most important and effective bombing missions of the war when they struck the port of Bari on the Italian east coast on December 2. The port was filled with 29 ships carrying aviation fuel, bombs, and ammunition waiting to be unloaded at the crowded docks. In a morning briefing at the new Fifteenth Air Force headquarters in the city, Air Force commander Lieutenant General Jimmy Doolittle had questioned Air Marshal Sir Arthur Coningham, who commanded the Desert Air Force units stationed in the region, about the security of the port and the possibility of an enemy attack. Coningham had replied that the Luftwaffe did not have sufficient bombers in the region to mount an effective attack.

That afternoon, a Luftwaffe reconnaissance flight overflew the port; Oberleutnant Werner Hahn counted the ships in the harbor, then turned east to return to Greece. Here, the Ju-88s of Lehrgeschwader 1 (Demonstration Wing 1), led by Geschwaderkommodore Joachim Helbig, the leading Ju-88 pilot of the war, were brought to readiness upon receipt of Hahn's report. The bombers took off at 1730 hours, flying at minimum altitude across the Adriatic to avoid Allied radar; 50 miles east of Bari, the bombers began climbing to bombing altitude, and 105 Ju-88s arrived over Bari at 1915 hours.

The first attacks were off target in the fading light and the bombs hit the city. The next group of bombers entered their dives and picked out ships moored in the middle of the harbor. The first hit was the Victory ship SS *John L. Motley*, which took a hit on its number five deck hatch; the deck cargo caught fire. A moment later, SS *John Bascom* was hit by bombs that ripped her from bow to stern and set her on fire. The SS *John Harvey*, moored at Pier 29, was hit and caught fire.

In the city, civilians unused to bombing attacks ran out of buildings to see what was happening; panic and confusion took over in the streets, as the rest of the bombers entered their dives and their bombs fell across Bari harbor. The crowds hampered the arrival of firefighters. The windows in Jimmy Doolittle's headquarters were blown out; he narrowly missed being hit by flying glass in his office.

A moment later, the bombs in the *John Harvey*'s hold went up. The explosion wracked the entire harbor as clouds of smoke erupted thousands of feet into the sky. Flaming pieces of the ship rocketed in all directions; these incendiary torches landed on other ships and set off a series of explosions in the harbor that turned it into a holocaust. Jimmy Doolittle, who had picked himself up off the floor and was standing by his shattered window staring at the incredible sight, was knocked down again by the enormous explosion.

Many Bari residents had run to the harbor to get away from the fires started in the old section of town and had gathered along the shore. They were decimated by the explosion, with bodies flying 25–30 feet high. The three military hospitals in the city were quickly overwhelmed as the wounded survivors were brought in.

The *John Harvey* had carried more than bombs and ammunition.

Within hours, hospital staffs saw remarkable symptoms among the survivors. Nearly all were experiencing eye trouble. Many began uncontrollably weeping, which was associated with eye spasms and fear of light. Many survivors claimed they were blind. Among patients supposedly in shock or suffering from exposure, their pulse beat was barely evident and blood pressure was extremely low; however, the patients did not appear to be in clinical shock.

By the next morning, skin lesions were noticed on many survivors, with striking coloration: bronze, reddish brown, or tan on some, red on others. A pattern of the distribution of burns began to emerge that depended on degree of exposure to the slimy harbor waters. Those who had fallen into the water were burned all over, while those whose feet or arms had been in the water were burned only there. Those who had been splashed by water had lesions where it hit them. Those who had washed the slime off their bodies and changed clothes had no burns. None of the usual treatment for burns, shock, or exposure was effective. Victims would improve temporarily, then take a sudden turn for the worse and abruptly die for no apparent reason. By the end of the second day, the mysterious deaths among both military and civilian casualties were increasing.

Word was sent to Eisenhower's headquarters in Algiers. Chief of Medicine General Fred Blesse sent Lieutenant Colonel Stewart F. Alexander to investigate. He had worked at the Medical Research Division of the Edgewood Arsenal, Maryland, before going overseas; his knowledge would be invaluable. When he entered the first hospital, there was a strange smell; he turned to the British doctor and asked why there was a smell of what seemed to be garlic. The doctor told him it seemed to be coming from the patients.

Alexander examined the small blisters on the patients and saw more evidence which fitted with the strange odor. Fluid accumulations in the blisters were diffused; in many cases it was difficult to determine the edges of the blisters. X-rays revealed that while few of the patients with the strange symptoms had suffered damage to their lungs, they all had lower-respiratory-tract symptoms. One patient appeared to be in marked shock but told a nurse he was feeling much better; he died seconds later with no sign of distress.

Given his experience, Alexander was quick to realize he was looking at the effects of exposure to mustard gas. Use of mustard gas had been outlawed after World War I, which had seen widespread use of the gas on the Western Front. However, in 1942, President Roosevelt had stated that any use of poison gas by the enemy would be met by "the fullest retaliation." The Allies produced and deployed mustard gas regardless of the Geneva Convention's rules.

The next day, a bomb casing was recovered from the floor of the harbor. Examination revealed evidence it had been filled with mustard gas. With this evidence in hand, the British port officials admitted there had been 100 tons of bombs containing mustard gas on board the *John Harvey*; it was intended the bombs would be stored in Italy for use in retaliation after an enemy poison gas attack. When the ship blew up, the mustard in the bombs had been released; some had mixed with the oily water of the harbor, while much of it was in the smoke clouds drifting over the city.

Eventually, 617 mustard-gas casualties were found among the military and ships' personnel, with 84 dead. The number of Italian civilians affected was never reported. Prime Minister Churchill directed that information of the Bari bombing be kept Top Secret. Other than two preliminary reports issued before his ruling that identified the agent responsible, all other reports listed the cause of the burns as "NYD"

– "not yet diagnosed." Because of the information blackout, staffs in the outlying hospitals where the majority of civilians were taken were never informed of the true cause until too late, leading to many unnecessary deaths. Britain has never officially declassified any of this information over the past 80 years.

Helbig's raid resulted in the complete destruction of 17 ships and significant damage to eight others. It was the worst Allied naval disaster during World War II, other than the Pearl Harbor attack. The destruction of aviation gasoline and ordnance resulted in a six-week delay in the new Fifteenth Air Force mounting significant attacks.

On January 15, the Fifth Army reached the Gustav Line, following six weeks of heavy fighting breaking through the Bernhardt Line, during which they took 16,000 casualties. Kesselring's strategy of making the Allies pay in blood for every foot of Italy was bearing fruit.

The air war had been nothing short of disastrous for the Luftwaffe. During the first six weeks of 1944, I./JG 4 lost 14 pilots killed, wounded or missing – including *Gruppenkommandeur* Major "Gockel" Hahn, killed on January 27 – of an authorized strength of 50.

The Allies were desperate to find a way around the formidable Gustav Line. Mark Clark was advised by Churchill to land at Anzio, which was less than 30 miles from Rome, to flank the Gustav Line. Rome could be taken and the Gustav Line cut off from the rear. In planning meetings, 3rd Division's commander General Truscott made the point repeatedly that success in landing in a basin surrounded by mountains was absolutely dependent upon surprise and swift movement. Any delay would result in the defenders occupying the mountains and trapping the defenders. Unfortunately, Clark's staff – working from fresh memory of Salerno, where a furious German response nearly threw Fifth Army back into the sea – were primarily concerned with the establishment of a bridgehead solid enough to contain what they saw as inevitable German counterattacks. Given that VI Corps, which would mount the invasion, would initially land only two divisions, Clark himself considered the Alban Hills too far away to be taken quickly.

The main Fifth Army assault against the Gustav Line started on January 20. Unfortunately, lack of time to plan and rehearse properly for an opposed river crossing meant the highly technical business ended in failure. The final assault by US II Corps and the French Expeditionary

Corps on January 24 against the northern part of the line raged for three weeks; in the end, the fought-out French and American units were withdrawn. Once again, Kesselring's strategy of blocking Allied advances as long as possible while inflicting maximum casualties was shown to be effective.

A bombing mission flown by the 321st Bomb Group on February 3 to hit Civitavecchia airfield was intercepted by 20 Bf-109Gs of II./JG 51, led by *Gruppenkommandeur* Hauptmann Herbert "Puschi" Puschmann. Turning onto the Mitchells' tails, Puschmann discovered the hard way that the bombers had been modified with tail gunner positions since he had last engaged B-25s in combat in North Africa. The withering defensive fire set Puschmann's fighter on fire and he crashed onto the airfield. Puschmann held the Ritterkreuz for 54 victories and his loss was sorely felt among the *Jagdfliegern* (fighter pilots).

The Second Battle of Cassino was memorable because of the bombing of the Abbey of Monte Cassino on February 15. Allied intelligence believed the ninth-century Benedictine abbey was in use by the enemy as an observation post able to observe the entire region from the commanding height. The bombing destroyed the abbey more fully than had invading Arab armies in the tenth century. The result was the creation of ruins that were turned into a perfect defensive position by German paratroopers who moved into the position after the event.

Imprecise bombing by B-17s and B-24s of the Fifteenth Air Force resulted in only 10 percent of bombs dropped hitting the abbey; the Fifth Army command compound at Presenzano, 17 miles from Monte Cassino, was hit by 16 500-pound bombs that exploded a few yards from the trailer in which Mark Clark was at his desk dealing with paperwork. B-25s of the 321st and 340th Bomb Groups also participated; the bombs dropped by the Mitchells were all "on target."

In the days following the bombing, the Indian and New Zealand Divisions tried to take the abbey. Unfortunately, winter rains that began on February 16 made movement on the steep slopes next to impossible, as well as limiting air support from Allied fighter-bombers. On February 23, the Indians and New Zealanders were withdrawn, fought out with heavy casualties.

As the Allied armies tried to batter their way through the Gustav Line, on March 11 Mediterranean Allied Air Forces (MAAF) began Operation *Strangle*. The air campaign's goal was to weaken the German armies by cutting their supply lines from the Alpine passes south throughout the Italian peninsula. This campaign would be carried out primarily by the B-25 and B-26 medium bomber groups, and the fighter-bomber groups that were now almost completely re-equipped with the far more capable P-47 Thunderbolt.

On March 13, four A-36s flying top cover for the rest of the 526th Squadron on a strike near Monte Cassino in cloudy skies were shot down when they were attacked by 20 Bf-109s of JG 53. Five days later, the crews at Pomigliano airfield witnessed the eruption of Mount Vesuvius; fortunately, the lava and the rocks spewed by the volcano did not reach the airfield.

The Third Battle of Cassino involved the launch of twin attacks from the north along the Rapido Valley – one against the fortified town of Cassino and the other against Monastery Hill; the goal was to clear the bottleneck between these two locations and allow movement on to the Liri Valley. It was hoped a preliminary bombing by Fifteenth Air Force heavy bombers would clear the way, something that had never before been attempted. The assault was postponed for 21 days as troops waited in freezing, wet positions for a favorable weather forecast, since the operation required three days of good weather.

The weather finally allowed the strike on March 15. The bombing began when several hundred bombers arrived overhead at 0830 hours, with the last departing three and a half hours later. A total of 750 tons of 1,000-pound bombs were dropped, many with delayed-action fuses.

After the bombers left, the New Zealand Division advanced behind a creeping artillery barrage by 746 guns; the attack's success depended on the attackers taking advantage of the bombing's paralyzing effect on the enemy. Unfortunately, the bombing was again inaccurate; only 50 percent of the bombs landed within a mile of their target point, with only 8 percent landing within 1,000 yards. The bombing and shelling killed 150 of the 300 defending German paratroopers, but the survivors rallied quickly. Allied armor was unable to advance quickly, held up by the bomb craters.

By that evening, when a follow-up assault on the left was ordered, it was too late. The German defenders had reorganized. Rain began again, contrary to forecast, and a torrential downpour flooded the bomb craters, creating huge lakes and turning the rubble into a muddy morass. Radio sets could not survive constant immersion, knocking out communications. Still, by March 18, the New Zealanders and Indians held positions around the abbey; a final attack was ordered on March 19. Before the attackers could set out, German paratroopers launched a surprise and fiercely pressed attack from the monastery, disrupting any hope of an assault. The paratroopers carried the new Panzerfaust anti-tank rocket. By mid-afternoon, the tanks – which lacked infantry support – were all knocked out.

Even so, the New Zealanders rallied and made small attacks over the next several days until the battle ended on March 22 with the withdrawal of the exhausted British and Indian units, with the Germans still in control of the abbey. The defenders had paid a heavy price: on March 23, the XIV Korps war diary noted that battalions in the front line had between 40 and 120 men, less than one-third to less than one-fifth of authorized strength. The Allies would now wait for the end of the winter rains before trying again to break the enemy's defenses.

As the fighting continued, the evening of Saturday, March 18, 1944, was quiet and cold, though not freezing. The twilight sky was partially overcast with the promise of rain; the new moon, visible through a break in the clouds, cast a faint light over 88 B-25s of the 340th Bomb Group lined up at Pompeii airfield; light drizzle spattered the bombers.

Suddenly, a distant, growling rumble came from the south, growing in intensity; momentarily, the ground shook. Then shook again. And again, stronger each time. In a minute, the rumble became a continuous, growing roar. Flight surgeon Dr Leander K. Powers wrote later in his diary: "While we were just finishing supper, someone called to say there were huge red streams of lava flowing down the sides of Mount Vesuvius. It was a sight to behold. Never had we seen such. As we watched the streams, like giant fingers flowing down the sides, we could see a glow in the sky."

The next morning, the 486th Squadron's First Lieutenant Dana Craig sat next to his ruined barracks and wrote a description of the first eruption of Mount Vesuvius in 150 years:

About midnight, I went out of my billet to answer the call of nature. While outside, in a mild drizzle, I was hit on the head by what I thought was a small rock. Suspecting some sort of joke, I went inside for a flashlight. When I returned, the light revealed a layer of damp cinders on the ground. We began to feel the earth shake as though a bomb had gone off. After each quake, a few minutes would pass before the debris blown out of the crater would hit the ground. We quickly understood that Vesuvius was erupting. About daylight, the rear of our building started to cave in. We then began to see larger rocks coming down. By this time everyone was wearing his steel helmet and heavy sheepskin flying jacket for protection from the falling rocks.

At Foggia, 90 kilometers north of Pompeii, men of the 321st Bomb Group gaped at the sky. A column of smoke and ash rose high in the southern sky. Within hours, smoke and ash descended on the base. By midday, the men had to use goggles to keep ash out of their eyes. That evening, Dr Powers recorded: "All during the night and Sunday there were quakes of the earth with tremendous roars similar to thunder from Vesuvius. The windows rattled, and the entire building vibrated."

A two-week-long series of eruptions began March 18. The mountain had "acted up" since the beginning of the month, so the only surprise was exactly when it began. Rocks as big as grapefruit fell from the sky, smashing cockpit canopies, plastic gun turrets and bombardier "greenhouses." The B-25s were dented worse than they had been back at Columbia Army Air Base in South Carolina in late 1942 when the 340th's entire fleet of 18 bombers was destroyed by a winter hailstorm. The Mitchells were covered in hot ash that burned away the fabric-covered control surfaces and crazed, melted, and cracked the Plexiglas turrets, canopies, and bombardier's greenhouses. Volcanic ash seeped through openings, filling the bombers and tipping them on their tails.

Dr Powers recorded, "The roars became more frequent and grumbled like a lion's roar. Streams of fire were shooting thousands of feet into the air, and the countryside was lit up for miles around. Oft times the entire top of the mountain looked as if it were a blazing inferno. It's really uncanny, yet amazing to look at this phenomenon. The vibrations of the building were truly uncomfortable." The rain of volcanic ash continued. On March 22, he recorded:

This morning, we rode down beyond Pompeii. The cinders were so deep that traffic was stopped. Along about noon, the wind changed and the cinders began falling on the town of Torre Annunziato.

Everything had a coat of black, just like light snow. We drove up toward Naples on the Autostrade, and, as the wind was blowing toward town, I got a wonderful view of the boiling inferno. Yesterday, I rode into a town that was destroyed by the flowing lava. Apparently, the flow was coming to a stop, but the devastation was terrific. Tonight, there is a lot of lightning coming from the clouds around the crater, accompanied by infrequent blasts from within the volcano.

Back at Foggia, winter weather finally eased as March turned to April; cold rain turned to less-cold rain as the 321st Group continued their participation in Operation *Strangle*. Bad weather over the next two weeks saw many missions scrubbed, with many of those actually flown hampered by poor weather over the target. Daily missions could be intense, whether one saw combat or not. On April 5, 446th Squadron bombardier Second Lieutenant James A. McRae and his crew were briefed at 1040 hours for a mission to bomb the Orvieto railroad bridge. After two hours on standby, they climbed aboard their B-25 at 1315 hours. Just as pilot First Lieutenant Dale Walker prepared to start engines, it began raining and the mission was canceled. Exhausted by the wait, McRae sacked out in his tent. After dinner, he learned there was a mission next morning. A stop by the meteorology section revealed the morning forecast was scattered showers.

Next morning, six bombers took off to hit Perugia airdrome. Halfway there, they flew into a rainstorm and aborted the mission. That night, McRae wrote about the frustration of preparing psychologically for a mission, only to abort, knowing a scrubbed mission didn't count for the 50 mission "tour." Tentmate Second Lieutenant Dale Walker wrote home, "Don't believe what they tell you over there about when we can come home because, believe me, they don't know one little thing about it. What you hear is a bunch of bologna."

The same day McRae's mission turned back for weather, 340th deputy group commander Lieutenant Colonel Malcolm Bailey led six shiny new B-25Js of the 487th Squadron through the cloudy sky to hit Perugia. Just after "bombs away," flak hit wingman Second Lieutenant Gerald Ashmore's bomber, setting the right engine on fire. Co-pilot Second Lieutenant Hamilton Finney, bombardier Second Lieutenant George Simpson, and radioman Corporal Bernard Burton bailed out and eventually got back to the squadron; Ashmore's parachute failed to open and flight engineer/turret gunner Sergeant Julius Iknus and tail gunner Sergeant Jesse Klein were unable to get out when the Mitchell entered a spin; they died in the crash south of the target.

Having finished loading 1,000-pound bombs for the morning mission, 448th Squadron armorer Sergeant Bernard Seegmiller sat down the evening of April 7 and waxed poetic in his diary regarding the bucolic Italian countryside:

> Tonight we have a beautiful full moon that I am sure I won't soon forget. There is something distinctive about spring in Italy that makes it different from anywhere I have been. The fields have been, for the great part, green all winter and the weather, though at times uncomfortable, has seldom reached freezing temperatures. From this state of semi-winter has suddenly dawned a condition of renaissance that cannot be mistaken, even though the trees have not yet put forth their shoots and the mountains, if we could see them for the haze that has covered the valley for several days, are yet splotched with white patches of snow.
>
> This morning as I returned from chow, I stopped to watch the Italian farmer who has a plot of several acres contiguous to our line area plant squash seeds. The seeds were pre-sprouted and he very painstakingly placed them in a hollow he had dug with his hands and covered them by pulverizing the damp clods. In three days, he said, they will be up.

By Friday, March 23, Vesuvius had inflicted more damage on the 340th than had the Luftwaffe since their arrival in North Africa 18 months earlier, destroying all 88 B-25s. Unlike the eruption in AD 79, no lives were lost at Pompeii airfield. But for the rest of the month, the skies across southern Italy were colored dull gray by ash and smoke that fell as far north as Rome. Between March 23 and 26, the 340th relocated to nearby Paestum airfield. American aircraft production was such that the total loss in the 340th was made good within a week as new, silver B-25Js arrived to replace the war-weary camouflaged B-25C and D models left behind at Pompeii. Formation training missions began within days of the replacements' arrivals; missions were flown soon after.

The 321st and 340th Groups had been flying missions together since they became part of the 57th Bomb Wing in January 1944. 321st commander Colonel Robert D. Knapp was promoted to brigadier general and became the wing commander. For the 57th Bomb Wing, the solution to the destruction created by Vesuvius was to move the 321st and 340th Groups to Corsica where they would join the 310th Group that had moved to the island in January. Operating from adjoining airfields, the wing would become a true thorn in the enemy's side over the rest of the Cassino campaign and beyond.

Corsica was already home to the 57th and 350th Fighter Groups. The 27th, 79th, 86th, and 324th Fighter Groups remained at their mainland bases, providing air cover and tactical support to the Cassino front, as well as supporting the Anzio beachhead.

A-36 pilot First Lieutenant Tom McElmurry had good reason to remember what he later called his most terrifying mission, when the 527th Squadron attacked the Viterbo airfields north of Rome on March 25.

I was leading the second element of the flight. During the dive, I noticed some gun emplacements firing from a small valley among low rolling hills just south of the airfield complex. I saw that they would be along my flight path during the exit from the target area. I decided to pull out of the dive below the tops of the hills separating the airfields from the gun emplacements, pop up over the hilltop and surprise the gun crews with a strafing pass.

It was okay to dump twenty degrees of flap at 250 miles an hour in the A-36. My plan was to do that and come over the hills with the aircraft nose depressed and all guns firing. I never pulled the trigger. Every gun in that battery must have had their barrels lowered, waiting for me to appear over the ridge. An explosive round detonated in the leading edge of the right wing. The metal peeling back from that sizable hole produced an aileron roll that almost put me inverted not much more than twenty feet above the ground. Fortunately, I had just enough aileron control to remain upright and escape. Looking back, I saw that my wingman had made a large fireball when he hit the ground.

Captain Carl Johnson of the 527th Squadron led a bridge-busting mission on April 1. With the experience of Lieutenant Colonel Tarrant's strafing mission back in November in mind, when he spotted a train that appeared when the Mustangs were over the target, he allowed it to enter the bridge before he executed a strafing run on it. This train was also loaded with ammunition. When Johnson hit it, the violent explosion also took out the bridge.

As the weather in Italy changed to spring and the ground at the front became drier and more solid with the end of the winter rains, preparations were under way to make a fourth attempt to break the Tenth Army and force its retreat.

5

ANZIO – THE LOST OPPORTUNITY

Field Marshal Kesselring's strategy of making the Allies pay for every foot they advanced up the Italian peninsula had paid off by the end of 1943 with the failure of the November offensive to come anywhere close to punching through the Gustav Line. The unyielding terrain and the onset of the worst winter in many years saw the advance grind to a halt as roads became muddy quagmires and mountain passes were washed out, while stormy skies kept Allied airpower from intervening successfully in the struggle on the ground. Put frankly, the Italian campaign was completely bogged down.

Allied leaders were now faced with the possibility that their failure to maintain a steady, relentless pressure on the Tenth and Fourteenth Armies meant that Kesselring could strengthen his positions in central Italy and hold up the Allies indefinitely, making it possible for the Germans to transfer divisions to other fronts. Such reinforcement in France could mean that Operation *Overlord*, the cross-Channel invasion, might fail. It was already clear that the proposed invasion of southern France, which had been hoped could be carried out close to Operation *Overlord*, thus dividing the enemy's defenses, could not happen as originally planned.

Something had to change, but a direct frontal assault was not the solution. Winston Churchill, who clung to his hope of decisive action in southern Europe, prodded and cajoled his military leaders to attempt something audacious.

At the end of December, Churchill proposed an amphibious operation that would create an end run around the Gustav Line. With the majority of Allied amphibious assault ships due to be sent to Britain in January to prepare for *Overlord*, what would remain would be insufficient to transport more than a single division a short distance. A series of single-division landings immediately behind the Gustav Line was considered, but that idea foundered on the fact it would not change the situation enough to force the Germans to retreat. Any landing had to threaten Rome with a large enough force to make the threat of taking the Italian capital believable to get Kesselring to divert troops from the Gustav Line to counter it. Churchill advised General Mark Clark to land at Anzio, which was less than 30 miles south of Rome. He then asked President Roosevelt to approve retaining 59 LSTs in the Mediterranean until late February to allow a multi-division operation, convincing the president with the argument that if the opportunity of such a landing was not taken, "we must expect the ruin of the Mediterranean campaign in 1944." The decision was made on December 28, 1943, with an invasion date of January 22, 1944. Operation *Shingle* was reality. VI Corps would carry out the operation.

In planning meetings, 3rd Division's commander General Lucian Truscott made the point repeatedly that success in landing in a basin surrounded by mountains was absolutely dependent upon surprise and swift movement. Any delay would result in the defenders occupying the mountains and trapping the defenders. Unfortunately, Clark's staff – still battered by fresh memories of Salerno, where a furious German response nearly threw Fifth Army back into the sea – were primarily concerned with the establishment of a bridgehead solid enough to contain what they saw as inevitable German counterattacks. Given that VI Corps, which would mount the invasion, would initially land only two divisions, Clark himself considered the Alban Hills too far away to be taken quickly.

The location appeared ideal. The villages of Anzio and Nettuno were an hour's drive south of Rome. Long empty beaches north and south of Anzio harbor fronted 20 miles of flat level ground before reaching the Alban Hills. The Appian Way and the Via Casilina – the two main military roads to Rome now known as Routes Six and Seven – were a matter of miles from the invasion beaches. Anzio harbor was big enough to allow follow-up forces to be landed in a protected harbor.

XII Air Support Command was reinforced in January. Among the USAAF units transferred to the command was the veteran 79th Fighter Group; the ground echelon departed the slushy mud of Madna on January 13, driving over treacherous ice-covered roads to cross the snowy mountains forming the spine of the peninsula, to arrive at the group's new base of Capodichino airfield outside Naples on January 15, and the group was ready for operations on January 18. For the ground crews, who had lived outside since they arrived in North Africa 18 months earlier, the discovery they would live inside – albeit in an unheated apartment building, which was, however, equipped with real toilets and bathrooms without hot water – meant they would be back in the "civilized world" again. Pilots and other officers were housed in another large apartment building that provided similar amenities. Food in the mess also improved from the heated C-rations at Madna, with fresh vegetables and meat making their appearance.

Capodichino airfield was filled with Allied air: a light bomber group equipped with A-20s, the P-40s of the 33rd Group, the B-25s of the 310th Bomb Group, and a C-47 squadron. With an orientation sweep by all four squadrons – the 99th Squadron having been reprieved in the Washington, DC hearings in November and December regarding their combat capability – up the coast to Rome and back on January 19, the group was ready to participate in Operation *Shingle*.

The invasion fleet dropped anchor off Anzio 30 minutes past midnight on January 22.

Two hours later, a five-minute rocket barrage of the harbor installations preceded the first wave of invasion craft carrying the troops ashore. All were surprised by the fact there was no answering fire, and the first 30 minutes ashore revealed the enemy was not present to oppose the landing. The hoped-for surprise had been achieved.

Intelligence estimates regarding the Luftwaffe were that 310 enemy fighters were within range of the beachhead, including 110 on airfields near Rome that were immediately available to attack the invasion.

In addition to Spitfires from the RAF's 244 Wing, Spitfires of the 31st Fighter Group provided air cover over the invasion fleet. Fighter control was provided by the 64th Fighter Wing's 82nd and 328th Fighter Control Squadrons, which had trained controllers to guide interceptions. The 308th Fighter Squadron had received 18 Spitfire VIII fighters in November, completely replacing the clapped-out Spitfire

Vs they had operated in North Africa and Sicily. The Spitfire IXs that equipped the 307th and 309th Squadrons made the 31st Group the American fighter unit best equipped to take on anything the Luftwaffe offered, though the latter two squadrons still had two flights each of Spitfire Vs due to the high demand for the Spitfire IX with the RAF.

Over the months of January, February, and March, the 31st Group flew air superiority/air defense missions over the beachhead, flying from Castel Volturno, an airfield located in the area of the Pontine Marshes. Mussolini's government had drained the marshes during the 1930s, but with the invasion of Italy, the pumps had been turned off and the fields were reverting to their previous condition. Thus, throughout the winter, the many rainstorms combined with the increasing water table to keep the airfield at Castel Volturno muddy even during the longer periods between rainstorms.

Radar spotted the first enemy aerial response at 0630 hours on D-Day when four Fw-190Fs of Schnellkampfgeschwader (SKG; Luftwaffe fast bomber wing) 210 attempted to attack the fleet. A flight of 244 Wing Spitfires intercepted and one was shot down while the other three turned away.

Between them, the 31st's three squadrons flew three missions each on D-Day to cover the Anzio invasion force from first light to dusk. The day was cloudy, which would have favored the Germans had they shown up, but the invasion was a complete surprise to the enemy; no enemy fighters showed up until late afternoon, when seven Fw-190 fighter-bombers appeared out of the clouds at 1600 hours and bombed "Peter Beach." The 309th Squadron intercepted them at 1,000 feet, flying through antiaircraft fire that made no distinction between enemy and friendly fighters. Major William Jared, the 309th's CO, damaged one Fw-190 that disappeared into the haze, while group commander Colonel Charles M. McCorkle had to break off when the four Fw-190s on the left turned into him. He then spotted six Bf-109s, two of which were shooting at a diving P-38 streaming glycol from its left engine. McCorkle turned into them to rescue the P-38, but then saw a single Bf-109 break from the pack almost in front of him. McCorkle chased the enemy fighter but was unable to get a solid hit. Suddenly the enemy fighter pulled up and the pilot bailed out in front of him!

At that moment, P-47s from an unknown unit dived into the fight, mistaking the eight Spitfires for enemy fighters and making a firing pass on them. Overall, the haze layer below 6,000 feet over the invasion made air combat difficult.

During a dusk patrol over the beachhead, Colonel McCorkle shot down a Bf-109G when the patrol was vectored onto an enemy formation. He later recalled:

> Major Thorsen, who commanded the 308th squadron, was shot down over the Anzio beachhead. He had to force land on the beachhead, and as he was going down with his engine puffing smoke and pouring oil, and looking for a place to set down, for some reason he didn't want to bale out. An ME-109 pulled up alongside him, skidded down to his speed, or approximately that, in sort of a slip and saw that he was going to have to land. The German then saluted Thorsen and flew away, rather than shooting at him. This was the last piece of chivalry I ever heard of in air combat.

The Luftwaffe's reaction to the landings at Anzio was fierce; there was heavy fighting over the beachhead throughout the rest of January and the month of February. On January 26, the 307th and 308th Squadrons flew escort for A-20s that bombed targets around Cisterna. On their return to base the pilots were ordered to land at a nearby airfield. When they arrived overhead, they discovered the field was under attack from 12 Bf-109s and Fw-190s! The 307th's CO, Major Virgil Fields, dived onto the tail of an Fw-190 and opened fire. The enemy pilot immediately bailed out to give Fields his fifth victory. Leading a patrol over the beachhead on January 28, Fields was attacked by a P-40, but was able to get home despite some damage. Flying a second mission that afternoon, his flight was vectored onto a formation of Fw-190 fighter-bombers. In the ensuing fight, Fields shot down one of the enemy fighters for his sixth and final victory.

The 31st was the only fighter group to operate from inside the beachhead. On February 1, the 307th Squadron was moved to the landing ground outside Nettuno. The field was under constant observation by the enemy from the surrounding hills, and was frequently shelled. The squadron lost more aircraft to enemy shelling while on the ground than they did from flak or enemy aircraft. During the two weeks the squadron remained on the field, four of their fighters were destroyed by artillery fire. When two RAF Spitfires landed on the field due to fuel shortage after engaging in combat with enemy fighter-bombers, the squadron saw their opportunity to obtain replacements. By the time the two fighters were refueled, night had fallen; the two pilots were put up for the night in the shelter where the pilots and ground crews slept.

During the night, the two fighters were "press-ganged" into the squadron; the RAF insignia was painted over with US insignia and the serials were painted out. When the two pilots emerged from the shelter in the morning, they were confronted with two burned-out, wrecked Spitfires in the shelter pens where their fighters had been parked, and were informed that enemy shelling overnight had unfortunately destroyed their airplanes. The 307th went out of their way to help the two gain passage to return to their squadron on an LST that arrived in the beachhead that morning. The squadron flew the two shanghaied Spitfires until they re-equipped with P-51s in early April.

On February 6, Colonel McCorkle joined the ranks of group aces during a patrol over the beachhead when he claimed a fifth enemy fighter. After the war, he recalled, "I had chased a German in a '109 to the deck. He was hit many times and was smoking. I was overtaking him very slowly, and I was just about out of ammunition, when suddenly he rocked his wings, in the old school signal of saying 'Okay, you win, I've had enough.' He pulled straight up in the air to a thousand feet or so, pushed over, and baled out. I think he was saying, 'Okay, no need to shoot any more, I'm bailing out.'"

The battle that saw McCorkle become an ace also marked the death of the 307th's CO Major Virgil Fields. A lone Bf-109G popped out of the clouds above the 31st's formation and set Fields' Spitfire IX on fire with a single burst that must have also killed Fields, since the fighter nosed over and went straight in to crash near Anzio. The 307th's war diarist wrote, "The patrol returned to base loose, scattered and badly shaken by the loss of their commanding officer. The entire squadron was stunned and mute at the death of Major Fields. Not only was he greatly liked and admired by everyone, of every rank, but he was also a great friend, a leader and a fighter. Now he was gone. It was beyond all comprehension."

The weather improved on February 7, allowing the 309th Squadron to send 12 Spitfires to patrol over Anzio at 0715 hours. Shortly after 0800 hours, a large formation of enemy fighters was sighted and the Spitfires immediately engaged. First Lieutenant Benzing shot down an

Fw-190 whose wingman in turn shot down Benzing's wingman. First Lieutenant Ray Harmeyer hit another Fw-190; it fell away, but recovered just above the beach and escaped to the north. First Lieutenant Richard Faxon chased another Focke-Wulf as far as Rome, where it escaped. Only one enemy fighter was destroyed with two damaged in exchange for four Spitfires.

An escort mission later that morning for B-26 Marauders by ten 309th Spitfires was intercepted by 14 enemy fighters near Bracciano. Lieutenants Charlie Souch and George Loving both fired at a Bf-109G. Loving later wrote about the fight:

> I was flying wing to Charlie Souch, who was Hobnail Red Leader. As he started out from our perch 4,000 feet above the bombers, I shoved my throttle forward and slid in a little closer. We headed down steeply on a path that would intercept the Me-109s before they reached a firing position. Souch began firing before we were within range, spewing a stream of 0.30-caliber tracers and 20mm shells ahead of the lead aircraft. I chimed in with a burst of fire. Moments later I saw an explosion on the port wing of the enemy leader, who broke off his attack on the bombers and turned toward us. As we passed through the enemy formation, aircraft were careering in all directions. I got off a good volley without observing any hits. Minutes later Hobnail Blue section fended off a second wave of attackers. That ended the German challenge. Souch claimed one damaged. Years later I learned that Souch was credited with a half victory, probably on the basis of gun camera film, with the other half credit going to an unnamed pilot − I may have been that unnamed pilot.

As dusk fell on February 12, 40 Ju-88s and Do-217s led by the redoubtable Joachim Helbig attacked the Anzio beachhead, starting fires throughout the area before escaping unharmed when the 307th's Spitfires were not scrambled. At noon the next day, a 309th patrol ran into another formation of Fw-190 fighter-bombers; First Lieutenant Ray Harmeyer destroyed two for his first victories. The fight was later described by his element leader, First Lieutenant John Fawcett:

> He was my wingman on the morning of February 13 over Anzio, when two Fw-190s flying in line abreast cruised right under us a

thousand feet below as though they were on a sightseeing flight! I called the break and we rolled upside down and went storming down behind them. In the process, Harmeyer, who was on my left, got about a hundred yards or so ahead of me. As we got close, he turned slightly to the right in front of me and got off a snap shot at the right-hand target, which immediately blew up in a great cloud of black smoke, flame and scrap aluminum, which I flew right through! Harmeyer then immediately turned left and got off a burst at the other Fw-190, which took fire and went straight in twisting and smoking. You can imagine my frustration in not getting one of those for myself, but the fact is that Harmeyer did exactly what a sharp fighter pilot should do. They were right in front of him, I was lagging behind, so he shot them both down within about ten seconds. I was in a few air battles that winter, but never a turkey shoot like that one.

The 309th had also been busy that morning. The dawn beachhead patrol spotted 20-plus enemy fighters at about 21,000 feet. First Lieutenant Mick Ainley chased a Bf-109 that turned for Rome; closing to 300 yards, he hit it with two short bursts that caused the enemy fighter to stream glycol and then thick smoke. Ainley overshot and lost sight of the enemy with the result that his final Spitfire claim was only for a damaged.

On February 20, the 308th Squadron flew a ground-attack mission near Anzio that ran across a small formation of enemy fighters. First Lieutenant Richard Hurd shot down one Bf-109G and damaged another, while First Lieutenant Leland "Tommy" Molland claimed an Fw-190 as a probable that was last seen limping away at very low altitude.

The next day, with the weather steadily improving, the 308th's First Lieutenant Fred Trafton damaged a Bf-109 for his first claim. The squadron's total increased on February 22, when the morning patrol spotted 30 enemy aircraft over Anzio just before 0900 hours. In the resulting fight, "Tommy" Molland shot down two Bf-109Gs, to give him a score of 4.5 victories. First Lieutenant Richard Hurd shot down another Bf-109 for his third victory, while Major Thorsen and Lieutenants Walker and Brown shot down one Bf-109 each. Sadly, First Lieutenant Hackbarth was lost when he was shot down in flames.

The 31st remained active over Anzio to the end of February, despite the almost-incessant rain, flying missions whenever the weather allowed. First Lieutenant Dick Faxon managed to catch a lone Fw-190 in the cloudy skies and shoot it down. He later described how "It seemed to open up like a can of chilli" as his hits struck the enemy fighter from nose to tail, causing it to disintegrate just as the pilot bailed out.

At the end of February, Colonel McCorkle confirmed rumors that the 31st would soon re-equip with a new fighter, the P-51 Mustang. This was not received as good news among the group's pilots, who had become attached to their Spitfires during battles over North Africa, Pantelleria, Sicily, and Italy. In mid-April, two P-51Bs and a pilot from the 354th "Pioneer Mustang" group in England arrived to initiate conversion training. The 31st's pilots were still unconvinced when told the new fighter was superior to the Spitfire, and had much longer range to boot. Their opinion started to change as they got the chance to fly the P-51s. At the end of March, the group learned they would join the Fifteenth Air Force in April to participate in the Ploesti campaign.

The 31st's last "big day" in the Spitfire came on March 18, when a morning mission flown over the Cassino battlefield engaged enemy fighters, with seven destroyed, one probably destroyed, and four damaged by pilots of the 307th and 308th Squadrons. A noon mission over Cassino by the 307th saw the Spitfires engage nine Fw-190 fighter-bombers as they headed toward the battle line to attack Allied ground forces; four Spitfires caught the enemy fighters as they attempted to enter their bombing runs and three were shot down. The second flight of four ran across 15 Fw-190 fighter-bombers and shot down three, while the third flight spotted another 12 enemy fighter-bombers and shot down two while scattering the rest. The evening patrol ran across 20 enemy fighters over the Liri Valley at 1645 hours and shot down six in a wild fight.

The final Spitfire missions were flown on March 30 over Anzio. That afternoon, the group learned they were leaving muddy Castel Volturno to move to San Severo, one of the established airfields in the Foggia complex. It had a 5,000-foot hard-surfaced runway and there were permanent buildings for quarters, the first time the pilots and ground crews of the 31st would live indoors since their arrival in North Africa 17 months earlier.

In addition to the Spitfires covering the invasion fleet, P-40s from the 79th, 33rd, and 324th Groups also engaged in combat over the beachhead.

On D-Day, Captain George Lee of the 79th was leading 16 P-40Ls when the 82nd Air Control Squadron (callsign "Grubstake") reported 20 Fw-190s and seven Bf-109s east of the beachhead and vectored the fighters onto them. The combat was sharp when the P-40s caught up with the enemy. Lieutenant "Butch" Owen shot down an Fw-190, knocking down a second only two minutes later. His wingman, Second Lieutenant David Vandivort, got on the tail of another Fw-190 closing on Owen and put several short bursts into the enemy fighter. The enemy pilot pulled up and bailed out. Lieutenant Walt Peterman took on an Fw-190 head-on, and when the landing gear fell down the enemy pilot jettisoned his canopy and went over the side. First Lieutenant Frank Nicolai closed on a pair of bomb-carrying Fw-190s; one went into Lake Albano inverted while he picked off the other as it attempted to escape at low level. With four others damaged, the enemy fighters turned away and vanished in the low-level haze. Lieutenant Jack Maye was shot down in the fight and captured on the ground to become a prisoner of war. In 11 patrols flown on D-Day, the 79th accounted for six of the seven enemy fighters shot down by the invasion air cover.

Despite two reconnaissance teams in jeeps finding there were no enemy units in the Alban Hills when they drove to the crest – from where they could see Rome only two hours after landing – VI Corps commander Major General John Lucas refused to believe their report. His orders were "1. Seize and secure a beachhead in the vicinity of Anzio; 2. Advance and secure Colli Laziali [in the Alban Hills]; 3. Be prepared to advance on Rome." Unfortunately, Lucas – who had never held battlefield command before – spent the first two days establishing defensive positions against a counterattack instead of pushing his forces out of the beachhead. An attack straight up the Appian Way the first day would likely have carried the Americans into an ill-defended Rome within 24 hours of arriving on the Anzio beaches.

The delay was fatal. Despite opposing the British at the Garigliano River crossing and the French and Americans at the northern end of the Gustav Line, Kesselring had stationed two reserve divisions south of Rome to counter exactly this possibility. When Tenth Army commander General von Vietinghoff requested the two divisions be sent to him for reinforcement on January 17, Kesselring listened to the Abwehr's intelligence report that, despite rumors of a possible Allied amphibious operation, they believed no such invasion was possible due to lack of sufficient shipping for transport. Based on that, Kesselring had sent the two divisions south, which was why there was no immediate German ground response to the landing that came as the rumors had said it would.

Upon hearing of the Anzio landing, Kesselring drove into the Alban Hills and personally observed the Allied landing. He later recalled, "The spectacle of Allied power was awesome: hundreds of ships; countless landing craft plying back and forth; everywhere troops, artillery, tanks; overhead a curtain of aircraft." Seeing that the troops were not moving swiftly to take control of the hills, Kesselring decided he would have time to get troops into the hills to block the invasion.

Gathering troops in rest camps and on garrison duty in nearby towns, the marshal personally moved units into the Alban Hills, ordering an artillery unit refitting outside Rome to rush to the hills. By nightfall, the artillery opened fire on the open beaches below. With the first defenders in place, Kesselring ordered General Eberhard von Mackensen to move the Fourteenth Army into the Alban Hills and surround the beachhead. Contacting Berlin, he obtained additional Luftwaffe squadrons from southern France and Austria, and two divisions – one from southern France and one from Yugoslavia. He also ordered von Vietinghoff to release troops, despite the state of battle against the Allied offensive. By the evening of D-Day, three German divisions were on the Appian Way headed from the Gustav Line to Anzio. By the next morning, the Alban Hills were occupied by German troops. From this position they were able to keep VI Corps surrounded and the beachhead under near-constant artillery fire directed from observation positions high in the Alban Hills.

General Lucas was fortunate that the day before the invasion, the 86th and 27th Groups' A-36s had hit the Luftwaffe headquarters at Frascati, only 5 miles from the Pope's residence at Castel Gandolfo, which was off-limits to any Allied air strike and why the Luftwaffe headquarters was located there. The pinpoint bombing wiped out the German headquarters, which controlled Luftwaffe operations in central Italy.

On January 23, D+1, the 86th Group suffered their blackest day in terms of losses. Fourteen of 32 Mustangs sent to strike the German counterattack at Anzio were either destroyed or damaged by enemy ground fire. These losses resulted in the 525th Squadron transferring their remaining A-36s to the 526th Squadron and receiving hand-me-down Warhawks from the 33rd Fighter Group following that unit's departure for North Africa and further transfer to India.

The 31st Fighter Group continued flying cover for the invasion fleet. The weather changed the day after the invasion with a solid overcast over the invasion fleet at 5,000 feet that never broke all day. The limited patrols that were mounted did not meet any enemy aircraft. The next day the overcast turned to rain which scrubbed almost all air operations.

On January 26, the 307th and 308th Squadrons escorted 36 A-36s that bombed the enemy airfield at Cisterna. The Spitfires shot down two Bf-109s and an Fw-190, and damaged three other Fw-190s. The 307th was alerted to move to an advanced landing strip at Nettuno in the beachhead. Arriving over the new airstrip, they found ten Bf-109s and Fw-190s strafing the field. Squadron CO Major Fields attacked an Fw-190 whose pilot jettisoned his canopy and bailed out. Lieutenant Tucker went after a Bf-109, closing to 50 yards at which point the enemy's engine spewed glycol and the pilot bailed out. Several other pilots went after Fw-190s but were forced to break off when enemy reinforcements showed up. After the enemy fighters flew off, Major Fields ordered the pilots to return to their regular base at Castel Volturno. The airfield at Nettuno would be used during the four months of the fighting at Anzio for refueling and rearming, but no American aircraft were permanently stationed there due to the danger of enemy attacks.

During the late afternoon of January 24, the 79th's Flight Officer Ed Bozzi – one of the most experienced pilots in the group – was leading eight Warhawks over the beachhead southwest of the Alban Hills when the P-40s were bounced by a mixed formation of 30 Fw-190s and Bf-109s. Bozzi and wingman Second Lieutenant Charles Trumbo became involved in a turning fight with an Fw-190. Bozzi managed to get in three bursts, at which the enemy's landing gear dropped down. Two more bursts set the fighter on fire, at which point the pilot bailed out. "Grubstake" called out another formation, but by this time the Warhawks were low on fuel. They made a pass on the new formation of Fw-190s, then were forced to turn back to Capodichino.

The next day, January 25, six 79th P-40s ran across ten Fw-190s. Captain John L. Beck and his wingman dived on the enemy and he shot one into the sea. The other Germans then evaded in the haze layer. Another patrol from the group ran across 15 Fw-190s and Bf-109s diving through a hole in the clouds to attack the invasion fleet. Lieutenant Gaston Collum got one with a long-range 90-degree deflection shot that set the enemy fighter's wing on fire. Element leader Lieutenant Bob Duffield – who in 63 missions had never engaged an enemy fighter – got on the tail of a Bf-109 and set it afire. The group was experiencing their best air-to-air success since the Pantelleria campaign.

The 99th Fighter Squadron engaged enemy fighters on January 27. Squadron commander Major George S. "Spanky" Roberts was leading the squadron on an early morning patrol when he spotted 16 Fw-190s pulling out of a bomb run over Anzio harbor. The pilots fell on the enemy airplanes, and, in a fast but brutal engagement that lasted only four minutes, Lieutenants Willie Ashley, Leon Roberts, Ed Toppins, and Bob Dietz each shot down an Fw-190, while Lieutenants Clarence Allen and Howard Baugh shared another, as did Lieutenants John Rogers and Elwood Driver. It was the squadron's biggest success since they arrived in North Africa the year before.

The 99th followed up that success in an afternoon patrol when they caught more Fw-190s over the beachhead and Lieutenants Lemuel Custis, Wilson Eagleson, and Charles Bailey each shot down one Focke-Wulf. Lieutenant Samuel "Lizard" Bruce was last seen chasing two Fw-190s toward Rome. His death was later confirmed and he became the first African American fighter pilot to die in air-to-air combat.

While this was going on, the 79th's "Flying Skulls" caught 20 Fw-190s and Bf-109s bombing Anzio harbor and broke up the attack when they dived into the enemy formation, shooting down one and damaging four. The day ended with the 79th Group claiming nine destroyed, four probables, and four damaged. The group would equal that score the next day, which was one of the best for Allied fighters in the entire campaign, with four groups submitting claims for a total of 21 enemy fighters shot down. Among the 79th's claims were four more from pilots of the 99th Squadron, with two claimed by Lieutenant Charlie Hall who had scored the squadron's first aerial victory back in July 1943, making him the leading African American fighter pilot with a score of three. Hall's claims came from one shot down in a deflection shot from 300 yards and the other from close astern the enemy fighter.

In two days, the 79th's pilots had claimed 18 enemy fighters shot down with five more probably shot down and ten damaged. They would go on to score first place among all Allied fighter groups during the invasion, with 29 destroyed, seven probably destroyed, and 18 damaged for two lost in air combat and a third when his engine overheated, forcing him to ditch at sea where he was captured and made prisoner.

During the first ten days of the invasion, the Luftwaffe managed to put up an average of 100 sorties per day over the beachhead; these were never enough to threaten the battle's outcome, but coupled with the near-constant shelling by German artillery looking down on the invaders from the Alban Hills, including the giant 280mm railway gun "schlanke Bertha" – known to the Americans as "Anzio Annie," firing 560-pound shells over a range of 38 miles – the air attacks harassed the invasion daily. By the end of January, the Allies had lost four ships sunk with two others badly damaged.

In return, the Allied fighters – including the P-40s of the 33rd, 79th, and 324th Groups and the Spitfires of the 31st Group and the RAF's 244 Wing – flew over 450 sorties per day over the fleet and the beachhead. Their claims since D-Day were 50 enemy fighters destroyed, while 15 Ju-88s and Do-217s were shot down by night fighters. The ships' AA batteries and those ashore accounted for another 100.

The Allied forces in the beachhead undertook an offensive at the end of January to break out of their encirclement and came heartbreakingly close to success. General Lucas's goal in the attack was to reach the villages of Albano and Valmontone, which would sever the lines of communication with Tenth Army to the south while opening the road to Rome for VI Corps.

The attack began at 0130 hours on January 30, when two battalions of US Rangers advanced silently down an irrigation ditch toward Cisterna to cut Route 7 at that point and move on to Valmontone, followed by 3rd Division. Unfortunately, when they were a matter of a few hundred yards from the village, they were hit with fire from a well-prepared German ambush. Carrying only small arms, the Rangers split up into small groups as they attempted to hold position until the arrival of 3rd Division. The division never made it because they were stopped cold by German armor and infantry a mile away from the Rangers. German tanks moved into position on the edge of the ditch and cut the Rangers to pieces from close range. Of the 767 men who had set out on the assault, only six would return to American lines. The 3rd Division was beaten back with heavy casualties.

The British 1st Infantry and US 1st Armored Divisions attacked on the northern edge of the beachhead toward Albano. The British infantry was able to break through the German main line of resistance and reach the village of Campoleone, but the 1st Armored Division's tanks bogged down on marshy ground left over from Mussolini's prewar draining of the Pontine Marshes that was not on any maps. This exposed the British flank and the troops were forced to pull back. Allied commanders now expected a German counterattack and ordered the units in the beachhead to go over to the defensive.

While it appeared the Allied offensive had run into overwhelming German strength, in fact the German resistance was composed of disorganized units and parts of units thrown into the breach as "battle groups." Had the Allies made one more determined push at either point, they could have broken through the thin line of enemy defenders. Kesselring had won the day by juggling his forces and throwing them into the battle piecemeal.

To top it off, the weather changed for the worse the next day, which grounded most of the Allied air units and prevented them attacking the German units now exposed on the line. The result was that Kesselring was able to build up strength over the week of really bad weather and additional week of unsettled weather; in mid-February, Fourteenth Army mounted a counteroffensive that nearly pushed the Allies into the sea that was as desperate as the fighting on the Salerno beaches eight months earlier.

February 5 dawned sunny and clear; the fighter groups were over the beachhead as early as possible to make up for lost time and effort. Captain Clarence Jamieson was leading seven 99th Squadron P-40s over Anzio town when "Grubstake" vectored them toward ten Fw-190s headed for the beachhead. Minutes later, Jamieson spotted the enemy fighters and the Warhawk pilots closed for the kill. Jamieson closed on Tail-End Charlie, but when he pressed the trigger as he came out of the steep dive, his guns jammed! Another enemy fighter turned into the Warhawk and opened fire. Unable to respond, Jamieson dived away but the persistent enemy pilot followed him, firing burst after burst as Jamieson roared over the countryside as low as he could get. The chase lasted some 20–30 miles before the Fw-190 banked away. Breathing a sigh of relief, Jamieson had only a moment to savor his escape before the Merlin began to sputter and miss. He tried to trade speed for altitude, but the P-40 lost power too quickly and he managed to set it down wheels up in a small clearing. With bullets flying overhead, he quickly realized he had managed to end up in no man's land. Looking around for cover, he saw three GIs beckoning him from some bushes 50 yards distant. He leaped out of the cockpit and with bullets chasing him managed to take a flying leap at the end that ended him safely behind the bushes with the soldiers, who guided him back to their lines.

The 99th's interception of the Focke-Wulfs had not gone as expected. Lieutenant George Crumby had his controls shot away by ground fire and took to his parachute, startling the herd of cows in the field below when he touched down. Lieutenant Elwood Driver managed to set one of the enemy fighters on fire, and it crashed into the grove of trees near the field that Crumby had landed in.

The weather remained clear with light clouds for the next several days. The conditions allowed the Luftwaffe to send 120 sorties a day over the beachhead. Two days later, on February 7, the 99th was able to even things out when an early morning patrol of eight Warhawks was vectored by "Grubstake" onto 16 Fw-190s that had just bombed the VI Corp HQ in Nettuno. The German fighter-bombers were just pulling off the target when they were caught by the Warhawks. The first flight, led by First Lieutenant Wilson Eagleson with wingman Second Lieutenant James Knighten, and element leader Second Lieutenant Clinton Mills with wingman Second Lieutenant Leonard Jackson, closed on the rear enemy flight. Spotting the P-40s, the Focke-Wulfs broke to the left. Jackson closed on the Fw-190 that flew right in front of him and hit it with a long burst from dead astern, sending the enemy fighter tumbling toward the ground out of control. The enemy pilot managed to get out and open his parachute moments before the fighter smashed into the ground. Eagleson and Mills also shot down one Fw-190 each before the rest disappeared in the morning haze.

It was the 79th's turn shortly before noon when eight 85th Squadron "Skulls" P-40s were vectored toward another enemy raid on the harbor. Moments later, they were hit by eight Bf-109s that were escorting 20 bomb-carrying Fw-190s. Lieutenants George Bolte and John Keene chased two of the Bf-109s 20 miles up the road to Velletri before Bolte shot down one with a 30-degree deflection shot; a moment later he met one of the Fw-190s head-on as it fled the battle after dropping its bomb. He scored a few hits before the Fw-190 dived away and outran him. Keene had become involved with a skilled Fw-190 pilot in a turning fight; he managed to put his sights on the enemy's tail and score hits that persuaded the enemy pilot to break off and dive away. Lieutenants George Nashold and Raymond Higgins of the second element had mixed it up with several gaggles of Fw-190s before Higgins managed to tag onto a Bf-109 that flew in front of him and set it on fire; the enemy pilot bailed out.

The second "Skulls" flight – Lieutenants Bob Duffield, Bob Bartlett, William McLane, and Don Gravenstine – went after the Fw-190 fighter-bombers as they entered their attack run over the harbor. Duffield caught one and gave it a short burst that set it afire. As the enemy pilot attempted to bail out, the fighter tipped over and dove straight into the ground below. Duffield and wingman Bartlett then chased another Focke-Wulf up the Appian Way at low level. Duffield got a hit that set the enemy fighter smoking; he turned aside to let Bartlett take it. Bartlett managed two bursts before the fighter smashed into the side of a stone building and blew up. As Bartlett took a moment to view the outcome, Lieutenant McLane shot down another Fw-190 as it tried to turn on Bartlett's tail. Just before fuel considerations forced them to turn for home, Don Gravenstine caught an Fw-190 with a deflection shot; the fighter flipped inverted and hit a row of trees before it ended up in an open field where it exploded in a fireball.

While the eight pilots had taken on almost 30 enemy fighters and managed to shoot down six of them without loss, the others had managed to get through to the harbor where they bombed and sank two small ships, killing 30 sailors.

A little more than 90 minutes later, at 1445 hours, ten Fw-190 fighter-bombers were picked up on radar at 12,000 feet over Nettuno. Again, it was a flight of eight from the "Skulls" that were vectored to intercept. Lieutenant Carl Stewart went head-to-head with one, turning to get on its tail where he gave it two more bursts that set the engine on fire. The enemy pilot got out just before his airplane exploded. At almost the same moment, Lieutenant Martin Granberg tagged onto Tail-End Charlie of three Fw-190s diving on the harbor, closing till the fighter filled his windscreen, at which point he raked it nose to tail with a long burst that sent it into a steep dive; that pilot managed to get out just before it went in. Lieutenant Alan Austin was hit in his engine by an Fw-190. As he set up to crash-land in the beachhead, he realized what he thought was an open field was occupied by a hospital. Turning away to avoid hitting anything in the crash, he ended up in a copse of trees. In what might have been a fatal crash, he managed to survive uninjured.

By the end of the day, the defending American pilots had claimed 17 enemy fighters shot down and destroyed. Of that total, the 79th claimed 12.

Despite the defenders' successes, the enemy was getting through. After the raids on February 7, the Fifteenth Air Force sent 100 B-24s to hit airfields the Luftwaffe was using at Viterbo, Tarquinia, and Orvieto on February 8. The bombers were accurate, and the damage inflicted was such that the enemy refrained from mounting more than a few hit-and-run raids for several days afterwards.

Over the next three days following their performance on February 7, the 79th's Warhawks took advantage of clear weather and flew 11 missions a day before the weather closed in on February 11. On February 10, the weather was worsening, but the 87th Squadron "Skeeters" flew a 16-plane mission that had the pilots dodging through snow and rain squalls in the vicinity of Lake Albano. Spotting Fw-190s bombing British ground positions on the northern edge of the beachhead, eight pilots in two flights dived on the enemy fighters. Frank Nicolai was first to close with the enemy, shooting an Fw-190's rudder off; the fighter hit the ground and shed its wings as it skidded 100 yards across the open field before ending up in a clump of trees. When the weather cleared on February 13, the 79th devoted its missions to interdicting enemy communications.

Kesselring had planned to launch a counter-offensive with the Fourteenth Army against the beachhead on February 1, but the attempted breakout by VI Corps on January 30 upset that plan. The German attack instead materialized on February 7 with ten divisions and air support from JG 4, JG 51, and JG 53. After retaking the high ground that VI Corps had managed to retain after January 30, the main attack came on February 16. General von Mackensen's plan was to split VI Corps down the middle and reach the Tyrrhenian Sea by February 19, pushing the Allies off the beachhead.

The opening German artillery barrage was heavier than any yet experienced at Anzio by the Allies. While 3rd Division managed to annihilate two inexperienced infantry companies from the Hermann Göring Division with an artillery barrage, the attack took the American defenders elsewhere by surprise; the enemy advanced by as much as 2 miles in several sectors.

Behind a curtain of smoke and shellfire, the main German attack went straight at the 45th Division, defending the center of the American lines. Outposts were overrun as companies disappeared, swallowed up without a trace, as the Germans advanced by sheer weight of numbers. The Americans committed all but their very last reserves, and while the line buckled, it held. With rising daytime temperatures, the Anzio plain became soft and muddy as frost in the ground melted in the warm air, which made it impossible for enemy armor to maneuver. The elite Lehr Infantry Regiment, which was composed of men who had been Hitler's guards, broke and ran when they came under intense artillery attack for the first time. By nightfall, the British and American lines had held.

The Germans were more successful when night fell. They forced a gap between the two front-line regiments of the 45th Division. General von Mackensen brought up his reserves, and shortly after 0800 hours, 35 Fw-190 fighter-bombers hit the American lines. This was followed minutes later by the advance of three *Panzergrenadier* divisions supported by 70 Tiger and Panther tanks. The Americans fell back before the onslaught, retiring across open countryside in daylight and taking heavy casualties. At noon, a massed formation of 48 Fw-190 fighter-bombers opened the American line, and the armor-supported panzergrenadiers split the 45th Division.

As the Americans fell back to the last defense line on the beachhead, the Allied forces at Anzio were on the brink of disaster. No further retreat was possible.

Thirty minutes later, the first of 800 Allied bombers and fighter-bombers appeared overhead. Warhawks, A-36s, and Spitfires bombed and strafed the enemy troops while A-20s, B-25s, B-26s, and even two squadrons of B-24s dropped 1,000 tons of bombs on the enemy. Martin Baltimore bombers from the Desert Air Force flew over the Apennines to add their weight to the attacks. The bombers unloaded within 400 yards of the American lines. It was the heaviest air attack in support of ground forces made by the Allied air forces in a single day ever recorded during the war.

The effect was devastating. The German assault was pulverized to an agonizing crawl. That night, von Mackensen urged his surviving troops to renew the assault, but the attacks were too weak to do more than harass the Americans. German regiments had been reduced to battalions; battalions to companies; companies to platoons.

The weather on February 18 turned terrible, with rain and snow showers throughout central and southern Italy, grounding all Allied air except a few sorties by P-40s and A-36s. The Germans took advantage of the break in attacks and advanced from Campoleone headed again toward the 45th Division. Allied artillery opened up and broke the attack. The enemy regrouped and renewed the attack; artillery again stopped the advance. The Germans tried twice more and could make no progress against the Allied artillery. They did manage to assault the 45th Division in the heaviest attack of the day. The division stood and held over four hours of desperate, hand-to-hand combat before this last serious bid to break through the American lines was beaten back.

The five-day offensive had cost the Fourteenth Army 5,000 men killed, wounded, and missing, but failed to dislodge VI Corps. The major crisis at Anzio was over.

Churchill had become increasingly upset with General Lucas's lack of initiative following the landing. He said to a close associate that it reminded him of the "bunglers" who had thrown away the opportunity provided by surprise in the Gallipoli landing in 1916 that he had advocated as a similar "leap" around the quagmire of the Western Front; that the failure of British military leaders at Gallipoli had nearly killed his political career was not lost on the prime minister. As the Anzio forces fought for their lives against the German offensive, Churchill pressed General Alexander to deal with the Lucas situation. Alexander visited Lucas on February 14 to inform him that a breakout from the beachhead was desired as soon as possible after the German offensive was defeated. On his return to Algiers, Alexander wrote Sir Alan Brooke, Chief of the Imperial General Staff, "I am disappointed with VI Corps Headquarters. They are negative and lacking in the necessary drive and enthusiasm to get things done. They appeared to have become depressed by events."

At about the same time Alexander was writing to Brooke, General Lucas confided to his diary on February 15, "I am afraid that the top side is not completely satisfied with my work ... They are naturally disappointed that I failed to chase the Hun out of Italy but there was no military reason why I should have been able to do so. In fact there is no military reason for Shingle." Further acrimonious arguments by the British with General Mark Clark regarding Lucas finally resulted in a decision by Clark on February 22 to replace Lucas with General Lucian Truscott, Jr., the commander of 3rd Division; Lucas was "kicked upstairs" and made deputy commander of Fifth Army until a more suitable position could be found for him back in the US.

The 79th Group had been in the lead of all the Allied attacks; on February 17 they had flown 103 of the 813 sorties flown that day by the Mediterranean Allied Air Force. The P-40s had staggered into the air from Capodichino carrying 1,000-pound bombs that day, and all but two of their missions were flown in direct support of the 45th Division. During the terrible weather on February 18, the group had still managed to fly 50 sorties, dodging local snowstorms and rain squalls. During those missions, they destroyed an 88mm gun emplacement, three machine guns, six armored cars, and shot up three Mark IV tanks, for a loss of only Lieutenant Albert Mace of the 86th "Comanches" Squadron who was hit by flak too low to bail out and died in the crash of his P-40.

Despite the successes the P-40-equipped fighter groups were achieving around Anzio, time was catching up with the old P-40; the last Merlin-powered Warhawk – P-40L-20 42-11129 – had rolled off the Curtiss assembly in April 1943. While the successor P-40N was supplied to the RAF and used by the Desert Air Force in Italy and over the Balkans until early 1945 as the Kittyhawk IV, the P-40 was no longer considered suitable for combat against the Luftwaffe by the USAAF. Now that production of the P-47 was hitting its stride at two factories back in the US, the time was coming soon when the P-40-equipped units would exchange their war-weary fighters for new Thunderbolts, which had already shown its potential as a superlative fighter-bomber.

Despite this, one more P-40 pilot was able to join the list of MTO P-40 aces before the changeover occurred. On February 16, Captain James E. Fenex, Jr., a flight leader in the 324th Group's 316th Fighter Squadron, had shot down an Fw-190 near Anzio, giving him a score of three confirmed victories. Fenex was one of the 316th's originals – known as a fearless low-level strafer – and had over 100 missions in his logbook. On March 29, two weeks before he was to return to the US having completed his tour, he led a dive-bombing mission to Anzio, where the target was a German supply dump in the Alban Hills. The Warhawks were successful, starting four large fires. As they pulled off the target, they ran into a mixed formation of Fw-190s and Bf-109s southeast of Rome.

Fenex engaged one Fw-190, then chased a second for 3 miles before pulling into range and setting it on fire. Two additional Fw-190s that attempted to intervene were damaged before he ran out of ammunition. Wingman Second Lieutenant James Dealy also destroyed another Fw-190 in the fight, while element leader First Lieutenant William R. King damaged a Bf-109. With the two Fw-190s confirmed destroyed, Fenex brought his score to five and entered the record books as the last P-40 ace in the Mediterranean Theater.

On February 19, the "Skulls" again ran across Fw-190s bombing British positions and attacked them. Lieutenant Carl Stewart scored his second victory when he set an Fw-90 on fire that exploded when it hit a small hill. The Skulls' operations officer had his aileron control knocked out by a burst of flak that put a large hole in his right wing, which allowed all his belted ammunition to hang into the slipstream, making the Warhawk almost uncontrollable. He managed to land at the Nettuno emergency strip, but the Germans opened up with artillery. In the midst of all that, with no tools but some safety wire, he managed to stuff the ammo belts back in the wing and secure them, then took off under fire to return safely to Capodichino.

Hitler urged Kesselring to mount a second counterattack. On February 29, four Fourteenth Army divisions struck the Allied line at Cisterna in a blinding rainstorm, heading for the 3rd Division's positions. The advance crumbled under pounding by 3rd Division artillery and after two days the Germans withdrew. Kesselring convinced Hitler that he should move onto the defensive and prepare the lines for the Allied breakout attack that had to come. Five divisions were left surrounding the Anzio beachhead in the Alban Hills while the others were sent south to reinforce the Gustav Line.

Both sides were exhausted. In the face of continuing rainy weather, each army settled in to await spring. There were no more major actions by either the Allies or the Germans for the next two months.

The first P-47s – early models handed down from the 325th Group after they were completely supplied with new-production Thunderbolts

– appeared at Capodichino airfield on February 8, with three aircraft provided to each squadron in the 79th Group for transition training. The 86th Squadron finished their transition training and began combat operations during the first week of March. The first mission on March 9 was an eight-aircraft patrol over the Anzio beachhead, flown at 15,000 feet, patrolling for enemy fighters that declined to appear. The 85th Squadron flew a similar mission on March 11.

While the regular squadrons of the 79th worked on transitioning to the Thunderbolts, the 99th Squadron was not included in this modernization program. In the meantime, they continued to operate with the 87th Squadron while the "Skeeters" awaited re-equipment.

On March 19, the 99th was ordered to find and knock out "Anzio Express," so named for the express train-like sound the shells made. The gun was one of two Krupp K5 280mm (11-inch) rail guns (the other known to the Allied troops as "Anzio Annie") – known to the Germans as "Robert" and "Leopold" – being used to shell the beachhead. That morning, eight P-40s took off to find tunnel openings where the gun might be hidden. The pilots spotted a suspect tunnel that attracted their attention when flak positions were spotted around it; four of the 500-pound bombs they dropped sealed the tunnel entrance. While they did not in fact destroy the gun, there was no more shelling since the entrance could not be cleared and the gun was removed from that position out the tunnel's other end. After the breakout offensive from Anzio began, the two guns were evacuated from the area to Civitavecchia for further evacuation on May 18, though in the end they were abandoned there by the enemy.

The 99th's dive-bombing skills made them a valuable addition to the 324th when they were transferred on April 2. They had proven their skill and ability while with the 79th, demonstrating that the criticism by Colonel Momyer of the 33rd Group had been unwarranted. Thus, there were no problems when the squadron moved on to the 324th, which would be the last USAAF fighter group in the MTO to operate the P-40.

The P-47's first combat over Anzio happened on March 14, the day after the 57th Group had moved over to the 324th Group's field at Cercola to join the force defending Anzio. The 66th Squadron flew a dive-bombing mission to hit the rail station at Fara Sabina. The "Exterminators" scored direct hits on the station and marshalling yards, dropping two 500-pound bombs each that started fires. As the first two Thunderbolts pulled up from their dive, they spotted three Fw-190s and gave chase. The enemy fighters split up, with two diving under the P-47s while the third climbed away and evaded the Americans. Lieutenant Donald Bell dived after the two and quickly latched onto the wingman's tail. Closing to 250 yards, he opened fire, hitting the fighter along the fuselage and wing roots. The pilot bailed out. Lieutenant Walter Henson went after the leader, closing to 200 yards and scoring numerous hits before he had to break off his attack as he overran the enemy fighter, which he lost sight of. Captain Thomas Liston confirmed the victory when he saw the Focke-Wulf go straight in and explode.

On St Patrick's Day, March 17, the 79th Group scored with their new Thunderbolts when the 85th "Skulls" and 86th "Skeeters" squadrons put up 18 P-47s to escort B-25s of the 340th Bomb Group to Roccasecca. Once the Mitchells were safely back over friendly territory, the P-47s broke away on a fighter sweep over the beachhead. Once there, a formation of 20 Fw-190s with a top cover of ten Bf-109s was spotted diving on targets in the beachhead. Led by Captain Carl Stewart, the "Skulls" were the first to engage, intercepting the Bf-109s at 12,000 feet. Stewart immediately got on the tail of a Bf-109. He later described the fight: "Closing in, firing dead astern, the ME [Messerschmitt] began smoking. At 2,000 feet the German aircraft half-rolled and plunged into the ground."

First Lieutenant Charles DeFoor, Stewart's element leader, tagged on to another Bf-109 and fired off nearly all his ammunition in a long burst that set the enemy fighter afire and sent it straight in to explode on impact. Second Lieutenant Maxwell engaged a Bf-109 and hit it when he opened fire, but lost it when he blacked out recovering from his dive. In their first air combat with the Thunderbolt, the "Skulls" were credited with two destroyed and one damaged.

With fighting having come to a standstill at Anzio from exhaustion and bad weather, Field Marshal Sir Henry Maitland believed that the stalemate on the Anzio beachhead could be broken by starving out the enemy and forcing them to retreat in order to shorten their supply lines. Operation *Strangle*, which commenced on March 19, was to utilize air interdiction to force a retreat from the beachhead and a withdrawal from the Gustav Line through relentless attacks on the supply network. The German forces in Italy depended on the extensive rail network that stretched from the Austrian border down through the Brenner Pass throughout the peninsula to the tip of the Italian "boot." The Mediterranean Allied Strategic Air Force (MASAF), which included the Fifteenth Air Force, was assigned the task of destroying marshalling yards in northern Italy, while the medium bombers of the Mediterranean Allied Tactical Air Force (MATAF) – composed of Twelfth Air Force and the RAF Desert Air Force – were tasked with destroying transportation infrastructure north of Rome between Siena and Genoa on the west coast, and from Ancona north to Rimini on the east coast.

South of this "interdiction belt," the fighter-bombers of XII Air Support Command (XII ASC) were turned loose to cut rail lines and junctions, attacking trains and any other transport. The 57th and 79th Fighter Groups focused their efforts on railway bridges, since the P-47's dive-bombing capability made it the weapon of choice for taking out the many smaller bridges dotting the Italian countryside.

The 57th's Michael C. McCarthy recalled, "We were to be a major player in Operation *Strangle*, the next big air-to-ground operation in the Italian theater. The plan called for full-scale interdiction of roads, railroads, bridges, marshalling yards, shipping lanes, ports, and airports from the northern Po Valley south through the Appenines [sic], the Arno river cities, and all roads south of Rome used to bring essential supplies to the German army. We would carefully avoid targets near historic sites in Rome, Florence, and Pisa."

While the medium bomber forces went after the larger bridges, XII ASC's P-47s, P-40s, and A-36s destroyed the remaining targets. The P-47 was able to carry double the bomb load of the P-40s and a heavier load than the A-36, which meant that the 57th's "Thunderbombers" of the fighter group were kept busy in March while the group geared up for the move to Corsica.

The 57th flew its first *Strangle* mission on March 24 when eight 64th Squadron "Black Scorpions" flew a railway reconnaissance mission between Civitavecchia and Capranica. Their primary target was the three-span, concrete rail bridge northeast of Civitavecchia. The P-47s began their dives from 3,000 feet, scoring numerous hits with their 500lb bombs on the bridge's western approach, successfully cutting the rail lines on all three spans.

First Lieutenant Paul Carll recalled, "Our flight formed up after the run and we did a turnabout to come home. It was at this point that we were attacked by ten-plus enemy aircraft." They quickly turned and engaged the ten Fw-190s from I./JG 2. Carll explained, "The enemy made a split attack, with two ships coming in on Lieutenant Loyst Towners' tail and three on my tail. Our element did a turnabout into the enemy and the last time I saw Towners there were two ships on his tail and he didn't appear to be making an attempt to shake them."

First Lieutenant Michael described the engagement:

These guys were aggressive, flew excellent formation, climbed quickly to attack out of the sun, maintained two-ship integrity and avoided the turning dogfight unless they had the advantage. I remember turning with one on the opposite side of the tight circle in a 90-degree bank, neither of us gaining on the other. I saw gun flashes from him, thought to myself "No way," but he actually put three shells in my P-47, one in front of the windshield and two more behind the cockpit. That is the lowest percentage shot in a dogfight, requiring the maximum lead and a full 90-degree deflection. I was impressed.

Michael's wingman, First Lieutenant Bill Nuding, was an equally good shot; he caught another Fw-190 with a 90-degree deflection shot, knocking pieces off the fighter and sending it out of control. When he followed it down, another Fw-190 attacked him and he was unable to confirm the first fighter's demise. First Lieutenant Bruce Abercrombie, who was chasing another Fw-190, saw a smoking fighter crash out of control, confirming Nuding's kill. Abercrombie's target billowed white smoke as the pilot struggled to maintain control. Abercrombie fired another burst, and the enemy fighter appeared to spin out of control. However, the pilot was able to keep flying and escaped.

While the "Black Scorpions" engaged the enemy fighters, the "Exterminators" of the 66th Squadron worked over a ten-wagon train. Initial results weren't good, but they strafed the train on a second pass, which destroyed the locomotive and damaged several wagons. Another 15 wagons were found on a nearby siding; they were strafed and set afire. Returning to Caserta, they spotted a lone Bf-109, which was shot down in flames by First Lieutenant Donald Smith.

On the Exterminators' second mission, four RAF Spitfires attacked the Thunderbolts, which were at 12,000 feet over the Tyrrhenian Sea. Second Lieutenant Leon Jansen, who was in the low flight, described the engagement:

When we were just west of the Anzio beachhead three bogies were called in at a position of three o'clock to our formation. As we proceeded north, I watched the three bogies going south. They turned ten degrees and began overtaking us. The flight of four P-47s that were giving us top cover were slightly to our right. The bogies were closing in on our top cover, and when they were within about 350 yards range I easily identified them as Spitfire VIIIs. One Spit closed right on in to a range of about 100–150 yards and fired a short burst at Lieutenant Coughlin, who was flying on Lieutenant McCoy's wing. Coughlin pulled up in sort of a wing-over and began a split-S. The Spitfire followed him. Coughlin's P-47 was smoking badly when he started down. He went straight down, hitting the water half-a-mile from shore. I watched him from the time the Spit began firing until he hit the water. When his P-47 struck the water it exploded, and flame was seen at that point for about two or three minutes.

Over the rest of March, each squadron of the 57th Fighter Group flew two or three missions a day south of the interdiction belt, hitting rail stations and marshalling yards. On March 29, Major Art Exon of the 64th "Black Scorpions" shot down a Bf-109 from a flight of four that attempted to interfere with the Thunderbolts, exploding the enemy fighter with a concentrated burst from his guns. First Lieutenant John J. Lenihan tagged onto a second Bf-109 and saw pieces fly off and smoke billow, but the enemy fighter escaped into the clouds before he could deliver a final burst.

Since the 79th Group's Thunderbolts had not yet received the modification the 57th Group had developed that allowed the P-47 to become such an effective dive bomber, the latter half of March saw the group involved in bomber escort missions. Prior to March 20, the 79th had flown just five escort missions since transitioning to the P-47. Once Operation *Strangle* began, the group flew 13 more escort missions over the last ten days of the month.

On March 24, the "Skulls" of the 85th Squadron escorted B-26s of the 320th Bomb Group to the Orvieto railway bridge. As the Marauders entered their bomb run, the escorts were bounced from out of the sun by 12 Bf-109s of 8./JG 53. The enemy fighters split into two sections of six, and each attacked one of the two four-plane P-47 flights. First Lieutenant Powell Schuemack, who was leading Yellow Flight section at 14,000 feet, warned Red Flight before the enemy hit them, but as he did, the second group of enemy fighters attacked his flight. Red Flight leader First Lieutenant Albert Benz saw the incoming enemy attacking from "seven o'clock high" as Schuemack radioed his warning, and turned his flight into them. As they did so, four more attacked from the rear, focusing their attention on Second Lieutenant Ward Pringle's Thunderbolt, P-47D, "Red Two." Just before he engaged the Bf-109s attacking his flight, Schuemack saw Red Two going down as it trailed thick black smoke with two Bf-109s on his tail. No one saw him crash, but no parachute was seen; Pringle was officially listed MIA.

On March 30, the 79th Group returned to Orvieto, escorting 24 B-25s of the 321st Bomb Group. As they crossed the coastline near Civitavecchia, they were attacked by a flight of 12 Fw-190s. However, the "Skulls" of the 85th and "Comanches" of the 86th Squadron kept the enemy fighters away from the bombers. The B-25 was lightly defended under its belly; the Fw-190s dove from 12,000 feet, then zoom-climbed underneath the bombers at 11,000 feet. Captain Stewart caught a Focke-Wulf from dead astern and set the right wing afire. The enemy pilot tried to maneuver but the wing separated from the fuselage and the Fw-190 spiraled into the ground where it exploded.

Free French Lieutenant Pierre Guachon, who was assigned to the 79th to train on the Thunderbolt, attacked four Fw-190s as they climbed toward the Mitchells; he fired several short bursts at one from less than 100 yards; the enemy fighter trailed black smoke and half-rolled into a steep dive. Not wasting time, Guachon climbed back to altitude, where he engaged a formation of Bf-109s from either JG 27, JG 53, or JG 77. Flying head-on at one fighter, he forced the pilot to break away, then dove on its tail, firing several bursts and getting hits on its fuselage, but it reached the cloud cover and escaped.

Two P-47s were lost in the engagement. First Lieutenant Milo Klear turned his stricken P-47 for home after he was hit by a Bf-109; he was forced to bail out over friendly territory when his engine seized and was returned to Capodichino by nightfall. First Lieutenant Schuemack was wounded when a cannon shell exploded outside his cockpit; he was hit in his leg by spraying shrapnel that knocked out his radio. He was able to nurse the stricken Thunderbolt back to friendly territory, but when the engine began running rough, he bailed out, landing safely among British troops, who tended his wounds prior to returning him to Capodichino.

As the bombers closed their bomb bays and turned for home, group operations officer Captain Edward Byron sighted a lone Bf-109 and dove to attack it. Firing at very close range, the enemy fighter slow rolled and its engine caught fire. Firing three more long bursts, the Bf-109 fell through the overcast at 9,000 feet out of control. He then sighted another Bf-109 as the Mitchells approached the coast and closed to within 100 yards. Firing four bursts from dead astern, he shot away a large section of the enemy fighter and smoke billowed from the engine. The Bf-109 fell off and spun through the overcast in the vicinity of Viterbo.

The cloud cover had become a solid overcast, making it almost impossible for the Thunderbolts to return to Capodichino. One landed safely, but the rest were then diverted to Taranto, while one landed at Pomigliano. Lieutenant Guachon bellied his fighter in near Benevento, escaping injury, while First Lieutenant Malin Eltzroth landed safely at Capodichino at 1700 hours.

Once the 57th relocated to Corsica in April, the new location allowed the Thunderbolts to attack many heavily defended targets throughout central and northern Italy above the Gustav Line. Lieutenant McCarthy remembered, "We flew several missions a day to destroy German road convoys. Power stations, marshalling yards, and bridges also received close attention. On one mission, I was leading three sections of four. We destroyed a power plant, a factory, two steam locomotives, an electric-powered locomotive on another train, several loaded freight cars, and found and strafed a motor convoy loaded with troops. We destroyed every target on that particular mission." Because of his leadership of this mission, Lieutenant McCarthy was awarded the Distinguished Flying Cross and was promoted to captain.

"The Jug" – the name pilots throughout the war called the P-47 – was a great dive bomber.

McCarthy recalled:

It had excellent stability at all speeds; it was easy to center the ball, trim, and keep the nose on the target. It was a relief not to stand on the left rudder just to keep the airplane from slipping sideways in a dive, as was the case with the P-40. This natural stability enhanced an excellent gun platform. Later in the war I was strafing a fast-moving train in the Po Valley and hit the locomotive with the cone of my eight guns. I knocked it completely off the tracks while the rest of the train, minus its locomotive, rolled on with no hesitation.

McCarthy later recalled just how dangerous the missions that the 57th Group and the other ground support units in XII ASC engaged in were. Dive-bombing exposed the fighters to enemy ground fire, and those units who took on the air support mission experienced higher casualties than did pure fighter units. McCarthy wrote in his memoir, "The air-to-ground environment is brutal, life threatening, and consistently dangerous. The fighter pilot population in our squadron changed 400 percent from May 1943 until the end of the war in June 1945. We lost airplanes and pilots on a regular basis. We changed tactics, varied approaches and routes to targets, and emphasized surprise at every opportunity. In the end, we learned that you must fly down the enemy's gun barrel to destroy the target."

Many pilots survived in this brutal environment due to the toughness of the Thunderbolt. McCarthy recalled how the airplane could absorb heavy flak damage and still fly. "The big Pratt and Whitney engine was incredibly tough. I flew one from Italy to Corsica taking 45 minutes with zero oil pressure minus two top cylinders that had been blown off by enemy fire. The engine ran until I pulled the throttle back for landing. That was not a fluke. Another squadron pilot repeated this later without three top cylinders and zero oil pressure. The secret was not to change the power setting."

While the other two squadrons in the 79th Group re-equipped with P-47s, the 87th kept its P-40F/Ls during March and April, flying dedicated fighter-bomber missions while the rest converted to the Thunderbolt. Had the "Skeeters" not kept on using their war-weary Warhawks in a role that only became increasingly dangerous, there would have been a significant gap in air cover over Anzio. The first ten P-47s arrived on April 18, while an additional ten arrived the next day; however, the squadron continued flying the P-40 until April 22. Since the Skeeters' pilots had previously gone through checkout with the Thunderbolt, they were able to fly the first P-47 mission on April 23, when the target was the marshalling yards at Orte.

While inbound to the primary target, two P-47s broke off and each dropped their two 500-pound bombs on the harbor at Gaeta Point. The rest of the formation attacked the marshalling yards and the surrounding infrastructure, dropping 19 500-pound bombs; direct hits on four warehouses and storage sheds resulted in massive explosions, while the rail lines were cut in two places. A second mission that took off at 1800 hours proved this wasn't a fluke, since the deadly accurate results were a significant contribution to *Strangle*.

April also saw the 79th fully engaged in the fighter-bomber business when newer bomb-rack-fitted P-47D-15s equipped the 86th and later the 85th Squadrons. The 86th's "Comanches" flew their first fighter-bomber mission on April 2, when squadron commander Major Melvin Nielsen led the attack on a key road junction. Eight Thunderbolts dove from 2,500 feet, and the 16 500-pound bombs landed in a loose pattern around the target. Lieutenant John McNeal led a second mission that afternoon, which saw another critical road junction hit with a similar number of bombs, with greater accuracy.

The "Comanches" flew similar missions throughout the first week of April, while the "Skulls" of the 85th flew fighter escort for the B-25s and B-26s. With new P-47D-15s arriving in greater numbers, the 85th flew its first bombing mission the afternoon of April 11, a dive-bombing mission to Gaeta by eight Thunderbolts. Despite very accurate 88mm flak, the pilots scored direct hits in the town center with six of the eight 1,000-pound bombs they dropped.

On April 15, the 86th set a new record, carrying a full 2,500-pound ordnance load for the first time on a combat mission. Three "Comanche" Thunderbolts took off from Capodichino at 1500 hours, each loaded with two 1,000-pounders on the wing pylons and a single 500-pound bomb on the centerline rack. Their target was Cassino. While two of the larger bombs failed to release, the four that did drop found their targets, proving the Thunderbolt could carry over twice the bomb load of the P-40, delivering the loads more accurately close to friendly forces.

Twelve "Comanche" P-47s took off at 0805 hours on April 18, led by First Lieutenant Saverio Martino to dive-bomb the railway bridge at Falerii. The Thunderbolts dived from 13,000 feet through intense light flak. A large formation of Fw-190s suddenly appeared and attempted to intercept the Americans in their attack. Captain Risden Wall, who led Blue Flight, pulled up to the left as he came off the target to see the bomb run of the rest. He recalled:

> The last aircraft of my flight was piloted by 2nd Lieutenant Don N. Mulkey; as he released his bombs and started to pull up, his P-47 received direct hits from very intense light ground fire and small arms fire. I saw him start climbing with flames coming from beneath the belly of his aircraft. He got to 4,500 feet, where he rolled over onto his back and his ship went in, flaming all the way to the ground, where it disintegrated. Though he had been hit repeatedly in his dive, Mulkey scored direct hits on the bridge span with his bombs.

Having now dropped their loads, the Thunderbolts turned to engage the enemy fighters, but only eight remained in the vicinity; six headed north while two chose to engage the P-47s. Wall closed on the first and opened fire, but broke off when the second closed from the rear. Turning into the attacker, he quickly got onto the Fw-190's tail and set it on fire with several bursts, following it down to observe the crash. At the same time, Lieutenants William West and Ray Hagler engaged the first fighter and destroyed it, sharing the credit.

On April 30, as the "Skeeters" pulled out of an attack on ten German vehicles, an enemy radar station with a large rotating aerial and several camouflaged buildings was spotted; 14 P-47s strafed the target, destroying the aerial and setting the surrounding buildings on fire.

While the 79th received new Thunderbolt fighter-bombers, the 27th Fighter Group – which had been forced to trade its beloved A-36s for war-weary P-40s when the supply of available Mustang dive bombers was insufficient to support two groups – learned they would soon receive new aircraft in May. Rumors of what new type they would get ran rampant, with many hoping to re-equip with new Mustangs, but the word was they would re-equip with the P-47. This was confirmed when the next group of replacement pilots to arrive turned out to have all been trained on the Thunderbolt. On April 10, the 524th Fighter Squadron received a few war-weary P-47s without bomb racks cast off from the 57th and 79th Groups for training. First Lieutenant Sayre was the first of the 524th's pilots to suffer an accident in the Thunderbolt on April 12 when he experienced a runaway prop on takeoff and was forced to belly land. On April 18, the 524th's pilots flew to Algiers in a C-47 to pick up and return brand-new P-47s to their Castel Volturno base.

On April 24, the unit's war diary recorded, "There are 27 P-47s assigned to our Squadron. Our Crew Chiefs are practically working double time maintaining both the P-40s and P-47s. Pilots are getting at least 15 hours of transition flying before any attempt will be made to fly any combat missions in the P-47s." Following the examples of the 57th and 79th, the 524th avoided the strain placed on ground crews and pilots during significant equipment transition with a three-week stand down to become familiar with the new aircraft.

USAAF P-40s engaged German fighters in combat for the last time on May 13, when Lieutenants Dealy and King of the 324th's 316th Squadron were each credited with a Bf-109, as was the 315th's First Lieutenant Ken Scheiwe. Immediately after scoring his Bf-109, Dealy was shot down, but he was rescued by partisans who helped him evade capture and return to the squadron when they moved to the Anzio beachhead on June 6. The group moved to Montalto di Castro airfield near Rome on May 30, from where they flew the last mission by USAAF P-40s in the MTO on July 18. The pilots had already transitioned to the P-47 over ten days before this. They ferried the war-weary Warhawks to Naples as soon as they were refueled after landing from the final mission, and traded them for new P-47Ds. With that, the long and bloody war fought by P-40s from the dark days in North Africa, through Sicily and Italy, was finally over.

The P-40, even with the Merlin engine powering the P-40F and L sub-types, couldn't fight effectively above 16,000 feet, where even the performance of the Merlin 20 series fell off, and was slow to get to that altitude like the rest of the early-war American fighters. The cockpit was cluttered and noisy, and the pilot found himself constantly applying rudder to keep it straight and level, while nearly standing on the right rudder to keep it aimed straight at a target when dive-bombing. Range was limited, particularly as a fighter-bomber, since the choice was either a drop tank or a 500-pound bomb on the centerline. Against that, the Warhawk was tough, and pilots liked that it could return safely even after suffering major battle damage. It could turn with its opponents at the lower altitudes which favored the fighter, and the armament of six .50-caliber machine guns was effective. As one pilot put it, "You couldn't outrun a Messerschmitt and you couldn't outclimb one. You had to shoot it down in order to get home, it was as simple as that." The maligned P-40 had held the enemy at bay in North Africa and held its own over Sicily and Italy until more modern types could replace it.

The 27th Fighter Group completed their transition to the P-47 and were declared operational on the new fighter on May 16; the transition had been extended because the group continued to fly P-40 missions while the pilots transitioned to the Thunderbolt. On May 19, when the weather cleared, the 524th Fighter Squadron flew its first P-47 combat mission over the Anzio beachhead. While inbound to their target, the squadron encountered heavy flak as they flew over Fondi at 8,500 feet. Flight leader Captain Arthur "Red" Sortore, who was flying his 115th combat mission, took hits that forced him to bail out 5 miles north of Fondi, which was then nearly 15 miles behind enemy lines. While a few enemy soldiers shot at him as he descended, he landed safely and found cover, which allowed him to hide out until nightfall. Over the next two days, Sortore evaded enemy patrols and headed south, finally making contact with advancing American units north of Itri in the late afternoon of May 21.

On the afternoon of May 26, the 524th ran across enemy fighters for the first time. Eight P-47s strafing retreating German tanks and motor transport southeast of Lake Bracciano were intercepted by 20 Bf-109s and Fw-190s, which dove on the Thunderbolts and damaged two on their first pass. Second Lieutenant Elmer Carroll was able to damage a Bf-109 before another got behind him and shot out his rudder cables; Carroll was forced to leave the fight while Second Lieutenant Harold Hamner was forced to bail out of his P-47. First Lieutenant Robert LaFollette damaged another Bf-109, and First Lieutenant Clyde Brown was credited with an Fw-190 destroyed. As the Thunderbolts disengaged, two RAF Spitfires attacked the fleeing Germans, and the Thunderbolt pilots confirmed the destruction of two additional Fw-190s.

At about the same time, the 79th Group's "Comanches" destroyed a supply train carrying ammunition and fuel south of Rome that blew up in a huge explosion. They then wreaked havoc with a large truck convoy, setting a record 58 vehicles of 65 on fire with repeated strafing passes; huge explosions meant the trucks were also loaded with ammunition.

During a train-busting mission on May 27, the Skeeters' Thunderbolts were intercepted by 15 Bf-109s. Lieutenant David Shuttleworth shot down one with an 80-degree deflection shot while the rest turned away after their initial pass.

June 4 saw the "Comanches" set a record for a single squadron when they shot up and destroyed 114 German trucks and armored vehicles on the road north of Rome. The 79th's record as a whole that day was 275 trucks and other motor transport shot up, 154 of which were destroyed, while also blowing up an ammunition dump and knocking out a tank, leaving the area north of Rome a mass of flames described by one pilot as "a huge forest fire."

Despite such an outstanding effort by the 79th in the air and the relentless fighting by the troops on the ground, Operation *Buffalo* – the codename for the Allied breakout from the Anzio beachhead – failed in its goal to "shut the door" on the German forces retreating from the Gustav Line. The entire Anzio operation, from the initial invasion to the final breakout, had been nearly upended on several occasions by mistakes made by senior Allied commanders. With the final opportunity for real success botched by Clark's egotistical mistake, Anzio was a failed opportunity that Allied soldiers, sailors, and airmen paid for with their blood.

6

"USS CORSICA"

The Vesuvius eruption thoroughly disrupted Allied air operations over Italy. There was fear that there could be additional eruptions and more destruction. As the newly assigned bomb groups of the Fifteenth Air Force made their homes at the Foggia complex in south-central Italy, the XII Tactical Air Force units needed to find new bases. Since the beginning of the year, Allied air units had been moving to the newly constructed airfields on Corsica. In late February, Twelfth Air Force planners considered the options and determined that more units of XII Tactical Air Command should be based on the island.

Corsica, the northernmost and smaller of two large islands west of the Italian peninsula in the Ligurian Sea, had been part of France since it was purchased from the Republic of Genoa in 1764. In the aftermath of the Franco-German Armistice in June 1940, the Vichy government took control. Following the Allied invasion of French-held North Africa and the German occupation of Vichy France in November 1942, Corsica was occupied by the Italian Army, with 85,000 troops on the island by July 1943. After the Italian surrender in September, 12,000 Germans arrived and took control; initially, the Italian troops collaborated with them.

Resistance to the Italian occupation began with the arrival of Italian troops in 1940, following Mussolini's decision to enter the war. By 1943, the local resistance was well organized and General Charles de Gaulle sent Free French representatives to unite the local leadership. The partisan movement's morale was boosted by the elusive Free French submarine *Casabianca*, which landed personnel and arms six times that spring and summer. The Free French Armée de l'Air made arms drops in the summer after the Germans and Italians were defeated in North Africa. Thus, the resistance was able to establish stronger control in the countryside.

Corsican partisans were the first to be called "Maquis," a reference to the tough, small, dense scrub brush on the island, a name later applied to underground forces in rugged southwestern France. The growth of the resistance saw the Italian OVRA Secret Police and Fascist Black Shirt paramilitary groups engage in a large-scale crackdown in June and July that saw 860 Corsicans deported to Italy.

Following the Italian surrender proclamation on September 8, the self-liberation of Corsica began with an uprising the next day, when the newly arrived German units moved to disarm the Italians. While senior Italian military leaders on the island were ambivalent in their loyalties, the majority of the troops were loyal to King Victor Emmanuel III; many joined the partisans.

The Allies initially resisted invading Corsica. With the initial success of the anti-Fascist insurrection, General Eisenhower decided to land the Free French I Corps in late September. De Gaulle pushed things forward when a unit of elite French troops landed from the *Casabianca* near the village of Piana in northwest Corsica on September 10. The Corsican partisans and the Italian 44th Infantry Division "Cremona" and 20th Infantry Division "Friuli" engaged the Waffen SS troops of the Sturmbrigade Reichsführer SS and the 90th Panzergrenadier Division.

The situation was further confused when the Italian 12th Parachute Battalion of the 184th Parachute Regiment – the troops of which came from Sardinia and were loyal Fascists – joined the Germans. The German units and their Italian allies retreated toward the northern harbor of Bastia.

The Free French continued to move quickly. The Free French 4th Moroccan Mountain Division landed in the port of Ajaccio on September 15, blocking the 30,000 retreating enemy troops. The last German units evacuated Bastia the night of October 3–4, leaving 700 dead and 350 prisoners of war.

In late October, work began on four airfields planned for operations by the Free French Armée de l'Air over southern France. Since Corsica's strategic location put targets in southern France and Austria, as well as all of central and northern Italy and across the Adriatic Sea to

Yugoslavia within bombing range, the USAAF soon offered to assist in constructing and expanding the airfields in return for permission to base aircraft there.

The first American unit to transfer to Corsica was the 52nd Fighter Group, which learned they would make the move in December 1943, when their long boring assignment to Coastal Command (which had seen them practically excluded from the war over the previous six months since the end of the North African campaign) during the Pantelleria campaign, the Sicilian invasion, and the move into Italy, was ended with a transfer to XII Air Support Command. The 52nd's 5th Fighter Squadron relocated from Bari in southern Italy to Borgo Poretta airfield, outside the town of Aghione, when squadron commander Captain Everett K. Jenkins led two Spitfire IX and nine Spitfire V fighters to the island on December 1, with ground support and maintenance personnel traveling from Naples to Corsica by LST arriving on December 3. The squadron was joined by the 2nd Squadron at Borgo, while the 4th Squadron went to Calvi airfield, with both units arriving on the island on December 6.

The 5th Squadron flew their first missions from Corsica on December 2. One 12-plane flight made a shipping reconnaissance patrol along the central Italian coast that provoked no enemy response, while six Spitfire Vs escorted a Walrus air rescue amphibian in a search for a downed bomber crew. A gasoline shortage on Corsica prevented further operations by the other squadrons until a shipment arrived on December 6. The group's first aerial score was recorded on December 7, when 4th Squadron pilots Lieutenants James O. Tyler and W. E. LaBarge took off to intercept a bogie that turned out to be an Me-410. After chasing it in and out of the clouds for several minutes, Tyler shot it down 20 miles southeast of Calvi. The victory was the first for the 52nd Group since the previous summer.

Over the course of the remainder of December, missions were flown over mainland Italy and southern France when the rainy weather allowed flight operations. These were road and rail recces looking for targets of opportunity in Italy and shipping reconnaissance missions over France. On December 28, the group flew their first dive-bombing missions after bomb racks were fitted over the four rainy days before that allowed the Spitfires to carry a 250-pound bomb under each wing. The mission was unsuccessful, with the four river barges attacked at

Joseph Heller plays the role of "Pete, a replacement bombardier," in the training film *Training In Combat* directed by First Lieutenant Wilbur Blume and made between September and December 1944. The 20 missions Heller flew during this time were the only "milk runs" flown by the group. He departed for the United States in January 1945 with 60 missions flown, at a time when the "tour" was a rigidly enforced 70. Was this event – which he never spoke of again – the reason he wrote *Catch-22*? (Wilbur Blume Collection)

First Lieutenant Wilbur Blume (right, top) directs a scene for the film *Training In Combat*, one of several he made for 340th Group CO Colonel John Chapman, which Blume called "a boondoggle." (USAF Official)

Colonel Robert D. Knapp led the 321st Bomb Group in North Africa, Sicily, and Italy before being promoted to command the 57th Bomb Wing, despite being initially thought to be too old for combat. He led every tough mission flown – the polar opposite of Heller's General Dreedle. (USAF Official)

On February 15, 1944, B-17s and B-24s of the new Fifteenth Air Force, as well as Twelfth Air Force B-26 Marauders, B-25 Mitchells, and A-20 Havocs, bombed the Benedictine abbey atop Monte Cassino, established as the first monastery of the Benedictine Order in AD 529 by Benedict of Nursia. The Allied command mistakenly believed the abbey – which controlled the Volturno River Valley – was occupied by German troops. In fact, the Germans only occupied the monastery after the bombing, when its ruins became an excellent defensive position. German paratroopers held off the US Fifth Army through three major assaults between February and May 1944. (USAF Official)

Mount Vesuvius erupted on March 25, 1944, part of a series of increasingly violent eruptions in 1906, 1929, and 1944. The eruptions interrupted Allied operations in the middle of the attempt to break through the Germans at the Gustav Line. (USAF Official)

A Caterpillar tractor driver attempts to scrape away volcanic ash from Pompeii airfield as Mount Vesuvius continued to erupt a week after the initial blast. Vesuvius damaged or destroyed more Allied aircraft over that week than the Luftwaffe had scored in two years of combat. (USAF Official)

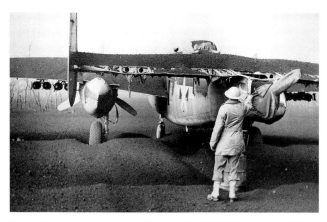

The 340th Bomb Group was based at Pompeii airfield just north of the volcano when it erupted on March 25, 1944. All 88 bombers were destroyed, with their plastic canopies melted and fuselages filled with hot volcanic ash. Everything inside was destroyed, along with the fabric control surfaces outside. The group received 88 new bombers in April when they moved to Corsica. Most of these were destroyed on May 8, 1944, when the Luftwaffe hit the island in the last bombing raids flown by the Germans in the Mediterranean Theater. That event – which happened five days before Joe Heller arrived on Corsica – was memorialized in *Catch-22* as Milo Minderbinder's "business deal" with the Germans. (USAF Official)

This B-25J of the 12th Bomb Group was given a publicity paint scheme celebrating the downfall of Mussolini in Italy and promising the same to Japanese emperor Hirohito. The Mitchell is flying over the Bay of Naples in the spring of 1944. (USAF Official)

Avignon bridge was where Joseph Heller had "the daylights scared out of me," which became the "Help the Bombardier!" scene in *Catch-22*. (USAF Official)

Production of the Fiat G.55 "Centauro" (Centaur) came too late to equip units of the Regia Aeronautica before the surrender of Italy in late 1943. Three *Squadriglie* of the ANR operated with 70 G.55s between December 1943 and April 1944 before reequipping to the BF-109G. The Germans stopped production of the fighter in September 1944. (Chronicle/Alamy Stock Photo)

Tents like this one used by a crew in the 340th Bomb Group on Corsica were the main living quarters for most American airmen in the Italian campaign from September 1943 to the end of the war. The winter of 1944/45, the coldest in Europe in a century, was particularly hard on crews living in tents like this. (USAF Official)

Most of the maintenance on aircraft of both sides during World War II was done outside. Ground crews became very adept at coming up with simple rigs that were easy to move from plane to plane for heavy work up to and including an engine change. This is a rig used by the 310th Bomb Group on Corsica. (USAF Official)

The Brenner Pass rail line ran from Bologna in the Po Valley to Munich, Germany, an eight-hour, one-way trip. At the beginning of Operation *Bingo* in November 1944, the German Tenth and Fourteenth Armies were receiving three times the minimum supplies needed to hold the Gothic Line, brought from Germany through the pass on the railway. *Bingo* aimed to cut off the German supply lines for the units manning the Gothic Line. On April 15, 1945, the Allied spring offensive began; the German armies surrendered unconditionally by the end of April, a week before the war ended in Germany. Operation *Bingo* was the most successful – and difficult – battlefield interdiction campaign ever flown by the US Air Force. (USAF Official)

B-25s of the 321st Bomb Group bombed the Galliate bridge in the Po Valley in October 1944 during the final Allied ground offensive to break the Gothic Line in 1944. (USAF Official)

The transformers at Trento, in the southern approaches to the Brenner Pass, provided all the power for the electric trains the railway used. The transformers were the first target hit during Operation *Bingo*, on November 6, 1944. Their complete destruction meant the Germans had to bring in coal-fired engines from other parts of the German railway system to replace the electric trains, and maintain the coal supply to keep the German armies in the Gothic Line supplied. (USAF Official)

Rovereto, at the entrance of the Brenner Pass, was the most difficult target to hit in Operation *Bingo*. The bombers could only approach from the south due to the winds in the pass and bomb from an altitude of 8,000 feet. The surrounding mountains on both sides of the pass were 7,000 feet high and the Germans had 88mm flak guns in position on the mountainside at 6,000 feet. Dan Bowling recalled that "Every mission we flew there, it was like the Charge of the Light Brigade – cannons to the left, cannons to the right, into the valley of death." (USAF Official)

P-47D-30 Thunderbolt "Torrid Tessie" of the 350th Fighter Group. It was part of a formation escorting bombers from 57th Bomb Wing during Operation *Bingo* in the spring of 1945. (USAF Official)

On April 16, 1945, Lieutenant Vladimir Sandtner of the Air Force of the Independent State of Croatia defected to Italy. He landed at Fano airfield just as Dan Bowling was taking off to lead a major mission, barely missing Bowling's B-25. The 321st's ground crews later sold the Bf-109G-10 to an RAF unit for three cases of Scotch whiskey. (USAF Official)

USS CORSICA, 1944–45

San Vicenzo surviving the attack. However, all was not lost when a second Me-410 was intercepted and shot down between Elba and the mainland. A final aerial victory on December 30 saw a Ju-88 shot down after being chased over the Ligurian Sea almost to the French Riviera coast. On New Year's Eve, a storm hit Corsica with driving rain and 40mph winds.

January 1944 saw the group make continued improvement in dive-bombing over several missions flown between storms. With the arrival of the 310th Bomb Group on Corsica, the 52nd also flew escort for their B-25s during anti-shipping missions.

The 52nd flew regularly during the first 30 days of the Anzio invasion, with successful ground support missions now that the group had mastered dive-bombing in a Spitfire. However, one of the most important missions saw Lieutenants Robert Liebl, James Bickford, Mike Encinias, and Arthur G. Johnson, Jr. spot a formation of 50 Ju-88s, He-111s, and Do-217s headed for Anzio as they crossed the Ligurian Sea for a close-support mission in the beachhead. Jettisoning their bombs, the four Spitfires dived on the formation. Lieutenants Bickford and Encinias got two He-111s and an He-111 and Ju-88 respectively, with Liebl and Johnson each shooting down a He-111. The attack forced the enemy bombers to break up their formation.

Lieutenant Bickford recalled:

It was a slow day with not much going on, so I convinced Bill Beard, the squadron ops officer, to let me lead a flight to hit the E-boat pens at Marina di Pisa. As we approached Marina di Pisa, we spotted this big formation of bombers just off the coast flying low over the water. When we attacked, the return fire was heavy, but nobody got hit bad. After we shot down the six we got, we ran out of ammo.

Mike Encinias remembered, "When I saw all those bombers flying past us, I thought at first they were friendly. I just couldn't believe we would have the luck to run across that many enemy aircraft. There were so many of them I didn't need to maneuver; I got behind them and fired till they went down. I stopped my attack when I ran out of ammunition after shooting down an He-111 and then a Ju-88."

Art Johnson reported, "I opened fire on one He-111. After several bursts its bombload blew up and I flew through the debris."

Bob Liebl recalled, "We left Borgo in the late afternoon, and came across the formation of bombers near dusk. We attacked and they scattered in all directions, dropping the torpedoes they were carrying. I picked an He-111 that headed inland on the deck. I got directly behind and fired five bursts and scored enough hits to see pieces of the left wing and engine fly off. A moment later the bomber dived into the ground but didn't burn." The battle was the biggest the 52nd had engaged in since North Africa.

The next day, four Spitfires were flying patrol over the invasion fleet when a formation of six Do-217s was spotted. One of the pilots was Art Johnson, who shot down one of the bombers for his second victory, while Lieutenant Clyde S. Cleveland shot down a second Do-217. Johnson recalled that his left cannon jammed, so that each time he opened fire, his Spitfire yawed to the right. "I began aiming at the left engine and would fire until the yawing brought the strikes to the right engine. After about three of these, the bomber plowed into the ground. Probably the yawing due to the jammed cannon saved me from being hit by return fire."

In early February, the 52nd was taken off dive-bombing missions when 90-gallon drop tanks arrived. With the increase in range provided by the new tanks, the group then flew escort missions for the B-25s of the 57th Bomb Wing for Operation *Strangle* missions. Several missions were opposed by the Luftwaffe, and the pilots showed that they hadn't forgotten how to shoot down enemy fighters during their six months on coastal patrol.

On February 19, the 52nd learned they would be trading in their Spitfires for new Merlin-powered P-51B Mustangs, and would transfer to the Fifteenth Air Force to fly long-range escort for the heavy bombers. They turned in the Spitfires – which were in turn handed over to the Free French – in early March 1944.

In early March as the Anzio operation turned into a stalemate, the weary P-39 Airacobras of the 350th Fighter Group touched down at Ghisonaccia Gare airfield to join the Spitfires of the Free French Armée de l'Air Groupes de Chasse GC II/7 "Nice" and GC I/3 "Corse," the first French units to be based on free French soil since 1940.

By late February, the 57th Group was well acquainted with their Thunderbolts following the rough start the 65th Squadron had experienced in their transition to the P-47 at the end of November

1943 – seen in retrospect as having contributed to the problems, since neither pilots nor ground crews were conversant with their new fighter. In January, first the 64th and then the 66th Squadrons had stood down from operations while all personnel received training about the new airplane, particularly its new powerplant, the Pratt and Whitney R-2800 radial, so different from the Merlin. Pilots were checked out by experienced P-47 pilots who explained to them how to get the most from the Thunderbolt as compared with the familiar P-40. The result was that when each squadron went operational, they did not suffer from the mechanical glitches that had plagued early operations by the 65th. By mid-February, all three squadrons in the group were fully checked out in the Thunderbolt.

Following the eruption of Vesuvius, the 57th received orders to transfer immediately to Corsica. Fortunately, the group's ground echelon was well versed in moving, and over a six-day period everything was packed and made ready for the move. On March 25, 1944, the group's ground personnel departed Naples on board a British-crewed liberty ship, headed for Corsica. The group's vehicles traveled on board two LSTs for the voyage. Departing Naples, the men were treated to a spectacular view from the harbor of nearby Vesuvius and the enormous ash cloud pouring from the peak. The voyage to Corsica was made through rough seas, with many crewmen felled by seasickness. Sergeant Gerald Schwartz, a crew chief in the 66th "Black Scorpions" recalled, "If there was any benefit to be derived from being seasick for many guys, it was that they were too sick to care whether or not we were to be bombed or torpedoed!"

The ship arrived at the port of Ajaccio, the capital city of Corsica, the afternoon of March 26, and the men spent the night under canvas in a nearby quartermaster camp. The next day, they departed at 0800 hours for a 170-mile trip to Alto airfield, located on Corsica's east coast, just south of the port of Bastia.

Lieutenant Colonel James Lynch, the ground exec of the 64th Squadron, recalled in his memoir that when they arrived at Alto, it was the best-prepared airfield they had come to in the 33 moves since they had first arrived in Egypt. A service group was already on the field and the mess and mess tents were already up. Amidst all the confusion of the arrival at Ajaccio, the only food they had received was cold C-rations the night before so the hot meal that was ready and waiting was remembered by all as the best welcome they had found at any of the fields they had operated from.

Alto airfield had been a swamp and was picked as an airfield because it would be the largest open area in the northern foothills when completed. The engineers had been working on the field since shortly after the new year, filling in the swamp. The PSP (pierced-steel planking) covering the ground meant they would be operating from an all-weather strip. After the muddy fields on mainland Italy where they had spent the winter, Alto was considered a great improvement all around.

The P-47s flew in from Italy three days later and flew the first mission from Alto on March 31. As XII Tactical Air Command's (TAC) only operational P-47 group, the 57th would operate from Corsica as a separate task force striking deep behind the enemy's right flank as the Thunderbolts went after the rail network and communications, with the top priority being destruction of locomotives, rolling stock, and motor vehicles.

Alto airfield was near the town of Folelli in the foothills. The scenery was beautiful: the islands of Pianosa, Monte Cristo, and Elba – the site of Napoleon's first imprisonment – could be seen in the distance. Newly promoted First Lieutenant Michael McCarthy – who had joined the 64th Squadron two weeks after the Palm Sunday Massacre of April 1943 – recalled, "Our squadrons made the transition to Corsica without incident. Advance parties had been in place long enough to set up tents and prepare mess halls, clubs, and maintenance facilities. Since they had been doing this for most of two years, they knew all the short cuts and problem areas." The 57th had a well-deserved reputation for being the best scroungers in the Air Force. If a needed item could not be borrowed or purchased, a team of "midnight requisitioners" would steal it. "Our road convoys were so diverse that it was difficult to identify the national identity of the group. We had more German, Italian, and British rolling stock than American."

After North Africa and Sicily, Corsica was a change for the better. McCarthy remembered, "After a tediously long hot day on the line, ground crews and pilots relaxed in the cool invigorating mountain stream. Improvised diving boards were constructed. Life in the mountains afforded a great many men a chance to rest in quiet and take things easy for a while, but for others who craved excitement, the complaint was that life was growing monotonous and dull." Passes were issued to the towns of Bastia, Ajaccio – birthplace of Napoleon – and Corte. Americans and Corsicans began to get to know each other.

Importantly, the group had modified the Thunderbolt to make it the effective fighter-bomber it became. While the initial equipment of the 65th Squadron had included some earlier P-47D sub-types, the other two squadrons received new P-47D-15s, which had the underwing pylons as factory-standard. Unfortunately, the pylons were set up to carry drop tanks, not bombs. The release for the wing tanks was on the floor of the left side of the cockpit, while that for the belly tank was on the floor to the right. Neither position was good for a pilot attempting to release bombs from those locations while keeping the airplane steady on a target in a dive.

The 65th's commander, Major Gil Wymond, had tasked Master Sergeant Bill Hahn, who brought Tech Sergeant Charles Appel into the project. An early fix had a cable from below the instrument panel attached to the release levers for the wing tanks. This worked, but as Hahn recalled it didn't allow them to drop a bomb from the fuselage. The final system had a bar welded to the wing tank release levers, running beneath the seat to the fuselage tank release lever, with one handle that allowed the pilot to release all three. Wymond had proven the system with a series of dive-bombing attacks on Yugoslavian targets in January. The system worked so well that XII Technical Command took the system and modified all P-47s arriving in Italy. Eventually, Republic took over and developed an electrical release system that appeared on the P-47D-25 and later sub-types. The P-47 was now an effective dive bomber. With the move to Corsica and the group's innovation and effectiveness in adapting the Thunderbolt as an effective fighter-bomber, the 57th Fighter Group was in high demand for tactical interdiction missions. Its designation as a separate task force specially assigned to the interdiction of Italian railway infrastructure eliminated any reassignment of the squadrons for escort or patrol missions.

Following the move by the "Exterminators" and the "Fighting Cocks," the "Black Scorpions" departed on April 2 for Corsica, flying a mission from Cercola with the other two squadrons to bomb different railway bridges and rolling stock in western Italy before landing at Alto. The 57th was ordered by XII TAC to generate 48 fighter-bomber sorties per day once established on Corsica. On April 3, the three squadrons flew two missions each – 96 sorties – exceeding all expectations.

The afternoon of April 6, two flights of eight P-47s led by Michael McCarthy left Alto on a railway recce mission to check out the rail line from Lake Trasimeno to Florence and identify possible dive-bombing targets while also engaging any targets of opportunity that arose. Within minutes of getting down low over the rail line, two trains were spotted and strafed; one locomotive was set afire and six wagons were damaged. Further on, several damaged but serviceable bridges were spotted, while a number of unbombed bridges and tunnels were spotted and noted for future reference. Finally, they spotted another train, which was unexpected in daylight.

McCarthy ordered two P-47s to cut the track ahead of and two to cut the track behind the train, then the other four strafed the locomotive, stopping the train. "I set up my flight to strafe freight cars immediately behind the disabled locomotive. I told my wingman to take enough space, keep me in sight, pick his own freight car, and do some damage. We were taking some light flak, less intense than usual. My wingman, Lieutenant Brown, stayed much too close to me on the first strafing pass, so close that his bullets flew over the top of my right wing, shooting at the same freight car." McCarthy curtly told the young lieutenant to move out further and concentrate on his own target to get some worthwhile results.

Brown moved out and his spacing was better, but unfortunately, he had lined up on the only obstacle in sight – a lone 100-foot pine tree. "Lieutenant Brown, who never saw that tree, hit it dead center with the hub of his four-bladed propeller, which sawed through the pine tree, and filled the engine space full of wood chips and sawdust." The collision knocked both wings out of alignment. With luck and the amazing toughness of the P-47, he remained in the air. "Understandably, he was in total panic. I caught sight of his airplane in a slight climb heading north, and pulled up on his wing."

Surveying the damaged Thunderbolt, McCarthy found it hard to believe any airplane could continue to fly in such condition. Keeping his voice calm to reassure Brown, he said they would keep climbing and that Brown should not touch the throttle. Brown complied with the directions, and after a few minutes, McCarthy believed they could try to return home and told Brown to follow his left turn back to Corsica. "If the controls responded well enough and the engine continued to run without drastic overheating, I planned to climb high enough to allow a safe bail out over water in case the engine quit. We had alerted the air rescue guys about that possibility." The P-47's windshield was covered with oil and debris and had been crazed in the collision. "I told him that I would navigate back to base. As minutes passed with the damaged airplane still flying, it was likely we would get home, but that raised a question. How do we get this wreck safely on the ground?"

They arrived over Alto at 6,000 feet. McCarthy told Brown to drop his landing gear. Without hydraulics, the main gear dropped out of the gear wells and looked to lock down. McCarthy made the approach on Brown's wing as the Thunderbolts made a circling descent and turned onto final approach. Brown managed to retard the throttle without killing the R-2800. Once on final approach, McCarthy moved ahead so Brown could fly formation on him as they descended toward the runway. When Brown touched down successfully, McCarthy accelerated and came around for his own landing. "Lieutenant Brown handled himself with courage and skill but decided his luck was gone. He did not fly another mission and neither did that airplane."

Another mission that day led by Captain Louis Frank finished their rail recce 6 miles south of Florence; climbing back to altitude, they sighted a formation of 11 Italian bombers flying low. The bombers were identified as ten obsolete Fiat BR.20Ms and a single Savoia-Marchetti trimotor SM.79. When the four dived to attack, the enemy pilots split their formation in two. Frank later reported, "We saw the formation below us and quickly positioned ourselves for an attack. The bombers split into two sections and I went after one with my wingman following. As one bomber came into my sights, I squeezed the trigger and saw my tracers hit the left engine and fuselage." The BR.20M was of wooden construction and quickly caught fire, spinning into the ground.

It couldn't have been more than ten seconds later that another bomber made the mistake of getting in my gunsight, and with only a short burst, he was on fire and spinning in. My wingman saw him hit the ground and explode.

I saw another bomber a short distance away. I fired on him and saw hits on the fuselage, and my wingman, Lieutenant Nevett, also got some target practice. His fire was true, with strikes near the cockpit, but this one was a little tougher. Our aircraft were faster and we overshot him; by the time we were able to turn around he had disappeared. When the flight landed, it was discovered Nevett's aircraft was the only one that had been hit by any return fire.

Second element leader Major Carlton Chamberlain also engaged the bombers, quickly shooting down a BR.20M.

I saw Captain Frank get one and Lieutenant Lenihan get another. I singled one out and fired a couple of bursts at him before he caught fire, but when it did start to burn, there was nothing that would have put it out. It hit the ground, a mass of flames. I did see one man jump and his parachute open before it started its last spin. I only had the opportunity to fire at one other bomber, and there were plenty of hits on it as many pieces flew off, but it wouldn't burn and I lost it before the job could be finished.

First Lieutenant John Lenihan, Major Chamberlain's wingman, went after the second formation of five bombers and downed three BR.20Ms.

I followed my leader down and then got in on the fun. One of the bombers was right in front of me so I pulled the trigger and it was soon in flames, spinning into the ground. I then banked to the left and another one was in my sights; with a short burst he too was set on fire and sent crashing to the ground in a mass of flames. I had to look around a bit for the third one, but after locating him, it didn't take long to finish him off. He caught fire like the first one and spun in. I've never seen anything like it. By that time there were no more to be found, so the only thing left to do was to get back into formation and come home.

The weather cleared on April 10. Missions flown that day resulted in claims for six locomotives destroyed, 40 wagons either damaged or destroyed, 27 motor transports of mixed types destroyed, one armored vehicle destroyed, and nine major rail cuts. Captain Marvin Parkhurst, who maintained the 65th's war diary, wrote, "If this keeps up, every pilot will have 100 missions or more and be on their way home by mid-summer. These kinds of operations sure keep the crews going, and they sure are doing a good job of it with plenty of spirit."

The 57th kept up the pace. On April 12, the 57th flew eight missions including the first mission over southern France. The 66th flew the most successful mission, destroying a series of seven ammunition and fuel dumps, with huge explosions. The largest of these saw flames shooting over 500 feet into the air; it was heard by other group pilots flying more than 2 miles away at 4,000 feet. One dump contained five camouflaged 10,000-gallon steel storage tanks that were partially destroyed. The mission's high point saw squadron commander Major William Benedict skip-bomb a thousand-pounder into a railway tunnel that was completely destroyed in the resulting explosion, with flames shooting out both ends and through the collapsing tunnel roof. Two days later the Thunderbolts bombed their assigned targets, then stayed low and shot up every moving train or motor transport they came across.

Luftwaffe fighters engaged the 64th Squadron, whose pilots acquitted themselves well, despite facing two-to-one odds. Captain Paul Carll shot down two Bf-109s while First Lieutenant Michael McCarthy destroyed one, and First Lieutenant G. P. Neese was credited with a probable; Carll's wingman, First Lieutenant Neal Gunderson, was shot up and became a POW when he was captured after he bailed out.

On April 18, Major Art Exon, commander of the 64th Squadron, flew through the secondary explosion on a bomb run, which set his P-47 on fire, forcing him to bail out; he was captured and taken prisoner within minutes. Major William J. "Jeeter" Yates – one of the group originals who had flown off the *Ranger* in July 1942 – returned to the group as deputy group commander on April 22 for a second tour.

At the end of the month, the group received word they had been awarded a third Presidential Unit Citation for "Pioneering in the adaptation of the high-altitude P-47 as a low-level strafing and dive-bombing aircraft." Over the course of the month, the 57th had dropped 1,346,500 pounds of bombs and fired 583,899 rounds of .50-caliber ammunition over 1,702 sorties. The group had averaged twice the number of ordered sorties on nearly every day.

An idea of just how dangerous the 57th's mission was can be seen from comparing the Missing Aircrew Reports (MACR) for the period between April 1943 and the unit's arrival on Corsica, which saw 20 pilots lost in that year, with the loss record over the second year of war in which the group flew as a dedicated fighter-bomber unit, losing a total of 84 pilots. The majority of losses were credited to ground fire. Of the 84 shot down, eight returned to the squadron after evading capture; only 18 emerged from POW camps at the end of the war.

The danger of their mission was not just from the enemy. Major Carlton Chamberlain, the group operations officer during the early days on Corsica, recalled his hairiest mission 50 years later:

One day when I was taking off on a mission from Corsica, the thrust from my propeller suddenly went to zero. We never found an explanation for it. I was just short of take-off speed, and was probably three-quarters of the way down the runway, when the thrust dropped away. I knew I wasn't going to take off, and I knew I wasn't going to be able to stop before I reached the end of the runway either. Therefore, I knew there was going to be a crash. I was carrying a full load of .50-caliber ammunition and two 500-pound bombs, and I didn't want to be in a fire with all those explosives, so I decided to jettison the bombs. I pulled the release, and those two bombs bounced end over end, keeping pace with me all the way down the runway! I had, of course, not armed the bombs, but I still didn't feel much comfort in that, inasmuch as they were bouncing on their fused noses every other cartwheel. They didn't explode, and I sailed off the end of the runway. I had taken every precaution that I could think of like turning off all electrical switches and closing the throttle. The area near the end of the runway had been built up so that it was level with the runway, and consequently there was a substantial drop-off past that. In addition, there was a small creek that ran cross-wise of the runway. My wheels caught on the far bank of the creek and caused the Thunderbolt to flip over onto its back. Because of the creek, the emergency vehicles had to go a long way to reach the crash. Several guys got there quickly on foot, however, and found me lying beside the inverted P-47 still wearing my parachute … I was not injured at all. The mystery lingers to this day.

The group was still experiencing equipment glitches with the P-47s, for which the ground crews found the solutions. 64th Squadron welder Corporal John L. Turnblom's solution to the problem of cowling brackets breaking, something that affected almost all new P-47s, was so good that Republic adopted it on their production lines. He recalled:

> They were getting persistent breakdowns in some of the airplanes. The lugs that held the cowling onto the airframe were molded into the aluminium cylinder heads of the engines. A lot of them broke, which grounded the aircraft. Republic sent three engineers to Corsica to examine the problem. Captain Frederick Ryan, our squadron engineering officer assigned me to work on the problem. I welded the broken parts. They tested the work for two days and did not have any trouble with the welding. After they accepted the welding, I had 79 airplanes to repair! They even sent some in from other outfits. If my welding had not been up to scratch the air force would have had to ship all these engines back to the factory and issue replacements. I got all them back in service in a short time and was awarded a Bronze Star for it.

The group was responsible for developing new tactics that were adopted by the other P-47 units in XII TAC. The 65th Squadron's First Lieutenant James "Wabbit" Hare recalled how they put new delay fuses to use in making extreme low-level attacks.

> We began to receive eight- to eleven-second delay fuses for our 500- and 1,000-pound bombs. The powers that be decided we could be more accurate in cutting the rail lines from low altitude, that is, from below 500ft. After a few missions, we started dropping the bombs singly in order to get more cuts. That meant putting your pipper a tad left of the tracks if you were dropping the bomb on the right wing, and vice versa. After we proved the effectiveness of this system, Major Dick Hunziker – our operations officer – decided that maybe we could skip-bomb railway tunnels. I was a flight commander, and my flight was selected to be the "Tunnel Busters." The other three were Stephen B. Secord, element leader, and wingmen Burton "Andy" Andrus and Herbert "Tommy" Thomas. We flew at least 20 of these hair-raising missions on the deck, strafing the target, dropping a single bomb and then immediately going into a high-G pullout to avoid the ridge the tunnel went through. On several occasions the bomb exited the other end of the tunnel before exploding, but

most of the time it detonated inside. I feel certain that we caught several locomotives hiding inside, thinking they were safer than safe. Before we finished that project, *Stars & Stripes* published an article and photo of my tunnel-busting flight.

The largest and busiest airfield on Corsica was Ghisonaccia Gare on the central east coast. The fighter units shared the field with the four squadrons of the 310th Bomb Group that arrived in late January from Philippeville, Algeria. The group had become anti-shipping specialists in operations across the Mediterranean after they were re-equipped with B-25G and later B-25H attack bombers armed with a 75mm cannon and 14 .50-caliber machine guns – sufficient firepower to shred nearly any maritime target.

From Algeria, the 310th's Mitchells ranged as far as the Greek islands of the Dodecanese and along the coasts of Italy and Yugoslavia. Following the move to Corsica, they went after enemy shipping in the Ligurian Sea and along the Italian coast, ranging as far as Toulon and Marseilles. Following the decision to base the 57th Bomb Wing's B-25s on Corsica, the 310th was transferred from XII Fighter Command and joined as the 57th Wing's third group. In April, their war-weary gunships were replaced by new silver B-25Js equipped for medium-altitude bombing.

Once the 57th Group was established on Corsica, momentum built for the final battles at Cassino, and the final days of March and the month of April 1944 were hectic. On April 16, the 340th's ground crews boarded trucks bound for Naples and went aboard an LST for the voyage to Corsica. On April 17, two B-25s left Gaudo-Paestum carrying the advance party, with a stop in Sardinia before flying to Corsica. After taking off in clear weather, they ran into a heavy storm over the Ligurian Sea and barely made it to their stop before severe weather closed in. The same day, three Mitchells from the 321st Group took off from Foggia, headed for Solenzara airfield on Corsica with the group advance party. By April 30, the rest of the group had made the crossing in small formations accompanied by ground crews to service the B-25s once there.

At Alesani, the 488th Squadron's Captain Thomas wrote that the living area was filled with cork trees amidst heavy underbrush: "It looks like it will be a nice set-up once everybody turns to and clears out his individual tent area." He noted the presence of fish in the nearby streams and wild boar in the nearby hills.

By the end of April, Corsica was an unsinkable aircraft carrier in the central Mediterranean; it would soon be known to the American aircrews there as "USS Corsica." However, the "unsinkable aircraft carrier" was in dangerous waters. The front lines on the Italian mainland were far to the south, while the enemy occupied all of Italy to the east and France to the north. Less than 30 minutes' flying time separated Corsica from German airfields on the mainland. XII Air Support Command was in effect operating behind enemy lines. No one paid attention to Axis Sally's May 1 broadcast, greeting the 340th Group and promising them a proper welcome, though this meant the enemy was now aware of their presence and planning action against them.

Michael McCarthy engaged a flight of Bf-109s while on a road-recce mission on May 2. "I found that the stories we had been told that the P-47 would come out second-best in a low altitude fight were wrong." While the rule was true for early model P-47s, McCarthy's new P-47D had water injection, which he used to give himself the winning edge and shoot down one of the Bf-109s before they flew off.

Following the fight, McCarthy heard a call for help from a pilot in the 65th Squadron, which had also been attacked by the Messerschmitts.

> I found him circling with his wingman in the area just vacated by the dogfight. One 20-mm shell had knocked out his instrument panel, leaving him without airspeed, altimeter, compass, or engine performance gauges. The second shell hit his right wing ammo compartment, exploding many .50-caliber bullets and forcing the door from its normal horizontal position to a vertical position that disturbed the aerodynamic flow across the wing, making the airplane fly in a severe crab. This was another example of a P-47 defying the principles of flight, flyable despite serious airframe damage.

McCarthy closed on the fighter and, after examining it from every angle, determined there were no leaking fluids or obvious structural damage other than to the right wing and cockpit.

> We decided I would lead back to Corsica with him on my wing. Because of the deformed right wing ammo compartment, we needed

to identify the airspeed at which the airplane would stall so we could pick a final approach airspeed for landing. At Alto, we circled the field high enough to permit a safe bailout. In the landing configuration, I slowed from 220mph calling the airspeed in 5mph increments. He found the pre-stall shudder began just below 170mph so we chose that speed for our final approach. I held 185mph as we turned to line up on final, slowing very smoothly to 170mph as we crossed the fence. He held excellent position, rotated, and touched down nicely with plenty of room to slow to taxi speed on the available runway.

Following the loss of 88 B-25s to Vesuvius in March, April saw the 340th Group start to receive new B-25J Mitchells right off the production lines in Kansas City and Tulsa. After the group moved to Corsica, they were completely re-equipped by early May. Sergeant Seegmiller wrote in his diary of the work necessary to modify the new airplanes for their role as medium-altitude level bombers:

Just now our Group is in process of being equipped with new airplanes, bright new B-25Js. They look sleek and shiny with their silver skins, but soon they will be beaten up and patched just like the ones we are turning in. Already we have begun stripping off guns and excess equipment in the amount of many thousands of dollars, equipment that just as well have never been sent to this theater of operation. I have been assigned one of the new planes and today it flew its first mission. Everything went off OK.

The "stripping" Seegmiller referred to included removing the four "package" guns mounted two on each side of the nose below the cockpit of the B-25J as a factory "improvement"; these bombers would not be taking part in any ground-attack strafing missions, unlike their Pacific cousins, and the weight saved allowed a heavier fuel load and a longer range.

May 12 was one of the bloodiest days for the 57th Wing's 321st Bomb Group. Twenty B-25s each from the 445th and 447th Squadrons bombed the Portoferraio docks on Elba, while 19 Mitchells from the 446th and 448th Squadrons bombed the Orvieto South railroad bridge. The intense and accurate flak over the bridge saw the 446th Squadron lose four of nine B-25s. One made a wheels-up crash landing on German-held Pianosa, south of Elba, where the crew became prisoners of war.

Axis Sally's words of welcome to the 57th Bomb Wing became actions the night of May 12–13. At 2200 hours, the bridge game the 340th Group's Captain Thomas and three friends were playing in their tent was interrupted when they heard explosions to the north. It was soon obvious that it was an enemy air raid. The men stepped out to see explosions light the night sky on the northern horizon.

Oberst Joachim Helbig, who had devastated Bari harbor while leading the last major German air raid back in December 1943, led 90 Ju-88s of I. and II./LG 1 that crossed out of northern Italy at sea level, thus avoiding Allied radar on Corsica. Borgo Poretta airfield outside the port of Bastia – home of the 1st, 52nd and 324th Fighter Groups – was their target. The bombers dropped fragmentation bombs and incendiaries on the field. The damage was extensive; more than 50 Spitfires of the 52nd Fighter Group were destroyed, along with over half the P-47s of the 324th, as well as more than 20 P-38s. As quickly as they appeared, the bombers disappeared into the dark sky over the Ligurian Sea as they headed home.

Helbig's raid affected every base on Corsica. At Alto, Lieutenant Colonel Lynch recalled that it was one of the days a soldier would not forget. After the group mounted two missions in the morning and one in the afternoon, members of the "Black Scorpions" were invited to have dinner with the French unit responsible for antiaircraft defense at Alto, which resulted in what Lynch recorded as an excellent seven-course French meal with wine, provided by the unit's cook who had been a chef before the war, who made the most of the unit's limited food supply. Lynch turned in around 2230 hours, only to be awakened 20 minutes later by the sound of explosions coming from the direction of Borgo Poretta airfield. Lynch emerged from his tent to find the sky over Bastia harbor lit up with searchlights. Moments later, the main fuel dump on the island was hit and exploded with what he described as real fireworks. Though Alto didn't appear to be under direct attack, everyone quickly moved to the slit trenches their experience in North Africa had taught them to dig upon arrival at a new airfield.

After an hour, during which the Germans dropped parachute flares over northern Corsica, things died down; shortly after midnight, Lynch and the rest of the group climbed out of the trenches and returned to their tents with the field lit by the fires still burning in Bastia and at Borgo Poretta.

With the excitement over, the 340th's bridge players returned to their game, calling it a night and slipping into their cots shortly after midnight. At 0230 hours, Alesani airdrome was roused by explosions on the field. Helbig's bombers had returned, reinforced by 60 more Ju-88s of KG 76. The raiders achieved complete surprise and lost no bombers. As at Borgo Poretta, they dropped incendiaries and fragmentation bombs on the bombers lined up on the field. They quickly departed, leaving 22 Americans killed and another 219 wounded at the two airfields. A pilot of the 488th Squadron later explained, "We had all these nice new shiny silver ships, and they reflected the light from the fires so well that the Germans had no trouble spotting where to drop their bombs."

These two raids were the last major bombing attacks carried out by the Luftwaffe in the Mediterranean Theater.

The survivors surveyed the damage in the cold light of dawn next morning. The devastation was widespread at Alesani, with 65 B-25s destroyed, leaving only 20 flyable Mitchells. It was the third time the 340th had taken a roundhouse punch in 19 months. The war diarist for the 487th Bomb Squadron later wrote, "Picks and shovels were at a premium throughout the area all during the daylight hours while those who didn't have a slit trench dug one and others improved upon theirs." In a gesture of defiance, the group attacked the railroad tunnel at Itri with the surviving bombers the next day.

That morning, the 445th's Sergeant Seegmiller wrote:

The weather is good again and for the last two days we have been going all out to support the 8th and 5th Army push against the Gustav line. Yesterday our planes were badly shot up. Two of the new Js were sent to the Service Group [the major engineering overhaul unit]. No one was injured in our squadron. This morning about 0400 Jerry bombed the 340th Group which is situated some distance up the coast. I did not go out, but the boys who did say it was quite a show. Today we learned that fourteen persons, including the Group CO were killed, 81 wounded and only 20 planes were left serviceable. We half expected them to return again, perhaps to this field, their results last night being so good. Our planes make a perfect target on account of as yet the dispersal area is not complete and they are all bunched along one taxi strip.

After the day's missions were flown, camouflage nets were draped over the silver B-25s at dusk; the ground crews remembered this was a difficult job, since they had to stand on top of stepladders, staying up by holding onto the heavy netting, which had to be dragged across the wings and over the fuselages, with the job taking over an hour to finish; this would become a regular part of the day, and the men who caught the duty frequently ended up missing the evening meal. Fred Anderson recalled he was happy to have a long-lived bomber that survived the bombing and was given a camouflage paint job, which meant it did not need the netting. On Sunday, May 14, 445th war diarist Captain William J. Nickerson wrote that for the first time since they had arrived overseas, men complained about a shortage of shovels and pickaxes as they extended slit trenches and turned them into bomb shelters. "Ingenious foxholes and slit trenches have appeared from nowhere. Some sport twigs, branches and boarding, some tin covering, while others closely resemble the I.R.T. and B.M.T. Subway entrances in New York City."

The three days after Helbig's raid provided a period of clear weather that allowed the various units on the island to maximize their operations in support of the Cassino battles. The three squadrons of the 57th Group averaged three missions a day for each. Lieutenant Colonel Lynch recalled that though all the missions were battlefield support, no pilots were lost until the final mission of the third day, when the 66th Squadron's Thunderbolts ran into intense flak over their target, losing two P-47s shot down with the pilots killed, and six others retuning to Alto badly shot up. The next two days saw rain showers that reduced operations to one mission each day by each squadron, which allowed the shot-up Thunderbolts to go through the group heavy maintenance section where extensive sheet metal work was accomplished that left the fighters looking brand new when they emerged from the shop.

Two 12-plane formations of B-25s from the 310th's 380th and 381st Bomb Squadrons flew a mission to bomb a railroad tunnel guarded by "88s" manned by gunners of the Hermann Göring Division; the flak was "heavy, intense and accurate." 381st Squadron bombardier Fred Nelson was startled by four salvos so close he heard the explosions even though his ears were covered by his headset.

I called "Bombs Away" and watched the light on the intervalometer record each drop. I called "bomb doors coming closed!" We whipped over in a near-vertical bank and dived after our leader, Lieutenant McLaughlin, who was in close to a vertical dive. When the airspeed indicator hit 350, I stopped looking, I didn't want to see any more. I looked back to see how the others were doing and the sky was black with flak bursts. Six of our planes were hit so bad they turned for a base in Italy knowing they couldn't make it back.

As if the flak wasn't bad enough, Nelson went back to check the bomb bay after they recovered and crossed the coast. He squirmed into the tight space between the bomb bay and the top of the fuselage, and unscrewed the "manhole cover" to make a visual check. "Even though I had every indication the bombs had dropped, I was dumbfounded to find not one bomb had dropped. We had gone through all that for nothing!"

The 380th Squadron's Second Lieutenant Clifton Campbell was flying one of the B-25s hit by an intense flak barrage as the formation approached the target. The right engine nacelle took a direct hit by an "88" that severed oil lines to the engine and cut the aileron cable, damaged the engine, and holed the gas tank in the wing. Campbell held formation long enough for his bombardier to drop the bombs, then the Mitchell took a second hit that destroyed the instrument panel, showering Campbell and his co-pilot with shards from the instruments. Amazingly, he was able to keep the bomber airborne. Without any instruments, he flew across 250 miles of ocean on one engine and landed successfully at Ghisonaccia Gare; the Mitchell was immediately pushed aside to become a source of spare parts. Twenty-one-year-old Clifton F. Campbell was awarded the Distinguished Flying Cross for getting his crew home alive.

The 324th Fighter Group – now the last unit in XII Tactical Air Command still equipped with the P-40 Warhawk – had such a record for accurate front-line close support bombing that Fifth Army specifically requested the group attack the German positions on Monastery Hill on May 12 with phosphorus and fragmentation anti-personnel bomb clusters. The 24 group pilots fought their way through bad weather and heavy ground fire to drop more than 5 tons of bombs on the German positions with pinpoint accuracy, with friendly troops only 300 yards away from their targets. Twelve more Warhawks dive-bombed and strafed a narrow gully on the hill where enemy troops were massing for a counterattack, turning the gully into rubble as the enemy attack went up in clouds of smoke. With that, the Poles were finally able to clear the barrier at Monte Cassino. Over the course of 26 days leading up to the final battle, the 324th had flown over 100 sorties per day, for a loss of 21 P-40s to enemy ground fire; the effort resulted in the group being awarded a second Distinguished Unit Citation.

The German air raid that night destroyed so many of the 324th's P-40s that the decision was made to immediately re-equip them with P-47s. Over the rest of the month, they would fly ground-attack missions with their remaining P-40s while pilots checked out in the P-47s as they were delivered to Borgo Poretta. The first P-47 missions were flown by the end of May.

On May 17, the 321st bombed the German fighter airfield at Viterbo in a low-level raid, knocking out six Bf-109s as they blanketed the field with fragmentation bombs.

The next day, Thursday, May 18, the 340th's aircrews and ground crews were still busy with buckets, mops, and brushes, slathering green paint cadged from the French squadrons at Ghisonaccia Gare on the upper surfaces of the surviving bombers and new replacement aircraft flown in since Helbig's raid. No one paid attention to the C-47 that landed with a load of supplies and replacement aircrew.

On May 19, three second lieutenants, a warrant officer, and three sergeants among the newly arrived replacements were assigned to the 488th Bomb Squadron. Flight Officer Francis Yohannon, the warrant officer bombardier, was accompanied by a skinny Jewish kid from Brooklyn who had dreams of becoming a writer and had just celebrated his 21st birthday on May 1. Bombardier Second Lieutenant Joseph Heller had graduated in the lower half of his navigation school at Santa Ana Army airfield, thus failing to qualify for training with a specific crew. Writing in his diary a week before he arrived on Corsica, Heller recorded his belief that he was ready to see action: "I want to see skies full of flak, and fighters screaming past in life and death duels high in the clouds."

Clearing skies allowed the Mitchells to support the battle at Cassino. The 340th's losses had been made up sufficiently to allow them to join the others as they went after German communications; flak at all targets was reported as "heavy, intense and accurate," and

19 B-25s of the 445th Squadron returned to Solenzara with varying degrees of damage from the batteries of "88s" defending the Rignano rail bridge.

On May 24, the "Black Scorpions" found a site where German trucks were being hidden during daylight. The other two squadrons also had flights in the vicinity, so the entire group was able to concentrate on the truck park. When they ran out of ammunition, they flew back to Alto and reloaded. The final flights were over the truck park at 2045 hours, which was still daylight under British Double Summer Time. When the last P-47s returned, pilots had put in claims for over 200 vehicles destroyed by strafing and bombing; in the 57th's administration, a "destroyed vehicle" was one that caught fire; claims were made for another 120 "damaged," which had not been seen to catch fire.

As the operation tempo increased in May, the inherent danger of working on aircraft designed to carry and drop explosives made life difficult and dangerous. On May 24, B-25J 43-27483, so new in the 486th Squadron she had no name, was being loaded by a team of four privates and two noncoms. Four 1,000-pound high explosive bombs were in a cart near the airplane. The plane had aborted a previous mission due to weather; the bomb bay was still filled with cluster bombs: six 20-pound fragmentation bombs wired together on a steel pipe. As the men unloaded these, one band broke loose; the bomblets became armed as they tumbled to the ground. One loader caught two, but the third hit the PSP. The loading crew was scythed by the shrapnel with five killed outright and the sixth badly wounded. The bomber's fully fueled wing tanks caught fire.

The alarm siren wailed as the squadron ambulance sped toward the fire. Screeching to a halt, driver Corporal Charlie C. Parker and medic Private John Palsma jumped out and rushed to the injured man. Bystanders screamed at them from cover to get away because the bomb cart had just caught fire. Parker and Palsma loaded the man on their stretcher and ran as fast as they could. They were less than 100 feet away when the four "thousand pounders" detonated in a shattering explosion, disintegrating what was left of the burning B-25 and throwing them to the ground; pieces of molten shrapnel showered them. The ambulance was blown off the frame, leaving only the chassis. One R-2600 engine was later found 300 yards away. Somehow

– though badly wounded – the two rose, grabbed the wounded man, and dragged him to safety, discovering he'd been killed in the blast. Of the six dead, the injuries were so extensive only three could be identified. For their disregard of their own safety, Parker and Palsma were awarded the Soldier's Medal; many believed they deserved far more than the lowest award. Armorer Robert Silliman remembered, "There was never a loading operation you did where you didn't know the slightest mistake would likely be fatal."

Joe Heller flew his first mission on May 25, to bomb the Poggibonsi railroad bridge. He later wrote:

> Poor little Poggibonsi. Its only crime was that it happened to lie outside Florence along one of the few passageways running south through the Apennine Mountains to Rome. As a wing bombardier, my job was to keep my eyes on the first plane in our formation, which contained the lead bombardier. When I saw his bomb-bay doors open, I was to open mine. The instant I saw his bombs begin to fall, I would press a button to release my own. That was the theory.

Distracted when he looked down at the target below, he froze when he saw the lead bomber drop its bombs and was a few moments late dropping his load, which blasted a hole in a mountain several miles from the bridge.

The bombers maintained their campaign against communications lines on May 26. The 321st's two afternoon missions met heavy flak and missed the Incisa viaduct and the nearby bridge. 446th executive officer Major Hunter's B-25 was hit by the "heavy, intense and accurate" flak while leading the formation toward the viaduct; the flak scattered the flight; only six bombers dropped their bomb loads on the structure, with poor results. Hunter's Mitchell was last seen heading southeast past Arezzo. Hunter held the plane steady so that co-pilot Second Lieutenant Walter Brickner, navigator Second Lieutenant John Kinney, bombardier Second Lieutenant Laverne Reynolds, flight engineer Sergeant John Denny, radioman Tech Sergeant Alfred Todd, and tail gunner Sergeant William Lanza could bail out successfully. Unfortunately, the bomber went out of control when Hunter left the cockpit and he was unable to get out of the stricken B-25.

First Lieutenant Frank L. Lonsdorf, pilot of the rearmost Mitchell in the diamond formation Hunter led, reported seeing the B-25 explode on impact with the ground. Reynolds and Denny were quickly captured, while Brickner, Kinney, Todd, and Lanza managed to evade and contacted Italian partisans, who kept them safe until advancing Allied troops freed them in July.

Returning to Corsica, Kinney reported what had happened:

On the bomb run, about 35 seconds before bombs away, our ship was hit by enemy flak. The nose was hit first and then the right wing suffered two hits. The Major rang for all crew members to abandon ship. Two men in the rear jumped almost immediately. The engineer, gunner and the bombardier then bailed out, and I was about to jump when the co-pilot called me back. An attempt was made to trim the aircraft, but it proved impossible to hold altitude. I jumped at about 4,000 feet; the altitude of the country below was 3,000 feet, and I did not, therefore, have much time to observe the stricken aircraft. I do remember seeing one other chute, which I believe to have been that of the co-pilot. I hit the ground with some violence and was knocked unconscious.

Kinney managed to avoid capture, later hearing that a body had been found in the aircraft. "He had worn a golden oak leaf, as well as a shoulder holster and a .45 revolver and .38 pistol. Major Hunter had always carried two guns, and had worn a shoulder holster; I am therefore positive of his death. The partisans said one man had been killed by Fascists, one man had been killed when his chute failed to open, and one man had been taken POW by the Germans." In fact, all three were taken prisoner and survived to be liberated on May 26, 1945.

B-25 43-4050 took an "88" hit that blew off the right rudder and a section of the right stabilizer as the right elevator fluttered away in the slipstream. In such a situation, a B-25 was nearly uncontrollable, but pilot Second Lieutenant Groh performed what the war diary called "a miracle of flying to bring the plane back," as he fought the controls all the way home. Lacking the control to land, Groh ordered his crew to bail out over Ghisonaccia Gare airfield, holding the bomber in a circle long enough for them to get out.

The 310th's crew chief Sergeant Frank Dean recalled what happened next:

The plane circled our field and dropped out everybody except the pilot. He flew the plane out to sea on the north side of Ghisonaccia Ville, maybe a quarter mile offshore. The plane rolled over on its back and the pilot dropped out the top escape hatch. When we saw it, we thought this was an intentional maneuver, but I heard later that the plane rolled over when the pilot let go the controls. The pilotless aircraft then righted itself, flew around a bit, then entered a dive.

In practically every village in Corsica there was a small grassy area that contained a monument to the boys of the town who had been killed in World War I. There was such a plot about 65 feet across in the very small village of Ghisonaccia Ville, and the MPs had a tent nearby. The bomber chose that plot to land on. Most of the fuel must have been used up for there was little fire, although it did destroy the tent. I visited the site after the plane had been removed. There was a new tent up and a sign in front: OFF-LIMITS TO AIRPLANES!

The rest of the planes bombed the Cecina road bridge on the way home. Captain Nickerson recorded in the war diary that "Photos showed that bridge too added to the growing list of bridges knocked out during the month of May. Lieutenant Cormier made a fine single engine landing. Lieutenant Conover's eye was slightly cut from flying Plexiglass. Sergeant Reddy received a mean flak wound in his arm. All in all, the 445th can consider itself proud and fortunate."

That night, Sergeant Seegmiller wrote:

Considerable activity. Today we are sending a total of 26 ships on two missions. The 8th and the 5th Armies in Italy joined forces yesterday. The kitchen has moved into the club house and food and feeding conditions are generally good. There are loud explosions taking place hourly. They are due to an engineer outfit using German mines to blast gun pits, latrines, etc. Today is pretty, though for two days we had a strong miserable wind. Margaret's letters are most satisfactory. We have no time off but I don't mind that because we are busy towards winning the war. We have had several alerts, but no bombs have been dropped on us. The squadron bombing lately has been pretty good.

445th Squadron pilot Second Lieutenant Charles Frederick Ritger, Jr., known to his family in Newark, New Jersey, as Fred, wrote home:

Hello Folks,

I guess I am a bit early with this letter but I just have to do something. One of my best pals went down today and it hit me as hard as a thing like that could. Lieutenant Laverne Reynolds, the best damn bombardier in the world, was knocked down while on a mission over Italy. I have become pretty much used to such things but he was such a swell fellow it is mighty hard to see him go. Enough for that now because I can't express what I feel.

I haven't received any more packages lately but I did get the Diary and the pack of Edgeworth (excuse me I mean Briggs). I also got a couple of pictures of Marilyn that were mighty fine. Pop will have to teach me when I get home. And that family photo, that was the kind of thing I go for. Please keep them coming.

I don't remember whether I ever told you about the plane I am flying now. It is painted olive drab, all except the nose section which is bright red. On the sides in large white letters is printed "Red Nosed Beckie"! I guess it's the old McCaddin Irish but that ship has been darned lucky.

I am applying for an absentee ballot for the coming elections and I would like some dope about the caliber of the candidates in the local area. Open up Pop and let's hear what you think about the guys.

I don't feel like writing much tonight so I will hit the sack.

I will write again soon.

Love to all,

FC Jr.

There was no let-up in the fighting over the following days and the bombers flew as often as possible in support of the armies. On May 27, 445th war diarist Captain Nickerson recorded:

Continuing the accelerated pace, four missions, totaling over a hundred sorties, were flown this date and five bridges knocked out. 445th Squadron bombing the North Massa road bridge on the last mission of the day placed 96 500-pounders directly in the target area, chalking up another hundred percent bombing accuracy mark for this Group. The 447th put ninety percent of their bombs on the Massa South bridge making the total effort for the complete mission highly successful. Three other bridges smothered by our bombs were the Orvieto North and South bridges and the Massa Railroad bridge.

Mission 313: On the second mission today, against the Vado Viaduct, nine aircraft failed to rendezvous but the other sixteen continued and laid a devastating pattern through and around the target. Photo interpretation showed that once again the 321st had bombed the target with one hundred percent accuracy. The one hundred percent total was tougher to attain this time since the flight had to fly through several minutes of heavy, intense, accurate flak which tended to scatter the formation. The fact that they stayed in there all the way is a tribute to the high degree of tenacity and skill maintained by the combat members of this group, which at present is "hotter" than during any other period in its history.

The Germans were getting better at opposing the bombers. By keeping the "88s" mobile, a bomber crew could suddenly come under attack any time after they crossed the bomb line. One pilot later recalled, "You tensed as soon as you passed the line. Then when you weren't fired at where they'd fired at you before, you might relax; and then suddenly they'd fire at you from a new place. That tension took its toll over time."

On May 29, while the 321st knocked out the Viareggio railroad bridge with several direct hits, there was more important news back at Solenzara. Captain Nickerson wrote, "The squadron latrines have been placed in the surrounding woods and completely screened in. There are footpaths leading to them that are not unlike the winding pioneer trails. These are the best latrines we have had since arriving overseas."

On May 31, 69 321st B-25s smashed roads and bridges at Cave, Subiaco, and Civitella Roveta. One plane was lost crash-landing at a friendly base in Italy. It had received a direct flak hit in the tail that blew the gunner out of his turret while two other crewmen bailed out 2 miles south of the target.

Navigator Second Lieutenant Daniel Galindo later recalled:

The target was attacked from an altitude of 9,500 feet on an axis of 200 degrees. After the bombs were released, a hard right turn was made and the formation flew over Valmontone. During violent evasive action over the city, our bomber received its first flak hit in the tail section. The plane immediately began to go downward. Fifteen seconds later the plane received more flak hits. An 88mm shell went through the right wing and gas tank. Another hit holed the fuselage and wing. The gasoline line in the bomb bay was cut and gasoline began to gush out. Before fifteen seconds more had elapsed, the bombardier bailed out. He was followed by the turret gunner whose vest-type parachute caught in the escape exit on the way out and left him dangling. I made an attempt to pull him back in the plane but his weight was too great. I lifted him forward enough to permit his chute to slide out. The aircraft recovered at 6,500 feet.

Pilot Second Lieutenant Gerald W. Wagner later reported:

Meager, distant and inaccurate flak was encountered on the last of the bomb run. After the hard break to the right during violent evasive action, the plane received the first direct burst of flak in the tail section. The plane started downward nose first. A check on the instrument panel revealed that the ball on the flight indicator was on the extreme left. I tried to trim the plane to prevent a possible spin. The elevator gave very little response and the aircraft continued downward. The other crew members were immediately notified to be ready to bail out. Several seconds later the plane leveled out with the aid of more power on the engines and I called out that everything was OK. The second hit, believed to be an 88mm, went through the right front main gas tank. A few seconds later, the navigator informed me that Lieutenant Werrlein and Sergeant Eiff had left the plane, disregarding the suggestion to ask the pilot first. Another burst came, hitting the wing, fuselage and the gas line in the bomb bay. I tried to call the tail gunner. The radio operator came forward and told me that he was blown out when the first burst hit the tail. I notified the flight leader to slow up so that I could join the formation. Upon checking the bomb bay, the navigator discovered gasoline gushing out of a broken line. The doors were opened to air out the bomb bay. I notified the flight leader that I would land near Anzio. The landing was more of a three-pointed landing because of the crippled elevator. Fuel and ignition were out on the approach and we rolled to a stop with the engines off.

Radioman Staff Sergeant James E. Kintly witnessed what happened to the tail gunner:

> We broke away to the right after dropping the bombs and the first hit blew me from my seat. While I was in mid-air – which to me seemed an eternity – I saw the tail gunner blown out of the plane. When the pilot got the plane under control, I fell on my back. As I got up, I heard the pilot calling the tail gunner. I notified him that he was blown out of the plane. The pilot notified me to stand by. We received another hit that shook the plane very badly. Somewhere along here I saw a chute open through the opening in the tail. Being under the impression that no one had bailed out, I called over the interphone to the pilot and told him that the tail gunner's chute had opened. It was only later that I discovered that his chute was still in the tail of the plane.

In the B-25 immediately to the rear in the formation, pilot First Lieutenant Damon McLain saw the whole event.

> On the turn off the target, I had just regained my position behind Lieutenant Wagner's plane when it seemed to explode and flare out. Quite a bit of debris came out of the tail with the tail gunner. He was spread eagled with his face and chest facing the sky as he went by, passing about ten feet below our left propeller. I did not see a parachute on his chest as he went by and I don't believe that he was wearing one. His clothes seemed to be badly torn and smoking. It was my impression that he was not conscious.

May 1944 saw the 321st Group take the heaviest aircraft losses in any single month since they arrived in the Mediterranean 16 months earlier; 14 bombers were lost, though fortunately most crewmen managed to get out.

As the Battle of Cassino reached its peak on June 2, the 57th Group sent out a flight of four P-47s from the "Black Scorpions" led by Captain Robert B. Abercrombie, to search for targets of opportunity as the Tenth Army struggled to retreat from the battlefield. If they found anything worthwhile, he was to radio, "Bananas are ripe."

Shortly after the Thunderbolts arrived in the area they were to search, they spotted artillery and trucks that were later identified as belonging to the Hermann Göring Division; Abercrombie sent the message, then led the flight in a bombing and strafing attack on the spotted vehicles.

Back at Alto, the rest of the group's aircraft were at readiness with pilots in the cockpit. Within minutes of receiving Abercrombie's message, the field reverberated with the sound of P-47s taking off. Flights went off individually to the target, and the afternoon was spent with planes taking off, hitting the target, returning to gas up and reload ammunition and ordnance, and return to the target. The missions continued until 2200 hours; final claims included 80 vehicles and several artillery pieces destroyed. It was the second heavy strike against the Wehrmacht the group had been able to pull off in ten days and marked the end of effective resistance by the Tenth Army.

The road to Rome appeared open and with it the end of the war in Italy.

7

THE COLOSSAL MISTAKE

Following three failed attempts to break the German lines on the Cassino front, in preparation for the fourth, the staff of Mediterranean Theater commander Sir Harold Alexander presented a battle plan that – had it been followed and carried out as described – would have led to the end of fighting on the Italian peninsula by the summer of 1944 following such breakthrough. That it did not was due to the inability of Fifth Army commander General Mark Clark to distinguish wider war goals from his ego-driven desire for fame as the "Liberator of Rome."

The Fourth Battle of Cassino was planned to begin in mid-May. British Field Marshal Sir Harold Alexander – now Allied Supreme Commander in the Mediterranean in Eisenhower's place since January – informed Allied commanders that the primary goal was "to force the enemy to commit the maximum number of divisions in Italy at the time the cross-channel invasion is launched." It was hoped that once the Gustav Line was broken, a breakout from the Anzio beachhead by a reinforced VI Corps would push across the major roads south of Rome and link up with the British Eighth Army attacking west across the Apennines. The linkup would block the retreat of the German Tenth Army and force its surrender. This could then result in a retreat from Italy by the remaining German forces in the north, ending the Italian campaign as the Allies crossed the Channel to invade Normandy.

US II Corps was to attack up the Ligurian coast along Route 7. To their right, the French Expeditionary Corps would attack out of the Garigliano bridgehead into the Aurunci mountains between the coastal plain and the Liri Valley. In the center, British XIII Corps would attack along the Liri Valley. To the British right, the 3rd and 5th Divisions of the Polish II Corps, newly arrived that spring from Iran, would take Monte Cassino and push into the Liri Valley to link with XIII Corps. The pinching maneuvers by the Poles and British were the key to success. Once the Tenth Army began to withdraw, VI Corps would cut off the line of retreat in the Alban Hills.

The battle opened at 2300 hours on May 11, with a massive artillery bombardment by 1,060 artillery pieces on the Eighth Army front and 600 on the Fifth Army front. Within 90 minutes, the attacking units were to move forward. In the event, US II Corps had made little progress by dawn of May 12, but the French Expeditionary Corps – led by Moroccan tribesmen from the Atlas mountains – captured their objectives and moved into the Aurunci mountains, considered impassable and therefore undefended. A crucial requirement was that Tenth Army be cut off from supply and reinforcement to the maximum extent possible.

The 57th Bomb Wing began flying two missions a day when Operation *Diadem* – a combined air/ground campaign designed to join II Corps, which was stopped at the Gustav Line, with VI Corps, which was in a stalemate on the Anzio beachhead – began on May 11, though operations were jinxed by the rapidly changeable spring weather, which saw rainstorms every few days. The three groups followed an operational profile in which two squadrons in a group launched 12 planes each for the morning mission, while the other two squadrons flew the afternoon mission. On some days during the battle, each squadron might fly as many as four missions, but such a "maximum effort" was difficult to sustain when half the squadron aircraft might be unavailable, being repaired from flak hits or undergoing engine changes. Tire changes hadn't been important in Africa, but on Corsica the PSP runways were bound together with wire; this frequently broke, allowing the sections to separate and creating runway surfaces that "ate tires morning, noon and night," as crew chief Sergeant Frank Dean recalled. Some bombers might fly every day, while others required additional maintenance restricting them to two or three missions a week. Aircrew could fly two to three missions a week, or nearly ten a month in normal operations. With a 50-mission tour, a man could see his tour completed in five months. This was a much shorter time than a tour in the heavy bombers, which flew perhaps three missions a week, with individual crewmen flying one or two of those missions.

Since the bombers were participating directly in the battle zone, it was crucial they know the exact positions of Allied ground units, to avoid the terrible consequences of bombing their own troops. Each group had an air liaison officer assigned from the ground forces. His duty was to keep a large map showing up-to-date Allied positions and to brief crews on the state of the land battle so they understood the mission's value, and to debrief crews as to what they had seen, for intelligence updates.

British Army Captain Dan Gurney arrived at Solenzara to become the air liaison officer for the 321st Group in early May. He understood from experience the need for crews to have such knowledge. "In April 1943, shortly after the capture of Tunis, the armored division in which I was serving as brigade intelligence officer was pulled back to rest some fifteen miles from the front. Between us and the front was a large flat lake, an unmistakable landmark one would think. In clear sunshine one morning, we received the full bomb load of a squadron of B-25s onto our innocent heads!" Gurney quickly hit it off with the group's intelligence officers, including what would be a lifelong friendship with Hollywood actor Jeffrey Lind, of the 445th Squadron. He was also popular for what he could obtain that they could not. "As a British officer, I was entitled to a monthly ration of Scotch from the British NAAFI (PX). As I didn't go for Scotch myself, I used to trade this for Hershey bars, for which there was no shortage of takers!"

The night of May 11, 1944, Captain Nickerson, S-2 (intelligence) of the 321st's 445th Bomb Squadron and the most thorough of the 57th Wing's war diarists, wrote:

Tonight Group Commander Colonel Smith called a meeting of the crew members and S-2 officers for the purpose of discussing the major push contemplated by the Fifth and Eighth Armies on the Italian front. He discussed the plan generally, beginning with the 1,400-gun barrage of ours which was to start at 2300 hours. Captain Abbott, the Air Liaison Officer, covered the plan in detail, going over the assignments of each division involved. The 321st was scheduled for air support for the Fifth Army and a busy few days ahead was ardently promised.

The 57th Bomb Wing was tasked with destroying as many bridges between Cassino and Rome as possible.

The weather only began to clear on May 11. On May 12, the 321st flew five missions between dawn and dusk, recording 114 individual sorties and establishing a new group record. Morning clouds hindered several missions. At 0630 hours, 12 B-25s from the 448th Bomb Squadron took off on Mission 280 to bomb the German command center in Pico. The clouds obscured the target, but the bombers were visible to the gunners below; several bombers took flak hits, and one was forced to ditch in the Ligurian Sea on the way back to Corsica. Clearing skies allowed the other missions to be flown successfully.

The French Expeditionary Corps captured Monte Maio on May 12, which put them in position to assist the Eighth Army in the Liri Valley. Kesselring sought to buy time to pull troops back to the second defensive position – the Hitler Line – ordering Tenth Army to put in every available reserve.

On the ground, XIII Corps made two crossings of the Rapido, despite strong resistance. Crucially, the 8th Indian Division's engineers succeeded in bridging the river by late morning; the 1st Canadian Armored Brigade crossed and provided vital support to beat off the inevitable counterattacks by German armor. By the afternoon of May 12, the Rapido bridgeheads had been expanded despite repeated enemy counterattacks.

The Poles assaulted aptly named Mount Calvary; they were forced to pull back in the face of a counterattack by German paratroops. The Polish infantry's leading units were all but wiped out by devastating mortar, artillery, and small-arms fire. Between May 12 and 15, Polish attacks and German counterattacks created heavy losses on both sides. The 4th Fallschirmjäger Regiment was reduced to 800 men from an original strength of over 2,000, while the Poles lost 281 officers and 3,503 enlisted troops. Witnesses described the battle as a "miniature Verdun."

May 14 saw Moroccan Goumier soldiers lead three battalions of the French Expeditionary Corps over the mountains parallel to the Liri Valley that the Germans had left undefended because they believed it impossible to traverse such difficult terrain, to outflank the German defenses in the rear of Monte Cassino.

On May 15, the German right wing began to give way under Allied pressure. The British 78th Division passed through the divisions holding the Rapido bridgehead and executed the turn to isolate the enemy still on Cassino from the Liri Valley.

In addition to the commencement of the Fourth Battle of Cassino, the month of May saw several changes in the fortunes of the 79th Fighter Group, which would play a major role in the battle. The group had moved from Capodichino to Pomigliano airfield in early May, which gave them a much longer concrete runway with concrete taxiways, making it easier for the Thunderbolts to taxi with a full 2,500-pound bomb load. At the same time, group commander Colonel Earl Bates left the 79th in order to take up command of the 86th Fighter Group, which was transitioning from the A-36 to the P-47, and bring it into the P-47 era. Bates' replacement was Colonel Charles W. Stark, member of the West Point Class of 1937, who had considerable P-47 experience, having been Officer in Charge for Fighter Development at Orlando Army airfield after spending time assigned to the P-47 development project at the Republic plant in Farmingdale.

Unfortunately, Stark's command was brief, lasting just a week. Flying on May 7 leading Red Section of the group's 86th Squadron on a train-busting mission near Civitavecchia, he spotted two trains of 15 and ten wagons each. The Thunderbolts dropped 28 500-pound bombs, which destroyed a dozen wagons and cut the rail line at four separate places. Flak was intense and accurate; Stark – flying brand new P-47D 42-25660, "X01" – was hit in the engine pulling out from his bomb run. Calling local ground control, codenamed "Grubstake," he stated he planned to ditch the P-47 at the Tiber River's mouth. Following the return to Pomigliano by the rest of the flight, a search mission was flown to locate Stark and First Lieutenant Stafford, who had also been shot down. Stark's P-47 was identified lying in shallow coastal water 5 miles north of the Tiber; the open canopy was proof he had gotten out successfully, though a further search did not find the colonel. Stark was captured after evading search parties for three days on May 10. Group command in the meantime was assumed by Major Melvin Nielsen, who had commanded the 86th Squadron since the previous December, just before the outbreak of the offensive.

The air component was primarily tasked with continuing to attack and destroy Italian railway infrastructure when Operation *Diadem* began, as well as any other transportation available to the German Tenth and Fourteenth Armies. Additionally, these air units would be attached to advancing ground units to provide close air support over the battlefield as the Fifth and Eighth Armies pushed the advance.

Six weeks of constant destruction of Axis trains, motor transport, and anything that moved had taken its toll. The 79th Group's three squadrons changed their focus from railway infrastructure and began attacking road bridges and motor transport. Seeking targets northeast of Rome, 15 85th Squadron P-47s took off at 0515 hours, looking for the Tenth Army's main line of retreat. They carried no bombs, intending to strafe anything they came across. The Thunderbolts were over Foligno at 0615 hours. Spreading into line abreast, they took up the hunt from an altitude of 100 feet. The first vehicles they surprised had no chance to get off the road, and 17 trucks and other transport were on fire with another 12 severely damaged. Flak was intense; two Thunderbolts took hits but kept flying. The squadron returned to Pomigliano at 0745 hours to refuel and rearm, departing for a second mission by 1000 hours. Carrying 1,000-pound bombs, their target was a railroad bridge outside Acquapendente on the eastern side of Lake Bolsena. Weather closed in over the target, so they diverted south and scored three direct hits on a bridge 20 miles south of the original target, with the rest near misses.

The 86th Squadron took off 45 minutes later and managed to hit the Acquapedente bridge, dropping 30 1,000-pound bombs, and putting a 20-foot hole in the span while cratering the northern and southern approaches. Two hours later, the 16 87th Squadron Thunderbolts took off carrying 32 1,000-pound bombs to add to the destruction of the bridge. En route, they ran across 15 Bf-109s and five Fw-190s; eight P-47s jettisoned their bombs to take on the enemy. Another 10–15 Bf-109s entered the fight, while the other eight Thunderbolts attacked the bridge, scoring several direct hits. Three Bf-109s were shot down, with First Lieutenant Damon Adkins credited with two and Second Lieutenant Walter Petermann credited with one and an Fw-190 probably destroyed. One pilot was hit and was forced to divert to Anzio. Post-strike analysis noted that the P-47 – which was not considered a low-altitude fighter – was able to stay with the Bf-109s below 2,000 feet.

While the British moved forward, the Poles launched their second attack on Monte Cassino. The fight on the ruined heights was fierce and at times hand-to-hand as they advanced under constant artillery and mortar fire from the strongly fortified enemy positions with little natural cover. The survivors were so battered that finding men who had the strength to climb the few hundred yards to the summit was difficult. A patrol from the 12th Podolian Cavalry Regiment finally made it to the top and raised a large Polish national flag over the ruins.

The Poles had opened the road to Rome.

The Tenth Army's line of supply was now threatened by the destruction of several bridges and the Franco-British advance in the Liri Valley. On May 17, the Polish II Corps and the British 78th Division linked up in the Liri Valley 2 miles west of Cassino. Faced with encirclement, the Germans began withdrawal to the second line of resistance. Previously called the Hitler Line, the secondary defenses had been renamed the Senger Line at Hitler's insistence in order to minimize significance if it fell. While units of the Eighth Army advanced up the Liri Valley, the Fifth Army moved up the coast, having broken the Gustav Line at Formia.

Getting 20,000 vehicles and 2,000 tanks through the ruins of the Gustav Line took several days as the Allies dealt with the blasted bridges and roadblocks the Corsica bombers had created. The weather began to change on May 20 as rain showers spread, limiting the missions the 57th Wing could fly from Corsica. Rain kept the Mitchells grounded on May 21, while the next day the famous Corsica gales began blowing. Some men discovered they had not properly set up their tents when they were awakened by their collapse.

The Polish II Corps attacked Piedimonte San Germano in the continuing rains on May 23. The fight against the veteran 1st Fallschirmjäger Division was difficult. The attack by the 1st Canadian Division on the Hitler Line breached the defenses the next day, allowing the 5th Canadian Armored Division to pour through the gap in the enemy lines.

At Anzio, the panzer divisions had been pulled out of the German lines and ordered south to rescue Tenth Army at Cassino. The 26th Panzer Division's movement was halted when they came to the bridges that had been knocked down by the Corsica bombers.

By late May, approximately 150,000 Allied troops were in the Anzio beachhead, even after the 82nd Airborne's 504th Parachute Infantry was withdrawn on March 23 to join the rest of the division in Britain, preparing for the Normandy invasion. There were now five American and two British divisions facing five German divisions in prepared defenses; however, the enemy units were weak in officers and NCOs following more than three months of combat with few replacements since priority was given to units on the Gustav Line. The German units now lacked any reserves.

The breakout from Anzio was codenamed Operation *Buffalo*. General Truscott's meticulous plan called for the British 5th and 1st Divisions on the left to attack up the Via Anziate to hold the German 4th Fallschirmjäger, 65th Infantry, and 3rd Panzergrenadier Divisions in place while the American 45th Infantry, 1st Armored and 3rd Infantry Divisions made the main assault against the German 362nd and 715th Infantry Divisions, striking respectively toward Campoleone, Velletri, and Cisterna.

At 0545 hours on May 23, 1944, a bombardment by 1,500 Allied artillery pieces began; after 40 minutes of sustained fire, the guns paused as an all-out low-level bombing and strafing attack was made by the XII ASC fighter-bombers. The infantry and armor then advanced, covered by a rolling artillery barrage. Fighting was intense: 100 tanks of the 1st Armored Division were lost, and the 3rd Infantry Division suffered 955 casualties. The German 362nd Infantry Division lost half its fighting strength.

German General Mackensen expected the main Allied advance on the line of the Via Anziate. The ferocious British feint on May 23–24 had the general convinced he was right. However, Marshal Kesselring was convinced the Allied goal was to take Route 6 and block the retreat of Tenth Army, which by this time was withdrawing under fire from Cassino. Kesselring ordered the Hermann Göring Panzer Division to hold Route 6 open to allow Tenth Army to make its escape.

Cisterna finally fell to the 3rd Division the afternoon of May 25, after a house-to-house battle with the survivors of the German 362nd Infantry; refusing to withdraw, the 362nd ceased to exist as an organized unit. By nightfall, 3rd Infantry was headed into the Velletri Gap near Cori, while the lead elements of 1st Armored were within 3 miles of Valmontone, in contact with units of the recently arrived Hermann Göring Division. Over three days of fighting, VI Corps had taken over 3,300 casualties, but Operation *Buffalo* was on schedule and going to plan. General Truscott was confident the concerted attacks by 1st Armored and 3rd Infantry Divisions the next day would see his troops take Route 6, blocking the further Wehrmacht retreat from the south.

By May 24, the Germans were pulling back from the Anzio beachhead from their positions in the Alban Hills. The roads in all directions were filled with enemy motor transport as daylight dawned. An early morning patrol from the 86th Group spotted this movement. Radioing the news back to their base at Marcianise, the group quickly responded. Throughout the day, as planes returned and were refueled and rearmed, the A-36s made life hell for the retreating Wehrmacht. By the end of the day, their score was over 200 vehicles destroyed and likely double that number damaged. The German withdrawal became a rout under the relentless air attack. Overall, the Mustang dive bombers were responsible for nearly one-third of all enemy vehicles destroyed by all units of XII TAC command during the Fourth Battle of Cassino.

The 79th Group's 86th Squadron set several new records on May 24. The day's first mission took off at 0540 hours for a road recce to strafe targets of opportunity. An F-6 Mustang from the 111th Tac Recon Squadron guided the P-47s onto a 30-wagon train near Riano, north of Rome. The 20 1,000-pound bombs demolished the train and the rails beneath. No longer encumbered by bombs, the Thunderbolts looked for targets of opportunity as they flew back to Pomigliano. They found 20 vehicles that attempted to disperse off the road once they were sighted. The Thunderbolts' machine guns quickly set 17 soft-skinned vehicles on fire.

On the third mission of the day, the Thunderbolts were guided to an enemy tank concentration near Arce, northwest of Cassino, by an RAF Spitfire. They dropped 22 1,000-pound bombs on the tanks, scoring ten direct hits and 12 near misses. Five tanks were confirmed destroyed, with the explosions reaching an altitude of more than 1,000 feet. The P-47s stayed low, hunting more targets of opportunity, and caught a six-gun 40mm flak battery by surprise, destroying all six and setting the ammunition truck on fire.

Over 14 hours of continuous operation, the 79th Group had flown 12 complete missions, 156 sorties, with an average mission length of one hour, 45 minutes. The missions included armed reconnaissance, strafing, close air support of ground units, and rail busting. A total of 306 1,000-pound bombs were dropped, more than a heavy bomb group would drop in one mission.

While the 79th and the 524th were flying close air support mission to support the Allied offensive as it pushed north, the 57th Group on Corsica continued operating strictly in the interdiction role. May 25 was the most intense day, with the 66th "Exterminators" increasing its air-to-air and air-to-ground scores. After dropping a three-span railway bridge, the formation split into two flights, with six P-47s in each. 66th Squadron CO Major Benedict led one, with the other led by First Lieutenant George Kriss, with both seeking targets of opportunity.

Kriss's flight was jumped by eight Fw-190Fs of I./SG 4 that came in from "7 o'clock" high. The flight dived under the enemy fighters to gain airspeed for the fight. Kriss then turned 180 degrees; he immediately found two Focke-Wulfs in his sights. Opening fire on the wingman and then the leader, Kriss followed both until they hit the ground. Kriss's wingman, Second Lieutenant Edwin Flood, fired a 30-degree deflection shot at another Fw-190 that attempted to attack them; pieces flew off around the canopy before it also crashed with the pilot likely dead at the controls.

First Lieutenant William Ehney spotted another Focke-Wulf as it made a 180-degree turn to turn onto his tail. Ehney shoved his stock over and stomped the rudder pedals, pulling through the turn faster to come out on the Fw-190's tail and scoring multiple hits when he opened fire. The stricken enemy fighter hit the ground almost immediately. Second Lieutenant Robert Kaiser was last to score, leaving an Fw-190 smoking badly.

Two P-47s failed to return. After the formation split in two, Major Benedict's six P-47s came under intense antiaircraft fire; Benedict's wingman, First Lieutenant Mervin Hitchcock, was hit and his plane was badly damaged, with him bailing out to be taken prisoner. Kriss's flight lost Second Lieutenant William Dickinson, who was hit in the Fw-190's initial bounce; mortally wounded, he bailed out but had succumbed to his injuries when he was found by a German patrol shortly thereafter.

Victory was declared at Cassino on May 25. By dusk, the Poles held Piedimonte; resistance by the Tenth Army collapsed as fought-out units began surrendering. The road to Rome was clear, with Tenth Army units that could avoid the Allies now in full retreat.

Major John Dolny, commander of the 86th Group's 527th Squadron, had good reason to appreciate the rapid advance VI Corps made as the troops emerged from the Anzio beachhead. He later remembered the mission he and his wingman, Second Lieutenant Finlayson, flew on May 25: "My wingman and I attacked a group of enemy vehicles in the valley south of Rome. As I broke off my strafing run, I was hit in my coolant radiator behind and below the cockpit. My wingman told me I was streaming coolant, so there wasn't much time before the Allison would overheat." Dolny turned toward Anzio and climbed to 3,000 feet to get over the Alban Hills. "After I got over the hills, I reduced power and the engine kept running, but now I was over a solid undercast; the engine began to run rough and I prepared to bail out. I told my wingman to head on back to base."

Dolny unfastened his harness and oxygen mask as he descended into the clouds. "When I broke out below the clouds, I could see the beachhead in the distance and knew I couldn't glide that far. We had been told on briefing that the bomb line was east of the main Rome–Naples road, and I knew I couldn't get that far before I had to get out." With the temperature gauge rising and afraid the engine would blow, Dolny went over the side at 1,000 feet. The parachute opened and he made one swing before hitting the ground. His Mustang impacted nearby and exploded. "I figured I was in enemy territory. I looked down the hillside and saw what looked like a command car, so I gathered my 'chute and hunkered down in the tall grass." He soon heard an American voice nearby say, "I think he's over there." "I got up and made my position known."

The soldiers were an American reconnaissance patrol. They took him back to the field hospital at Anzio. "I was given medical attention, a martini, and I spent the night. The next morning, they fixed me up with a crutch and I caught a C-47 back to Pomigliano." Once there, a Red Cross girl drove him to the 86th's airfield. "Once back home, I found that the Army had broken out of Anzio and I had luckily bailed out on our side of the lines. My Assistant Ops Officer was also hit and bailed out, but he wasn't so lucky as I was and was captured by the Germans. In ten days I was back flying missions."

On May 25, the 79th Group's "Skeeters" shot up 25 trucks with another 40 damaged on one mission while losing two pilots to the vicious enemy light flak, indicative of the pace of operations. Though diminished, the Luftwaffe was still present over the battlefield. During an afternoon mission the same day, as the 16 "Skeeter" Thunderbolts pulled out of their bomb runs against a target north of Rome, they were intercepted by 20 Bf-109s. Lieutenant William Fuestal battled to get away from four Bf-109s, shooting down one, then sending the wingman to crash in a ditch and explode. Lieutenants James Blassingham, Ferdinand Tichenor, and Robert Noell each claimed one in low-level fights. With that, the surviving German pilots turned away to the north while the "Skeeters" headed home.

To this point in the battle, close air support by P-47s for advancing ground units was limited. Such activity was a "third phase" priority, following achievement of air superiority and successful interdiction of enemy supply lines. As the Fifth and Eighth Armies moved north, the Thunderbolt came into its own as the Air Force's best close air support assault fighter. The 524th Squadron's pilots may have been the first to use the Thunderbolt in this role, supporting the breakout from the Anzio beachhead. Such operations were inherently dangerous, which was proven by the fact that though their first week of operations was successful, they lost aircraft and their pilots. The squadron's operation report made at the end of May noted, "Flak was not much heavier than usual, but due to the fact that the unit was pressing its attacks very aggressively and also because a large amount of strafing was done, the enemy downed more of our airplanes during this period than at any time in the past ten months. Seventeen P-47s were damaged by flak and four lost." Fortunately, three of the four lost pilots were able to bail out successfully and return to base. The fourth was Captain Benjamin L. Rorie, the squadron commander, who was killed by a direct hit while strafing tanks and trucks.

In ten days of operations during the final breakout, the 524th Squadron claimed the destruction of 132 trucks, 15 tanks, two armored cars, seven artillery pieces, three motorcycles, and more than 100 wagons destroyed or damaged. On May 25–26, the 524th and other Thunderbolt units attacked targets in the heavily traveled escape route through the Velletri Gap. At the end, claims were made for 1,050 enemy cars, trucks and tanks destroyed, which was confirmed by advancing Allied units who made a ground count.

Just as all operations appeared to be moving as planned, with VI Corps and the Eighth Army set to link up the next day, the night of May 25 General Truscott received new orders from General Clark via Fifth Army operations officer, Brigadier General Don Brand, to implement Operation *Turtle* and abandon Operation *Buffalo*. This involved turning the main line of attack 90 degrees to the left, away from Route 6. While 3rd Division would continue to advance toward Valmontone and Route 6, 1st Armored was to withdraw and prepare to exploit the breakthrough along the new line of attack. Importantly, General Clark did not inform General Alexander of this change of orders until 1100 hours on May 26, by which time the change was a fait accompli.

The next day, as VI Corps initiated the difficult maneuver, Marshal Kesselring threw four divisions into the Velletri Gap, stalling the advance on Route 6 in a four-day battle with 3rd Division before they withdrew on May 30, keeping Route 6 open to allow seven Tenth Army divisions to withdraw from southern Italy and head north past Rome.

General Clark's order shocked Truscott, who later wrote:

I was dumbfounded. This was no time to drive to the north-west where the enemy was still strong; we should pour our maximum power into the Valmontone Gap to ensure the destruction of the retreating German Army. I would not comply with the order without first talking to General Clark in person. However, he was not on the beachhead and could not be reached even by radio. Such was the order that turned the main effort of the beachhead forces from the Valmontone Gap and prevented destruction of the German Tenth Army.

There has never been any doubt in my mind that had General Clark held loyally to General Alexander's instructions, had he not changed the direction of my attack to the north-west on May 26, the strategic objectives of Anzio would have been accomplished in full. To be first in Rome was a poor compensation for this lost opportunity.

In the early hours of June 4, 1944, reconnaissance units of the 1st Armored Division were the first American units to enter the city limits of Rome; within an hour, the 1st Special Service Force became the first Allied unit to move into the heart of the city. Over the course of the morning, Fifth Army entered Rome, which the Germans left as an "open city." General Eisenhower had refused to delay the Normandy invasion for General Clark's victory celebration, despite his entreaties. While his troops marched past the ruins of Imperial Rome, the Tenth Army managed to move to the east and north around the Eternal

City; with that, they broke out of the failed trap and continued north, pursued by the Canadians.

During the advance on Rome, air-to-ground and ground-to-air communication was found lacking. Requests for close air support had to move up the chain of command to Corps level, then sent through channels to the supporting aviation elements; this wasted precious time and potentially cost lives. The speed of the advance during the last week of May caught many supporting aviation units off guard; with friendly ground units not in their expected positions, friendly fire incidents resulted.

Two systems of forward air control had been developed since the Sicilian campaign. "Rover Joe" teams had been used since the Sicilian campaign. A "Rover Joe" team was composed of a fighter pilot, a ground officer, and an enlisted radio operator/driver, with a jeep fitted with an SCR-522 radio to talk to airborne fighters and an SCR-191 long-range radio for communication with higher headquarters. Once fighters had hit their primary targets, they checked in with "Grubstake," "Acorn," or another sector controller; the fighters were handed over to a "Rover Joe" team for direction to targets of opportunity. The fighter pilot on the team would talk the aircraft in on a target, using a "pilot's eye" to describe the target to the airborne hunters. This was an adaptation of the system developed by the Desert Air Force in North Africa.

The other method was developed by the 1st Armored Division, using the division's three Stinson L-5 spotter aircraft, which were nicknamed "Horseflies." They were equipped with High Frequency (HF) radios that enabled them to talk directly to P-47s operating in their sector. If there were no fighter-bombers immediately available, the L-5 pilot reported back to the division artillery fire direction center, and the mission request was passed through channels. Once the mission was assigned, the inbound P-47 pilots called in on the L-5's frequency and were talked onto the target by the "Horsefly" controller. This system was used to great effect on June 5, when the 524th Squadron's P-47s were assigned to cut the rail line between Orte and Capranica. Once they dropped their bombs, the pilots contacted "Grubstake" for targets of opportunity. They were vectored south of Monteresi and east of Lake Bracciano, linking up with a "Horsefly" controller who led them to a release point where they could make strafing attacks on a concentration of vehicles.

The pilots sighted 50 trucks parked under the trees just off the road. Defensive fire was mostly small arms and light machine guns, but was fairly intense and accurate. First Lieutenant Robert LaFollette's Thunderbolt took hits while strafing that caused him and his wingman, Second Lieutenant Shank, to divert to Nettuno. The 524th returned to Pomigliano claiming seven "flamers," one truck destroyed, and 16 damaged. When LaFollette and Shank returned, an additional four trucks destroyed and two damaged were added to the day's tally.

Over the next six weeks, Eighth Army harried the retreating enemy over 225 miles to Perugia; in mid-July, seven Tenth Army divisions linked up with the Fourteenth Army, which held the Trasimene Line. Both armies then made a fighting withdrawal to the formidable Gothic Line, where they arrived in early August. Clark defended himself regarding his desire to take Rome, writing after the war, "We not only wanted the honor of capturing Rome, but felt that we deserved it. Not only did we intend to become the first army to seize Rome from the south, but we intended to see that people at home knew that it was the Fifth Army that did the job, and knew the price that had been paid for it." A greater price for Clark's ego would be paid by American, British Commonwealth, and Brazilian soldiers and airmen over the next 11 months in a war that wouldn't have happened had the general been able to keep his ego in check and his eyes on the greater goal. As correspondent Alan Whicker observed, regarding Clark having failed to follow orders, which led to the perceived waste of lives as a result: "If he had been German, Hitler would have had him shot."

8

PURSUING THE WEHRMACHT

While General Clark reveled in his victory parade through Rome, the Tenth Army poured across the 11 of 14 bridges over the Tiber River that were undamaged, headed toward the refuge of the Gothic Line in the mountains south of the Po Valley. VI Corps left the liberation of Rome to others, crossing the Tiber in pursuit of the enemy on June 5. Two days after Rome was liberated, the Allies landed at Normandy. The good news led to feelings of euphoria among the exhausted men of the Fifth and Eighth Armies and Twelfth Air Force, as it now seemed possible the war might end soon. However, it was soon clear the Germans had not received the message that they should now quit.

On June 9, the Allies took the ancient Roman port of Civitavecchia. As they continued north, VI Corps ran into stiff German resistance at Grosseto; the enemy was not defeated until June 16. After a four-day battle, the island of Elba – once Napoleon's prison – fell on June 19. As VI Corps fought on, the French Expeditionary Corps, Polish II Corps, and Canadian I Corps kept close on the Germans' heels. Following a four-day house-to-house battle, the ruined city of San Vicenzo was taken on June 27. The French pushed forward west of Lake Trasimene; by the end of June, they were 5 miles from Siena.

As the Allied force chased the enemy to the Arno River, there was a major shift in XII TAC planning. The changed battle situation required a change in basing of the fighter-bomber groups for the coming operations. While Pomigliano and Ciampino airfields were well within range of Rome and the vicinity, as the Allies advanced to the Arno River, they were moving out of operational range for the P-47 groups based on the mainland. Fighters flying from Corsican bases had to cross 100 miles of the Tyrrhenian Sea to reach mainland Italy, while southern France was almost 200 miles from the P-47 bases at Alto, Serragia, and Ghisonaccia. Borgo Poretta, on the northeast coast, was just under 200 miles distant. By mid-July, all units had been moved to Corsica, and the summer of 1944 saw P-47s of the 57th, 324th, and 79th Groups and the 57th Bomb Wing's B-25s hitting roads, bridges, and railroad infrastructure, as well as road traffic and trains throughout northern Italy.

June saw the 57th Group receive new replacement P-47Ds with bubble canopies. What was most memorable to the pilots was that the airplanes were not painted with camouflage, but were rather a shiny silver. As "Wabbit" Hare recalled, "The fact these airplanes were silver, and not camouflaged, was taken as proof we must be winning the war." Michael McCarthy remembered:

> We expanded our operations to the Po Valley between Bologna, Turin, Milan, and the main railroad line running through its center along the Po River. German supplies had to transit through this rich, fertile, industrialized part of Italy in order to have any chance to benefit their forces holding the Allies. Activity in the Po area was incredible. Marshalling yards in each city were bustling where the Germans assembled trains during the daylight to make runs to the front at night.

Italy was now a secondary theater of operations to the overall Allied war effort. With the targeting focus of Operation *Strangle* expanded in light of the likelihood of operations soon stretching into southern France, XII TAC was able to interdict enemy supply lines and infrastructure there as well as the enemy supply support in Italy.

The 79th Group, which was still based at Pomigliano, near Naples, was now out of range of the front lines; on June 7 the group was ordered to move to Corsica where they would be based at Serragia. The Thunderbolts arrived on June 11 and flew their first combat mission the next morning. By June 15, the ground echelon arrived by sea and moved over the next three days to their new base.

Pilots of the 79th had grown used to plush, indoor quarters at Pomigliano; they were now living in a crowded tent village a mile's walk from the airfield. Many complained about the food quality and how slowly the "literally mile-long chow line" moved. With the move to Serragia, bridge- and train-busting became the mission. Two missions per day with three flights in each became the standard schedule again. On June 13, 12 P-47s of the 87th Squadron were taxiing for takeoff on a bridge-busting mission when a flash message canceled the mission. A recon flight over Genoa had spotted the Italian aircraft carrier *Aquila* in the harbor, moored under camouflage netting and flying the German flag.

The Thunderbolts were hastily reloaded with 500-pound bombs and took off shortly thereafter for Genoa. While one pilot aborted just after takeoff when he discovered his gear would not retract, the others continued on; after 45 minutes, they were over Genoa at 1515 hours. The P-47s spread into three line-abreast formation and headed toward the target at 1,000 feet. The first two bombs penetrated the carrier's starboard bow just above the waterline and exploded inside; two more direct hits amidships were followed by four on the stern. The ship caught fire and the flames spread. More direct hits were scored on the pier, resulting in new fires and a massive explosion. Four P-47s strafed the flight deck from bow to stern. As the Thunderbolts headed back to Corsica, the *Aquila* emitted columns of white and black smoke that rose above 1,000 feet. The defending flak was the most intense any pilot had seen in months; First Lieutenant Tom Hawk and his P-47 both took severe hits; fortunately, he was able to fly the barely flyable Thunderbolt back to Serragia. When a 3rd Photo Group F-5 Lightning flew over Genoa harbor 18 hours later, the carrier was still on fire.

Throughout June, the 57th Bomb Wing flew missions against road and rail bridges to block the German retreat. Missions fell into a rhythm of two per day per squadron; most aircrew had a day off between missions, but the pace was fast. By the end of June, after 16 missions, bombardier First Lieutenant Tom Cahill could tell his mother more about what he was doing:

I found out yesterday that I can write about flak and fighters, though give no specific instances. No doubt you have been wondering about them. Missions are generally classified as "milk runs," "beaucoup," and "beaucoup-beaucoup." Beaucoup means, in our parlance, flak. Flak can generally be evaded if you see it coming – one-two-three and don't be around for four. The colonel says it's just a "harassing agent," but when I'm the guy being harassed it makes the cheese decidedly more binding. The fact that Jerry is on the run helps considerably, but as their positions keep moving, a flak-free target yesterday may be Hitler's hideout today. For my money, any trip you come back from is a milk run, so don't worry about that stuff anymore. A real milk run comes frequently enough so that you don't get the idea you are personally getting the whole German artillery thrown at you.

Staff Sergeant George B. Underwood – who had arrived as a replacement gunner/armorer in the 310th Group's 381st Bomb Squadron in November 1943, while they were still in Algeria – had grown up in Hollywood, California, after his parents moved there when he was six months old. There were 55 airfields in Los Angeles County, and he soon looked up every time he heard an airplane overhead. In 1932, his father took him to the National Air Races at Mines Field, where he saw Roscoe Turner set a transcontinental speed record from New York City in the Bendix Trophy Race, then later be disqualified from taking first place in the Thompson Trophy race for cutting a pylon. He enrolled in the Junior Reserve Officer Training Corps at Fairfax High School. "The fact they had a rifle team, of which I became a leading member, was the one thing that kept me in school til graduation." Graduating in 1941, he went to work over the hill from Hollywood at the Lockheed factory in Burbank. He was restrained from joining up after Pearl Harbor by the need to repay his mother $100 for the operation to fix his nose after it was broken in a basketball game. "When I went to the Army enlistment office in Hollywood, the sergeant told me they weren't accepting anyone for pilot training at the time, but he assured me I would be first on the list when it opened up after joining the Air Corps. I was anxious to get to the war and signed up anyway." His talent with a rifle got him assigned as a gunner.

Sergeant Underwood would have good reason to call his 57th mission, flown on June 22, 1944, "the scariest one of all."

The morning was cloudy with a hint of rain; flying for the day might be canceled. Shortly after lunch, the crews of the 381st Squadron were told to stand by for a mission. The weather stayed "iffy." They spent the afternoon in card games, reading, and trying to sleep. Finally, at 1600 hours, the other crews were called to a briefing, but not Underwood's. The crews were informed that the 380th and 381st Squadrons would each put a 12-plane formation, joined by six Mitchells from the 379th Squadron, forming two 18-plane formations, to hit the Vernio rail bridges east of Florence, known as "beaucoup" flak targets, but no one was particularly worried. The bombers were all airborne and on their way by 1720 hours, with the target approximately 90 minutes' flying time distant. Within minutes, the 12 RAF Spitfires rendezvoused to provide escort. A mission this late was cutting things close; they would return just before sunset.

Just as the second Vernio mission was taking off, word came the Germans in Leghorn were spotted preparing to sink four hulks in the southern harbor entrance, to block the use of the harbor when it fell to the Allies. Leghorn was expected to be taken; this had to be prevented. A "quickie" mission was laid on – three bombers from the 380th, three from the 381st, and 12 from the 428th Squadrons, to sink the hulks before they could be position in the harbor entrance. Underwood's crew was one of the three from the 381st. For once, they would fly "their" B-25J, 43-27507, the one with their names on it. Known as "507" in the squadron, she had arrived on Corsica the week before and had yet to be named.

First Lieutenant Glenn T. Black of the 381st was assigned as leader. He later recalled, "I didn't like the arrangement, for we had our best missions when the whole mission was made up of crews from one squadron. We all knew each other and were able to work together better. Although I didn't like it, I expect the second element lead crew liked it much less." That crew – the 380th Squadron's pilot First Lieutenant Peterson, co-pilot First Lieutenant Lightsey, bombardier Staff Sergeant Hunt, gunner Sergeant Earl Petach, and tail gunner Sergeant Pizzimenti – had just completed their tour of 70 missions. They had orders to return to the States the next day; their B-4 bags were packed in their tents. When they were assigned to the mission, all the other 380th crews were upset, but no one complained, and manned their aircraft. They took off 20 minutes later.

Nearing Leghorn, the formation became scattered in the clouds. Black's formation – including "507" – was to bomb from 12,500 feet, left of the other two flights bombing at 8,500 and 10,000 feet. Black turned wider over the Initial Point (IP), putting the flight well behind the rest. Black puffs of 88mm shell explosions around the formations ahead made it certain the Germans were ready and waiting. Black lowered his seat to concentrate on the Pilot Direction Indicator, which moved right or left as the bombardier lined up. He was unaware his wide turn had added 90 crucial seconds to the bomb run.

Flak burst around the second formation as their bombs fell away. Suddenly the wing of the lead B-25 erupted in flame. The Mitchell fell into a steep dive while fire spread to the engine nacelle and then the fuselage. At the last moment, a body exited the rear escape hatch. The parachute began streaming, but it was too late; the crewman fell all the way to the harbor below while the bomber exploded on impact. Peterson's crew wouldn't catch their flight home. The second B-25 took a hit in the bomb bay and the right engine caught fire. Pilot First Lieutenant Quitta nosed over in an attempt to douse the flames and headed out to sea.

George Underwood glanced over his shoulder at the other planes as they entered the bomb run. They formed as tightly as possible to insure a good concentration. The bombers were quickly surrounded with exploding shells, some close enough the explosion could be heard over the engines.

Black realized the run was taking longer than it should. In Underwood's Mitchell, bombardier Smith watched Black ahead, his hand on the panel to toggle the bombs. Underwood glanced over his shoulder to see the leader's bomb bay doors come open and heard Smith's call, "Bomb doors open." A moment later Smith called, "Bombs Away! Bomb doors closing. Let's get the hell out of here!"

Black's formation was too far from the others to join up for evasion.

Originally I had planned to turn left and climb as soon as the bombs were released, since that would put us on a heading out to sea, away from the target and above the altitude the Germans had their shells set to explode at more quickly. I had noticed before that the Germans had come to expect this maneuver, since they would fire to our left after we dropped our bombs. Since we were so far back, I elected to turn right and dive, since they wouldn't expect us to turn toward them.

As the other five followed Black, the Germans got the range in a series of lucky shots.

Underwood later remembered, "We took a close burst just ahead of the right wing outboard of the engine, and it was very quickly apparent the engine had taken the worst of the hit when smoke poured out of the cooling flaps." "507's" Lieutenant Prasse broke left out of formation and dove for the open sea. A second 88mm burst near the left wing. Prasse feathered the right engine and headed for Corsica. Underwood kept his eyes on the "good" engine, where smoke from burning oil streamed from the cowling flaps.

Black felt his whole plane seemed to stand still in midair as several shells exploded close by.

> I looked down at my right hand, which had been on the throttles – it lay limp in my lap. I looked at my right arm and could see the jagged end of the lower part of the bone in my upper arm and the jagged ends of the bones in the lower part of my arm. My elbow was no more. My lower arm reminded me of the drumstick of a freshly-butchered chicken. The only connecting flesh I could see holding my lower arm looked like raw meat. I turned the controls over to my co-pilot, but he pulled up straight and level so I took over again and did evasive action one-handed that was probably more violent than was necessary. After we were out of range of the flak, I turned the controls back over to him and called for the bombardier to give me first aid.

Co-pilot Jerry Gerg managed to head out to sea; when he attempted to apply power and climb to a safer altitude, he found the control cable of the right prop pitch control lever was cut; he could not add power, since increasing manifold pressure without increasing propeller rpms would blow the engine. Black ordered the crew to get rid of everything they could throw overboard in hopes they could make it to Corsica. The sun was just above the western horizon, creating a kaleidoscope through the badly fractured windshield. During the long flight home Black had to tell Gerg what was out front as they flew on into the setting sun. "There was a neat hole through the center of our artificial horizon, and the normally-horizontal bar was straight up. The hydraulic pressure gauge registered zero, which meant we couldn't lower the flaps or gear." Hydraulic fluid sloshed in the bomber.

The oil system fire in Lieutenant Quitta's bomber burned itself out; whatever was on fire in the bomb bay departed, and their dire situation seemed resolved. With the right engine feathered with the potential to catch fire again at any moment, Quitta turned toward Corsica as the sun lowered over the western horizon.

At Ghisonaccia, the air was filled with the approaching roar of the B-25s returning from the Vernio mission as the Mitchells appeared overhead and broke for landing. Red flares were fired from several, indicating wounded on board. Shaken crews climbed from the planes, telling of heavy, accurate, "beaucoup-beaucoup" flak, with continuous bursts among the formations. Everyone marveled that only one crew was lost over the southern bridge and no one else was killed. When 380th maintenance sergeant Frank Dean examined "The Little King" for new flak holes, "I found a small hole right beneath the bombardier's compartment, where it had been stopped by an extra piece of armor plate we had installed for just such purpose. Had it not been in place, there could have been a fatality. Most of the other aircraft bore mute evidence of the accuracy of the German gunners."

First Lieutenant Storey D. Larkin remembered:

We took the worst pasting of our lives in one of the bloodiest battles we were ever in. The minute we started the bomb run, their accuracy was deadly. Just as the lead ship dropped, they got hit in their left engine and the pilot had to feather it. They got back. The Germans concentrated on us and got in some excellent shots but we got off with just one hole in the gas tank. At the south target one ship went in head first, as well as one of the escorting Spitfires. Nobody saw any 'chutes. We managed to overfly a flak position on the way home and they opened up on us. Our element drew the brunt of their fire. The plane on the right got it in the left engine. He seemed OK for a few minutes and then the main wheels dropped and the bomb bay came open which meant they had no hydraulics. The engine caught fire and he continued to lose altitude as we crossed the coast. We stuck with him and at 2,000 feet a 'chute came out the rear. He circled back over land and another five 'chutes came out. Then the plane went out of control, dove to tree top height, pulled out and went into a stall and flat spin. Another crew saw the pilot's chute at the last minute when it stalled. When we got back to Ghisonaccia, we orbited while planes with wounded landed ahead of us.

In the fading light over the Tyrrhenian Sea, Lieutenants Quitta, Black, and Prasse nursed their crippled Mitchells home. Quitta saw the dark shape of Corsica on the horizon. Suddenly, the bomb bay fire caught again, spreading rapidly to the gas tanks. Quitta pancaked the bomber onto the sea below, but only co-pilot Second Lieutenant W. B. Helgeson got out the upper escape hatch, dragging the badly injured Quitta, before the B-25 sank out of sight. A nearby rescue boat pulled both from the sea, but Quitta was already dead, while Helgeson died a few hours later. The other four crewmen were lost with the plane.

George Underwood thought they might make it when he heard Sergeant Smith announce, "Corsica dead ahead." They were soon over Ghisonaccia, but when pilot Prasse tried to lower the gear, it didn't operate; Underwood and radioman Jim Heany hand-cranked it down, and Prasse elected to land beside the PSP runway. "507" touched down nose high on the main gear; as the nosewheel touched ground, it collapsed from flak damage. "We got thrown around inside from that fast stop." Tail gunner Campbell wrenched his back when he stepped out the open rear hatch and fell 20 feet to the ground. "We counted 200 flak holes, including one 88mm hole in the left wing where a shell had passed through without exploding." "507" had barely lasted a week before being dragged to the boneyard where it was turned into spare parts.

Black's B-25 was the last one to land.

We had been steadily descending on the way home, and I worried that the mountains of Corsica rise to about 8,500 feet. I was worried about descending below the clouds and running into one of them. However, we broke out of the clouds north of Corsica and as soon as I saw the island I knew right where we were. The closest airfields were fighter fields with short strips. The only base hospital was on the south end of the island, a ways from Ghisonaccia. The 340th's base at Alesani was the closest to the hospital, so that's where I decided we'd land.

Gerg called the Alesani tower; they were cleared straight in. Bombardier Nick Paul tried pumping the emergency hydraulic system to lower the gear unsuccessfully and couldn't find the crank to lower the gear manually. "We were then too low to give the crew the opportunity to bail out, and we couldn't climb back up. A belly landing was our only alternative. Hydraulic fluid and 100-octane fuel was sloshing around in the lower fuselage. When I looked in the navigator's compartment, I saw a fog of fumes. There was a great possibility of fire and explosion in our crash landing."

Black held the controls with his left hand, with Gerg following on his yoke. As they approached the runway, Paul called out the airspeed so Black could keep his attention outside. "I had a thick yellow cushion placed vertically on my lap. If I was thrown forward on landing, hopefully it might protect my chest and face."

At 200 feet, Black retarded the right engine. Paul called out 135mph airspeed, then moved to take crash position. "As we flared over the runway, Jerry started to pull back, but I said let's get this on the ground and he pushed forward with me. The tail touched and we slid on the ground so smoothly that we didn't feel anything but the rapid deceleration."

Once they stopped, they had to get out fast. Tail gunner Morris pushed open the rear escape hatch and quickly crawled out with the radioman while Paul pushed open the cockpit escape hatch and climbed out onto the nose, followed by the turret gunner. "I had never considered my crew an eager-beaver crew, but they did move quickly that day!" Black tried to stand up, only to discover the parachute's right leg strap was still fastened. He couldn't work it loose with his shattered arm. When Gerg reached over to unstrap him, Black realized his co-pilot had a deep flesh wound in his left hip. Gerg pushed Black out and followed.

"Men were swarming toward us from all directions. Some of my crew shouted at those approaching with lighted cigarettes to get out of there since the plane was full of gas. Fortunately, it did not explode or burn. I was later told by the 340th's engineering officer that we did very little damage on landing, but when they had to get it out of the way for other emergency landings, they dragged it over boulders and damaged it beyond repair."

Black would spend the next two years in hospitals, undergoing surgery and therapy to regain some use of his arm. A week later, Jerry Gerg returned to flight status.

The 380th lost two B-25s of three sent out, with all killed, while the 381st lost two of three with no fatalities on the Leghorn mission. The hulks were sunk away from the harbor entrance. The 381st lost a plane at Vernio while the 380th lost none. The approaches to both bridges were "heavily damaged." The "lucky" 428th had only one plane holed over Vernio, while the 379th's planes were undamaged. Of 58 aircraft that flew the missions, three were lost, with two so badly damaged they never flew again. Thirty-eight others had flak damage. Two crewmen were dead, and five wounded. Ground crews robbed crashed aircraft of valuable parts. All the aircrews received the Air Medal. June 22, 1944 – the longest day of the year – was the worst day the 310th experienced in the entire war.

Due to the losses, the 310th received a two-day stand-down; afterwards, they went back to war and flew seven more missions by the end of June. All crews returned smiling. Sergeant Dean wrote in his diary, "No flak. No fighters. We had no explanation as to how this could happen." The tempo continued through July as the bombers concentrated on transportation targets in the Po Valley.

The 27th Fighter Group was still at Rome's Ciampino airfield, which meant a 300-mile round trip for a mission to the front. On June 29, the Thunderbolt's combat radius was put to the test. A photo-recon flight found nearly 500 rail wagons carrying armored vehicles in the Rimini–Forli area. Each of the group's squadrons were sent, so that when the 523rd had dropped all its ordnance, the 524th would arrive overhead, followed by the 522nd. The 523rd's monthly report stated:

… the cars were located and very accurately bombed, direct hits being obtained on the train at four separate places. Many cars were left burning and many others damaged as a result of the bombing and fire from the guns of the aircraft. Other bombs were dropped on the rail yards at Forli, two of them direct hits on the tracks and four others landing on a large building believed to be a power station. The building was set on fire and numerous blue explosions were observed, each one creating additional damage. The formation then turned on 30 box cars and a locomotive, damaging all. Leaving Forli and continuing along the tracks, an additional 25 box cars were attacked and all of them damaged by strafing, with some left burning.

The 524th took over from the 523rd, claiming another 100 wagons damaged or destroyed.

The 86th Fighter-Bomber Wing finally ran through all the available A-36s; the 526th and 527th Squadrons said good-bye to the A-36 when the first war-weary P-47s – hand-me-downs from the 27th Group – arrived at the group's operating airfield, Orbetello, on June 23. The 525th Squadron, which had been forced to exchange their remaining A-36s for P-40 hand-me-downs from the 324th Group back in May, began receiving other war-weary P-47s from the 332nd Group at the end of June when the "Red Tails" transitioned to P-51s and joined the Fifteenth Air Force.

The pilots of the three squadrons were not happy to exchange their A-36s for P-47s; the Thunderbolts were experiencing repeated failures of the bomb and wing tank releases; the fighter began to receive nicknames like "Old Overbolts," "Republic Repulsive Fat Boys," and "Flying Milk Bottles." Captain Howard Decker led eight A-36s for the group's last mission with the North American dive bomber on July 14. That week, the 86th moved to Borgo Poretta airfield, 20 kilometers south of Bastia on Corsica, to take part in the coming invasion of southern France.

The pursuit of the Tenth and Fourteenth Armies significantly changed the tactical airpower situation. The P-47 had proven itself to be the dominant aerial weapon supporting the advance.

Marshal Kesselring had kept his strategy, forcing the Allies to pay in blood for their advance. The Tenth and Fourteenth Armies' leading units entered the Gothic Line in early July. With the defenses based on the supply center at Bologna – the southern terminus of the Brenner Pass rail line that carried supplies from Munich to Bologna in eight hours – the pillboxes, with their interlocking fields of fire on the steep, heavily forested Apennine mountainsides, could block the Allied advantage in armor and motorized transport.

The Gothic Line had been designed by Erwin Rommel, with construction beginning in the fall of 1943 and extending into the spring and summer of 1944; more than 15,000 slave laborers worked on it. Construction was slowed by poor quality concrete deliberately provided by local Italian sources. Captured partisans forced into the construction gangs supplemented the lethargy of the slave laborers with clever sabotage. The line was 10 miles deep; it extended from south of La Spezia on the Ligurian coast to the Foglia Valley, then along the natural defensive wall of the Apennine mountains, 50 miles deep with peaks covered with thick forests rising to 7,000 feet. It ended on the Adriatic coast between Pesaro and Ravenna. There were 2,376 concrete machine-gun pillboxes with interlocking fire; 479 anti-tank, mortar, and assault gun positions; and 390,000 feet of barbed wire coupled with several miles of anti-tank ditches. The steep hillsides did not allow the Allies to make use of their superiority in vehicles, reducing combat to a small-unit infantry struggle. The fighting in northern Italy would last an additional ten months as the Allies tried desperately to find a way around or through the defenses Rommel had designed so well.

At the end of June, the 65th Squadron's Michael McCarthy completed his tour. Most pilots held themselves fortunate to survive their deadly work and looked forward to returning stateside and the opportunity for a new assignment, preferably in Training Command. The group leaders asked McCarthy to consider volunteering for a second tour. If he did, he would go home for 30 days' leave, returning to a position of responsibility in the unit as one of the "Wheels." "I had volunteered in the first place to defeat the Germans and had discovered I was good at the job, so I took their offer and returned to Boston." McCarthy discovered his girlfriend had joined the SPARS, the women's division of the Coast Guard, and was home on leave from basic training. They got engaged but decided they would not marry until after the war was over. Captain McCarthy returned to Alto in time to participate in the invasion of southern France.

On July 7, "Wabbit" Hare led 12 65th Squadron P-47s on what he later considered his most memorable mission, to attack fuel dumps and rail tracks in the Po Valley.

We got some good hits on suspected fuel dumps but no outstanding fires. We made a few cuts in the rails, strafed a few vehicles and were searching for more when someone called on the radio, "Bogey at one o'clock low!" I saw a black dot moving northwest at about 200 feet above the ground, seemingly unaware of our presence. The dot soon became an aircraft about ten miles ahead of my formation. I replied "I have him." Every pilot in the formation had him by then and poured on the coals, and it became a race to see who would get there first. I think I had the advantage of making the decision to go after the bogey and got to full throttle first. None of the fellows could catch me, and as I got closer, I recognized it as a Caproni-133, an Italian transport plane. My fighter was going so fast that when I got in range it was almost like a stationary target. I would have time for just a one-second burst at most before overshooting him. I put my gunsight pipper barely in front of the nose of the target and squeezed off my one-second burst of eight .50-caliber machinegun fire. The poor guy probably never knew what happened. His airplane exploded in a ball of flame and plunged 150 feet into the Po River. All the pilots on the flight slowed down to cruising speed and we flew back to our field on Corsica. I really looked forward to showing off my spectacular kill with my gun camera film but was sorely disappointed when our gun camera technician, Sergeant Francis Hudlow, informed me that all the film had been used up by the previous pilot flying my airplane. Well, no film but 11 good witnesses.

Hare had scored what would turn out to be the last confirmed aerial victory for the 65th Squadron in the war, bringing the squadron's grand total to 49 German and Italian aircraft shot down. Hare had joined the 57th in August 1943 on Sicily; by the time he went home on leave in October 1944, he had survived 169 missions. He was one of a few to return for a second tour as assistant group operations officer, flying 24 missions before war's end.

The 57th Group planned to mark the second anniversary of its arrival in the Mediterranean combat zone on July 1 with a celebration party. That morning, four "Exterminators" from the 66th Squadron encountered enemy fighters, now a rare event since most Luftwaffe units had been withdrawn from Italy after the defeat at Cassino. The claim for six Bf-109Gs shot down without a loss made a most appropriate beginning to the group's 25th month in foreign service.

Once the Germans arrived at the Gothic Line, it was imperative to attack their supply lines in the Po River Valley. XII TAC began Operation *Mallory Major* – a series of missions to destroy all the bridges on the Po River from the Ligurian Sea to the Adriatic Sea in an attempt to starve the Tenth and Fourteenth Armies into submission. On July 12, Thunderbolts of the 57th Group's 65th Squadron escorted B-25s of the 310th Bomb Group to bomb bridges outside La Spezia; three more missions were flown that day. Phase 1 of the operation, flown on July 12–13, destroyed or severely damaged all the Po River bridges, cutting off the enemy between the river and the Allied front lines. Follow-up missions by the Thunderbolts of the units now on Corsica were flown over the next two weeks to disrupt the German repair units.

The morning of July 13, 12 Thunderbolts of the 79th Group's 86th Squadron led by Captain George Ewing were southwest of Ferrara when Blue Flight was jumped by several Bf-109s. Ewing downed one during the initial bounce; Yellow Flight turned into the enemy fighters and chased one several miles before they broke off and returned to the formation. On their return, they came under fire from flak and Second Lieutenant Robert Ryan's P-47 took a direct hit in its oil reservoir, which resulted in oil streaming from his cowl flaps to cover the airplane all down the left side and half of the right, completely covering his canopy. Flight leader First Lieutenant Alan Austin joined with him and told him to open the canopy. Ryan's receiver worked but the transmitter was out. With Austin questioning him by hand signals, Ryan nodded that his engine seemed OK, that he was uninjured, and that he thought the fighter would make it to the coast. Austin turned back heading west.

Austin later reported that:

For the first two minutes, five Me-109s flew to our right and slightly above, but did not attack. There were seven of us. After five minutes on course, the receiver in Ryan's X53 apparently stopped working as he drifted continuously to the left. We were at 6,000 feet, about four miles north of Via Reggio, when I noticed his prop start windmilling. The ship slowed down noticeably, and a few seconds later Ryan was seen to bail out. His 'chute opened at approximately 5,500 feet and he drifted eastward. When last seen, he was at about 200ft dropping into a wooded area between two hills. We did not circle him as we did not want to give his position away.

Ryan was fortunate that he was able to make his way to the American lines and returned to the group in two weeks.

At the end of July, the 57th Group was the first P-47 unit in the MTO to receive a new weapon, 3-inch rockets fired from an 8-foot-long plastic "bazooka tube." Mounted in a group of three, the "bazookas" were slung under the wing between the main gear and the underwing pylon. It was soon discovered that the rockets were inaccurate due to distortion of the tube when the rocket was fired. Michael McCarthy recalled one hair-raising mission in which the rockets arced back over his wings, narrowly missing the Thunderbolt's fuselage. "Nevertheless, these rockets got a lot of use because whether they hit what we were firing at or not, they forced the enemy to keep his head down, which made it harder for them to shoot at us."

On July 28, George Underwood flew his 68th mission to hit the Borgoforte railroad bridge, returning unharmed. On August 1, he took off for number 69; weather intervened and they were forced to return – the mission didn't count. On August 2, mechanical problems forced an abort – again, it didn't count. After a night tossing and turning through nightmares, the next morning he went to the flight surgeon and said he couldn't fly again, that he knew he'd never survive number 69 of the 70 needed to go home. The next week he had orders home. "I was lucky."

Operation *Anvil*, the invasion of southern France, had been first adopted at the Tehran Conference in November 1943. Churchill wanted an invasion of northern Yugoslavia, to allow the Western Allies to move up to the Hungarian plain in an obvious effort to block a Soviet advance into eastern Europe. Stalin opposed the idea. Eisenhower, with the support of Roosevelt, then proposed an invasion of southern France to happen simultaneously with Operation *Overlord* and thus split the German defenders. Churchill opposed the decision over the following months and claimed the Allied force would necessarily be too small and thus liable to be surrounded as had happened at Anzio. The difficulties at Anzio led to cancellation of *Anvil* because the necessary forces were still directly involved in combat operations in Italy.

With the breakthrough in May freeing up the forces originally scheduled to participate in *Anvil*, the difficulties faced by the Allied armies in the Norman bocage led to the invasion being revived as Operation *Dragoon*, to take pressure off the Allies in Normandy. The invasion of southern France would now take place on August 15, the earliest date that allowed naval transports used at Normandy to return to the Mediterranean and carry the invasion forces to the French Riviera. Shortly after Rome was taken, the highly experienced 3rd, 36th, and 45th Divisions of VI Corps were pulled from the Fifth Army's order of battle to prepare to lead the invasion, along with the First Free French Army. Units of XII Air Support Command began flying more missions to southern France after the decision was made to mount the invasion; XII ASC supported the invasion until the end of

August, when several units were transferred to what would become XIX Tactical Air Command to support the invaders as they advanced up the Rhône Valley. A reduced XII ASC returned to the fighting in Italy.

After the decision was made to proceed with *Anvil*, the combined strength of the US Fifth and British Eighth Armies fell from 249,000 to 153,000 by the end of August. The veterans were replaced by inexperienced troops of the Brazilian Expeditionary Corps and the American 92nd Infantry Division. By September 1, there were only 18 Allied divisions in Italy to confront the German Tenth and Fourteenth Armies' 14 front-line divisions, plus four to seven reserve divisions.

The 57th Fighter Group had been so successful in Operation *Strangle* that famed Hollywood director William Wyler – who had made the acclaimed documentary *Memphis Belle* about the first Eighth Air Force B-17 to survive 35 missions the year before – brought his documentary crew to Alto on July 10 to film the group's story for a second documentary. Their filming was complete by the end of July, just before operations for the invasion of southern France began. The result was the film *Thunderbolt*, which was finally shown in the United States in 1947.

On August 8, the 340th Bomb Group flew their 500th mission since arriving in North Africa 18 months before. The target was the three bridges over the Rhône River outside Avignon, France. Captain James E. Nickerson wrote that the bridges were considered "the roughest target in the theater," known to the crews as "The Dreaded Avignon Bridges." The mission was one of 11 that the 340th would fly that day in support of the invasion. The mission was number 37 for newly promoted First Lieutenant Joseph Heller; he would remember it forever.

As the formation of Mitchells cruised over the coast of southern France headed toward Avignon, Heller looked out of his greenhouse "office" at the peaceful countryside below. The navigator – a history teacher before the war who loved it whenever a mission took him to places he had studied – announced over the intercom, "On our right is the city of Orange, ancestral home of the kings of Holland and William III, who ruled England from 1688 to 1702." The worried voice of the radioman chimed in, "And on our left – is flak."

The Germans were ready for them as the sky ahead filled with yellow and orange explosions surrounded by ominous black clouds. The Mitchells turned on final approach and Heller concentrated on his leader. The bridges were now visible through the flak – it was a matter of moments before "bombs away!" Heller glanced out just in time to see the B-25 to his left struck by a direct hit in its bomb bay. The bomber disintegrated in the explosion, leaving only one of the rudders, which fluttered through the formation. The pilot and co-pilot were among Heller's best friends in the group.

As bombs fell from the leader, Heller hit his release switch and checked the intervalometer to ensure the bombs were falling as they should. When he saw the fourth light, he closed the bomb doors and reported, "bombs gone – doors closing." Suddenly they were bracketed by three close "88" flak bursts, so loud Heller could hear them through his headset over the engine roar. Shrapnel rattled against the aluminum skin like rocks on a tin roof.

With bombs gone, the pilot banked away to the right. More flak exploded, blowing off the right wingtip, which fluttered away. Someone shrieked over the intercom, "Help me! I'm hit!" The co-pilot, with nothing to do but observe the terrifying moment, gave in to his terror, grabbing his control yoke and whipping hard right as he pushed forward. The bomber banked into a wild dive. "Help him! Help him!" the co-pilot cried over the intercom.

Heller suddenly was thrown around by the rapid wingover and dive; G-force pinned his head to the bulkhead behind him and his feet thrashed the air over the machine gun mounted in the nose. He steadied himself and readied for the pull-out, but there was none. The voice shrieked again, "I'm hit! I'm hit!" just as his headset was pulled out of its jack by sudden movement.

The pilot fought with the co-pilot for control. The navigator tried to restrain him but was shoved aside. The pilot grabbed the throttles and pulled back to slow the dive. The navigator landed a lucky punch that knocked the co-pilot back in his seat. The pilot pulled out of the wild dive, momentarily squashing everyone with the G-force. The terrified co-pilot recovered and grabbed his controls, fighting the pilot in his panic until the flight engineer restrained him. The Mitchell bucked and reared as the pilot fought to prevent a catastrophe. Finally, several thousand feet below the others, they pulled level, low enough to be bracketed by light flak. The pilot turned sharply to get away.

In the nose, Heller managed to steady himself and get his headset plugged back in. "Help who?" he shouted. "Help him! Help the bombardier! He doesn't answer!" Surprised, Heller checked himself and found he was unhurt. "I'm the bombardier! I'm OK! I'm OK!" "Help him! Help him!" the voice cried.

Heller shoved himself through the narrow tunnel back to the cockpit. The turret gunner and navigator restrained the co-pilot as the pilot concentrated on their escape. Heller plugged into the intercom and heard "Help him!" He climbed into the narrow space between the roof of the bomb bay and the top of the fuselage, squeezing through to the rear.

He found the radioman and tail gunner together. The radioman had a large oval wound in his thigh and there was a hole in the plane just behind the waist window, where the shrapnel that hit him had entered. Nauseated at the bloody sight, Heller opened the first aid kit and spread sulfa over the wound, then bandaged it and gave the radioman morphine. He returned to the cockpit.

The pilot set course for Corsica while the co-pilot regained his composure. No one said anything about the fear he had given in to. They'd all been there, so terrified they were "all up in my flak helmet," as they described that kind of terror. Heller glanced at his watch; the entire event, which had seemed to last for hours, had actually taken place in a matter of four minutes since he had closed the bomb doors. Heller later remembered that on the way home to Corsica, "I finally admitted to myself that they really were trying to kill me. That they were trying to kill all of us was no consolation. They were trying to kill *me*!"

On Operation *Dragoon*'s D-Day, August 15, 94,000 men landed; there were only 395 casualties. Marseille and Toulon were quickly surrounded by the French First Army, and were liberated on August 28, a month earlier than expected. The US Seventh Army tried to encircle and cut off the German Nineteenth Army near Montélimar; the following battle left the Nineteenth Army badly damaged and in full retreat through the Rhône Valley.

Operation *Dragoon* saw the return of US Navy fighters operating from aircraft carriers for the first time in Europe since VF-9 and VF-41 had flown their F4F-4 Wildcats over Casablanca during Operation *Torch* nearly two years before. While seven British escort carriers operated a mix of Wildcat V and Hellcat I fighters, American escort carriers (CVEs) USS *Tulagi* (CVE-72) and USS *Kasaan Bay* (CVE-69) operated brand-new F6F-5 Hellcats.

Tulagi was home to the unique VOF-1 (Observation Fighting Squadron 1), whose pilots had received training at Fort Sill, Oklahoma, as artillery spotters in order to direct supporting gunfire from the cruisers and destroyers of the invasion fleet. The squadron had been created after it became obvious during Operation *Torch* that traditional US Navy spotting aircraft like the SOC Seagull or OS2U Kingfisher floatplanes were unlikely to survive in the European combat environment.

Kasaan Bay's VF-74 had the assignment of flying strike-recon missions. Despite having no formal training in photo reconnaissance or artillery spotting, and having only fired rockets once during training, VF-74's pilots ran up respectable bombing and rocket scores of 35 percent hits during the invasion. The Hellcats had the longest range of any of the carrier fighters involved in the invasion and could fly missions as far as Toulouse to the west or Macon, which was 200 miles north up the Rhône Valley, or to Cannes and Nice to the east.

Both squadrons flew a strike mission at dawn on D-Day, which began as a misty morning. Their target was four coastal batteries at Isle de Porquerolles. *Tulagi's* and *Kasaan Bay's* Hellcats flew a total of 100 sorties during the course of D-Day. The two squadrons would gain the honor of being the only US Navy Hellcat pilots to score against the Luftwaffe.

At 0805 hours on August 19, VF-74 CO Lieutenant Commander Harry B. Bass spotted a Ju-88 near the Rhône River. He led his division in a dive onto the bomber's tail where all four pilots opened fire and quickly sent it down. Shortly after 1600 hours, two other divisions of VF-74 Hellcats spotted a Do-217 south of Lyons. Wild firing from six pilots failed to hit the bomber as it evaded at low level, but Lieutenant (j.g.) E. W. Castandeo and Ensign C. W. Hullard waited till they were in range and split the victory.

At around 1700 hours that evening, two divisions of VOF-1 Hellcats flying a tactical recon mission up the Rhône Valley spotted two low-flying He-111 bombers headed south. The Hellcats dived on them, but the two enemy aircraft split up. Lieutenant Rene E. Poucel and wingman Ensign Alfred R. Wood closed on one from astern and set it afire to crash in a ball of flame. VOF-1 executive officer, Lieutenant Commander John H. Sandor, and his wingman, Ensign David Robinson, closed on the second Heinkel, which was flying at 700 feet, and raked it from nose to tail with full deflection shots.

The enemy bomber crash-landed in a field and was set afire by the two naval aviators in a strafing run. The Hellcats continued on their mission; 20 minutes later Ensign Wood spotted a third He-111. Diving on it from 2,000 feet, he fired a long burst that set both engines on fire; the bomber crashed in the woods below. In addition to the three aerial victories, the Hellcats returned to *Tulagi* with claims for the destruction of 21 trucks, a locomotive, and ten rail cars.

August 20 was a bad day for both squadrons. VF-74 lost three Hellcats and two pilots, including Lieutenant Commander Bass, who was hit by flak on a strafing run near Chamelet and crashed out of control with the pilot likely already dead. Over Toulon, VOF-1's Lieutenant David S. Crockett was spotting gunfire when he was hit by flak and bailed out to become a POW for the next four days before he was handed over to American troops by the surrendering enemy soldiers who captured him. Lieutenant James Allson was strafing vehicles near Villefranche when he was hit. Pulling up, he bailed out at 5,000 feet just as the Hellcat's right wing came off. He was rescued by American ground troops.

The next day, August 21, VOF-1 pilots Lieutenant (j.g.) Edward W. Olsewski and Ensign Richard V. Yentzer ran across three Ju-52 transports over the Rhône Valley. Despite both Hellcats having sustained minor flak damage in an earlier strafing attack, Olsewski attacked the Vee-formation from the right and shot down the number three enemy plane in two passes, then – with only one gun firing – took out the other wingman. Yentzer took three passes to shoot down the leader with a left side deflection shot. VOF-1 took one loss when Lieutenant (j.g.) J. H. Coyne's Hellcat disintegrated under fire while attacking a truck convoy near Sainte-Anastasie. Coyne managed to bail out at the last moment, with his parachute opening just before he hit the ground.

That evening, the two CVEs retired out to sea to resupply, returning on August 24. Between then and August 29, VOF-1 lost two Hellcats, one flown by squadron CO, Lieutenant Commander William F. Bringle, who was hit over Marseilles and had to ditch halfway back to *Tulagi*. The other was also lost in ditching and both pilots were picked up successfully.

Over the 13 days they participated in the invasion, the two squadrons lost 11 Hellcats, one-fourth of their number. In return, they were credited with the destruction of 825 trucks and other vehicles, with damage to 334 others, wrecking or stopping 84 locomotives, and shooting down eight Luftwaffe aircraft. It was a record equal to that of the Wildcats over Casablanca.

On D-Day, August 15, the 57th Wing's B-25 groups flew multiple missions; the first departed at 0200 hours while the last returned at 1900 hours. While air cover was provided by fighter groups of both Twelfth and Fifteenth Air Forces, the Luftwaffe failed to appear.

First Lieutenant James Jackson, the 445th Squadron's assistant intelligence officer, flew a D-Day mission as "bombing accuracy photographer." He later wrote of the mission in his diary:

> We took off at 0205 hours. In all there were 36 planes. Our course led over Ajaccio and then north west to the French coast which we followed due east past Toulon, Marseilles and the Rhone estuary. At this point we headed inland, weaving and turning to avoid flak positions. None was sent up at us and at 0413 hours we were over the target in good formation and with good visibility. The lead element missed the bridge but plastered the approach. Lying on my stomach over the camera hatch, I watched our bombs leave the ship and lose shape in the sky below.

Antiaircraft guns opened up as the formation took evasive action.

> As we came over the water and headed west it seemed to me as if all of southern France was blowing up. I counted six targets that had been hit heavily. One large area of dust and smoke assumed the aspect of land fighting but I could not be certain of that. We were now out of danger from the enemy and began taking off our flak suits. Everyone was relaxed and grinning and felt good. From the time of starting engines I had carefully observed my own reactions by checking my pulse and noting other evidence of emotional strain. I was scarcely nervous the entire trip and was in all pleased with my reaction … Of course the raids now are in no degree of comparison as hazardous as they used to be and it seems hardly sporting to fly against so worn an enemy.

At 0500 hours the radioman hooked the crew into a BBC newscast. "The announcer told of the landing in southern France and said the sky was literally filled with aircraft. I looked out of the window at the scores of B-25s, B-26s, B-17s and fighter planes and thought, 'Brother, if you only knew.'" Attacks continued for two more days before the weather closed in again for a few days.

August 17 saw the Thunderbolts of the 86th Group attack the rail yards at Cavaillon. Once their bombs were gone, the fighters dropped down to strafe locomotives and rail cars in the yard. One train was spotted trying to get away, and several fighters went after it. The train was transporting ammunition in several rail cars. When the bullets hit those, the resulting explosion nearly knocked the strafing Thunderbolts out of the sky with several being near-missed by railroad ties thrown as high as 200 feet into the air. The explosion was heard across the invasion area, and it left a crater over 200 feet wide. The mission marked the first time pilots dropped still-full drop tanks and then set them afire by strafing.

On August 18, 36 B-25s of the 321st Bomb Group flew one of their most dangerous missions of the war. The French battleship *Strasbourg* and cruiser *La Galissonnière*, which were under the control of the Germans, had been spotted positioned in Toulon harbor where they could fire at the attackers. Weather conditions were such that other Corsica-based units turned back, but the 321st's formation navigated by dead reckoning over the cloud cover to reach the target. Toulon's 82 heavy antiaircraft guns opened fire as they turned to make their bomb run at 13,000 feet. The intense flak hit 27 Mitchells, wounding 12 crewmen. The semi-armor-piercing "thousand pounders" were dropped with 100 percent accuracy, sinking both battleship and cruiser as well as a submarine and destroyer. It was the most successful medium bomber attack against enemy warships from a high-altitude horizontal bombing run in the war. In February 1945, the 321st received a second Presidential Unit Citation for the mission.

The 86th's Captain Bert Benear had reason to remember his 67th mission, flown on August 19. One of the "old hands" who had joined the group a year before and participated in the Salerno invasion, he led a flight of four Thunderbolts to bomb the Avignon bridge. Shortly after crossing the coast inbound to the target, he spotted three Bf-109s. He ordered his wingman to follow him, and the two pilots jettisoned their bombs. As he closed on the three fighters, Benear saw that they had airscoops under their left wing. Thinking he might have misidentified

Spitfires as Messerschmitts, he banked to the side; in an instant one of the three banked toward him and he saw the German insignia.

The German pilot broke to the right and Benear was quickly on his tail. Two bursts from his eight machine guns set the enemy fighter on fire and it went in. Benear then turned on the second Bf-109 and fired into the cockpit; the fighter rolled over and went in, with the pilot likely dead. He quickly found himself under fire from the third Messerschmitt, now on his tail. The Thunderbolt took hits, and black smoke suddenly streamed from the left wing. Thinking he was on fire and spotting other enemy fighters approaching, Benear split-essed and hit the water injection. With black smoke pouring from his exhausts and the wing, the other enemy fighters decided he was on fire and going in.

Benear then got caught in the Thunderbolt's deadly compressibility dive. Frantic to break free, he put his feet on the instrument panel and pulled back on the stick. Just at that moment he blacked out; a moment later the fighter hit thicker air and the controls responded. The P-47 rocketed back up into the midst of the enemy formation as he came to. He opened fire on a Bf-109 he was headed toward, hitting it in the belly and setting it on fire. As it rolled and went in, he banked away and dove for the deck again with full power. Leveling off at 50 feet over the Mediterranean, he set course for Corsica. When he landed, there was a grinding noise and the big fighter veered left. After finally stopping the Thunderbolt and shutting down, he climbed out. He quickly discovered the source of the fire in the wing – his left main tire had been hit and set on fire, burning the tire off the hub. The fighter was badly shot up and was soon dragged off to the boneyard to become spare parts.

In the aftermath of Seventh Army's lightning advance, the 27th, 79th, and 324th Groups were given movement orders on 18 August; within 48 hours, advance parties of all three groups were preparing the airfields at Le Luc and San Raphael in southern France for the arrival of the Thunderbolts. Twelfth Air Force was now engaged on two different fronts.

The secondary status of the Mediterranean Theater was driven home in the 57th Bomb Wing on August 20, when General Robert Knapp announced that a combat tour – which had been raised from 50 to 55 missions on August 1 and then to 60 on August 15, was now indefinite, with the crews to fly missions "until they can fly no more." Unannounced was the fact that the wing was not receiving replacements as they had, since those men were being diverted to units fighting in northern France. The 340th Group's war diarist wrote on August 21:

> Something entirely new in the way of disciplinary problems cropped up today. The up-cropping is the result of the recent order of this Wing that the men are to fly till they can fly no more. So many of the men having come into combat with a seeming understanding that at 50 they would be entitled to furloughs or rotation back to the States, and later to have the ante raised to 55, then 60, and now raised indefinitely find themselves grumbling quite loudly. On the morning of the completion of their 55th mission two gunners and several officers turned to the Squadron C.O., telling him that they thought they had done enough flying and hoped to be taken off combat status. The two gunners are now in the guard house under charges of misbehaving before the enemy. Actually all that was involved was their telling the C.O. their intentions to no longer fly. It is apparent that the Group Commander and Wing Commander are both interested in having the charges pressed if for no other purpose than to have a test case upon which to base further action. Other combat members of the Group have grievously resented this reaction of the Colonel and have lost much of the respect previously held toward him.

While the two gunners went to the stockade, three officers – including Joe Heller – who protested the new order were placed "in hack," confined to their quarters, though still expected to fly missions. On August 24, Twelfth Air Force commander Lieutenant General Cannon ordered Knapp to rescind the order; Knapp in turn ordered 340th Group commander Colonel Chapman to reverse his orders regarding the protesting gunners and officers. A week later, a group of replacements arrived on Corsica.

In the midst of this internal disruption, the 340th was ordered to fly a "road blocking" mission on August 23. While crews thought nothing of orders to bomb railroads, rail bridges, highway bridges, military bases, or any target considered "war related," no one liked the "road blocking" missions that involved bombing civilians in undefended towns and villages to knock down buildings and leave the wreckage to slow movement of enemy units. B-25s bombed from 8,000 to 12,000 feet, low enough for anyone to see the results of the words "bombs away!"

The target was the Settimo bridges outside Ponte San Martino, located in the Val d'Aosta (Aosta Valley) in northwestern Italy. The bridges had been built by Julius Caesar's legionaries during his invasion of Gaul, in 55 BC. The Roman Via Settimo ran from the Gran Pass, across the Val d'Aosta to the Piccolo San Bernardo Pass; it was the direct route from the Po Valley to the Rhône Valley in France. Napoleon had crossed the bridge in 1800 on his way to Marengo.

Italian partisan units had destroyed highway and rail bridges in northwestern Italy, leaving the Germans in control of Piccolo San Bernardo Pass and the Via Settimo. Following the invasion, orders came down to redouble efforts to disrupt traffic on the road. The mission was scheduled following "Ultra" intelligence reports that the Germans planned to move two panzer divisions from Austria to France via the road, to attack the Allies at Grenoble. Thus, there was a perceived military need to block the Via Settimo; the bridges were to be destroyed.

Mission 522's 18 B-25s – 12 from the 488th, including Joe Heller in one, and six from the 489th Squadron – took off at 1500 hours, each carrying four "thousand pounders"; 20 minutes later, two bombers aborted with "mechanical problems." They reached the target at 1730 hours. What happened next created controversy for 60 years.

Lead bombardier First Lieutenant Robert Burger recalled in 2003, "I was ready to start sighting in on the target; I thought there must be some mistake and I very nearly aborted the mission. I started my bomb run. As my five wingmen saw my bomb bay doors open they in turn opened theirs. When they saw my bombs drop they triggered their load." The bombs struck the plaza in the center of Ponte San Martino – where many townspeople had gathered to see what the 18 silver dots in the sky were doing – rather than the bridges. Of the 130 people who died in the bombing, 40 were children.

While 15 bombs hit the town center, three exploded harmlessly in a field outside the town. B-25 "8K" had turned away from the target while in formation, causing its bombs to go astray. The return flight was uneventful except for "8K." The maneuver that caused three bombs to fall wide caused the fourth to jam in the bomb bay, where the tail gunner unsuccessfully tried to kick it free. During the post-strike debriefing, Second Lieutenant Clifton C. Grosskopf – the pilot of "8K" – stated he had executed an evasive maneuver to "avoid flak." There was no flak; the only weapon protecting Ponte San Martino was a machine gun that did not fire a single shot; Grosskopf refused to bomb the wrong target. Beyond that, it was an iron-clad rule that a bomber held formation regardless of flak while on the bombing run.

That night, when post-strike bomb damage assessment photos were developed, showing the town center had been hit, there was major concern in the 340th regarding the military significance of what they had bombed. The 489th Bomb Squadron's debriefing report noted, "the town center is believed to be the command headquarters of an armored division."

No one questioned Grosskopf's statement about taking evasive action despite the fact that doing so was specifically against the rules. No one in the rest of the crew substantiated or denied his statement. As the actual results of the mission became clear, Grosskopf's action was "swept under the rug"; making an example of him would bring unwanted attention from higher authority, while punishment would have had an adverse effect on crew morale.

The Settimo bridge mission was a watershed moment for Joe Heller that he never explained in interviews after *Catch-22* was published. The mission was his 40th; he had flown an average of a mission every other day since his arrival on Corsica in late May. After August 23, he flew only 20 more missions before returning to the United States in January 1945.

Michael McCarthy returned to the 57th Group two days before the invasion. He later recalled:

I came back to flying missions with no drop off in efficiency. We had several new guys who demonstrated the ability to learn, showed leadership potential, and had the courage to endure fierce enemy antiaircraft fire, whose effectiveness continued to be awesome. I was not surprised that my airplane took heavy damage on my first missions to marshalling yards in the Po Valley cities. The Germans were serious about making us pay for the privilege. My reaction to facing lethal antiaircraft fire again startled me. I found my system for dealing with personal fear during my first year in combat needed some "tinkering" to be effective during this last year. The fact that I chose to come back to this dangerous occupation led me to wonder whether God was ready to continue His role in keeping me safe. I finally realized God was very good at His job. He did not need my help. When I left everything in His hands, quit worrying, and slept soundly, I regained my ability to control fear.

In late August, McCarthy led a dive-bombing mission to a marshalling yard outside Bologna. As he dived on the target, he spotted a long train pulling out of the yard. "I told Chad Reade, my wingman, to take spacing. We would hit the train with two or three strafing passes. I stopped the double locomotive on our first pass and continued around for another." McCarthy turned around over a dry riverbed south of the rail line and aimed the Thunderbolt at the train. "I was low and very fast, just lining up my firing pass when I saw a huge barn door moving away from a gun emplacement hidden in the riverbed." As the P-47 passed directly overhead, the German Flak-37 opened up with a long burst; one shell hit McCarthy's fighter behind the cockpit. "I felt the airplane shudder and the cockpit filled with smoke. As I rolled the canopy back, the smoke cleared. Chad pulled up on my wing and told me there was a large hole over the supercharger in the fuselage, forward of the tail, and that the supercharger was smoking. He could see daylight through the fuselage from one side to the other." McCarthy stopped unbuckling his harness to bail out when he realized he was too low. "The engine was still running. Chad saw no more smoke so the fire was out. We decided to turn gingerly back to Corsica in a gentle climb." McCarthy suspected his rudder and elevator control cables were damaged; in fact, there was only one of each left. He held a very gentle touch on the controls as the two Thunderbolts took course for Corsica.

Arriving over Alto airfield, McCarthy felt there was the possibility of making a safe landing and decided not to bail out. As he descended, he put the gear handle in the down position; the main gear dropped out and locked down, but the tail wheel was up. "We let the others land, then, with Chad on my wing, we came around for a smooth no-flap touchdown. Chad told me later there was no sign of structural support that he could identify from his examination of the damaged area." McCarthy held the tail off the runway as long as he could. When it dropped and touched ground, the fuselage buckled where it had been hit. "Chad's comment about no visible means of support was accurate. This airplane had flown for the last time."

First Lieutenant Dan Bowling arrived on Corsica at the end of August, reporting to the 57th's 321st Bomb Group after a 21-day voyage in a Victory ship converted to a hospital ship from Norfolk, Virginia, to Naples. He turned 22 three weeks after arriving at Solenzara. The son of a miner's union organizer later elected to the Arizona state senate on the Socialist Party ticket, Bowling grew up in the hardscrabble mining town of Bisbee, Arizona, which he remembered as "a company town for the Phelps-Dodge Corporation through and through." He learned early to never back down from a fight, as children of the miners the company turned against his father picked on him at school. At age 11, the family was run out of town and left for Los Angeles. Once in the USAAF, he had quickly gained a reputation of not "taking guff" from anyone, regardless of rank.

During training, Bowling's leadership qualities had seen him make cadet company commander of each unit on the way to pinning on his pilot's wings. Before being posted overseas he received additional training; as a result, he was unique among all pilots in the 321st other than the group commander, holding a "green card" identifying him as fully capable of instrument flight. On his third training flight after being assigned to the 445th Bomb Squadron, the check pilot noted Bowling had more hours as a B-25 first pilot than he did. After a week, he flew his first combat mission as first pilot; four missions later, he began training to become a "lead pilot." By the end of September, Dan Bowling was made a flight leader for two wingmen.

In late August, the 486th's Tom Cahill's ability as a bombardier was noticed; he became a designated "lead bombardier" in the squadron. In a letter to his mother, he explained the new assignment was a double-edged sword: "It kinda looks like I may not be home for Christmas. When I first got here I was getting 12–15 missions a month, but since I have been leading I am lucky to get half that many and when Fall arrives, perhaps less. How many more I'll have to fly I don't know."

On August 25, the 57th Fighter Group received word they would be departing Corsica to return to the Italian mainland, since the line of battle on the peninsula had moved far enough north that the battlefields were too far from the island for the Thunderbolts to carry enough fuel as well as enough ordnance to make a mission worthwhile.

On September 9, the "A Party" – half of the enlisted men and ground officers – was loaded and ready to depart for the new base at Grosseto. Each squadron's advance party went aboard an LST at Calvi with their loaded vehicles for the move. The ships departed at 0230 hours on September 10; the trip to the mainland took a day, with men again experiencing seasickness as they had when they moved to Corsica six months earlier before arriving at the port of Piombino at 1630 hours. Grosseto was 50 miles from Piombino, a large flat area near the beach that had three airfields. After several days of preparing the field, the 66th Squadron was the first to move over from Alto, arriving the afternoon of September 17 after flying a mission. There were no operations for the next three days, as all flying operations in northern Italy were canceled in the face of the first major rainstorm of the fall. The group made the discovery that their airfield in the Grosseto was subject to flooding, and were able to prevail on being moved to Grosseto Main airfield, which had been developed as an all-weather airfield, where they started operations on September 25, with the other two squadrons finally moving over from Corsica. A week after the 57th moved to Grosseto, they were joined by the 86th Group.

Normandy's success notwithstanding, Churchill and the British Chiefs of Staff were still keen to break the Gothic Line and open the "Ljubljana Gap" in northern Yugoslavia, allowing movement into Austria and Hungary. For Churchill, this was a way to forestall the Russian advance into central Europe. While US leaders saw this as a diversion from the main focus in France, the Americans agreed at the Second Quebec Conference on September 12, 1944, to support the offensive that had begun in northern Italy immediately after *Anvil*'s initial success.

Operation *Olive* called for an attack by the Eighth Army up the Adriatic coast toward Pesaro and Rimini, to draw in German reserves. The US Fifth Army would attack the weakened central Apennine front north of Florence, advancing toward Bologna with the British XIII Corps on the right fanning toward the east to create a pincer with Eighth Army.

Over 1,200,000 men saw combat in Operation *Olive*, making it the biggest battle ever fought in Italy. Eighth Army commander Lieutenant General Sir Oliver Leese stated, "The battle of Rimini was one of the hardest battles of Eighth Army. The fighting was comparable to El Alamein, Mareth and the Gustav Line."

Italian partisan forces were so effective in disrupting German operations that by September, German commanders were unable to freely move about; Generalleutnant Frido von Senger und Etterlin, commander of XIV Panzer Korps, later recalled traveling in a Volkswagen "displaying no general's insignia of rank – no peaked cap, no gold or red flags." Brigadier General Wilhelm Crisolli, commander of the 20th Luftwaffe Field Division, was captured and killed by partisans returning from a conference at headquarters.

The Germans were taken by surprise when Eighth Army attacked on August 25, catching the LXXVI Panzer Korps in the midst of a withdrawal to the Green I fortifications of the Gothic Line proper. Kesselring, unsure if the attack was a major offensive or whether the main Allied attack would come on the Bologna front from the US Fifth Army, refused to commit the reserves. On August 28, when Kesselring was presented with a captured copy of Leese's order of the day to Eighth Army for the 25th, he realized this was a major offensive. Reinforcement divisions from Bologna would need two days to arrive in position – if the trains and rail lines were not destroyed by the Allied air forces.

On August 30, the Canadian I and British V Corps reached the main defensive line on the far side of the Foglia River; the Canadians punched through and advanced 15 miles to the Green II line on August 30; Eighth Army was close to breaking through to Rimini and the Romagna plain, but fierce resistance from the 1st Fallschirmjäger Division halted the Canadian advance.

British V Corps' advance slowed in the difficult mountain terrain. On September 3, armor attacked to dislodge the Coriano Ridge defenses and reach the Marano River, opening the gate to the Lombardy plain. The paratroopers held after two days of gruesome close-in fighting, with heavy losses on both sides. The British tried to outflank the enemy by driving west to reach the Marano valley which curved behind the Coriano positions.

Called "The Cassino of the Adriatic," the battle for Gemmano, fought September 4–13, saw the 56th Division and then the 46th Division make 11 unsuccessful assaults. On September 15, the Indian 4th Division attacked a 12th time at 0300 hours, securing the German positions in the Conca Valley. At Croce, on the northern side of the valley, 56th Division fought a five-day, door-to-door and hand-to-hand battle against the German 98th Infantry Division before the Germans were forced to withdraw.

The attack on Coriano was renewed. Advancing behind a paralyzing bombardment from 700 artillery pieces and bombers of the Twelfth and Desert Air Forces, the Canadian 5th Armoured and British 1st Armoured Divisions attacked the night of September 12, emerging victorious on September 14.

Again, the way was open to Rimini. However, the weather intervened, with four days of torrential rain turning rivers into unbridgeable torrents while halting air operations. The Germans seized the opportunity to reorganize and reinforce their positions. When the weather cleared, Eighth Army was confronted by the Rimini Line. The offensive resumed.

At the same time Eighth Army commenced Operation *Olive*, US II Corps and British XIII Corps advanced into the mountains for the main assault. The Germans gave fierce resistance, but after three German divisions were withdrawn to reinforce the Adriatic front, the advance forced the enemy to withdraw into the main Gothic Line defenses. Fifth Army's main assault began on September 12 at dusk. Progress was slow at Il Giogo Pass, but British XIII Corps made better progress, and General Clark called up the 337th Infantry from the reserve, to exploit the British success. The unit fought its way onto Monte Pratone, a key Gothic Line position 3 miles east of Il Giogo Pass, by September 17, when II Corps renewed their assault on Monte Altuzzo, which fell that morning.

The 57th Wing's Mitchells went after German transport routes in the Po Valley to support the offensive. The main enemy was the weather; many days, the fall rains brought low clouds covering the targets. On September 10, supporting the British troops fighting at Rimini, the 310th Group bombed the Guerra ammo and fuel dump and got an unexpected taste of air combat when they ran into the 2° Gruppo Caccia of the Aviazione della RSI, now flying Messerschmitt Bf-109Gs after recently turning in their Macchi C.205 "Veltro" fighters. As the bombers approached the target, First Lieutenant Warren M. Wolfe experienced engine failure and was forced to feather the prop and drop out of formation. He continued on regardless, and his bombardier hit the target successfully. As the Mitchells withdrew, six of the Italian-flown Bf-109s spotted Wolfe's B-25 and attacked. Wolfe took evasive action, throwing the bomber around the sky in evasive action and avoiding further damage until the 57th Fighter Group's P-47 escorts arrived on the scene, forcing the enemy pilots to break off their attacks. It took two hours flying slowly south before Wolfe spotted a friendly airfield and landed safely.

Fifth Army's success allowed the army to outflank the formidable Futa Pass defenses, which forced the enemy to fall back and leave the pass to fall on September 22. Fifth Army had fought their way to the main Gothic Line. The 370th Regimental Combat Team (RCT) of the 92nd Infantry Division had pushed the enemy in its sector beyond Highway 12 to Gallicano; the Brazilian 6th RCT took Massarosa and Camaiore. By September 30, having taken Monte Prano, the Brazilians took control of the Serchio Valley region. Then Fornaci and Barga in early October, while the 370th RCT, reinforced by units from the 365th and 371st RCTs, held the line on the Ligurian coast.

Joe Heller flew his last "beaucoup" mission on September 23, a month after the Settimo bridge mission. Late in the afternoon of September 22, a photo-recon flight spotted the previously damaged Italian light cruiser *Taranto* being towed out of drydock in La Spezia harbor, likely to be scuttled in the harbor mouth to block Allied access after the port's impending fall. The 340th's 488th Squadron was ordered to sink the ship in place the next morning.

Eighteen B-25s took off at 0815 hours and headed off across the Ligurian Sea. They arrived off La Spezia an hour later. Heller's bomber was part of the "chaff flight" that would drop strips of aluminum to confuse radar-directed antiaircraft fire. The three bombers crossed the harbor at 8,000 feet as the tail gunners and radiomen tossed chaff out the rear hatch. As they turned back toward the sea, Heller saw the 12 B-25s bracket the cruiser with their 1,000-pound semi-armor-piercing bombs, causing it to roll on its side. Flak was heavy but inaccurate, and no bomber was hit. The mission resulted in a second Presidential Unit Citation awarded to the 340th.

When 18 B-25s of the 310th's 428th Bomb Squadron attacked a troop area near Rimini on September 28, the crew of B-25 Number 771 – pilot First Lieutenant Louis Schovanec; co-pilot Second Lieutenant George Rorer; bombardier Sergeant Edward Stroyke; turret gunner Sergeant Anthony Ruggiero; radio operator Sergeant MacMakin Collier; and tail gunner Sergeant Luis Martinez – discovered just how tough the Mitchell was. When Stroyke shouted "bombs away!"

Schovanec remarked to Rorer they were lucky there didn't seem to be any flak. As Rorer later recalled, "Suddenly, a burst went off right under us and pitched our tail straight up." An instant later, a second flak burst exploded under the nose of the lead bomber, flown by First Lieutenant Harold Iverson. Rorer continued, "When the second shell hit, we were looking down at them through the overhead windows of the cockpit. Iverson's ship was thrown into a steep bank to the left, directly toward us. Louis and I manhandled the ship into a steeper bank and climb, trying to get away. We wrapped the ship around but it was no use – with a terrific crash they slammed into our belly."

When Iverson's Mitchell slid away, Rorer could see the canopy was caved in as Iverson and his co-pilot desperately tried to cover their heads with their arms. "That was the last we ever saw of them." There was no time to worry about Iverson's fate as Storer and Schovanec fought to save their plane and crew. The right wing had buckled at the point between the outer end of the flap and inner end of the aileron in the collision, causing the bomber to act as if full "up" right aileron had been applied; forced into a steep right bank, the B-25 fell off right and began to spin. "We both stood on the rudder and forced the control wheel to the left as we pushed the yoke forward, pointing the nose down. The wild gyrations ended as airspeed was restored and we regained a semblance of control. We recovered at 5,000 feet after falling from 13,000 feet in a matter of minutes."

Once the bomber leveled off, Sergeant Ruggiero clipped on his chest parachute, kicked open the lower forward escape hatch, and threw himself through it. "We never saw Ruggiero's chute open. We were still flying, going straight but the right wing was way down, and we were headed deeper and deeper into enemy territory." They couldn't turn right without entering a spin, but by standing on full left rudder and holding full left up aileron, they were able to make a sliding turn to the left. "It took about ten minutes to get turned around back toward our lines, but it seemed like an eternity."

Crossing the Allied lines, they gave some consideration to bailing out, but it was impossible; if one pilot let go his death-grip on the controls, the other could not have held the Mitchell level long enough for others to get out. "I asked the crew if they wanted to bail out while we held it or ride it down. They all agreed to stick it out." The two pilots began considering making a belly landing at the first flat spot they sighted. A moment later, they saw the British airbase at Fano in the distance and decided they'd attempt a wheels-down landing there. "The first thing to find out was would it glide? Back came the power and we slowly lifted the nose; after several tries we found it would only glide at 180 miles an hour, which was fast in any man's book."

Again, they managed to turn and line up for a long straight-in approach, keeping the throttles at full power and waiting till the last moment to lower the gear. "We touched down at 180 and got on the brakes as soon as the nose wheel was on the ground. The plane swerved from side to side, and threatened to collide with the tower at the last moment, but somehow we got stopped before we ran out of runway."

Once on the ground, Rorer began shaking as he climbed down the ladder. The crew checked the Mitchell, shaking their heads in disbelief. The right rudder didn't work, the fuselage underside was bashed in at aft of the rear hatch and bent to the right, so the tail was no longer aligned with the rest. Iverson's propeller had sheared off the right engine nacelle rear section, and about a square foot of rubber was gone from the right main tire. That it hadn't torn loose in the landing was a miracle. Second Lieutenant Rorer was awarded the Distinguished Flying Cross in recognition of his herculean effort saving his plane and crew,

The beginning of the end of Operation *Olive* came on September 20, when the Canadians managed to break through the German positions on the Ausa River, moving onto the Lombardy plain; the 3rd Greek Mountain Brigade entered Rimini the next day. In response, the enemy withdrew from the Rimini Line, taking up new positions behind the Uso River a few miles beyond Rimini. Before further progress could be made, the autumn rains came early, pouring in unexpected torrents. Field Marshal Kesselring's dogged defense had won the day.

What progress the Commonwealth forces managed was very slow; the torrential rain closed roads and tracks, creating a logistical nightmare. Eighth Army was out of the mountains, but they now confronted the waterlogged Lombardy plain; swollen rivers crossed the line of advance, preventing armor from exploiting the breakthrough, as had happened the previous autumn. The infantry forced their way through Tenth Army's fallback position on September 26, reaching the Fiumicino River on September 29. At that point, a four-day torrential downpour forced a final halt. V Corps was fought out. During the five weeks since the start of the offensive, Eighth Army suffered 14,000 casualties, enough to force a reduction in British infantry battalions from four to three rifle companies due to a manpower shortage. Tenth Army suffered 16,000 casualties.

With the situation in southern France well under Allied control, Eighth Army requested that the 79th Fighter Group return to Italy and rejoin the Desert Air Force, since their P-47s were the best airplane for effective close air support. The group had established a reputation for accuracy in their close support with the Commonwealth forces during the fighting in south-central Italy. On October 3, the air echelon landed at Jesi airfield on the Adriatic coast; they would operate from the field for the next 60 days. Their arrival coincided with the increased rain and cold weather of the oncoming winter and the airfield was soon a sea of mud. Jesi was crowded with the six squadrons of RAF 239 Wing, the B-26 Marauders of the South African Air Force (SAAF) 3 Wing, and the 167 Maintenance Unit that provided Spitfire replacements to the Commonwealth squadrons. The grass airfield was short and slick when wet, which made P-47 takeoffs with a full ordnance load "adventurous," as recorded in the group's war diary. The weather was terrible, and during their time at Jesi, all flying operations were canceled for a total 17 days. Still, they managed 2,099 sorties over the other days, primarily missions against enemy lines of communication and supply lines. During their time at Jesi, the 79th lost 29 P-47s to the deadly enemy flak.

US II Corps pushed through Raticosa Pass and reached Monghidoro on October 2; they were 20 miles from Bologna. The weather intervened as had happened on the Adriatic front. The weather made air support impossible due to rain and low clouds, while rain turned the roads to the ever more distant supply dumps at Florence into muddy morasses.

Weather over the Po Valley cleared enough on October 3 to fly a mission against the Po Valley railroad. For the 321st Group's Mission 578, the 445th and 446th Squadrons put up 12 B-25s each; the 447th Squadron added eight more, for a total of 32 B-25s. The target was the Galliate railroad bridge in the northwestern Po Valley, known with dread as a well-defended target. The German repair crews were considered to be among the best in Italy, since the bridge never got completely knocked out.

Captain Lawrence "Ace" Russell, one of the most respected pilots in the 445th, flew the lead plane with his bombardier Danny Galindo as lead bombardier. For both, this was number 70, after which they would go home. Russell, known as "Iron Man" for his size and physical ability, was one of the best-liked men in the 321st, particularly among the enlisted men. Dan Bowling remembered there was a high-stakes poker game in his tent the night before. When it broke up around 2300 hours, Russell commented, "Hey Bowling, I bet you wish you were in my boots. In two weeks I'll be home and a war hero because I survived seventy missions." The mission was number 18 for Bowling in the 30 days since his first.

The morning of October 3, they manned their planes. Bowling was second element lead in "Pistol Packin' Mama," right behind the three B-25s led by Russell and Galindo in "Scrap Iron." None of the crews were told at briefing that the Galliate bridge was now the most important bridge in the Brenner Pass. On October 2, fighter-bombers had hit the rail line north of the bridge, blocking troop trains carrying reinforcements to Bologna. Photo-recon flights found the enemy had positioned several new 88mm guns. On the morning of October 3, 1944, the Galliate bridge was the most well-defended target in northern Italy.

The bombers droned north-northeast at 10,000 feet over the clouds covering the Po Valley. When the target was sighted, Russell led them in a turn at the Initial Point. Bowling remembered, "Russell and Galindo always had long bomb runs, straight and level for three to four minutes." This allowed the Germans to fire at least six or seven volleys. The flak field's black clouds ahead of the formation was thick.

Bowling recalled, "Two minutes into the bomb run, my left wingman exploded and I could see his co-pilot trying to get out." Russell's right wingman started smoking and dropped out of formation. "With thirty seconds to go, Russell's plane pulled up and to the right. I could see their right wingman smoking and also pulling to the right. I told my bombardier Joe Silnutz we were taking lead, and just then Russell radioed they were all bailing out."

Sergeant Gerald M. Bertling, tail gunner in B-25 44-28948, the right wing plane of the fourth element of the formation, later reported:

After we began our bomb run we encountered heavy, intense and accurate flak. A few seconds before the bombs were released, I saw two large pieces of metal fly past our element. I turned in time to see the left wing plane of the first element on fire sliding under the formation and losing altitude quickly. It began to spin and after it lost 3,000 feet, one wing fell away and it began to spin faster. I saw the plane crash and burn a few miles from the target. I did not see any parachutes.

Staff Sergeant William A. Smith, tail gunner of B-25 43-4008, the right wingman in the rear formation, reported:

Just before the bomb release point, I noticed a trail of flame coming from behind our left rudder. The next instant the aircraft came into view. The entire left side of it seemed to be engulfed in flames. Then the plane rolled over on its left side and started downward out of control leaving a trail of burning fragments. I did not observe any parachutes. We then went into a steep bank and I was unable to see the plane in question after we leveled off.

Around five seconds before the bomb release point, Russell's B-25 had taken a direct hit in the right engine, which caught fire. Bowling's co-pilot, Second Lieutenant Harold L. Cox, reported:

The plane jerked sharply to the right and left formation several times, but he kept it under control until the bombs were away. As we broke away from the target, Captain Russell completed a 180 degree turn and went off to our right. At this time he had not feathered the right engine. After making our 180 degree turn, I observed Captain Russell's plane under control and holding altitude well, but the right engine was still smoking. As we turned to the left, it appeared as if Captain Russell was turning to follow. He was in the vicinity of Novara. Approximately 30 seconds after we completed our turn on course, Captain Russell called, saying "Anyone in the Drybeef formation. This is 740. I'm going down." I was on VHF at the time and heard his call loud and clear. Immediately I asked for his position. His only reply was "This is 740 going down." I called again for his position but received no answer.

Bowling and bombardier First Lieutenant Joe Silnutzer made an accurate drop. "We pulled up and broke right and I noticed solid flak at our previous position. There were two close explosions I could hear over the engines, followed by the sound of hail on a tin roof as we were showered with shrapnel." "Pistol Packin' Mama's" rudders were damaged, leaving only the trim tabs for directional control, while the hydraulic system took a hit and lost pressure. Shrapnel tore several large holes in the wings. Back at Solenzara, Bowling orbited to allow other damaged aircraft with wounded on board to land first. After landing, the crew counted 64 holes in "Pistol Packin' Mama." "She was reconditioned with so many patches everywhere that her new nickname was 'Patches.'"

Of the 445th's 12 B-25s, two were lost, seven took flak hits, and four crewmen on two different planes were wounded. They made 100 percent drops, which knocked out the bridge. It was the toughest mission the squadron had flown since their arrival in North Africa 18 months before.

The next week, the men of the 57th Wing exchanged their lightweight summer gear for winter uniforms. Only a few missions were flown throughout the rest of October; most missions that did take off were recalled due to weather. Dan Bowling remembered, "A mission that was scrubbed for weather didn't count for your total to finish a tour. But try telling your mind and body it didn't count!"

Fifth Army made a last effort to take Bologna on October 20. The forces in Italy were short of artillery ammunition due to a reduction in ammunition production in anticipation of imminent German defeat. The artillery batteries were rationed to the point that fewer rounds were fired in the last week of October than during one eight-hour period on October 2. US II Corps and British XIII Corps fought for the next 11 days but made little progress on the road to Bologna.

The 321st was ordered to attack the Galliate bridge again on October 20. The Germans were close to making it operational. The announcement of the target was met with shock by the crews, many of whom had flown the devastating October 3 mission. Dan Bowling remembered many planes returned to Solenzara full of shrapnel holes, but all crews returned unharmed. The bridge was reported knocked out.

On October 25, 1944, Captain Michael McCarthy learned he had been promoted to major and was now operations officer of the 65th Fighter Squadron. He was four months away from his 21st birthday. He later wrote of the war situation:

> Offensive pressure by Allied forces pushed the Wehrmacht back to the Appenines [sic] north of the Arno River where they could again use high terrain to delay the Allied advance despite our greater numbers, excellent weapons, and air superiority. In this final winter of the war, the Germans took advantage of bitterly cold winter weather to prevent the Allies from advancing over the Appenines [sic] into the Po Valley. Efforts to dislodge German defenses along the east coast also would not succeed until the brutal winter weather loosened its hold on the Italian peninsula.

Snow began falling across the Apennines on October 24, spreading to the Lombardy plain. By the end of the month, the European continent had entered what would be recorded as the coldest winter in a century.

9

THOSE LITTLE BLACK FLOWERS
THAT GROW IN THE SKY

The miserable weather that arrived in October meant there were only 14 days when the weather was sufficiently clear for pilots to acquire their targets visually, a crucial requirement for a successful bombing attack. Missions were usually possible by late morning when the clouds broke, but it was clear the weather would be the decisive factor in the offensive's final success. Close air support missions were flown on troop concentrations, gun emplacements, and storage depots, particularly along Fifth Army's main axis of advance, Highway 65. Interdiction missions ranged across the Po River Valley to Lake Maggiore on the Swiss border.

On October 20, the 27th Group's 522nd Squadron caught a diesel engine pulling 20 wagons in the open on the railway line between Bologna and Ferrara. First Lieutenant William Kropf led Red Flight in a dive on the train; they hit the engine and cut the rails ahead in two places, then strafed the train while White Flight gave high cover. When Red Flight completed their run and pulled up, White Flight dived on the target and dropped their bombs, after which the Thunderbolts climbed for altitude and headed for home.

As they departed, the Thunderbolts were targeted by accurate 40mm flak, and Captain Robert Fromm, the 522nd's CO, was hit in his engine. His wingman, First Lieutenant Bernard Hartman, pulled close to see if Fromm was OK. "He put the P-47 in a dive and then without calling bailed out at approximately 9,000 feet. He appeared to have cleared the airplane without trouble. I lost sight of him as he fell, and could not spot his 'chute." Unfortunately, Fromm's parachute never opened.

By late October, it was clear that Operations *Olive* and *Pancake* – the efforts to break through the Gothic Line and into the Po Valley – had failed. Fifth Army's units had given their all, fighting vicious close-range battles in incredibly difficult terrain against a well-trained, dug-in enemy. The shortages in both replacements and ammunition the Allies experienced only reinforced that the Italian Theater was now considered a backwater to the main event in France and the Low Countries. Despite making the greatest advance toward Bologna in the offensive's final days, troop strength in the 88th Division had dropped below 60 percent.

The winter of 1944–45 would see the Italian campaign take its final turn.

The clear lesson of the failed campaign was that – as they were presently constituted – the Tenth and Fourteenth Armies were too strong for the Allied Armies in Italy (AAI) to defeat, with their best units having been transferred to France and replaced with the inexperienced Brazilian Expeditionary Corps and 92nd Infantry Division, no matter the willing spirit of the men in those units to close on the enemy. The two German armies had to be weakened over the winter of 1944–45, when there would be no major fighting in the snowy mountains of northern Italy, in order for the Allies to end the war in the spring.

The Germans were supported by a supply line that ran from Munich through Austria into northern Italy through the Brenner Pass, ending at Bologna in the Po River Valley. The Brenner was the most famous of the passes through the Alps that separate Austria from northern Italy, and the lowest, at a maximum altitude of 4,511 feet, making it the only pass that could be kept open in the winter without undue hardship. Before there were roads, the Brenner was the primary invasion route from the north into Italy. As of November 1, 1944, 24,000 tons of supplies were flowing through the pass each day, six times the minimum daily requirement for the German armies. Even after the bombing campaign against the Brenner railway over the summer, the trip from Munich to Bologna took only eight to 12 hours. With the Allies unable to undertake offensive operations, only airpower would be able to reduce the German advantage. 57th Bomb Wing commander General Robert Knapp set his planners to work to develop a successful plan.

Seventy-two trains a day ran through the route. Three main lines from Munich and Augsburg joined at Innsbruck, Austria, the northern end of the pass. Two lines ran south through the pass to Verona, where they again branched out into the Po Valley. The main lateral line ran from Verona east to Vicenza, and west to Milan and Turin. Three single-track lines ran south to Bologna, the main supply point. Because the system ran on electric power, there was no need for the Germans to use their coal-fired trains or divert dwindling coal supplies to the southern front. If the power system could be destroyed, it would force the enemy to replace electric locomotives with steam locomotives; this required diversion of locomotives and crews from elsewhere in German-controlled Europe, when the entire rail system was under attack. Additionally, shipping space in the southbound trains would be diverted from military supplies to coal for the replacement trains.

Knapp's planners believed that cutting electric power would drop the carrying capacity to 10,000 tons a day, since the enemy could not replace the Brenner locomotives one for one. That was still 250 percent of the minimum requirement, but there would be little margin for error. After reducing the number of trains, bombers would target the marshalling yards, line stations, storage areas, repair depots, and all 24 bridges. Success would require multiple missions to each target in a contest with German repair units. The campaign could cut off the Gothic Line over the course of the winter. The codename was Operation *Bingo*.

General Knapp presented his plan to his old friend General Ira Eaker, with whom he had served on the Mexican border following World War I. Eaker, now commander of the Mediterranean Allied Air Forces, saw the proposal's promise – that the Air Force could make it possible for ground forces to smash through the Gothic Line after the spring thaw and thus bring the war in Italy to a rapid end. With his approval, the campaign would begin on November 6.

On November 2, the 86th and 57th Groups' base at Grosseto was almost completely flooded out when a dike north of the town overflowed due to the weeks of continuous rain. The pilots' quarters on base for both units were completely deluged; the first floors of each building were under 4 feet of water. The 66th Squadron's Staff Sergeant George Coyle obtained a fishing boat, which he rigged to a truck winch, allowing it to be used to ferry men out of the flooded area. The group's enlisted men moved into the villas near the beach where the ground officers had been quartered, while the displaced officers moved into a large farmhouse. The 86th Group moved north to Pisa, but the 57th remained behind and cleared out the mess, declaring themselves able to return to operations on November 6.

The M10 4.5-inch "bazooka" rocket tubes used by the Thunderbolts took a heavy toll on enemy installations and supplies. However, the tubes carrying the rockets were plastic and inevitably deformed after only a few firings, making them less accurate. Additionally, the rockets themselves had folding fins which did not always fully deploy, sending the missiles into wild gyrations. The rockets had been introduced in-theater by the 79th Fighter Group, which flew their first "rockets mission" on October 19 when group commander Colonel Nielsen led an armed recce mission up the Adriatic coast.

Michael McCarthy recalled that out of six rockets fired, at least one could be expected to come out of the tube and execute "a looping roll" that could scare the pilot with a near miss. The rockets were not particularly accurate, but were good enough to make flak gunners take cover as the P-47s made their dive-bombing attacks. As close-support missions allowed the troops below to actually see the destructive power of a rocket attack, the result was that both Fifth and Eighth Army units made increasing requests for Thunderbolts to make rocket attacks on targets they called in for close support.

October also saw the P-47s start using new 110-gallon incendiary tanks. These tanks were filled with gasoline and a gelatinous substance, which became known as "napalm"; the tanks were ignited on impact by small grenades. The 527th Squadron's morning mission on October 3 marked the first use the new tanks. As flight leader First Lieutenant John Boone was flight inbound to the target, he was hit by flak. Despite his engine catching fire, Boone managed to keep control of the P-47 and dropped his napalm on target. He pulled up to 3,000 feet, initially intending to bail out, but when the engine fire went out, he decided it was possible he could make it back to friendly territory. Second Lieutenant John Robinson, Boone's wingman, reported that the stricken P-47 steadily lost altitude until, at about 1,000 feet, the right wing dropped and the fighter "dived into a hillside and exploded." The rest of the flight reported that when they dropped their napalm, there was "a dazzling display with flames and smoke covering a large area," but the initial assessment of the new napalm tanks was not enthusiastic. They were difficult to drop effectively since they tumbled once released; in order to hit the target, a pilot had to fly at a much lower altitude, where he was more vulnerable to flak. Once the tanks were fitted with fins for 500-pound bombs, they did the job and became a valuable weapon in the mountainous terrain. The new weapons were complemented with fragmentation cluster bombs that could be dropped on antiaircraft positions to kill their crews.

In addition to new weapons for the Thunderbolt, the pilots received the G-3A G-suits in mid-October. The suits, which VIII Fighter Command began using in the summer of 1944, allowed a pilot to engage in high-G aerial maneuvers without blacking out. The benefits of such equipment for pilots performing a high-G pullout from a dive-bombing attack were quickly obvious, particularly in the Apennines where the Thunderbolts were now operating.

The 350th Fighter Group – which had completed their transition to the Thunderbolt from the P-39 Airacobra in July and August – was augmented in October by a fourth squadron, the Brazilian 1st Fighter Aviation Group (Portuguese: 1º Grupo de Aviação de Caça, 1st GavCa). Brazil had declared war on Germany on August 26, 1942, and the 1st Fighter Aviation Group was authorized in December 1943. The pilots, who were all carefully selected from the ranks of the Brazilian Air Force for experience and demonstrated ability, arrived in Orlando, Florida, in January 1944. After 60 hours' training in the P-40, they moved to Panama, where they received another 110 hours' training in the Warhawk. In June 1944, they moved to the Suffolk Country Army airfield, close to the Republic Factory, where they undertook a further 80 hours' training in the P-47. Following this, the unit arrived in Italy on October 6, 1944. Along with the Brazilian Expeditionary Forces that joined the Fifth Army in August and participated in the Gothic Line battles that fall, these Brazilian units were the only Latin American force to engage the Germans in the European Theater.

Second Lieutenant Paul Young – a farm boy from Indiana who joined the Air Force in 1942 and originally trained as a glider pilot – arrived on Corsica in October. "Fortunately for me, they decided in the spring of 1944 that they had enough glider pilots, and I was sent on to powered flight training instead of to the infantry, since I had demonstrated some aptitude as a pilot." He was assigned to the 445th Squadron of the 321st Group at Solenzara. "The weather was bad most of that month, but fortunately there was enough clear weather over Corsica that I was able to get in some training and demonstrate to them that I was good at flying the B-25. I was assigned as a co-pilot with the understanding that if I showed I had what it took on operations, I'd be moving up to first pilot pretty quickly."

Monday, November 6, 1944 saw the first Operation *Bingo* mission, which was also Paul Young's first mission. "There was no 'sunny Italy' that I ever saw. It was cold and damp on Corsica, which made it hard to sleep through the night in our tents without waking up shivering. Coupled with the fact I had the jitters for my first mission, I had no trouble getting up when they woke us at 0500 hours to get ready."

The 340th and 321st Groups were assigned the transformers at Trento and Ala respectively, while the 310th Group was assigned those at San Ambroglio. If the bombers were successful, trains as far north as Balzano would lose power.

The mission to Ala was the 321st Group's 600th since their arrival in North Africa 20 months earlier. The nine 445th Squadron B-25s were led by Captain Gerald Wagner in "Vicious Vera"; Paul Young flew as co-pilot for Second Lieutenant Max Poteete in "Val"; the 446th Squadron's nine Mitchells were led by commander Lieutenant Colonel Paul Cooper; First Lieutenant Marion Walker led the 447th's nine in "Cover Girl"; Captain Harold Farwell led the 448th in "Out of Bounds." All were loaded with eight 500-pound high-explosive bombs.

The transformer was a small target that required real skill to take out. There was no defending flak or fighters to contend with, allowing each squadron's lead bombardier to zero in perfectly on the target; the 321st's war diarist recorded that the 100 percent concentrations were so accurate it was "pickle barrel bombing." The Ala transformer was so thoroughly destroyed it was not replaced until after the war. Results were similar for the 340th at Trento, and the 310th at San Ambroglio.

The 79th Group's Thunderbolts made rocket attacks against the power station near Verona, covering two squadrons of RAF bomb-toting Kittyhawk IVs which dive-bombed the target, putting it out of operation. The attack scored 18 direct hits on the main buildings in the complex, and 23 against the transformers themselves. As the fighter-bombers departed, they reported the sky was filled with vivid blue flashes of electricity. Electric power for the line between Verona and Trento was knocked out for the rest of the war.

Additionally, B-24s of the Fifteenth Air Force were sent to hit power stations in the Brenner Pass. Bombing from altitude, the heavy bombers were adversely affected by the winds over the Alps and most missed the target. Thus, the Germans were able to continue to use electric power in the pass itself.

The predicted power outage did stop trains as far north as Balzano; within days Ultra picked up reports of a supply delivery drop to the predicted 10,000 tons, accompanied by orders to divert coal-fired locomotives. Operation *Bingo* was off to a roaring start.

On November 7, the first mission against the bridges was flown by the 321st Group. The bombers dropped a string of "thousand-pounders" right through the center of the Sacile railroad bridge for a 97.2 percent score; the center span of the Motta di Livenza railroad bridge fell into the river, despite the 5/10 cloud cover that prevented six of the 18 Mitchells from dropping their bombs.

The 321st's toughest mission of the campaign was flown on Friday, November 10. The target for the 44 Mitchells was the temporary rail bridge and a ferry terminal at Ostiglia the Germans had recently completed. Dan Bowling flew second group lead with co-pilot Second Lieutenant Jay DeBoer, bombardier First Lieutenant Joe Silnutz, and navigator First Lieutenant Phil Starczewski. First Lieutenant Sam Monger was Bowling's wingman with co-pilot Paul Young on his third mission. The bridge was fiercely defended. The 446th Squadron lost B-25J "Leydale," hit in the right engine moments before "bombs away." Pilot First Lieutenant Walton Ligon's left arm was nearly amputated by a piece of flak. Co-pilot Captain Gale Dickson took over while bombardier First Lieutenant Lawrence Clausen ministered to Ligon and tried to help him with his parachute when they took a second hit. Dickson ordered the crew to bail out. The navigator, bombardier, radioman, and tail gunner managed to bail out while the two pilots were lost in the crash. The other 11 bombers were holed by the intense flak, with wounded crew in each.

The 447th Squadron took heavy losses. Lead pilot Captain Maurice "Wigs" Wiginton's "Ready Teddie" took flak hits in both main gas tanks and the electrical system was knocked out, which prevented a drop. Wiginton was able to land back at Solenzara despite a full bomb load and the plane full of gas fumes. B-25 "Traveling Comedy" was hit by flak and lost an engine; the bomber crashed attempting an emergency landing at Pisa. Four other B-25s were lost, and the surviving bombers were all hit by flak that killed four crewmen and injured 12 others.

Just as the 448th Squadron's lead pilot First Lieutenant Douglas Anderson reached the Initial Point (IP), his B-25 "Desirable" had its left engine shot out by flak. Anderson continued to the release point as other hits knocked out the hydraulic system, destroyed the compass, covered the pilots with shattered plexiglass, and cut one of the rudder control cables. "Desirable" remained airborne till the right engine failed, and all seven crewmen parachuted safely. Douglas was captured while partisans found the other six, and they returned to Corsica in mid-December.

"The Duchess," flown by First Lieutenant Milford Kruse, was hit by flak that knocked out the right engine and wounded turret gunner Sergeant Nico Pined, bombardier Staff Sergeant Woodward Pealer, and radioman Staff Sergeant Irving Schaffer. Another hit took out the hydraulic system, which lowered the main gear halfway. Kruse was able to successfully belly land back at Ghisonaccia.

The bombers knocked out seven spans of the pontoon bridge at a cost of 32 aircrew wounded. Paul Young remembered, "It was my first mission where the Germans made a serious attempt to kill me. It wasn't easy to sit there as co-pilot and take it as all that flak exploded around us, but in retrospect it was better I had that first experience as a co-pilot where I wasn't responsible for a crew while I put everything I'd heard people say about how to control fear to work."

Only half the days in November were suitable for flying due to bad weather. The 86th's 525th Squadron sent a flight of eight P-47s to attack Villafranca airfield near Verona on November 10. One Thunderbolt turned back with mechanical problems but the other seven continued on, led by First Lieutenant F. C. Brinley in his P-47 "Love 'n Stuff." Arriving over the field and making a bomb run, several of the 500-pound bombs the Thunderbolts carried exploded close to a Ju-88 and two Bf-109s, but none were destroyed. Brinley led them on a second run, strafing the field in the face of intense flak; they were credited this time with the Ju-88 and three Bf-109s confirmed destroyed, with Second Lieutenant Walter Reiber scoring the three confirmed fighters. As they pulled up from the attack and headed back to Pisa, they discovered five of the seven P-47s had been holed by flak and damaged to varying degrees, but all returned safely.

More aircrew replacements in the bomber and fighter groups arrived over the course of November. On October 21, 1944, 18-year-old Second Lieutenant Henry Harmon "Harm" Diers and 50 other brand-new second lieutenants, all recent Air Force flight school graduates, reported to Newport News, Virginia, for transport to the Mediterranean. They soon went aboard what he later recalled as "a big Liberty ship." The convoy spent 12 days crossing the Atlantic to Casablanca, with six days in the mid-Atlantic spent in a storm that confined many to their racks with sea sickness. From there, the young pilots were transferred to an older liner for the three-day voyage to Naples. Diers remembered, "We boarded a Mediterranean cruise ship for the final leg to Naples, Italy. It was a touch of posh early 20th century luxury class travel, a nice finish to our transatlantic journey." They arrived in Naples on November 7:

We had spent almost a month preparing to be shipped overseas, all ground duty, no time in the air. Added to this were nearly two weeks of flightless days at sea, crossing the Atlantic. None of us had flown for a seemingly interminably long time. When we finally arrived in Italy and found that we had yet more days to wait before being assigned to a Fighter Squadron, we were bored, depressed, and impatient, loafing around in a "Repple Depple" (Replacement Depot) outside Naples near Caserta ...

One hot day, we frustrated pilots were all standing around in an athletic field engaging in calisthenics; there must have been about fifty or sixty of us. Suddenly a P-47 Thunderbolt came roaring over us, very fast and very low. We brand spanking new replacement pilots were ecstatic! We jumped up and down, threw our hats in the air, waved and shouted! "A real combat plane!" We were absolutely thrilled at the sight. Then and there I promised myself that if I ever had a similar chance to buzz this field, I would (as a morale booster, of course). Months later I had my chance. When I left Caserta to return to Grosseto, I wanted to locate that "Repple Depple." It took a bit of time, but I did find it, and sure enough, there they were, fifty or more newly arrived pilots on that same athletic field. I buzzed down across the field; reenacting the flight of my predecessor, only this time I made three low passes. Hats flew in the air, everyone waved, but then on the third and lowest pass I flew through some treetops.

Leaves came blowing into my cockpit through the cockpit air intake. "That was low enough," I thought, and headed for home. When my crew chief checked the plane after I landed, he looked at me and said in his southern drawl, "My, Lieutenant, the trees sure do grow tall down there, don't they?"

After three weeks in the replacement depot, Diers and two others received orders to report to the 57th Fighter Group at Grosseto, for flying duties with the 65th Fighter Squadron.

After two weeks of "clobber college" spent learning the operation policies and procedures his predecessors had discovered might keep him alive, Diers flew his first mission over northern Italy, dive-bombing antiaircraft sites in support of an Operation *Bingo* mission. It was an event he would long remember. "I was flying tail position in the formation, the last in line. All of a sudden there appeared small puffs of smoke – tiny clouds – right there around me, just a few at first, then many, many more. I was fascinated. I didn't notice that the other seven planes in my flight were weaving, climbing and diving. I heard a shout over the radio, 'Diers, wake up. Get your ass moving, that's flak they're shooting at you!' I complied at once!"

Diers later recalled what it was like to dive-bomb a German antiaircraft position.

Once we were over our target and began our dive to release our bombs, all evasive action ceased. We just dove down as fast as possible from about 4,000 feet to a few hundred, pulled the release lever, and dropped the bombs on our target. During those few seconds I felt no sense of danger, no fear of the guns, just concentration on my dive. Bravery was not a factor. Being young and feeling immortal was. But, post dive, I'll admit to a bit of anxiety as I climbed upward out of range and out of the area as fast as possible, full throttle, with flak chasing me!

On December 2, the 79th Group was happy to receive orders transferring them from Jesi to Fano airfield. Fano was a prewar Regia Aeronautica field, and had PSP steel matting, which gave it all-weather capability. Unfortunately, it was 1,500 feet shorter than the performance manuals listed for a safe takeoff by a P-47 with a full load. The aircraft had to be in perfect flying condition and pilots had to handle them skillfully, as any mechanical defect or pilot error would result in disaster when the airplane crashed at the end of the runway with a usual load of two 1,000-pound bombs, two sets of three-tube rockets, and a 110-gallon belly tank. Pilots almost always used the P-47's water injection system to provide sufficient power for a safe short-field takeoff. Due to bad winter storms, only six days had weather clear enough for operations.

Cold was something everyone dealt with in the winter of 1944–45. Paul Young remembered, "We boarded up the tents as best we could, and we would supplement the coal ration by going out in search parties to cut down trees for fuel. A lot of the guys made stoves that burned avgas. We were cold on the ground, we were cold in the planes. I was just cold all the time."

There was only limited heating in a B-25 and the oxygen systems in all planes had been removed because of the fire danger from flak hits. 488th Squadron radioman Staff Sergeant Jerry Rosenthal, who arrived in late November, remembered:

Anoxia was a big problem, since the missions into the Brenner Pass were generally flown at 11,500 to 15,000 feet. We would take our gloves off to check our finger nails for signs of anoxia even though we couldn't do anything about it. We also got to know all about Aerotitis Media, the inflammation of the inner ear from changes in altitude. The air temperature in the airplane at my station as radioman was around 25 below, and if you took off your glove and touched anything, you could freeze your skin to whatever it was. The pilots and bombardier and turret gunner in the nose had a couple heaters there that probably got the temperature up to 10 below, as did the tail gunner. But the radioman's position was unheated and drafty since it was right behind the bomb bay.

A veteran Rosenthal shared a tent with taught him how to prepare for the cold.

I acquired a blue wool electric flight suit, even though there was no electricity available for it in the airplane, but I wore it over my GI long johns, then a wool shirt over that followed by my A-2 jacket with a super heavy sheepskin coat over that! Wool socks, then GI shoes with the wonderful sheep lined flying boots over them. I had sheepskin overalls to cover the wool GI pants, and with all that, I was able to prevent frost bite!

Wearing all that, movement inside the fuselage "wasn't easy."

Mountain weather was also an enemy. In the Alps, turbulent winds swept down at speeds of 50–60mph, making accurate bombing difficult. In the Brenner Pass, the mountains on either side were 8,000–9,000 feet high; some reached 10,000 feet. 445th Squadron co-pilot Second Lieutenant Victor Hanson recalled a mission where his plane was hit and dropped out of formation. The pilot turned into what ended up being a box canyon too narrow for them to turn around. "We were climbing against downslope winds that were only a little bit slower than we were going up. We were holding maximum power and just barely climbing. All those rocks out front definitely had my attention as we got closer and closer. In the end, we cleared the ridge by maybe 20 feet. That was my scariest mission and it didn't have anything to do with the Germans."

57th Wing leaders ordered crews to fly their bomb runs straight and level for at least four minutes from the Initial Point to "bombs away." Crews were reluctant to do this since it gave the enemy gunners time to fire several volleys; it was the moment in a mission when most shoot-downs happened.

Dan Bowling was one of the top pilots in the 57th Wing; his bombardier Joe Silnutz was the 321st Group's best bombardier. They were determined to find a tactic to avoid exposure and still hit the target accurately. Bowling recalled:

Joe and I decided the only way to survive was by taking evasive action. We practiced many times on the bomb range and developed a process in which we would fly a certain compass heading to the target circle, then turn 10–15 fifteen degrees right or left, then change again to a different heading, then change course to the target. Joe got the timing with the Norden sight so accurate we would only fly 30–40 forty seconds straight and level to the target.

Since Bowling was a squadron lead pilot and Silnutz a lead bombardier, they were able to put the tactic into action.

When I was out front, everyone else had to do what I did, so they followed me. I could look out just after we changed course and see a barrage go off right where we would have been had we continued on. Then we'd turn and there would be another barrage go off where we would have been. When we turned on to the bomb run, the gunners were so confused they didn't have the time to put up that last volley before we dropped and broke formation.

321st Group commander Colonel Smith was quite open that "I want a star when I leave" and held bombing accuracy as the key to that. Whenever he gave the order to fly straight and level during a pre-mission briefing, Bowling would later tell the other pilots to follow him. "I was proud of two things about the missions I led. One was that we had the highest bombing accuracy of anybody in the group, and the other was that I had the lowest losses. We got the target and we didn't lose our friends." Eventually 445th Squadron commander Colonel Cassidy ceased arguing with Bowling, giving him the highest unspoken praise by making him lead pilot on every tough mission during the worst period of the Battle of the Brenner.

December 9 was a "bad day" for the 57th Fighter Group. At 1030 hours a 66th "Exterminators" flight found a train pulling flatcars loaded with motor transport headed south near Vicenza. The pilots made a strafing pass and got good hits, damaging several of the flatcars. However, the gunners in the train's flakwagon were extremely accurate. When First Lieutenant Charles Dehmer pulled up from his dive white smoke poured from his engine and supercharger. Others in the flight calling for him to bail out were met with no response; the P-47 reached an altitude of approximately 500 feet when it rolled over and plunged into the ground.

As the others formed up, Captain Thomas Callan radioed that he had been hit and his oil pressure was zero. Pulling the nose up in hopes of using the last of the engine to get sufficient altitude to glide east and ditch in the Adriatic, it was clear when the rest of the flight caught up with him that he would have to bail out. Rolling the stricken Thunderbolt inverted, Callan fell out of the cockpit and pulled the ripcord of his parachute once clear of the tail. He parachuted safely but was quickly captured by a German patrol.

The 66th's second mission of the day was an armed reconnaissance in the same area where Dehmer and Callan went down; enemy trucks were spotted on a road, and the Thunderbolts dived to strafe them. When Second Lieutenant Robert Lown pulled out of his dive, he "mushed" into some trees and the P-47 exploded.

An hour later and a few miles east, a fourth "Exterminators" Thunderbolt was shot down during a bombing run. First Lieutenant Wayne Dodds was able to ditch his P-47 into the Venice lagoon in about 3 feet of water. He was the only pilot lost that day who would return, after a month of adventures behind enemy lines. The next day the squadron lost Second Lieutenant Eugene Smith. In an eerie twist of fate, five replacements reported to the 66th Squadron that afternoon.

Sergeant Jerry Rosenthal flew his first mission on December 10 and remembered it well. Thirty-six 340th Group B-25s from the four squadrons were briefed to hit the deadliest target in northern Italy – the Rovereto railroad bridge.

Rosenthal and the other crews ate a "mission breakfast" of fried fresh eggs, real bacon, and hot cakes at 0600 hours. At the 0800 briefing, they learned there was a possibility of enemy air activity; ten 57th Fighter Group P-47s would escort them. Rosenthal's B-25, "8K," was number four in the third six-plane box with First Lieutenant J. H. Kroening, pilot; Second Lieutenant V. Fortuna as co-pilot; Second Lieutenant Norman Rosenthal, bombardier; Sergeant H. Lisby, turret gunner; and Sergeant P. Sims, tail gunner.

The 488th Squadron's 18 Mitchells crossed into Italy just north of La Spezia. The crews donned their flak vests and watched for strangers as the P-47s joined up and took position.

We were at 12,000 over Lake Garda and climbed to 13,400 on the bomb run. No Oxygen. On the bomb run I pulled my helmet down around my ankles and picked up the K-20 camera to shoot the bombs away and maybe the bomb strike of the leading boxes. The first box caught heavy, intense, inaccurate flak at the beginning and we got heavy, intense, accurate flak just before bombs away. I dropped my camera when it got hit by a flak burst that came up through the floor.

Following "bombs away," the bombers broke away and Rosenthal watched six Bf-109s jump the lead squadron, while the 488th's formation was attacked by two Bf-109s from left low and one from left high. The enemy fighters hit a B-25 that exploded while another spun, its engines on fire. One fighter flew through the formation; Rosenthal saw it coming but wasn't able to track it with his gun. Formation gunners shot down one attacker and the P-47s got four. The bombers put 64 1,000-pound bombs on the bridge. Ten B-25s were holed by the Rovereto gunners, wounding one crewman. "It was a rough four hours," Rosenthal remembered.

December 15, 1944 was a date Harm Diers long remembered; the target was a major bridge over the Po River near Piacenza.

We began our bombing run at about 3,000 feet, peeling off to the left in a single file as we dove down. The sky was filled with puffs of smoke from the anti-aircraft guns. As I pulled out of my dive after releasing my bombs, I saw a flash of fire from a gun emplacement on the ground to my left, and swerved left to strafe it. The pilot who preceded me in the bombing run had missed the bridge with his bombs. They had fallen to the left and exploded directly under me and I flew through the fragments! Luckily, the plane seemed to be flying normally. The sturdy P-47 prevailed and I arrived back home safely at Grosseto. The crew chief counted well over a hundred holes in the plane's metal skin.

Being the first American fighter unit to enter combat in the MTO, the 57th set records no other group could match. In December, the three squadrons became the first and only USAAF fighter squadrons to each fly 1,000 missions. The 66th Squadron recorded Mission 1,000 on December 13, followed by the 64th on December 22, and the 65th on Christmas Eve. The group flew Mission 3,000 on New Year's Eve, with the 66th "Exterminators" marking the record. By the end of February 1945, Mission 4,000 was flown. Their concluding record at the end of the war in Italy on May 2, 1945, was a total 4,651 missions since August 1942.

XXII TAC lost the B-26 Marauders of the 17th and 320th Bomb Groups in December when they were transferred to France. Not only was the 57th Wing left alone on Corsica, but so few replacements had arrived since October the mission tour was raised from 60 to 65 in November, when 45 340th Group crews completed their tours, leaving only 22 crews, with no replacements. The group's war diarist wrote about "a severe loss of morale" among the men at the news of the tour extension.

The situation was the same in the 321st and 310th Groups, particularly after the tour was raised to 70 in December. Paul Young, who had been promoted to first pilot in early December, told the squadron operations officer he would fly first pilot or co-pilot on any mission. "It was the only way I could think of to get all the way to 70 missions and get home." Winter weather reduced the missions flown, making the strain on men of trying to get enough missions to go home worse.

The day after Christmas, 1944, the German Fourteenth Army gave American troops in the Fifth Army a surprising and unwelcome delayed Christmas gift. In the early morning hours of December 26, eight German and Italian infantry battalions, supported by artillery, attacked positions held by the "Buffalo Soldiers" of the African American 92nd Infantry Division. The 92nd had manned their positions along the Serchio River since early November. While they had conducted extensive patrolling, they had not met the enemy as a division. The attackers initially overwhelmed the 366th Infantry Regiment, but the troops regrouped and fought to delay the onslaught with what was available.

Due to the failure of division commander Major General Edward Almond to communicate the severity of the attack to higher authority, the Thunderbolts of the four units available were not given orders to fly close air support for the beleaguered troops when daylight came. Almond, a native Virginian, had been highly regarded by US Army Chief of Staff General George C. Marshall, who made him the 92nd's commander. The division was segregated, manned by African American draftees. Marshall believed Almond would bring enlightened leadership, but he did not. With almost all the white officers being Southern, the division was remembered by the men as being run "like an old plantation," with the "Jim Crow" social system strictly enforced. As a result, the unit was plagued by low morale, which Almond attributed to a lack of skill by the African American troops.

By the time the severity of the attack and breakthrough became known at XXII TAC, there was little that could be done. The majority of missions flown on December 27 were close air support for the counterattack. Any Axis troops spotted became targets for the Thunderbolts, which dropped fragmentation cluster bombs and napalm on the enemy, then strafed them. The line was stabilized by the end of the day on December 27, with the enemy withdrawing on foot under cover of darkness. The front lines had been restored to roughly their positions on Christmas Day by midday of December 30.

On December 31, the 1st Brazilian Fighter Squadron celebrated two months of successful combat operations as part of the 350th Fighter Group, flying three missions that day. The first, composed of eight P-47s, took off from Pisa airfield at 0755 hours to dive-bomb the Trento rail marshalling yards. They were met by intense flak between Ostiglia and Melara as they departed the target area, having cut the tracks in the yard with 16 500-pound bombs and strafing rolling stock, destroying eight wagons and damaging ten more.

A second flight of eight, sent an hour later to follow up the first strike at Trento, was forced to hit an ammunition dump near Genoa when the weather closed in over Trento. The Thunderbolts dropped 13 bombs, destroying six storage sheds with spectacular results. Once through their bomb runs, they strafed vehicles near the dump, with two trucks destroyed in huge secondary explosions. As they headed back to Pisa, a train with 100 wagons was spotted at Novi Ligure. Strafing holed the locomotive's boiler and damaged several wagons.

December finally saw US forces in Italy provide effective military command leadership. General Mark W. Clark, vainglorious Fifth Army commander, was promoted to command the Allied 15th Army Group, formerly the Allied Armies in Italy (AAI), as successor to British Army General Sir Harold Alexander. More important was Clark's replacement as commander of Fifth Army. The appointment of Lieutenant General Lucian K. Truscott, Jr., was the most important assignment of senior leadership in the entire Italian campaign. Truscott had a record as the most successful American senior commander in working with the other nations' armed forces, a skill Mark Clark completely lacked. Fifth Army was the most international of the Allied armed forces in Europe, with more British, South African, Brazilian, Polish, and Italian troops than American. He was gruff and intent on getting things done, not a posing prima donna like Clark. Known for decisiveness and competence, the lack of which qualities had sunk the careers of so many others in North Africa and Italy, Truscott never, ever treated his men with the contempt Douglas MacArthur was so well known for. The morale of all units in Italy benefitted from the change of command. On Corsica, Dan Bowling recalled, "Things changed for the better after Christmas. There was a different attitude everywhere."

Truscott faced a daunting situation. Winter weather and difficult mountain terrain negated Fifth Army's power of armored maneuver, while exploitation of now-overwhelming air superiority was nearly impossible. Additionally, the Army lost needed units when British troops were sent to Greece following the German evacuation in December, while the British 5th Division and Canadian Corps were transferred to northwest Europe.

In his new position, Truscott managed to convince General Marshall that this was the time to commit the most unique combat unit in the Army – the 10th Mountain Division – to combat. The success of Finnish ski troops who humiliated Soviet armored units in the Winter War of 1939–40 led to the formation in 1942 of a regiment to fight in mountain environments during winter, with the full division formed at the end of the year. The unit's ranks included Olympians who would have competed in the Helsinki Winter Games of 1940, cowboys, lumberjacks, All-American athletes, members of the National Ski Patrol, and others with "outdoor" backgrounds. They trained at Camp Hale, Colorado, 8,000 feet high in the Rocky Mountains. Marshall held back committing the unit to combat until there was a situation only they could handle. War in the Tyrolean Alps in the coldest European winter in a century qualified. The division arrived in Italy in mid-December 1944 and entered combat in late January. They would remain on the front lines for the 110 days left of the war in Italy, though Sergeant Tony Sileo recalled, "they took our skis away from us after our first couple weeks of patrols."

The antiaircraft artillery was always present. On November 1, IV Flak Korps fielded 366 88mm antiaircraft guns stationed from Verona to Innsbruck. Sixty-nine more 88mm guns were moved into the Brenner Pass at the end of November, for a total of 435 heavy weapons. By January 1945, the guns were located as far north as Bressanone. Paul Young's bombardier kept a map on which he marked flak positions with a red dot. By February 1945, the map had a solid red line half an inch wide, which ran from Verona to Innsbruck. Young remembered:

The Germans had a nasty trick of moving the guns around. You'd tense up as you approached the place you got shot at on the last mission, and there'd be nothing, so you'd relax. And then five minutes later as you flew over a place where you'd never been shot at, all of a sudden you were surrounded by those little black flowers with the red center in them. It finally got to the point where I was tense from the minute we crossed the front lines headed north till the minute we crossed them headed south. Over time, that takes something out of you.

By January 1945, the Germans had built flak positions in the mountains at altitudes up to 3,000 feet. One battery west of Ala was positioned at 4,100 feet – 3,000 feet above the target and only a few thousand feet below the altitude the bombers flew at. Rovereto was considered the worst flak trap in Italy, because bombers could only attack from one direction. The concrete gun pits were halfway up the mountainsides to either side of the town. Fortunately, the enemy never developed a proximity fuse like that used by Allied antiaircraft guns, but they did position lookouts atop the mountains with equipment that allowed them to fix the bombers' altitude within a few feet, which added to the danger, especially with radar-guided guns.

In answer to this, formations included three anti-flak planes, which dropped strips of aluminum foil called "Window" to defeat radar. Beginning in January 1945, the anti-flak flight began using 100-pound white phosphorus bombs to burn out the gun crews, damage the weapons, and explode stored ammunition. This was considered "chemical warfare" by the Germans, who announced that captured crews identified as dropping white phosphorus would be subject to summary execution as war criminals. Such executions happened at least three times between February 1945 and the war's end.

The 350th Group's 346th Squadron began 1945 with an attack on the heretofore-untouched Milan rail marshalling yards by two flights of Thunderbolts in the waning daylight hours on January 2. The first flight knocked out the western roundhouse with two 1,000-pound bombs that partially collapsed the structure, badly damaging three locomotives inside. The rest of the P-47s in the first flight then destroyed half of the eastern roundhouse, destroying four locomotives inside and damaging four more. The second flight dropped "frags" that destroyed 15 wagons on the side tracks and cut the rail line in two places. All eight Thunderbolts then gave the yard a thorough going-over with their machine guns. When they departed, they left behind 70 locomotives damaged or destroyed, and more than 100 wagons destroyed or damaged.

The morning of January 3, three P-47s of the 86th Group led by deputy group CO Lieutenant Colonel George Lee executed a "Rover Joe" ground support mission against a company-sized enemy unit in the town of Montesino. Keeping low to surprise the enemy, Lee led Captains James Covington and Vincent Relyea on a run into the target despite intense small-arms fire. All three dropped their 110-gallon napalm tanks on target, wrecking a German counterattack against American infantry dug in on the opposite side of the street. The three then made several strafing passes.

On January 20, a flight of eight 346th Squadron Thunderbolts led by First Lieutenant Elmer Belcher spotted a formation of eight Bf-109s at 10,000 feet near Vicenza. They were from the Aeronautica Nazionale Repubblicana's (ANR) 2° Gruppo Caccia. The enemy fighters broke left, diving on the Thunderbolts. Belcher turned the flight into the attack, meeting two Bf-109s head-on. The first six made their initial pass and disengaged with a chandelle into the clouds. One P-47D took a hit. Belcher and his wingman chased the two that stuck around. They split up; the two Thunderbolts followed one and Belcher closed on its tail and got a good burst, killing pilot Tenente Enrico Brini.

With the battle lines stalemated by the winter, the 79th Group returned to participation in Operation *Bingo* beginning on January 20. The P-47s flew escort for the bombers due to the activities of the ANR squadrons now based near the Swiss border, and also dive-bombed and rocketed enemy gun positions at the targets. At the end of January, the 79th – which had been the second USAAF unit to enter combat in North Africa during the Battle of El Alamein over two years earlier – recorded their 30,000th sortie on January 27, 1945. The mission was flown by deputy group commander Lieutenant Colonel Johnny Martin in "Ten Grand," the 10,000th Thunderbolt produced at Republic's factory in Farmingdale, which had been specially christened at the factory by famed aviatrix Jacqueline Cochran and painted in special markings to celebrate the achievement. Martin's task was an uneventful mission to bomb the railroad tracks north of Bologna. The next day a snowstorm blew out of the Alps and closed Fano for three days till the snow could be cleared from the runway and taxiways. Four train-hunting missions to Austria were flown in the clearing weather. The group would continue such missions throughout February; the mission involved a 400-mile flight over the wintry Adriatic Sea, with water so cold a man would freeze within ten minutes if he crashed. The area between Villach and Klagenfurt in the narrow Drau Valley provided excellent train hunting, though pilots had to be careful flying in the valley, due to the winds coming off the surrounding mountains. Over the course of the month, the group claimed over 30 locomotives destroyed.

The marginal weather throughout January allowed the enemy to extract two full divisions out of the Gothic Line. The 16th SS Panzergrenadier Division and the 356th Infantry Division were both evacuated back to Germany by rail, while the weather kept the Corsica bombers and the Thunderbolts out of the Brenner Pass. The Thunderbolt units averaged only two missions per day throughout January, with many days of weather so poor no missions were flown. On the days where missions could be flown, the emphasis was still on the destruction of rail transport to cut down the supplies available to the Tenth and Fourteenth Armies.

The harsh conditions of mountain flying could create freakish accidents in a moment. On January 21, Jerry Rosenthal lost his friend Staff Sergeant Aubrey Porter in such an accident.

> Our mission was to Ora-San Michelle Railroad Diversion. Porter was flying as tail gunner in "8P" which was number three in the second box. There was very rough air over the target, the planes were bouncing around very violently with great fluctuations in altitude. We made three runs over the target because the bombardiers couldn't get lined up and the flight leader was gung ho. On the third run there was heavy, accurate flak. "8U" was in number six position, directly below "8P." Just before bombs away, "8U" bounced up and struck the right tail section of "8P" with its left propeller, which cut away the rudder and stabilizer and continued into the tail gunner's compartment and part of the left stabilizer. Porter was actually cut out of the tail! "8U" lost its left wing, fell into a flat spin and went down.

Gil Hartwell, tail gunner of the lead ship, saw the whole thing and reported that "Porter fell through space without a 'chute. I saw his 'chute and 8U's wing fall past us. There were no 'chutes from 8U."

The 340th Group's war diarist reported, "Second Lieutenant William B. Pelton and his co-pilot, Flight Officer Harry K. Shackelford, of the 488th pulled an aerodynamic miracle this afternoon when they brought their B-25 back from the mission to Ora-San Michelle without its right stabilizer or right elevator. How they landed the plane safely is still bewildering our operations officer and the hundreds of men who saw the damaged craft come in." Afterwards, "8P" was rebuilt and continued to fly missions.

The 57th Wing's B-25s flew 48 missions over the Brenner in January 1945; 39 missions drew flak that hit 224 aircraft with five shot down. The pass was closed to through traffic on five separate days. The 340th Group's war diarist recorded that "milk runs are getting few and far between in northern Italy." With replacements few and far between as Army leadership looked to finally defeat the Nazis in Germany itself, the mission total was changed in late January, with the announcement that the tour of duty was changed from 70 missions to "the war's duration." Some tried to turn in their wings and take transfer to the infantry, but were refused. Paul Young remembered, "It really was you had to be crazy to continue, but if you tried to get out that meant you were sane and you had to stay. It wasn't called Catch-22 or anything, but the policy was there."

Joe Heller, who had been a "loud voice" against tour increases in August, was not among those affected by the changes. He had been given another assignment. 340th Group commander Colonel Chapman was very aware of his public image and had placed First Lieutenant Wilbur Blume, a bombardier with an extensive background in photography, in charge of what was called the "9th Photographic Unit." The unit's photographers accompanied missions to get "official photographs" of the results. Blume was also assigned as group public relations officer and made several short documentaries for the colonel.

In September, Blume was ordered to make a documentary titled *Training In Combat*, about the colonel's new program for replacement crews. Blume chose his actors from group members in late September; among them was Joe Heller, chosen to be "Pete," a replacement bombardier. He and the other "actors" were put on "limited duty," assigned missions that were considered "safe," so the project wouldn't lose any cast members. Bad weather days in October limited shooting. Progress was made in November, and the project was completed shortly before Christmas; "Pete" is in several scenes in the documentary, which was restored at the National Archives between 2012 and 2014.

Three weeks before the new tour was announced, Joseph Heller climbed aboard a C-47 at Alesani on January 12 that took him to Naples, where he boarded a ship bound for New York. His logbook recorded 60 missions that he later described as "mostly milk runs," a statement that applied only to the final 20. How he was able to leave when he did has never been explained.

On January 29, a 346th Squadron flight led by First Lieutenant Richard Sulzbach ran across seven Ju-87 Stukas, 25 miles north of Bologna. The P-47s were in perfect position to attack the enemy dive bombers. Warning the others to watch out for the rear gunners, Sulzbach scored hits on the nearest one, which went into a dive out of control. Second Lieutenant Clark Eddy got hits on a second, but could only claim it as a probable since he did not see it crash. The other five ungainly bombers dove for the deck where they split up, evading the Thunderbolts in the mountain shadows. Since they had jettisoned their bombs to make their escape, their mission had been foiled.

When President Roosevelt and Prime Minister Churchill met at Malta on February 3, it was agreed to transfer the Twelfth Air Force from Italy to southern France to support the main effort. In the week that followed, General Ira Eaker, commander of the Mediterranean Allied Air Forces, met with General Carl Spaatz, commander of US Strategic and Tactical Air Forces (USSTAF) to argue against the move. Eaker pointed out that doing this would leave two Allied divisions facing the Gothic Line without tactical air cover. The Desert Air Force would be forced to shift units to compensate for the loss of airpower in the western half of Italy.

On February 9, USSTAF agreed that two of the five P-47 groups in Italy would be shifted to the First Tactical Air Force, which was supporting 6th Army Group on the Franco-German border. XXII TAC would be forced to do more with less, but Fifth Army retained its air cover.

On February 8, the reorganized 92nd Infantry launched Operation *Fourth Term*, a new limited ground offensive with the objective of securing better positions from which to commence the Fifteenth Army Group push to destroy the Tenth and Fourteenth Armies, scheduled when the spring snow melt arrived in the Apennines. The offensive was covered by the 27th and 86th Groups.

At 1245 hours, the "Rover Joe" controller assigned four 524th Squadron Thunderbolts to hit the coastal guns near La Spezia, which were harassing the 92nd Division's positions with artillery fire. Each Thunderbolt in the flight carried two 165-gallon napalm tanks – a new weapon using the P-38's drop tank. These were aerodynamically superior to the 110-gallon tanks and could be dropped more accurately since they had tailfins from 1,000-pound bombs. As the P-47s came in on their attack run, several 20mm antiaircraft guns opened up on them. Second Lieutenant Charles Young, Jr., was hit over the target. Element leader First Lieutenant Irwin Lebow saw pieces fly off of Young's wing and the P-47 rolled inverted before it crashed straight into the ground. The eight napalm tanks had found their mark, scoring two direct hits and several near misses on the coastal gun emplacements, silencing them.

On arrival back at Pontedera airfield, the three Thunderbolt pilots were met by Twelfth Air Force commander Major General John Cannon, Colonel S. F. DuToit of the South African Air Force, and 27th Fighter Group commander Colonel William Nevitt. As he climbed out of his cockpit, Lebow was congratulated by General Cannon for completing the 500,000th Mediterranean Allied Tactical Air Force sortie since the invasion of Italy 18 months before.

The 92nd continued the offensive, supported by the 27th and 86th Groups. On February 9, a series of tactical blunders stymied the division, allowing the defending Germans to mount a counterattack against the 370th Infantry Regiment. Faced with withdrawing or being overrun, the troops pulled back. By February 10, the offensive ground to a halt. With P-47s overhead throughout the day and "Rover Joe" controllers ready to call in the Thunderbolts, enemy daytime movements were severely restricted, which saved the 92nd Division from complete disaster.

On February 11, the 27th and 86th Groups prepared to move to France and rejoin XII TAC. By February 15, the 27th arrived at Saint Dizier airfield. Two days later, the 86th arrived at Tantonville. The two groups began flying combat operations over the Western Front on February 20, 1945.

Allied troops had failed to take Monte Belvedere, the key to Bologna, despite making three assaults at the end of the fall offensive against the Gothic Line. Operation *Encore* was now planned to take Monte

Belvedere. To do so, Riva Ridge had to be taken first. The ridge was considered impossible to climb and the Germans defended it with one battalion of mountain troops. On the night of February 18–19, 1945, 1st Battalion and Fox Company of 2nd Battalion, 86th Mountain Infantry, made the 1,500-foot vertical climb in a blizzard. By dawn, the enemy had been driven off the ridge. On the 19th, 85th and 87th Regiments made a bayonet attack on Monte Belvedere without covering artillery fire. The surprise assault was successful and the peak was captured after a hard fight. When the Germans attempted the first counterattack, the regiment's assigned "Rover Joe" team was able to call in the 65th Squadron P-47s orbiting overhead, which quickly located and silenced the enemy with bombs, rockets, and machine-gun fire. Over the next two days, the Germans made six more unsuccessful counterattacks. The enemy was at a severe tactical disadvantage with "Rover Joe" teams with the troops and "Horsefly" spotter aircraft overhead. The 87th Regiment's war diary stated:

> The frontline troops came to love Rover Joe, and Jerry was forced to keep his weapons silent while airplanes were overhead. The sight of a diving airplane, the falling bombs or flash of rockets, and the following sound of strafing or a tremendous bomb blast, was a heartening one to the soldier lying in his hole, harassed by artillery. The strongest and most coordinated counterattack the enemy seemed able to put on against our air power and superior observation was withstood on the morning of the 21st, with a very great percentage of enemy troops involved killed or captured. The enemy couldn't move his armor up into position under the watchful eyes of Rover Joe. The only effective force the enemy seemed to bring on our troops was his artillery and mortar fire, and this remained heavy throughout the week.

In three days of close combat in conditions no other American unit ever fought in, the 10th Mountain Division suffered 850 casualties, including 195 dead. Fifth Army was now in position to breach the Gothic Line, take Highway 65, and open the way to the Po Valley when spring arrived.

Operation *Encore* had achieved every objective with effective employment of infantry, artillery, and airpower in concert. The front lines now extended almost straight across northern Italy from the

Ligurian to Adriatic Seas. Fifteenth Army Group was now poised to deliver the final blow on Army Group C's Tenth and Fourteenth Armies.

With the Russian offensive threatening the enemy in eastern Austria, the Germans attempted to move troops from northern Yugoslavia and northern Italy up to Austria to provide reinforcement. Despite the adverse weather conditions in the Austrian Alps, the 79th Group was able to average ten missions a day for the last four days of February, attacking the rail line in the Ljubljana–Klagenfurt–Villach–Dobbiaco area and destroying numerous trains. Amazingly, there were no losses in the group during this four-day period of maximum-effort missions, despite intense enemy defenses. Between March 3 and 6, the group flew missions from dawn to dusk as the weather cleared. Their score of ten trains destroyed on March 6 by five missions resulted in the award of a second Distinguished Unit Citation. Overall, the 79th's P-47s and the 239 Wing's Kittyhawks claimed a total of 200 rail cars destroyed or damaged. Operations continued at a similar level during every clear day in March. On March 21, an advance party of the 79th left Fano to set up a new landing ground at Cesenatico, 40 miles north of Fano. The group moved to the new airfield at the end of March.

During February, the Corsica bombers flew missions as far north as Innsbruck, Austria. Even in Austria, the Luftwaffe was now so depleted there was no opposition. German gun batteries were increased at Trento and Bressanone, and new batteries appeared at Laves; there were now 482 guns in the Brenner Pass and it was a rare mission that did not draw flak. The enemy's early warning system was refined: when an incoming formation flew within 200 kilometers of a defended area, the batteries were alerted. When the bombers passed 80 kilometers, the guns were manned. Course and altitude were provided by the mountaintop observers. There were no surprise attacks. Crews described the flak as "murderous."

February 1945 saw the worst losses of the war for the 340th Bomb Group. During the month, six Mitchells were shot down, with 37 aircrew listed MIA and 11 wounded in the B-25s that returned to Corsica. The three groups flew 82 missions during February; 62 missions drew flak, while 14 B-25s were lost and 305 were damaged, despite the introduction of white phosphorus for anti-flak operations.

From January 30 through March 26, 1945, the Brenner line was cut at some point every day. That did not mean no traffic was getting through. The Germans were forced to run separate trains through different sectors, forcing them to unload and reload supplies that added an additional delay in delivery. The trip from Munich to Bologna that had taken 8–12 hours in October 1944 took four to five days by March 1945.

Oberfeldwebel Werner Mork returned to northern Italy from Germany in late February. Writing after the war, he recounted:

> Once we got to the Brenner in Northern Italy, it was the train itself that suddenly became the target. From this point on there were many disrupted stretches of track and in particular damaged bridges. At those points we had to exit the train and make our way across the rickety rail bridges by foot to where another train waited on the other side. The Brenner train was no longer a reliable means of transportation; I frequently had to get out and walk. Sometimes there wouldn't even be a train, but rather a line of trucks that would take us to the next rail station that was still intact. All this sure raised our confidence that we would win the war.

The dangerous life of a fighter-bomber pilot was shown in the experiences of one group of 16 replacement pilots who joined the 57th Fighter Group on November 4, 1944, as recorded in the diary of 21-year-old Second Lieutenant Ken Lewis, who was assigned to the 66th "Black Scorpions" Squadron. On February 4, 1945, he wrote:

> Flew my 36th mission this afternoon against Castle Franco, east of Citadella. Quite a hot spot. Pop Heying was leading the show, and was hit on his dive-bombing run. We completed our runs through heavy flak and joined up with Pop, who was in trouble. His plane was on fire in the fuselage just forward of the tail. The control cables burned through, leaving him only aileron and trim tab control – we headed for home wide open. There was a slight explosion, and the fire then burned itself out, so Pop flew that crippled plane all the way home. It was impossible to land it, so he bailed out just off the field.

Lewis wrote five days later on February 9:

> Another one of those bad days. Lyth and Matula both got it today and bailed out just behind the lines, and Paine had his canopy shot off, was wounded in the head, neck and shoulders, and is in the

hospital here now. Matula was hit in a strafing run, his plane was a mass of flames. He bailed out from low altitude and was either hit himself or hurt on landing, according to Blackburn who circled over him. Several Italians were seen to come from a nearby house and carry him over to the house. Lyth was on a two-ship show with Mosites. They bombed a train and Lyth got a direct hit. It was an ammunition train, and the whole thing blew up right in front of him. The huge sheet of flame thrown up covered his plane, and set it on fire. He pulled up and bailed out, just short of the bomb line. Some son of a bitch was shooting at him with 20mm as he came down in his chute, according to Moe.

Eight weeks before the end of the war, on March 6, 1945, a now-veteran Lewis sat alone in his room and wrote:

Just returned from rest leave in France this evening. Bad news awaiting me. While I was gone, we lost three more men. Jeep Norris killed, Phil Lehman the same, and Kruse bailed out over the Brenner Pass. Phil was in France just before I was. We spent the first day of my leave and the last day of his together. Since I was in France, they just locked up our room, so everything is just as he left it. Tomorrow they'll take his things away. I sure feel funny tonight – sitting here alone in the room, looking at Phil's bed, his clothes and things, knowing he won't be back.

On March 10, the 310th Group flew their toughest mission in the Brenner Pass campaign. The two targets were a bridge near the town of Ora that had been previously knocked out and had been recently repaired so that a single track was operational, and a new line that had been constructed around a previously bombed stretch of line. Forty-eight B-25s from the 379th, 380th, 381st, and 428th Squadrons carried four 1,000-pound bombs each. A seven-plane anti-flak flight from the 379th Squadron was armed with 100-pound white phosphorus bombs and 20-pound fragmentation bombs, while a six-plane anti-flak flight from the 381st Squadron was similarly armed. The mission was led by group operations officer Major Royal Allison and 379th Squadron operations officer Major Carl E. Rice. Thirty-two enemy guns were reported in the area, both German 88s and Italian 105s.

The attack plan had the 381st's six anti-flak bombers precede the main formation to hit gun positions, with the 379th's anti-flak flight taking out any that were missed. Twenty-four bombers from the 379th and 380th Squadrons would bomb the railroad bridge, while 18 B-25s from the 428th Squadron bombed the diversion line.

The formation crossed the Italian coast north of La Spezia and climbed to cross the snowy peaks. The six anti-flak bombers ran into heavy flak before they could drop their loads. Smoke pots obscured the targets. Box after box of B-25s flew into the worst flak their crews had ever seen. Three were shot down on the bomb run while a fourth crashed after dropping its bombs, with ten more crippled by flak hits. Major Rice remembered, "Never have I heard so many flak bursts as on the bomb run that day." Major Allison reported, "The flak was everywhere – intense, heavy and accurate. Going into it seemed like a suicidal act. The first box was badly shot up and their plight could be seen by the others. The succeeding boxes went right in regardless."

In the first box, First Lieutenant George F. Tilley, Jr.'s "Puss and Boots" was severely damaged and forced out of formation. Bombardier Second Lieutenant Russell Grigsby recalled, "We had broken away from the main formation a few minutes away from the IP, when wham-wham-wham-wham, four bursts of flak exploded fight below us." Flak riddled "Puss and Boots," tearing gaping holes in the wings and both engine nacelles; large fragments smashed all but three instruments in the cockpit. Flak severed the main hydraulic lines and shot away the emergency system; the landing gear and flaps were inoperable. Grigsby later wrote, "The right engine was smoking and several gas lines had been cut so that fuel began to pour into the turret gunner's and radioman's compartments."

Miraculously, no one had been hit. When Tilley feathered the right engine, the flames were extinguished. Their choice was to bail out or try to restart the engine, which might explode. After three tries, Tilley got the engine running again, then realized he had no airspeed indicator. First Lieutenant Victor Irons brought his Mitchell alongside the wounded "Puss and Boots" in response to Tilley's cry for help.

Once over Corsica, Grigsby and Staff Sergeant George McTavey tried unsuccessfully to crank open the bomb bay doors to drop the bombs, then tried unsuccessfully to crank down the landing gear. "By this time the fuel was ankle deep in both forward and rear compartments, and with the fumes we had to fight nausea as well as broken controls and flames."

When a second attempt to lower the wheels failed, Tilley told the crew to bail out. Grigsby went out the forward hatch, followed by the navigator and co-pilot, while the radioman and tail gunner went out the rear hatch. Tilley trimmed "Puss and Boots," headed out to sea, and bailed out successfully. The pilot was awarded the Distinguished Flying Cross for saving his crew.

The B-25 flown by First Lieutenant George Rorer – who survived a midair collision back in September – caught fire in the right engine nacelle, and flak wounded his co-pilot too seriously to bail out. Rorer attempted to crash land, but as the B-25 touched down, the right wingtip hit a tree that caused the Mitchell to cartwheel, burst into flames, and break in two. No one survived.

First Lieutenant Jordan Keister's 428th Squadron B-25 was hit and fell behind the formation when the right engine and nacelle caught fire. Keister fought to maintain control, which allowed four crewmen to bail out. Moments after the last one got out, the right wing came off; the bomber spun in, exploding on impact.

The 379th Squadron's Lieutenants George Parry, Richard McEldery, Andrew Dennis, Noah T. Shirley, and Gordon M. Jacobs brought their badly shot-up bombers back successfully, saving their crews. Each was awarded the DFC.

Despite 18 bombers damaged by the deadly flak that also destroyed four of the 48 attackers, there were few men wounded. Multiple hits in areas occupied by the crews should have caused wounds but didn't. Gas sprayed into fuselages from ruptured lines, yet no one was burned.

The line was cut in several places, while the bridge was so badly damaged it was not repaired before the end of the war. The 310th Bomb Group was awarded a second Distinguished Unit Citation for the mission.

Paul Young never forgot his 37th mission, flown on March 24, 1945:

As we flew away from the target, the guys in back called on the intercom to ask if we had taken a hit up front, since things were "very windy back here." We checked everywhere, but there was no damage. Our radioman then crawled into the space over the bomb bay and opened the inspection hatch to discover that one of our thousand pounders had hung up by its tail shackles. It was hanging out the bomb bay, preventing the doors from closing. Not only that, but the arming propeller on the nose was spinning. I looked over at my co-pilot. Our first reaction was to bale out before the bomb was fully armed. But we were still 30 miles behind the lines, over enemy territory. There was a quick crew conference on the intercom and the radioman said he'd try something first before we bailed out. He then shucked his gear and lowered himself through that small inspection hatch in the roof of the bomb bay to hang by his arms while he repeatedly kicked the bomb. After what seemed an eternity, the tail gunner reported the bomb had fallen free. He then pulled the radioman out of the bomb bay. When we got back to our base, the first thing I did was write up a recommendation for a Distinguished Flying Cross for our radioman.

The 321st's war diary took no special notice of the terrifying event, noting that three 1,000-pound bombs were jettisoned: two at sea, one "over enemy territory."

The 310th Group suffered their last loss from enemy air action on March 23. While flying a mission to bomb the Pordenone railroad bridge, the Mitchells were attacked by 20 Italian-flown Bf-109s, just as the formations broke from their bomb drops. Five enemy fighters caught the 380th Squadron's Second Lieutenant James J. Summers flying the trailing B-25 in the box of six. The bomber was hit by cannon fire in the left engine and wing, knocking out the oil system and the hydraulic system, which dropped the landing gear. With the extra drag, the bomber dropped out of formation. Summers and co-pilot First Lieutenant Alex Zebelian, Jr., fought to maintain control as the bomber dropped toward the mountains below. The tail gunner and radioman bailed out through the rear hatch while the bombardier kicked the forward hatch open and threw himself out. Several Bf-109s pressed a second attack; the damaged engine caught fire, which spread quickly to the wing. The Spitfire escorts finally drove the enemy off as the pilot, co-pilot, and turret gunner got out and the B-25 exploded when it crashed into a mountainside. The co-pilot, turret gunner, and bombardier were rescued by partisans and returned to Corsica at the end of the month. Unfortunately, the others were captured and became POWs.

The Italians' second attack hit Captain Everett Robinson's lead B-25 from the 380th Squadron, damaging his left engine before they were driven off by the escorts. Robinson kept the badly damaged bomber airborne and returned to Ghisonaccia where he made an emergency landing; he was awarded a DFC for getting his crew home uninjured.

The 12 B-25s of the 379th Squadron were the last to bomb the bridge. First Lieutenant John M. Ford and co-pilot First Lieutenant William Poole were flying lead for the third box. Their B-25 was hit by two Bf-109s that set the right engine afire. Ford held formation until his bombardier made the drop, then dived to put out the flames and brought the Mitchell home.

First Lieutenant Walter E. Grauman was Ford's wingman. His turret gunner opened fire when the Bf-109s flashed past, setting one on fire as it turned away. The bombers and their escorting Spitfires claimed four enemy fighters shot down and three damaged.

The Fourteenth Army's Quartermaster General reported on April 6 that it took five to six days for a supply shipment to get through the Brenner Pass. Only an average 1,800 tons of supplies arrived each day in March, less than half the daily minimum necessary to sustain operations.

10

THE ITALIAN AIR FORCES

A major factor regarding which side an Italian soldier, sailor, or airman ended up on after the September 1943 surrender depended on where in Italy the individual was when the surrender was announced. While 4° Stormo – the leading Regia Aeronautica fighter unit, with more victories between 1940 and 1943 than all other Italian fighter units combined – maintained its traditional royalist connections and moved as a group with the royal family and the Badoglio government, becoming the main fighter unit of the Regia Aeronautica/Italian Co-Belligerent Air Force (Aviazione Cobelligerante Italiana, or ACI) that was organized on October 13, 1943, several units that were part of the ANR, the Fascist air force proclaimed by Mussolini on October 10, 1943, were those already stationed in northern Italy when the surrender was announced. Another consideration was what region of Italy a man came from, with northerners largely remaining with the Mussolini government and southerners remaining with the regular armed forces.

There were exceptions, such as *Aerosiluranti* (torpedo bomber) ace Leo Buscaglia, who took off from La Spezia on what he said was a night mission with his regular crew and flew to Malta, arriving over the island at dawn and landing at Hal Far to surrender in accordance with the terms in the surrender announcement. He would lead the Co-Belligerent Air Force's bomber unit until the summer of 1944 when he was killed in a crash of an ex-RAF Martin Baltimore bomber, which the unit was converting to from their S.79 Sparviero bombers. Conversely, Major Adriano Visconti, a committed Fascist who became the leading fighter ace of the ANR, flew with three comrades from Sardinia to northern Italy after the surrender.

The Italian armed forces – the Regio Esercito (Royal Army), Regia Marina (Royal Navy), and Regia Aeronautica (Royal Air Force) – that fought on the Allied side after the Declaration of War against Germany by the Kingdom of Italy on October 13, 1943, were known as "Co-Belligerent," resulting from the "Co-Belligerent" status of the Kingdom of Italy; officially the Kingdom of Italy was not abolished when the Badoglio government surrendered to the Allies, and as such was officially acknowledged by the Allied Powers as the legitimate Italian government. Thus, the Italian armed forces kept their official name, with the additional "Co-Belligerent" definition. The air force dropped usage of the fasces national insignia and adopted the tricolor roundels – red, white, green – that had been used during World War I until 1927. The Co-Belligerent Air Force did not fly any combat missions in Italy during the war in order not to come into conflict with the ANR. Instead, the Italian air units operated in the Balkans theater, providing air support to the Yugoslavian and Greek guerillas and protecting those Italian units that had been "marooned" in the Balkans by the Italian surrender.

The ANR – the main combat arm of Mussolini's puppet state – fought the Allies until the end of the Italian campaign in April 1945, though their missions became less and less frequent due to lack of equipment and fuel. The Co-Belligerent Air Force was also the most active of the Italian government's armed forces. Both initially used Italian aircraft.

The development of the three fighter designs known in the Regia Aeronautica as the *"Serie 5"* (fifth generation) demonstrates that, contrary to Allied wartime propaganda, the Italian aviation industry was capable of developing world-class combat aircraft. The one negative was that all three were forced to use the German DB 605 engine, due to the inability of the aviation industry to develop high-powered aircraft engines in the class of the DB 600 series, the Merlin, or the American Pratt & Whitney R-2800.

The Re.2005 was a progressive development of the Re.2001. It was the fastest of the three fifth-generation fighters at high altitudes and the best in dogfights due to excellent maneuverability with what test pilots called "finger light" controls, but it suffered from a vibration which turned out to be a propeller balance problem that was corrected. Unfortunately, the Re.2005 was the most intricate, and therefore time-consuming, of the three to produce, which made it unattractive at that stage of the war; additionally, by this point Reggiane fighters had gained a bad operational reputation with Regia Aeronautica pilots. Thus, the Re.2005 was only produced in a small pre-production batch and only saw brief combat in Sicily with a single *Squadriglia* before the unit was wiped out.

Aeronautica Macchi, which had produced the previous best Italian fighters, the C.200 "Saetta" (Lightning) and C.202 "Folgore" (Thunderbolt), developed two designs for the competition. One was the C.205N ("N" standing for "new"), an aircraft specifically designed to take full advantage of the power of the DB 605, while the other – the C.205V – was a modification of the successful C.202, with the airframe "beefed up" to absorb the additional power. The C.205V, which was developed as a "stop-gap" pending the full development of the C.205N was, in the end, the design that was ordered into production and service.

The C.205N "Orione" (Orion) had a redesigned forward fuselage with strengthened longerons to absorb the full power of the DB 605. The effort was time-consuming, but, after a delay of several months, the C.205N1's first flight was on November 1, 1942. Armament included an MG 151 20mm cannon firing through the propeller hub with 300rpg, and four cowling-mounted 12.7mm (.50-caliber) Breda-SAFAT machine guns with 350rpg each. The aircraft had a top speed of 391mph. The second prototype, the C.205N2, first flew on May 19, 1943, equipped with three MG 151 cannons – one engine-mounted and two wing-mounted, with 300rpg each, and two fuselage-mounted 12.7mm machine guns with 300rpg each. This was a much heavier armament than that of the C.205N1, as well as more than the Re.2005 and G.55. Its top speed was 390mph, marginally slower than the C.205N1, with a correspondingly slower climb to reach operational altitude. An order was placed for 1,200 aircraft, but production was abandoned due to the Italian armistice.

The C.205V "Veltro" (Greyhound) was a straightforward modification of the successful C.202 "Folgore" (Lightning) with minimal changes to the airframe other than strengthening the engine bearers to take the increased power while the vertical fin and horizontal stabilizers were larger. Like the C.202, the C.205V's left wing was 8 inches greater in span than the right, an elegant aerodynamic method to compensate for engine torque. Apart from all-metal flaps, the other control surfaces were metal-framed and fabric-covered. The C.205V had self-sealing fuel tanks, an armored seat, and armored windscreen as standard. At a distance the two fighters could be mistaken for each other; in fact, many C.205s were actually C.202 airframes with beefed-up engine mounts and the more powerful engine installed. The C.205V prototype first flew April 19, 1942.

The 100 C.205V *Serie I* aircraft had the same armament as the late-series "Folgore": two 12.7mm machine guns in the fuselage and two 7.62mm machine guns in the wings. The *Serie III*, the most-produced version, had two Breda/SAFAT 12.7mm machine guns in the upper forward fuselage with 320rpg each and two wing-mounted MG 151 20mm cannon with 250rpg each. A 30-gallon drop tank or a 160kg (350lb) bomb could be carried beneath each wing outboard of the landing gear. The C.205V's performance was good at low and medium altitudes, with a top speed of 399mph at 24,000 feet – which could be reached in 7 minutes, 6 seconds – and good dive characteristics; handling and speed dropped considerably over 26,000 feet.

Since the C.205V could be introduced into production with a minimum of disruption to the line, it was adopted in May 1943 pending production of the G.55 and Re.2005. More C.205 airframes were produced before the September surrender than the Re.2005 and G.55 combined. The Veltro matched the performance of the North American P-51B Mustang, with which it fought in a series of spectacular air battles over northern Italy in June and July 1944. Italy's highest-scoring ace, Major Adriano Visconti, achieved 11 of his 26 credited victories in the few weeks he was able to fly the Veltro during the Sicilian campaign, while Sergente Maggiore (Sergeant Major) Luigi Gorrini shot down 14 enemy aircraft with the C.205 in the same time period.

The third fighter, the Fiat G.55 "Centauro" (Centaur), was a completely new design, and was judged by those who flew it to be the best Italian fighter of the war, clearly demonstrating parity with, if not superiority to, the Bf-109G-6, Fw-190A, P-51D Mustang, and Spitfire IX. Unfortunately for Italy, it came just too late to equip units of the Regia Aeronautica before the surrender.

The Fiat G.55 was designed from the outset to take advantage of the Daimler-Benz engine, while the Macchi C.205 and Reggiane Re.2005 were both developments of earlier radial-powered designs modified to use the Daimler-Benz DB 601. Fiat had already been working on an advanced design planned to use a domestic high-performance engine which had not come to fruition when the Regia Aeronautica decided to develop a "fifth-generation" fighter. Modification of the advanced design to replace the powerplant with the DB 605 engine was relatively uncomplicated and put Fiat ahead of its competitors. The G.55 prototype made its first flight on April 30, 1942, well before its competitors, and demonstrated a top speed of 390mph, fully loaded, without using war emergency power, at 23,000 feet. The only negative assessment noted by test pilots was a pronounced left-hand yaw at takeoff due to engine torque; this was partially remedied by positioning the vertical stabilizer at a slight offset right to counteract torque.

Armament of the G.55 was originally designed around an engine-mounted MG 151 20mm cannon, with four Breda-SAFAT 12.7mm machine guns mounted in the forward fuselage, firing through the propeller. This became the *Serie O*; 34 were ordered but only 19 were produced, and six of these were converted to become the first *Serie 1* G.55s. The *Serie O* fighters were the only G.55s to see any service with the Regia Aeronautica prior to the Italian surrender, though their use was limited to intercepting Allied bombers in the vicinity of Rome.

The *Serie I* was modified to an armament of the engine-mounted MG 151 with 250rpg, and two 12.7mm machine guns in the upper forward fuselage, with an MG 151 with 150rpg in each wing. Test pilots were delighted to discover in tests during the summer of 1943 that the *Serie I* was more maneuverable than either the Bf-109G or the Fw-190A. The G.55 could accelerate away from both German fighters in a dive that was only inferior to the Fw-190 in roll.

Italy had surrendered by the time production of the G.55 *Serie I* commenced in the fall of 1943. The *Serie O* aircraft were in use by Regia Aeronautica squadrons in northern Italy that became units of the ANR. Since Fiat was based in Turin in RSI-controlled Italy, it was logical the fighter would now become the main equipment of the ANR. Prior to the surrender, 1,800 G.55s had been ordered; the ANR upped this to 3,400. Unfortunately, the Italian license-built DB 605 was unsuccessful and Fiat was forced to depend on German production for their engines, as had happened with both the Macchi C.202 and Re.2001. This meant Fiat was at the end of the priority list after DB 605s were produced for the Luftwaffe. The Fiat factory in Turin kept the G.55 in production for six months. On April 25, 1944, the Fiat factories were heavily bombed. By that point a total of 164 G.55s had been completed, with 97 produced after the armistice and delivered to the ANR. In the aftermath of the bombing, G.55 production was dispersed to small cities, with the final assembly in Turin. Production was slowed as a result and the Germans stopped all production in September 1944.

The Luftwaffe paid both the C.205V and G.55 the compliment of considering them for use by the *Jagdfliegern*. The C-205V did equip JG 77 when it became the sole *Jagdgeschwader* (fighter wing) remaining in Italy after the withdrawal of the other units in the summer of 1944.

In December 1942, a Luftwaffe delegation visited Guidonia. They were favorably impressed by the promised performance of the *Serie 5* fighters. In February 1943, a German commission led by Oberst Petersen was sent to evaluate the new prototypes. They brought an Fw-190 A-5 and a Bf-109G-4 for direct comparison tests in simulated dogfights. The tests began February 20, 1943; the G.55 was competitive with both the Fw-190 and Bf-109 in speed and high-altitude climb rate, while still maintaining superior handling characteristics. Oberst Petersen called the G.55 "the best fighter in the Axis" in a report to Göring, stating that since it was bigger and heavier than the Bf-109G it was a good candidate for the new DB 603 engine, which was significantly larger than the DB 605. After listening to Petersen in a meeting held with Göring in late February, Erhard Milch and Adolf Galland voted to produce the G.55 in Germany. The DB 603 was installed in what became the G.56 prototype, which was equipped with a pressurized cockpit and armed with five 20mm cannon.

Interest in the G.55 program was still high after the armistice. An October 1943 meeting of the Reichsluftfahrtministerium (RLM; Ministry of Aviation) considered removing the G.55 jigs from the Fiat factory to put the fighter back in production in Germany. Göring and RLM head Erhard Milch listened to a presentation by Kurt Tank, who had personally tested a G.55 at Rechlin, the RLM technical center; he had nothing but praise for the aircraft. Oberst Günther Lützow stated that the C.205 and G.55 were "equivalent to our Bf-109G-6 ... also in terms of armament and flight characteristics, they are sometimes better," and that they were "much easier to take off and land than the 109."

However, the G.55 program was eventually abandoned by the Luftwaffe, since production required 15,000 man-hours. The RLM estimated that this could be reduced to 9,000 man-hours in a German factory, but German factories were assembling Bf-109s in only 5,000 man-hours. In the end, it proved impossible to move the jigs before the Allies bombed the Fiat factory. After the war, the G.55 was put back into production and used as front-line equipment by the new Aeronautica Militare air force. The fighter was further developed postwar as the G.59, using the British Merlin.

The C.205V's combat debut came during the Battle of Pantelleria on June 8, 1943, when "Veltros" from 4° Stormo escorted SM.79 "Sparviero" torpedo bombers and C.200 "Saetta" fighter-bombers attacking Allied warships shelling the island.

Eight "Veltros" from the 3° Stormo and ten from the 51° Stormo were among the fighters available for the defense of Sicily when the island was invaded on July 9, 1943; they were quickly overwhelmed by the Allied air forces.

When Italy surrendered on September 8, 1943, six "Veltros" were among the aircraft that flew south to become part of the Co-Belligerent Air Force in addition to the C.205Vs of 4° Stormo already in the south. However, lack of access to spare parts meant the Veltro could only remain in operational use by cannibalization of damaged airframes, which led to the fighter being withdrawn from operations by the summer of 1944. 4° Stormo was re-equipped with hand-me-down P-39Q Airacobras previously flown by the 350th Fighter Group after the group switched over to P-47s in May; the Italian pilots were not impressed with the older American fighter, which by 1944 was no longer competitive in aerial combat.

The C.205V and G.55 were the initial equipment of the ANR, which had access to the Macchi and Fiat factories in northern Italy to maintain support for spare parts. The ANR had an initial strength of two *Gruppi Caccia Terrestre* (fighter groups). 1° Gruppo Caccia (fighter squadron) and 2° Gruppo Caccia were initially equipped with the C.205V in November 1943, operating them until May 1944, when they re-equipped with Bf-109G-6/R6 fighters left behind by I./JG 53 and II./JG 77 when those units departed Italy after the fall of Rome.

The three *Squadriglie* (squadrons) of 2° Gruppo Caccia – 4ª Gigi Tre Osei; 5ª Diavoli Rossi; and 6ª Gamba di Ferro – were equipped with 70 G.55s, operating them from December 1943 to April 1944, at which time the *Gruppo* began progressive re-equipment with the Bf-109G. The *Gruppo* was initially commanded by Tenente Colonel (Lieutenant Colonel) Antonio Vizzoto, who was relieved in May 1944 by Tenente Colonel Aldo Alessandrini.

Because the ANR units remained in front-line combat, the pilots serving in those units became the top-scoring Italian fighter pilots of the war. The two top-scoring Italian fighter pilots were Ugo Drago and Mario Bellagambi, both of whom flew as squadron commanders in the ANR's 2° Gruppo Caccia.

Born March 3, 1915, Ugo Drago obtained his flying certificate early and worked for a time as an instructor before joining the Regia Aeronautica, where he graduated from flight school and won his wings in 1939, commissioned as a *Sottotenente Pilota* (second lieutenant pilot).

Drago was posted to the CR.42-equipped 363ª Squadriglia, 150° Gruppo, in which he served throughout his career in the Regia Aeronautica until the armistice was announced, becoming commander in June 1942. He scored his first victory flying a CR.42 on November 2, 1940, during the Greek campaign, shooting down a Greek PZL P.24 on a bomber escort mission to Salonika. On November 12, he scored a double, shooting down two P.24s over Koritza, and shot down an RAF Blenheim on February 13, 1941.

Equipped with C.200 Saettas by the end of the Greek campaign, the *Gruppo* stayed in Greece until December 1941, when it was posted to North Africa. Escaping Tunisia at the end of the North African campaign, 150° Gruppo was transferred to Sicily in May 1943, becoming the first Regia Aeronautica fighter group to re-equip with the Bf-109G. After initial teething troubles during the brief work-up period, the *Gruppo* first engaged the enemy during the Pantelleria campaign in June. Drago and his pilots scored their first victories on June 9, when four Bf-109s of 150° Gruppo along with 14 C.202s of 51° Stormo engaged a formation of 50 Spitfires and P-38s, with the Bf-109s shooting down four Spitfires, including two by Drago, who was then shot down with two other Italian pilots and bailed out over Pantelleria. These were his last victories with the Regia Aeronautica.

Following the armistice, Drago joined the ANR, joining 2° Gruppo Caccia as commandeer of 1ª (later renumbered 4ª) Squadriglia, which flew the first G.55s in the ANR before converting to the Bf-109G in the spring of 1944. Between June 24, 1944 and March 23, 1945, Drago was credited with 11 victories, consisting of four P-47s, two P-51s, a P-38, a B-24, a Boston III, a B-26, and a B-25. Capitano Ugo Drago flew over 400 combat missions during World War II and was awarded three Silver Medals for Military Valor by the Regia Aeronautica and another awarded by the RSI, two War Crosses, and the German Iron Cross, First and Second Class.

Capitano Mario Bellagambi obtained his civil flying license in 1934, then joined the Regia Aeronautica a year later and won his wings in 1936. Promoted to *Sottotenente Pilota*, he was assigned to 362ª Squadriglia, 52° Stormo, 24° Gruppo, flying the CR.32. In April 1938, Bellagambi went to Spain, flying the CR.32 with the "Gamba di Ferro" ("Iron Leg") Squadriglia, led by Tito Falconi. He was later assigned to the ground attack Squadriglia "Ocio Che te Copo" ("Attention! I'm going to kill you!") led by Tenente Ido Zanetti. In April 1939, he returned to Italy and went back to duty with 362ª Squadriglia. The unit re-equipped with the Fiat G.50 Freccia (Arrow) in the spring of 1940, just prior to going to war. Bellagambi's unit took part in the Greek campaign in 1940–41.

In 1942, Bellagambi joined 150° Gruppo and flew in the North African campaign. Bellagambi scored his first individual victories during the Sicilian campaign after the *Gruppo* converted to the Bf-109G. Following the armistice, Bellagambi joined the ANR and was assigned to 2° Gruppo Caccia in G.55s, where he was named commander of 2ª Squadriglia "Diavoli Rossi" ("Red Devils"). He remained with that unit to the end of the war, by which time Bellagambi had engaged in 45 air combats, and was credited with 14 victories, making him the leading ace of the ANR and the top-scoring Italian pilot of the war. His victories included one B-17, one B-25, one B-26 Marauder, three P-51 Mustangs, five P-47s, and three Spitfires.

The leading Italian fighter commander of the war was Adriano Visconti, who scored with both the Regia Aeronautica and the ANR, flying combat through to the end of the war. Visconti was born in Tripoli on November 11, 1915, where his father, Count Galeazzo Visconti, who had served in the North African colonization expedition of 1911, remained in search of his fortune. When he completed his studies he applied to and was accepted by the Accademia Aeronautica (Air Force Academy). Graduating in 1939, he was commissioned as a *Sottotenente*

Pilota and assigned to 59ª Squadriglia, 12° Gruppo, 50° Stormo, which was equipped with the Breda Ba.65 and based at Tobruk. When war broke out in 1940, Visconti was posted briefly to 2° Gruppo Aviazione Presidio Coloniale's 23ª Squadriglia. After escaping three Gladiators of 33 Squadron while flying a Caproni Ca.309 "Ghibli" reconnaissance aircraft and saving the lives of his crew, he was awarded his first Medaglia di Bronzo (Bronze Medal) and returned to flying the Ba.65 with 159ª Squadriglia. The Breda was thoroughly inadequate for the role of a ground-assault aircraft, and 50° Stormo suffered such appalling losses with the vulnerable Bredas the unit was disbanded in January 1941.

Tenente Visconti was transferred to 76ª Squadriglia, 7° Gruppo, 54° Stormo, based at Treviso and equipped with the Macchi C.200 Saetta. With his background in reconnaissance, Visconti flew both bomber escort and aerial reconnaissance in C.200s fitted with cameras over Malta, where he was credited with a "probable" Hawker Hurricane on December 22, 1941; in 1942 the unit received a small number of C.202 Folgores modified for photo recon which he also flew on recon missions to Malta.

Visconti scored his first confirmed aerial victory, a Blenheim, shot down on June 15, 1942 during the Battle of Pantelleria, following that up with two Spitfires shot down on August 13. By March 1943, Visconti had been promoted to *Capitano* and was appointed commander of 76ª Squadriglia; the unit was re-equipped with C.202s and flew in the final air battles in Tunisia. On April 8, 1943, accompanied by his wingmen, Laiolo and Marconcini, Visconti spotted three Spitfires; each Italian pilot was credited with one. By May 13, he had added a Spitfire and P-40 to his score. That day he squeezed his friend Capitano Fioroni into the cockpit of his C.202 and managed to reach Sicily.

In August 1943, Visconti was appointed commander of the newly formed 310ª Squadriglia Caccia Aerofotografica (Aerial Photography Fighter Squadron) at Guidonia airfield outside Rome, equipped with six specially modified C.205Vs. In early September, he led a detachment to Decimomannu. On September 9, following the armistice, he and his wingmen Laiolo and Saieva flew back to Guidonia, each with three ground crew in the rear fuselage of the Veltros.

A committed Fascist, Visconti joined the ANR when it was formed, initially commanding 1ª Squadriglia Caccia and then the entire I° Gruppo "Asso di Bastoni," from February 1944 to the end of the war. He was credited with his first ANR victory when he shot down a P-38 on

January 3, 1944, flying a C.205V. He personally claimed ten victories during the war but has been credited by other sources with as many as 26.

On April 29, 1945, Maggiore Visconti negotiated the surrender of his unit, 1° Gruppo Caccia, to Communist partisans near Malpensa airfield, Milan, after being promised that none of his men would be killed. He and his officers were then put aboard buses and taken to the Savoia Cavalleria barracks in Vincenzo Monti. Visconti and his adjutant, Tenente Valerio Stefanini, were then taken to another room for interrogation, where they were both shot in the back by the Russian bodyguard of the partisan leader Aldo Aniasi. The Russian was later charged with murder but was discharged since the murder occurred before May 2, the official end of the war in Italy, and was considered an act of war. Visconti and Stefanini were hastily buried in the barracks courtyard.

The last Luftwaffe fighter unit had departed Italy following the invasion of southern France, leaving the ANR with responsibility for air defense of northern Italy. Following organization of the two fighter groups in October and November, the ANR began combat operations in December 1943. 1° Gruppo "Asso di Bastoni" flew the C.205V Veltro, while 2° Gruppo was equipped with the G.55 Centauro. In January 1944, the C.205Vs of the 1ª Squadriglia were the first to engage in combat, shooting down three from a formation of P-38 Lightnings. In April 1944, German military authorities ordered that the ANR be incorporated into the Luftwaffe. The Italian pilots burned their C.205 and G.55 fighters in protest. In June 1944, the two fighter groups were re-equipped with Messerschmitt Bf-109G-6 and later G-10 and G-14 fighters. 1° Gruppo Caccia "Asso di Bastoni" suffered such heavy losses during the Cassino campaign the unit was withdrawn to Germany for training from October 1944 to February 1945, when it returned to Italy and operated from airfields near Milan and Varese until April 1945, when it was transferred to airfields at Parma and Pavia, before being transferred again to Brescia and Verona near Lake Garda. Between October 1944 and February 1945, 2° Gruppo Caccia "Gigi Tre Osei" was the only ANR fighter unit active in northern Italy. After November 1944, casualties began to outnumber victories for the pilots.

Throughout the Brenner Pass bombing campaign, the ANR squadrons never had more than 40 fighters available at any given time, spending long periods without sufficient fuel to make an effective defense.

The 350th Fighter Group became the last P-47 group to engage in air combat in Italy in two air battles against the ANR in March and April 1945. On a cloudless March 14, 15 P-47s of the 346th and 347th Squadrons escorted 321st Group B-25s. At 1115 hours, Second Lieutenant C. C. Eddy, flying Yellow Three in First Lieutenant John Bergeron's Yellow Flight, spotted 16 Bf-109G-10s climbing away from Lonate airfield. When he called them in, he was told to stay with the bombers. Yellow Flight continued on while Eddy kept an eye out for the enemy fighters. After several minutes, he realized they had gained the altitude advantage and headed toward the bombers. This time his warning was followed by Yellow Flight climbing to intercept the Bf-109s before they reached the B-25s.

The enemy fighters took the bait and dived on the Thunderbolts. The leader turned in to make a pass on Bergeron, but a long burst from Eddy's guns convinced the enemy pilot to break off. Second Lieutenant Roger Ellis took a 20mm hit in his engine; he broke off and turned for home with oil spraying from the engine. Bergeron broke away from the fight to escort Ellis, leaving Eddy and Flight Officer Walter Miller to deal with the enemy fighters. Miller shot a Bf-109 off Eddy's tail, which fell toward the ground below, trailing thick black smoke. Eddy later recalled, "One Me [Messerschmitt], apparently the leader, decided to get things over with. He did a wingover and came down in a steep dive. I broke into him head-on. We both started firing at long range and closed at a high rate. I saw that I was getting solid hits in his engine and wing roots. He kept firing, and as we passed within inches, I could still hear his guns. After he went by, Walt and I turned into the others."

The two Americans thought they were fighting Germans, but Eddy's target was Adriano Visconti, 1° Gruppo Caccia commander. He bailed out moments before his mortally wounded fighter impacted the ground. With their leader out of the fight, the remaining enemy pilots broke contact and turned away for home while Yellow Flight stayed with the bombers.

"Rhubarb," the local fighter controller, advised First Lieutenant Belcher's Green flight that the enemy were headed west, and cleared the P-47s to pursue them. Hoping to catch the enemy, Green Flight headed directly to Bergamo airfield. The gamble paid off when First Lieutenant Robert Thompson caught a Bf-109 and put a burst into the engine. He turned away and claimed a damaged; in fact, Thompson actually scored a destroyed, since it was subsequently determined that he had fired at Capitano Guido Bartoluzzi, who was killed when his mortally wounded Bf-109 exploded on Malpensa airfield. The crash led to the destruction of another 1° Gruppo Caccia fighter when Maresciallo (Marshal) Danilo Billi's Bf 109G-10 landed and ran into the crane being used to remove Bartoluzzi's fighter from the runway. Billi was miraculously unhurt, but the Bf-109 was destroyed.

Green Flight found Bergamo airfield surprisingly active; there were freshly painted Ju-88s and Bf-109s in the dispersal area with yellow theater ID bands. Belcher, Thompson, Parish, and Allen made 15 strafing passes over the field. When they headed home, they left one Ju-88 on fire and five more Ju-88s plus an SM.79 Sparviero and a Bf-109 badly damaged. The Thunderbolts also knocked out seven 20mm gun positions.

With the RSI squadrons more active, March 18 and 20 saw the Campoformido airfield near Udine where 2° Gruppo Caccia was now located attacked both days by Thunderbolts of the 79th Fighter Group. On March 18, 50 P-47s attacked the field with rockets followed by multiple strafing runs that damaged the airfield but only caught two Ju-88s on the ground. The airfield defenses shot up four of the attackers and shot down First Lieutenant Clarence E. Paff, a 55-mission veteran who died in the explosion when his Thunderbolt hit the ground. On March 20, a photo-recon flight spotted the Bf-109s of 2° Gruppo Caccia on the ground at Campoformido. When the 79th's Thunderbolts appeared an hour later, they had learned from the previous mission; one squadron went after the known gun positions with fragmentation and white phosphorus bombs and rockets while the other two squadrons went after the aircraft on the field with the same ordnance. Once they had unloaded, the squadrons returned to Fano to rearm and returned, flying 260 sorties and keeping P-47s overhead for nearly all the daylight hours as they thoroughly wrecked the airfield, setting buildings on fire, cratering the runways, and bombing revetments. When the last P-47 finally departed, 21 of the Gruppo's 29 Bf-109s were destroyed. The wartime career of 2° Gruppo Caccia was over.

On April 2, the 346th and 347th Squadrons each added six enemy fighters to their score when they engaged 28 Bf-109s of the 1° Gruppo Caccia attempting to intercept the B-25s in a fight over Lake Garda. The Italians failed to see there were two separate bomber formations with fighter escorts on parallel courses. When they intercepted the first bombers they saw, they flew directly in front of the 346th Squadron. First Lieutenant Richard Sulzbach turned on the tail of the enemy fighter that flew in front of him and opened fire, setting the airplane on fire and killing the pilot, Tenente Aristede Sarti.

The 347th Squadron engaged a second formation nearly simultaneously. Within a minute, Captain Frank Heckencamp shot down three Bf-109s in flames. 346th Squadron commander Major Gilbert claimed two, while Sulzbach shot down a second in the swirling fight. When the Italians were able to finally disengage, they had lost 12 of their number without even hitting a single Thunderbolt in return.

Just before sunset, the 345th Squadron's Lieutenants Horace Blakeney and Darwin Brooks sighted three Bf-109s bearing down on them about 3 miles away. These three had been involved in the battle over Lake Garda and were trying to get home. Blakeney and Brooks dropped their belly tanks and gave chase. In a ten-minute dogfight over Verona, they chased the three Bf-109s through flak barrages, damaging one and forcing the second to break away. They continued after the third, gradually closing until they were able to get good hits. The enemy pilot bailed out, and the 350th Group's 13th Bf-109 of the day crashed and burned.

The last ANR interception mission was carried out on April 19, 1945 when 22 Bf-109s of 1° Gruppo Caccia took off to intercept the B-25s of the 57th Bomb Wing in the Brenner Pass. They were intercepted by two squadrons of the Fifteenth Air Force's 322nd Fighter Group, the "Tuskegee Airmen," and never got close enough to the B-25s for anyone in the bombers to be aware of their presence. Between January 1944 and April 1945, six ANR pilots scored five or more victories against the Allies.

The Italian Co-Belligerent Air Force (ACI), or Air Force of the South (Aeronautica del Sud), was the air force of the Royalist Badoglio government. The ACI was formed in October 1943 after the Italian armistice in September. By the end of 1943, 281 Italian warplanes had landed at Allied airfields. The crews of these aircraft became members of the ACI, re-equipped with Allied aircraft and engaged in transport, escort, reconnaissance, sea rescue, and limited tactical ground support operations. They flew 11,000 missions from 1943 to 1945. The ACI never operated over Italian territory, to avoid encounters between the ACI and ANR.

290

Four groups formed the ACI. They were: 2° Gruppo, 3° Stormo Trasporto, formed in November 1944 and operating C-47s; 10° Gruppo, 4° Stormo, operating the Bell P-39 Airacobra; 20° Gruppo, 51° Stormo, operating the Spitfire V; and 28° Gruppo, Stormo Baltimore, operating the Martin Baltimore light bomber.

Leading pilots of the ACI included Carlo Emanuele Buscaglia, one of the most famous Italian pilots of World War II as an ace torpedo bomber. Born in Novara, Piedmont, in 1915, Buscaglia entered the Accademia Aeronautica (Air Force Academy) in October 1934. Graduating with his wings in 1937, he was promoted to *Sottotenente Pilota*. On July 1, 1937, he was assigned to the 50ª Squadriglia, equipped with the obsolete Savoia-Marchetti SM.81 Pipistrello, but soon replaced with the superior SM.79 Sparviero. In 1939 he was promoted to *Tenenta* and transferred to the 252ª Squadriglia. He flew with this unit on his first combat mission, on June 21, 1940.

On July 25, he volunteered for the Reparto Speciale Aerosiluranti ("Special Torpedo-Bomber Detachment") of the Regia Aeronautica, later renamed the 240ª Squadriglia Aerosiluranti, based in Libya. On the night of September 17, 1940, Buscaglia attacked and heavily damaged the Royal Navy cruiser HMS *Kent*. In early December he attacked the cruiser HMS *Glasgow*.

In January 1941 Buscaglia's unit was transferred to Catania, where he took part in the attack in which the British aircraft carrier HMS *Illustrious* was badly damaged. Promoted to *Capitano*, Buscaglia was named commander of a new unit, the 281ª Squadriglia, and took part in the Battle of Cape Matapan in March 1941. By January 1942 Buscaglia had been awarded the Silver Medal of Military Valor five times, and the German Iron Cross Second Class. That April he was selected to command the new 132° Gruppo Aerosiluranti, subsequently sinking several ships. On August 12, he and German ace Hans-Joachim Marseille were received in Rome by Mussolini, who promoted him to *Maggiore* (Major).

On November 12, 1942, during a mission against the Allied invasion of North Africa, Buscaglia's aircraft was shot down and he was declared "killed in action"; a Gold Medal of Military Valor was awarded posthumously. However, Buscaglia had survived, although wounded and badly burned. Captured by Allied troops, he was transferred to a POW camp in the United States at Fort Meade.

Following the armistice, Buscaglia asked his captors for permission to join the ACI and fight alongside the Allies. At the same time, the ANR 1° Gruppo Aerosiluranti was named after him.

On July 15, 1944, Buscaglia assumed command of 28° Gruppo, newly equipped with Martin Baltimores and based near Naples. On August 23, attempting to fly one of the new aircraft without an instructor, Buscaglia crashed on takeoff and died the next day in a Naples hospital.

Sottotenente Carlo Negri, an engineering student before the war, enlisted in the Regia Aeronautica in 1941. After graduation from the Accademia Aeronautica, he was assigned to 4° Stormo in June 1943. Following the armistice, Negri, together with most of 4° Stormo, flew to Apulia where the royal family had found safe haven after fleeing Rome. The unit had very strong ties with Prince Amedeo, Duke of Aosta, who had commanded the group in the 1930s.

4° Stormo became the first fighter groups of the Co-Belligerent Air Force, flying ground-attack and supply missions to support the Regio Esercito (Royal Army) in the Balkans embedded in the local resistance movements. On September 21, 1943, Negri volunteered to drop a message to an Italian unit encircled in Koritza, Albania. His C.202 was hit by flak, and Negri made a forced landing; he was immediately captured by the Germans. Tried in a show trial, because he did not have the protection of the Geneva Convention since there had not yet been a formal declaration of war between the Kingdom of Italy and Nazi Germany (which would occur on October 13, 1943), he was sentenced to death and shot on September 23. He received a posthumous Medaglia d'oro al Valor Militare (Gold Medal of Military Valor) for this action.

Tenente Teresio Vittorio Martinoli was credited with 22 air victories and 14 shared destroyed in 276 sorties in the Regia Aeronautica, flying in the North African, Pantelleria, and Sicilian campaigns. Graduating from the Regia Aeronautica flying school at Ghedi in 1939, he was assigned to 366ª Squadriglia of 151° Gruppo, 53° Stormo, with the rank of *Sergente Pilota*.

Shortly before the outbreak of war, he was posted to the 384ª Squadriglia, 157° Gruppo, stationed in Trapani, Sicily. He claimed his first air victory on June 13, 1940, a French Potez 630, shot down over Tunis. In September he was posted to 78ª Squadriglia, 13° Gruppo of 2° Stormo. On October 13, he claimed a Gloster Gladiator of 112 Squadron RAF. Transferring to 4° Stormo – which became his permanent unit – in November, he claimed a Bristol Blenheim shot down on January 5, 1941.

During 1941–42, Martinoli flew fighter sweeps over Malta, flying the new C.202 Folgore. He claimed two Hurricanes on October 19, 1941, and a Blenheim and a Hurricane on November 2. He was credited with three Spitfires shot down between May 4 and 16, 1942, over Malta. During the Battle of Bir Hakeim in North Africa, he shot down two Kittyhawk fighters and damaged a third on June 9. One of four 73ª Squadriglia C.202s that attacked a formation of 12 Kittyhawks, he shot down one. His final North African victory was a Kittyhawk from 260 Squadron RAF shot down on October 23, 1942. In July 1943, he claimed a P-38 Lightning shot down and a shared Boeing B-17 Flying Fortress over Sicily.

With the rest of 4° Stormo, Martinoli joined the Co-Belligerent Air Force, flying missions to Yugoslavia. His last victory was a Junkers Ju-52/3m transport shot down over Podgorica, on November 1, 1943, after a dogfight with two Luftwaffe Bf-109s. Vittorio Martinoli was killed in a flying accident on August 25, 1944, while undergoing flight training on the secondhand Bell P-39s that had just been delivered to 4° Stormo. He was posthumously awarded the Medaglia d'oro al Valor Militare. He had been previously decorated with two Silver Medals and the German Iron Cross Second Class.

Following the end of the war, the Italian monarchy was brought to an end by popular vote on July 18, 1946, and the Republic of Italy proclaimed. A new air force, the Aeronautica Militare Italiana (AMI), was formed. In 1949, former ANR pilots who swore an oath of allegiance to the new republic were allowed to join the new air force. Mario Bellagambi was one who did so. He retired in 1967 as an air vice-marshal, having commanded several units of the AMI before retiring as the air attaché accredited to Japan, South Korea, and the Philippines.

11

VICTORY IN ITALY

At the end of March, the 57th Group's Lieutenant Lewis wrote in his diary about "the big picture" as he saw it. "During the last weeks of the winter, the fifteen daily missions the group flies had become somewhat frustrating because there weren't as many juicy targets left to shoot up, but the flak was still intense. Everyone was thinking that the way had been cleared so when does the offensive start? On a few occasions, the group escorted bombers into Austria without losing a single bomber under its control."

The finale to the war in Italy saw the 57th Wing's Mitchell bombers leave Corsica in early April 1945, a year after their arrival, for bases on the mainland. With new targets in Austria and northern Yugoslavia, and the front lines in the Apennines moving north, Corsica was too distant to allow the bombers to operate with full loads.

The 310th Group began the move from Ghisonaccia to Fano, an airfield on the Adriatic coast, on March 30. The main group arrived on April 6 and the entire move was finished by April 10. Everyone was impressed that Fano was a well-built seaside town located at the end of the old Roman Via Flaminia, which had escaped the ravages of war when the Allies advanced up the Adriatic coast. The airfield was located a mile south of the town. The new quarters were long, single-story masonry structures which had been divided into three-room apartments. Most important to the ground crews, there were hangars for maintenance work. The group shared the field with RAF and SAAF squadrons operating Spitfires, P-40 Kittyhawk dive bombers, Beaufighters, Mosquitos, and B-26 Marauders the South Africans flew.

The 321st Group commenced their move from Solenzara to Falconara airfield on the Adriatic coast on March 31, when the advance ground echelon departed for the mainland. The group flew their first mission from Falconara on April 5, when Dan Bowling, now a newly promoted captain, led 20 of the 445th's bombers as the 321st's contribution to an 80-plane group strike against German Defense Area "Harry," where they dropped fragmentation bombs on troop positions and gun emplacements. While *Bingo* missions were still flown to hit targets in the Brenner Pass, the focus was now missions directly supporting the coming Allied ground offensive.

On April 4, the 340th Group commenced its move to Rimini, south of Venice on the Adriatic coast. Morale perked up when it was discovered their quarters were in Miramare and Riccione, which were fashionable summer resorts that had been popular for vacationers before the war. After nearly three years under canvas from North Africa on, they would be indoors at last. The 340th's war diarist wrote, "The rooms have running water, are wired for lights, and have suffered no bomb or shell damage. Everybody is blinking with amazement at finding himself plunked down in these pleasant little towns with fairly well-dressed people, attractive girls, and small shops."

The group flew its last mission from Alesani on April 6, attacking a ship in La Spezia and the Poggio Rusco rail bridge, both of which were missed; that was made up by the successful bombing of a coastal gun near La Spezia holding up the 92nd Division's advance on Massa. The Mitchells then landed at their new airfield outside Rimini.

Sergeant Bernard Seegmiller, who arrived at Falconara on April 7, wrote his impressions of the new base in his diary on April 9.

We arrived here the afternoon of the 7th by C-47. The weather was quite bad and we flew blind most of the way. Some of our B-25s were forced to turn back on account of icing conditions. We are quartered inside a huge compound which accommodates the entire group. Each squadron occupies a barracks that is complete with showers, kitchen, administration and latrines. The construction is brick with tile floors and a great deal of marble. Some improvising has been done to convert the squat-down latrines into showers. I am told this place was built as a cavalry base by the Mussolini gang. It is very elaborate. The field is very well laid out and steel planking covers

the runway and taxi strips and hard stands. A British outfit built
the landing facility and are still operating with Spits, Beaufighters,
Mosquitos and PBYs. Fifteenth Air Force heavies frequently land
here on emergency returns from targets in Germany and Austria.
Several have come in badly shot up since we came over.

The fact there were large hangars at Falconara made the ground crews
happy, since difficult jobs like engine changes could finally be done
inside, where there was proper equipment for removing and replacing
engines and for major repair of shot-up airplanes.

All three groups quickly discovered the widespread presence of
military police. The days of not worrying whether one had shaved,
if clothes were oil stained, and that all officers were saluted properly
by enlisted men, and junior officers showed seniors proper "military
courtesy" were gone. Crew chief Fred Lawrence wrote in his diary,
"people are complaining about having rejoined the Army."

The final Allied offensive began with massive aerial and artillery
bombardments on April 9. The 57th Fighter Group flew 30 missions
that day, targeting enemy command posts and heavy artillery positions.
Ground crews worked with renewed vigor, seeing the tangible results
of their work.

Sergeant Seegmiller wrote his memories at the day's end: "Today has
been a big one. Every available aircraft in the theater operated in preparing
a push-off for the Eighth and Fifth Armies. It began about 1300 hours
and we watched every type of plane in the American Air Force go over
like great flocks of geese as our own were taking off. It was an impressive
sight and I could not help thinking, 'Those poor damn Germans.'"

First Lieutenant Glenn Pierre, the 340th's war diarist, wrote:

A terrific air pounding of German positions northeast and east of
Bologna by 600 bombers and hundreds of fighters starting shortly
after one o'clock. Our 340th group put up 76 aircraft, almost half
the wing effort. Our targets were two artillery concentration areas
near Imola. Photo Interpreter says most of the 13 boxes of six aircraft
bombed very accurately. After the air attacks had ceased – about
1800 hours – the artillery got going and the Polish corps and the 10th
British Corps, whom we were supporting, jumped off over the Senio
river, bound for the banks of the Santerno river, the first pause point.

The 57th Wing now operated at "maximum effort" to support of the Allied armies. All three groups and the 12 component squadrons flew multiple missions every day. Captain Jackson, the 321st Group's war diarist, wrote on April 11:

> With the new Italian offensive rolling along, the target for today was the Argenta Reserve Area. Wing called for another maximum-effort day and we came through with 48 Mitchells taking off at 0758 hours and 24 more taking off at 0853 hours. The past three days, briefings have begun in the early morning darkness; but no one seems to mind it, just so the offensive keeps going. The combined frag-load this morning was 8,520 fragmentation bombs and it forebodes another bad day for German GIs. The first formation over ran into heavy, moderate, accurate flak and one plane received a hit in the tail while on the bomb-run. It was last seen turning east and losing altitude rapidly. The second formation also ran into heavy flak and returned with three aircraft holed. The consolation was a 99 percent accuracy. After a hurried noon chow and darn little sack time, 24 planes went out for the San Ambrogio Rail Culvert at 1430 hours, and 18 more headed for the Volargne Rail Fill at 1540 hours.

Mission 846 – bombing the troop assembly area at Argenta in front of the Eighth Army's Australian division – was Dan Bowling's 60th and most memorable mission of the war. He led 18 445th Squadron Mitchells at the head of 48 B-25s from all four 321st Group squadrons in "Flo," one of the newest bombers in the 445th; Second Lieutenant Paul Riggenbach was co-pilot; navigator First Lieutenant Robert Mitchell guided the formation to the target; bombardier Joe Silnutz was group lead, on whose aim all others would depend. Bowling's formation led 14 bombers of the 446th Squadron headed by Major Robert Smedley in "Merrily We Bomb Along." They were followed by six 447th Squadron B-25s led by First Lieutenant Norman Rose in "Number 62," while First Lieutenant W. F. Autrey, in "Number 86," led ten 448th Squadron B-25s bringing up the rear.

Their pre-mission briefing had emphasized that timing was of the essence. It was feared that the two German divisions at Argenta were ready to mount a counterattack. Bowling, Silnutz, and Mitchell were told Allied troops would light smoke pots to mark their lines; the target was very close to the Allied positions. "If the white smoke changes to yellow, do not bomb." Yellow smoke meant the Allied troops had started their attack. There had been numerous events throughout the war when Allied bombers hit their own troops at places like Cassino and St Lô; it was crucial that the bombers arrived over the target on time, ahead of the attack. The thousands of fragmentation bombs they showered over the enemy would give Allied troops the cover needed when they commenced their advance. Bowling asked for information regarding the defenses and was told there were over 200 antiaircraft guns. "We were to bomb at 10,500 feet and 200 miles per hour. This was the most heavily-defended target we had gone against. I knew it was going to be tough."

Takeoff time was 0758 hours. Silnutz and Mitchell had both argued against taking a new plane on its first mission with Bowling. A preview of things to come came when it took three tries to get the right engine to turn over and start. When Bowling stopped short of the runway to make his pre-takeoff check, there was a sharp drop on the right engine magnetos. With one turn over the field for join-up, Bowling led the 48 Mitchells on a 40-minute flight over the Adriatic to Ravenna, the point where they turned inland to head for Argenta. "When we were climbing to 10,500 feet, I realized the plane was very sluggish. When we got to altitude, I had to set the engines at nearly full-throttle to maintain 200 miles an hour, and the cylinder head temperatures on both engines were nearly at the red line." Bowling was now eight minutes ahead of schedule.

"I had to do something to save the engines, so I notified the formation I was reducing speed by 20 miles an hour and climbing 500 feet. Three minutes from the target, we would dive back down to the correct altitude and pick up the right speed." It was crucial that the bombers be at the right speed and altitude when they dropped their loads; those were the settings in the Norden bombsights – any variance would prevent an accurate drop.

The formation arrived over the target three minutes early; Bowling increased power and dived back to 10,500 feet, picking up speed to 200mph. "Suddenly all hell broke loose with black flak puffs right where we would have been had I not dived and picked up speed. Those flak gunners were right on us. Joe opened the bomb bay."

When the bombers turned onto their run, Mitchell called there was yellow smoke on the ground. Silnutz replied, "bomb doors closing."

Sensing something wrong, Bowling screamed at Silnutz to re-open the doors. "Roll forward six or seven hundred feet and bomb! I'll take the blame!"

Mitchell argued they were too late, that they had to abort. "Then the flak was all around us. The plane on our right was hit twice and gone. I pulled to the right and had both engines past the red line, waiting for the explosion." The formation followed, evading with Bowling's tactic. Enemy gunners put a solid field of explosions where they would have been. "They were ten seconds too late to get us." Bowling turned back left and 45 seconds later Silnutz called, "bombs away!"

With bombs gone, Bowling immediately rolled left and reduced power. "The engines sounded ready to blow, so I got us headed back to the Adriatic, where at least we'd have a chance of being picked up. Moments later, the cylinder head temperatures came back down to red line. Still dangerous, but now that we were in a dive for the coast, cooler air was circulating through the cowling."

The bombers returned to Ancona 40 minutes later. There were two jeeps with four officers waiting at "Flo's" hardstand. "I thought we'd done it, hit our own troops." Silnutz and Mitchell climbed out while Bowling shut down. "I saw it was the intel officer, ops officer, group bombardier and the deputy group CO. I figured we'd had it. And then they grabbed Silnutz and Mitchell and were shaking their hands." When Bowling crawled out, he was told by deputy group CO Colonel Camara that the mission had been perfect; they had hit the enemy directly on target with a 100 percent drop.

The next day, Bowling was informed by line chief Master Sergeant Mitchell that "Flo's" engines had not been re-set after she arrived in the group. When crossing the South Atlantic, engine power settings were adjusted for long-range cruise power needed for the long delivery flight. Indeed, it had been a very near thing Bowling had not lost both engines on his attack run.

The Argenta success was marred by the loss of "Maggie," flown by First Lieutenant Lewis Dentoni. She had taken a hit in the tail and been forced out of formation as the bombers turned onto the bomb run. Everyone who saw the tail hit and shattered believed tail gunner Staff Sergeant David Morisi had been killed when they saw him blown out of the tail. One gunner thought he saw two parachutes pop open before "Maggie" crashed just behind Allied lines and caught fire, but no one was found. Joe Silnutz was hit hard by the loss; he had shared his tent with Dentoni and Lewis since his arrival on Corsica – the three were close friends who had gone to Rome and Capri together on leaves. Bowling had flown several missions with tail gunner Morisi.

Amazingly, Morisi survived. The hit's impact knocked him unconscious and blew him out still in his seat with all equipment attached. When he came to, he unhooked his seatbelt so the seat and armor plate fell away, then pulled his ripcord and landed just north of the front line, where he was captured and spent the war's final weeks as a prisoner.

The next day, Bowling learned the officer in charge of setting the smoke pots had mistakenly fired the flare for lighting the yellow smoke pots, rather than the white pots. Troops reported the Germans were in shock from the bombing. Several thousand were killed and wounded; the Australians took over 3,500 prisoners.

On Saturday, April 14, Fifth Army's offensive toward Bologna began. The attack was preceded by B-25s dropping fragmentation bombs while P-47s rocketed and strafed the enemy positions, followed by a 30-minute massed artillery barrage. Sergeant Hugh Evans of Item Company, 85th Mountain Infantry, remembered, "I had never seen anything like that, seen so many airplanes. You couldn't believe anyone could survive that."

The 86th Mountain Infantry's morning report recorded:

Promptly at 0830 the airplanes began to circle lazily over the front lines, to be greeted with shouts and waves from the troops below. The planes moved over the valley and let loose with firebombs over Rocca di Roffeno. Great geysers of flame and heavy black smoke rose up to 200 feet in the air, and the concussion could be felt 3,000 yards away. When the planes had finished, the artillery opened up, seemingly pounding every spot that the Air Corps had missed. In a few moments the valley was almost completely obscured by a fog of gray, black, and white smoke. The bursting shells started rockslides on the shale slopes of Rocca di Roffeno, and buildings were reduced to irregular piles of rubble.

Unfortunately, the bombing and barrage were not as effective as they had been at Argenta, since hazy weather prevented fully accurate bombing.

Fighting was fierce when the 85th and 87th Regiments attacked Hills 903 and 913 near Castel d'Aiano; 553 men were killed, wounded, or missing that day.

That afternoon, as Dan Bowling rolled down the Falconara runway on takeoff for another mission to hit German artillery outside Bologna, he was surprised to see a Bf-109 flash past, as defecting pilot Lieutenant Vladimir Sandtner of the Croatian Air Force barely missed him as he dropped his landing gear and put his fighter down on the runway. Bowling managed to get airborne despite the near collision. When he turned over the field and looked down, he saw the fighter parked beside the runway, as the pilot climbed out of the cockpit surrounded by ground personnel. "It turned out he was in the Croatian Air Force fighting for the Germans, and had decided today was a good day to end his war, so he flew over from Yugoslavia and landed at the first field he found, which happened to be ours."

The Battle of the Brenner had succeeded, cutting supplies available to the enemy armies by 80 percent compared to what they had received at the end of the fall 1944 battles. On April 18, Eighth Army units broke through the Argenta Gap, sending armor to encircle the Tenth Army and meeting the American IV Corps advancing from the Apennines. The remaining defenders of Bologna were trapped.

Dan Bowling flew what turned out to be his final mission on April 19. The target was the Vignola road bridge between Bologna and Modena, which separated the 90th Panzergrenadier Division's headquarters from the unit's vehicle storage park. Bowling's six 445th Squadron bombers led seven from the 446th. Despite heavy fire from two six-gun 88mm flak batteries, they put bombs along the 300-foot bridge's entire length, destroying four spans and seriously damaging the fifth. The mission was named "Mission of the Month" in the 321st record book.

When he returned to Falconara, Bowling found he had been taken off flying duties. Offered a promotion to major if he remained with the 321st, he declined and happily accepted the orders that sent him home two weeks later.

On April 21, the Eighth Army's Polish 3rd Carpathian Division and Italian Friuli Group, and Fifth Army's 34th Infantry Division, entered Bologna. The 10th Mountain Division bypassed Bologna and reached the Po River on April 22. Eighth Army's 8th Indian Infantry Division arrived at the river the next day. The 340th's war diarist recorded,

"Bologna has fallen to the Fifth and Eighth Armies, it was announced today. Air support undoubtedly was a big key in making the Germans release their iron grip of last autumn and winter. With their supplies cut off by bombing and communications badly slashed, the Germans could only fall back under the tremendous armored drive of our Allied 15th Army Group."

Harm Diers' second most-memorable mission occurred on April 25. Now an experienced pilot, Diers was an element leader. He was flying an "armed reconnaissance" mission with his wingman near Lake Garda – a beautiful long narrow lake in northern Italy, walled in on its eastern bank by steep cliffs rising vertically and pierced by highway tunnels. The main route ran to the Brenner Pass along the lake's eastern edge. "Flying over the lake, I noticed a large oil or gasoline tank truck stopped near the mouth of a tunnel through the cliffs." Since he was out of position to make a run at the truck, Diers called his wingman to attack it. "He claimed he couldn't see it, so I got into position and dived to strafe the truck, wondering why it hadn't taken cover in the tunnel opening. I soon found out. It was a trap, using the truck as bait!" Antiaircraft guns opened up on Diers' P-47, firing from the tunnel, the cliff above the tunnel, and hillside positions to either side of the road. "I was flying almost at water level over the lake when I was hit. I called on my wingman to come down and help me but he said, 'They're shooting at you!' (As if I didn't know it) so I just radioed back, 'Let's get out of here!'"

Diers engaged the emergency water injection system, giving him a 20 percent boost in horsepower. "The system was intended for just such a time as I was having. But it has one negative draw back – when used, it created a dark trail of smoke, which the German gunners saw and interpreted as evidence that they made a hit. They thus assumed that I was really damaged and so concentrated their fire. Black puffs of explosions surrounded me, but that wonderful P-47 roared on." Diers pulled back on the stick and gradually gained altitude. He found his wingman, and made it back home safely, "thanking the 'angel on my shoulder' once more."

While the end of the war was expected at any time, there was still time for fighting and dying. On April 25, the 321st Group flew Mission 895, to bomb the Cavarzere road bridge. The mission was led by the 445th Squadron's Captain Wayne Kendall in "Spirit of Portchester" with nine other Mitchells, including "06," flown by Paul Young. The nine accompanying 446th Squadron bombers included the veteran "27," flown by First Lieutenant Roland Jackson. The formation was rounded out by three bombers from the 447th Squadron.

The mission proved to be "hot," with German flak again reaching for the bombers. B-25 "27," survivor of Cassino, southern France, the first assault on the Gothic Line, and the Battle of the Brenner, had its left engine knocked out by flak and set afire. Shrapnel slashed the thin aluminum skin, wounding bombardier Sergeant Robert Lattin, turret gunner Staff Sergeant Joseph Dalpos, radioman Sergeant Henry Nichols, and tail gunner Sergeant George W. Darnielle, who bailed out; Darnielle's parachute failed to open. Lieutenant Jackson was able to keep "27" in the air until they crossed the Allied lines and he crash-landed at the first airfield he spotted. Jackson and his co-pilot pulled the wounded bombardier out of the nose and ran from the burning bomber before it exploded minutes later.

Sergeant George W. Darnielle was the last member of the 57th Bomb Wing killed in action. Mission 897 proved to be the 321st's last mission of the war.

That same day, Eighth Army units advanced toward Venice and Trieste. Fifth Army drove north toward Austria and northwest to Milan. A rapid advance toward Turin by the Brazilian division took the Army of Liguria by surprise; it surrendered that evening.

For Italians, April 25 became Liberation Day when the Committee of National Liberation called for a general uprising in remaining German-held towns and cities across northern Italy. Genoa, Milan, and Turin were liberated by April 27.

Benito Mussolini and his mistress Clara Petacci were stopped – headed for Switzerland to board a plane and escape to Spain – near the village of Dongo on Lake Como, by Communist partisans. Urbano Lazzaro, Political Commissar of the 52nd Garibaldi Brigade, identified them. They were both summarily shot in the village of Giulino di Mezzegra on April 28, with 15 other officials of the Italian Social Republic. Their bodies were trucked south to Milan on April 29 and dumped on the Piazzale Loreto, renamed "Piazza Quindici Martiri" in honor of the 15 anti-Fascists executed there five days earlier. The bodies were shot, kicked, and spat upon, then hung upside down on meat hooks from the roof of an Esso gas station, where they were stoned by civilians.

The 445th's Captain Jackson wrote On April 28:

Well, it looks like the inevitable has happened, because without doubt, we have run out of targets. Today was a good flying day, but wing did not assign any targets and approved local transition flights. The battle lines are more fluid than ever before, and wherever our troops haven't entered, reports are that the Partisans are holding the towns. Milan, Turin and Venice were taken over by the Partisans and our forces moved up to make connection with them. It seems that the Allied command is reluctant to assign targets to us because of the possibility of assigned objectives already taken by rapidly moving ground forces. The day was climaxed with an announcement from General Clark that "German resistance in Italy has virtually been eliminated."

Army Group C retreated on all fronts, having lost most of its fighting strength. By April 29, General Heinrich von Vietinghoff, the commander who had stymied Allied armies from Salerno to the Gothic Line, had little option left but to surrender. That morning, he signed the instrument of surrender, with hostilities to formally end on May 2, 1945.

Captain Jackson wrote:

After almost two-and-a-half years of slugging, bombing, mud and mountains, the enemy collapsed practically overnight and the Italian campaign closed in a blast of superlatives. We've made greater gains than any other theater; we've taken the biggest bag of prisoners on all fronts; we're the first theater to wind up; and we're the first to receive an unconditional surrender from an army group. As for the group, we just wound up our busiest month in existence and set a lot of records for future operations to aim at.

During the Battle of the Brenner Pass between November 6, 1944 and April 9, 1945, the 57th Bomb Wing flew 6,839 individual sorties in 380 missions. A total of 10,267 tons of bombs were dropped. Forty-six B-25s were lost, while 532 were damaged. Five hundred aircrew were killed or wounded. Losses in the 57th and 350th Fighter Groups – the P-47 units most directly involved in the campaign – were 35 and 40 percent of flying personnel, respectively. By the end of the war,

64th Fighter Squadron commander Lieutenant Colonel Gil Wymond, the only original member of the group still in combat, who had flown across Africa to Egypt, then fought over the Western Desert, Tunisia, Pantelleria, Sicily, and Italy, was flying a P-47D-30RE Thunderbolt named "Hun Hunter XVI."

Looking back at how he and the 57th Fighter Group survived the war, Michael McCarthy wrote, "One distinguishing characteristic of our performance was the willingness to take care of each other. True leadership is unselfish. When you take risks to care for your people, the attitude is contagious and will always pay dividends far beyond your expectations. The fallout in loyalty, respect, dedication, and esprit de corps contributed to the ability of the unit to get tough jobs done with better results."

General Lucian Truscott came to the Sicily-Rome American Cemetery in Nettuno, Italy, on Memorial Day, May 30, 1945, to give a speech dedicating the cemetery on behalf of America and President Harry Truman. The speech was not recorded, but GI cartoonist Bill Mauldin, who chronicled the Italian campaign through his characters "Willie and Joe," was there. He later wrote of the experience in his memoir *The Brass Ring*:

The general's remarks were brief and extemporaneous. He apologized to the dead men for their presence here. He said everybody tells leaders it is not their fault that men get killed in war, but that every leader knows in his heart this is not altogether true. He said he hoped anybody here through any mistake of his would forgive him, but he realized that was asking a hell of a lot under the circumstances. He would not speak about the glorious dead because he didn't see much glory in getting killed if you were in your late teens or early twenties. He promised that if in the future he ran into anybody, especially old men, who thought death in battle was glorious, he would straighten them out. He said he thought that was the least he could do.

BIBLIOGRAPHY

Ambrose, Stephen E., *Eisenhower* (New York: Simon and Schuster, 1983)

Bernstein, Jonathan, *P-47 Thunderbolt Units of the Twelfth Air Force* (Oxford: Osprey Publishing, 2002)

Beschloss, Michael, *The Conquerors: Roosevelt, Truman and the Destruction of Hitler's Germany, 1941–45* (New York: Simon and Schuster, 2002)

Blake, Steve, with John Stanaway, *Adorimini: A History of the 82nd Fighter Group in World War II* (Boise, ID: 82nd Fighter Group History Inc., 1992)

Blake, Steve, *P-38 Lightning Aces of the 82nd Fighter Group* (Oxford: Osprey Publishing, 2012)

Bowling, Dan, *Follow PDI: My Experiences as a B-25 Pilot During World War II* (Lomita, CA: Cambria Publishing, 2009)

Cleaver, Thomas M., *The Bridgebusters: The True Story of the Catch 22 Bomb Wing* (Washington, DC: Regnery History, 2016)

Collier, Richard, *The Freedom Road: 1944–1945* (New York: Atheneum, 1984)

Garland, Albert N. and Howard McGraw Smyth, *Sicily and the Surrender of Italy* (Washington, DC: US Army Center of Military History, 1993)

Goldman, Kenneth H., *Attack Transport: USS Charles Carroll in World War II* (Gainesville, FL: University Press of Florida, 2008)

Goodwin, Doris Kearns, *No Ordinary Time: Franklin and Eleanor Roosevelt in World War II* (New York: Simon and Schuster, 1994)

Green, Herschel H., *Herky: The Memoirs of a Checkertail Ace* (Atglen, PA: Schiffer Military History, 1996)

Hamilton, Nigel, *The Mantle of Command: FDR at War* (New York: Houghton Mifflin, 2014)

Hammel, Eric, *Aces Against Germany: The American Aces Speak*, Vol. 2 (Novato, CA: Presidio Press, 1993)

Hewitt, H. Kent, "The Allied Navies at Salerno: Operation *Avalanche* –
September 1943," *United States Naval Institute Proceedings*, Vol. 79, No. 9,
September 1953

Innfield, Glenn, "Disaster at Bari," *American Heritage*, Vol. 22, No. 6,
October 1971

Ivie, Tom and Paul Ludwig, *Spitfires and Yellow-Tail Mustangs: The 52nd
Fighter Group in World War II* (Manchester: Hikoki Publications, 2004)

Keegan, John, *Intelligence in War* (New York: Alfred A. Knopf, 2003)

Kucera, Dennis C., *In A Now Forgotten Sky: The 31st Fighter Group in WW2*
(Stratford, CT: Flying Machines Press, 1997)

Lambert, John W., *The 14th Fighter Group in World War II* (Atglen, PA:
Schiffer Military History, 2008)

Lawrence, Frederick H., *Untold and Unsung* (Victoria, Canada: Trafford
Publishing, 2004)

Lawrence, Frederick H., *Mediterranean Mitchells: History of the 445th Bomb
Squadron* (Victoria, Canada: Trafford, 2005)

Luce, Steve W., *The 86th Fighter Group in World War II* (Hamilton, MT:
Eagle Editions Ltd., 2007)

Lynch, James A. and Gregory Lynch Jr., *The Black Scorpions: Serving With the
64th Fighter Squadron in World War II* (Philadelphia: Casemate, 2023)

Matteoli, Marco, *53° Stormo* (Oxford: Osprey Publishing, 2010)

Mauldin, Bill, *Up Front* (New York: H. Wolfe, 1945)

Mauldin, Bill, *The Brass Ring – A Sort of a Memoir* (New York: W. W.
Norton & Co., 1971)

McCarthy, Michael C., *Air-to-Ground Battle for Italy* (Maxwell AFB: Air
University Press, 2012)

McDowell, Ernest R. and William N. Hess, *Checkertail Clan: The 325th
Fighter Group in North Africa and Sicily* (Fallbrook, CA: Aero Publishers,
1969)

Miller, Merle, *Ike The Soldier: As They Knew Him* (New York: G. P. Putnam's
Sons, 1987)

Molesworth, Carl, *The 57th Fighter Group: First in the Blue* (Oxford: Osprey
Publishing, 2011)

Molesworth, Carl, *P-40 Warhawk Aces of the MTO* (Oxford: Osprey
Publishing, 2002)

Mullins, John D., *An Escort of P-38s: The 1st Fighter Group in World War II*
(St Paul, MN: Phalanx Publishing, 1995)

Overy, Richard, *Why the Allies Won* (New York: W. W. Norton, 1995)

Pace, Steve, B-25 *Mitchell Units of the MTO* (Oxford: Osprey Publishing,
2008)

Perry, Mark, *Partners in Command: George Marshall and Dwight Eisenhower in War and Peace* (New York: Penguin, 2007)

Scutts, Jerry, *Bf 109 Aces of North Africa and the Mediterranean* (Oxford: Osprey Publishing, 1995)

Stout, Jay A., *The Men Who Killed the Luftwaffe: The US Army Air Forces against Germany in World War II* (Mechanicsburg, PA: Stackpole Books, 2010)

Tillman, Barrett, *Hellcat: The F6F in World War II* (Annapolis: Naval Institute Press, 1979)

Weal, John, *Jagdgeschwader 53 "Pik-A's"* (Oxford: Osprey Publishing: 2008)

Woerpel, Don, *The 79th Fighter Group over Tunisia, Sicily and Italy in World War II* (Atglen, PA: Schiffer Military History, 2001)

GLOSSARY

The list below contains acronyms and non-English terms used in the text.

ACRONYMS

ACI: Aviazione Cobelligerante Italiana (Italian Co-Belligerent Air Force)

ANR: Aeronautica Nazionale Repubblicana (Italian Fascist Air Force)

ASC: Air Support Command

CAD: US Army Civil Affairs Division

DFC: Distinguished Flying Cross

DUC: Distinguished Unit Citation

JG: *Jagdgeschwader* (Luftwaffe fighter wing)

KG: *Kampfgeschwader* (Luftwaffe bomber wing)

LCT: Landing Craft, Tank

LST: Landing Ship, Tank

MASAF: Mediterranean Allied Strategic Air Force

MTO: Mediterranean Theater of Operations

NASAF: Northwest African Strategic Air Force

OKH: Oberkommando des Heeres (German Army High Command)

OKW: Oberkommando der Wehrmacht (Wehrmacht High Command)

PSP: pierced-steel planking

GLOSSARY

RAF: Royal Air Force

RSI: Repubblica Sociale Italiana (Italian Social Republic)

SAAF: South African Air Force

TAC: Tactical Air Command

USAAF: United States Army Air Force

VF: Fighter Squadron (US Navy)

NON-ENGLISH TERMS

German

Experte(n): German term for "ace"

Freie Jagd: free hunt patrol

Geschwader(n): wing(s)

Gruppe(n): group(s)

Jagdflieger(n): fighter pilot(s)

Jagdgeschwader(n): fighter wing(s)

Jagdwaffe: Fighter Force

Luftflotte(n): air fleet(s)

Luftwaffe: German Air Force

Schwarm: flight of four aircraft

Staffel(n): squadron(s)

Italian

Gruppi Caccia Terrestre: fighter groups

Gruppo/Gruppi: group/groups

Squadriglia/Squadriglie: squadron/squadrons

Regia Aeronautica: Royal Italian Air Force

Stormo/Stormi: wing/wings

311

INDEX

Note: page numbers in **bold** refer to illustrations.